WIZARDS

WIZARDS

David Duke, America's Wildest
Election, and the Rise of the Far Right

BRIAN FAIRBANKS

VANDERBILT UNIVERSITY PRESS
Nashville, Tennessee

Library of Congress Cataloging-in-Publication Data

Names: Fairbanks, Brian, 1981– author.
Title: Wizards : David Duke, America's wildest election, and the rise of
the far right / Brian Fairbanks.
Other titles: David Duke, America's wildest election, and the rise of the
far right
Description: Nashville, Tennessee : Vanderbilt University Press, [2022] |
Includes bibliographical references and index. | Summary: "An account of
the 1991 Louisiana gubernatorial race between ex-Klan Grand Wizard David
Duke and former Louisiana Governor Edwin Edwards, and its
consequences"—Provided by publisher.
Identifiers: LCCN 2022007215 (print) | LCCN 2022007216 (ebook) | ISBN
9780826505019 (paperback) | ISBN 9780826505026 (epub) | ISBN
9780826505033 (pdf)
Subjects: LCSH: Duke, David, 1950– | Ku Klux Klan (1915–)—History—20th
century. | Right and left (Political science)—History—20th century. |
Governors—Louisiana—Election—History—20th century. |
Louisiana—Politics and government—1951–
Classification: LCC F376.3.D84 F35 2022 (print) | LCC F376.3.D84 (ebook)
| DDC 976.3/063—dc23/eng/20220225
LC record available at https://lccn.loc.gov/2022007215
LC ebook record available at https://lccn.loc.gov/2022007216

CONTENTS

Introduction

He is not a George Wallace. He is beyond that. He is truly a type that one
would find in the 1930s in Germany. He sees himself as this Messiah, that he's
going to save the white race.

BETH RICKEY, in the *New York Times*, Nov. 10, 1991

The Far Right didn't come out of nowhere in the United States; in fact, it
came from Louisiana.

The voters, "Yankees" and foreign observers who were surprised by the
Proud Boys, Donald Trump, the Oath Keepers, and the "Stop the Steal" rally
must have overlooked the Pelican State's politics over the previous century
and a right-wing uprising seeded there and throughout the South. Beginning a
century ago, the glitz and glamor of the Roaring Twenties clashed with a widening income inequality, alternately inspiring and enraging middle class and
poor folks, although those blocs initially surged toward a *left*-wing populism
to even the score. Louisiana governor and US senator Huey Long emerged
from the crackling, volatile Great Depression a towering figure of unfathom-
able popularity despite exhibiting unprecedented delusions of grandeur, as
befitting of the title of his self-penned theme song, "Every Man a King."[1] He
once told writer James Thurber, "I've saved the lives of little children, I've
sent men through college, I've lifted communities from the mud, I've cured
insane people."[2] Long, though, was more accurately the political equivalent
of a raging drunk in a bar, held back by both arms, purplish and seething,
growling that his target was lucky he couldn't reach. Though 5' 10", his con-
temporaries described him as a "scrappy, portly little feller." Long emerged
as a litigant against the state's domineering oil monopolies, kicking and
screaming his way into the hearts of underdogs in every parish, including the
"coloreds." In an era beset by sixteen senators, sixty congressmen, and eleven
governors who were known Klansmen, Long broke new ground in the South

by refusing to race bait, focusing instead on "the social and economic problems of the present," as biographer T. Harry Williams suggested, including
after the murder of two anti-Klan activists.[3] The "Kingfish" threatened a Klan
Imperial Wizard, saying he would go "toes up" if he "dared" visit Louisiana,
and when asked about his plans for black people, Long said firmly that he
would "treat them just the same as anybody else, give them an opportunity
to make a living, and to get an education."[4]

Buoyed by his election to the US Senate while still in the Governor's
Mansion, Long immediately threatened to challenge Franklin Delano
Roosevelt for the presidency—a move backed by the nation's most popular
radio broadcaster—if FDR refused to enact socialist economic programs
like wealth redistribution.[5] Long likely planned to challenge President
Roosevelt from a third-party platform and either split the left-wing vote or
slip through the cracks to win in 1936. Instead, before he could run in earnest, he was felled at the state capitol by an assassin's pistol. Eyewitnesses
claimed his last words were, "Oh God, don't let me die. I have so much left
to do."[6] No Louisiana politician seriously threatened for the presidency
again until the rise of David Duke.[7]

The meteoric ascension of a Louisiana Democrat not named Long has similar parallels. From the first months of the 1970s to the early 1990s, when
conservatives finally achieved power and squeezed out the last remnants
of liberal welfare programs and civil rights initiatives, Edwin Washington
Edwards, a sharecropper's son born shortly before Long's first victory,
served as Kingfish under a similar moniker: "the Cajun Prince." He had
other nicknames, too, like Fast Eddie (he won $15,000 playing craps on a
campaign-related trip to Monaco[8]), the Silver Fox (his slicked-back graying
hair caused screams when it was sighted emerging from a limo, even at age
sixty-four), and the Crook, but the Cajun Prince stuck. Like Huey Long, he
embraced labels, for whether laudatory or derogatory, they were free publicity. A dry-witted, handsome card player but a teetotaler and a nonsmoker,
Edwards built his awe-inspiring million-plus-voter following through what
LSU professor Wayne Parent called "Made-For-TV Longism," crushing sleepy
opponents like Republican Dave Treen, of whom Edwards famously said, "It
takes him an hour and a half to watch '60 Minutes.'"[9] Like his contemporary
Bill Clinton, Edwards's magnetism and ability to connect one on one with
voters helped him remain undefeated in sixteen consecutive elections, but
being seemingly unbeatable didn't render him impervious to self-inflicted
wounds, and those wounds eventually doomed him.

In tandem with the decline of a progressive national Democratic party in the post-Roosevelt era, Louisiana moved further right. Divisive social issues festered to the point that, following a 1980s Supreme Court ruling allowing states to set restrictions on abortions, Louisiana made pregnancy termination illegal even in cases of rape or incest and set an astonishingly high sales tax rate, a consequence of conservative officials fearing any income tax increase would alienate their IRS-obsessed base.[10]

Into Louisiana's declining economy and social unrest plunged the youngest-ever Grand Wizard of the Ku Klux Klan. With his trademark crisp gray suit, megawatt smile, soft-spoken voice, and the political smarts to focus on campus and youth recruiting, David Duke oversaw a stunning revitalization of the KKK. Born after World War II and having embraced the Third Reich as a teenager, Duke headed a growing anti-government, separate-but-equal and anti-racial-tolerance protest movement;[11] that it positioned itself firmly on the country's pro-business, anti-communist wing gave the capitalist establishment something to work itself into a froth debating: *do we accept a candidate who thinks like us but is politically toxic?* Duke made local headlines for blaming the state's economic ills on welfare "giveaways" and rising crime rates on affirmative action initiatives.[12] He built a personal brand of the Long variety, a demagogical organization through which he could actually *sell* political propaganda like yard signs, hats, or buttons emblazoned with his last name, contrary to his opponents, who often resorted to begging supporters to take swag gratis. And despite mockery in the press for being a supposed "also-ran yahoo," Duke eventually tapped into a growing conservative movement that prized "aw shucks" personas and tough-love family values (Ronald Reagan) over substantive debate and progress (Michael Dukakis) or peacenik liberalism (Jimmy Carter). Moreover, Duke had a secret weapon. Unlike Edwin Edwards, a legendary but increasingly unwelcome figure in the political scene in the eighties, Duke's support base was largely composed of enthusiastic voters. *Rabidly* enthusiastic voters.

Following the ballot count in his 1991 race, Duke's message continued to spread to the point that it became clear he had been ahead of his time, not so much a product of it. Terrorist attacks, right-wing rhetoric, and the Klan's popularity online in the nineties indicated, or led to, a radical realignment of the country's two political parties. The white nationalist movement, behind the Oklahoma City and Atlanta Olympics bombings, also rose in power.[13] It all pointed back to one campaign, one election, one candidate. While the runoff drew consecutive front-page stories in major newspapers, there is another, even more compelling tale from 1991, one mostly kept out of the panic-stricken op-eds and self-congratulatory postmortems: little-known Republican Beth Rickey, through her relentless pursuit of the truth about Duke, almost single-handedly turned the tide in the 1991 governor's race, the most controversial and widely watched local election in American history.[14] Her story, never thoroughly investigated or reported in full, is a prime example of the adage "country over party" and a blueprint for antifascist efforts today.

The final tête-à-tête involving Duke and Edwards, held on November 17, 1991, would mark the end of "the New South" and the birth of a darker yet more invigorated political era, one that ripples through our politics three decades later in ways both mysterious and deeply disturbing. But for a month that autumn, while brilliant fall foliage lit up Kisatchie National Forest, crisp peppers, collards, and turnip greens lined grocery aisles, and football fever swept weekend campuses, two self-proclaimed "wizards" put their radical beliefs on hold and let activists on both sides create the fireworks. And then, having slain the most towering dragon of them all, Louisiana's left-leaning coalition patted itself on the back, unaware the movement had won a battle, not the war. This was the unnoticed Lexington and Concord, the first firefights in the larger political struggle that led to Trumpism.

As Huey Long once said: "I used to get things done by saying please. Now I dynamite 'em out of my path."[15]

Prologue

October 19, 1991

If you're not from the South, you really don't understand us.

BUDDY ROEMER

It was election night, and the governor of Louisiana was bored out of his skull.

Program options for Charles "Buddy" Roemer III boiled down to two choices: the first game of the World Series or the live news updates on his race. Neither offered riveting footage, especially so soon after polls closed.

Buddy adjusted his La-Z-Boy and tried to concentrate on the public-television commentators discussing his primary race, but the Twins and Braves beckoned from the Baton Rouge CBS affiliate. He hovered his thumb above the up and down channel buttons and waited for a commercial break. At any moment, he knew, a reporter would break in and read the results sealing Roemer's first-place showing and spot in the runoff election. In the interim, however, he brooded over the surprising resilience of his opponents, Edwin Edwards, an ex-governor and Roemer's mentor, and David Duke, former Grand Wizard of the Ku Klux Klan and now essentially a political neophyte. At worst, the good people of Louisiana imagined Duke would finish a strong third in the primary. A handful of insiders considered the possibility that Duke might stumble his way into second—a *distant* second—behind Buddy, but even that seemed too doom-and-gloom for most to stomach. Regardless, the superstitious governor decided to wait to savor his victory until *after* the results were ironclad; in the interim, Roemer dialed a dozing aide, who had waited two hours for Buddy to come out to the idling state police cruiser and zoom across town to celebrate at the Baton Rouge event. Roemer considered asking for someone to join him in a game of poker.

The TV, however, would be too interruptive. Besides, were he to lose—the election—he wouldn't have a salary to gamble with. He instead gave himself a shot of insulin and picked up a book.[1]

With hard data remaining sparse, the lone local broadcast following the returns stalled for time. One newscaster, seemingly impressed, noted that Roemer's organization had put together three simultaneous election night parties. Roemer, of course, wasn't in attendance at any of them, which the station declined to mention. Showing up could only jinx it. (He'd stationed his campaign staffers at an event at the Sheraton Hotel, two hundred miles away, that had welcomed the hometown hero in '87 and been booked a second time for kismet's sake.[2]) The celebrants included business leaders in oversized aviators, devout buttoned-up Christians in short sleeves, old school conservatives dabbing at their foreheads and stirring gin and tonics with miniature straws. To mitigate the suspense, attendees dipped into the champagne before it reached room temperature. Most had seen the polls, which, after months of Roemer leads, had suddenly shown the three primetime players essentially tied.[3] No matter who led going into the runoff, though, the sitting governor would likely be one of two to qualify, and, as the first or second choice of the majority of voters, would crush Candidate TBD.[4] Roemer, a onetime campaign strategist, knew he needed only to outpace half a dozen perennial losers and also-rans across a single day's voting in his rural northern Louisiana strongholds. Heck, he had done it before under more trying circumstances. As a congressman and dark horse candidate four years earlier, Buddy Roemer blew past Edwards, the incumbent dogged by corruption allegations; a rematch in this year's two-candidate runoff would make for a landslide in Roemer's favor.[5] There was just one problem: the governor couldn't decide whether he wanted to win reelection or quit politics forever. (Danny Walker, a childhood pal and close confidante, confessed he rooted for Buddy's elimination, explaining, "If he loses, he wins."[6]) Roemer's wife had divorced him after a brief separation, taking their adolescent son and hiding out at a small-town Colorado motel.[7] The governor's major proposals had died in the legislature and again in the voting booth when voters shot them down as ballot initiatives. He had abandoned the Democrats for the GOP, which thanked him by instead nominating a little-known congressman for governor over their own incumbent. Roemer rarely ventured out of the mansion regardless. He had kicked off his campaign only after the legislative session ended a few weeks earlier and appeared in a mere handful of ads and live debates, yet, he promised aides, momentum remained on his side. "Forgive me," he kept asking voters on the trail, and so far, judging by exit polling, they had.

Reclined on the La-Z-Boy in a tan suit, arm resting on a slim volume by Descartes, Buddy held the remote in front of him like a taunt.[8] He betrayed no outward emotion, and his bodyguards and campaign team didn't get any answers when they tried to check in. They ducked back out of the office with the "HONOR" plaque on the door and resumed their silent vigil. Roemer flicked over to check the score of the more interesting contest and tried to get jazzed about how the Atlanta Braves were doing. Georgia, after all, might be a swing state in the 1996 presidential election.[9]

When his nerves got the best of him and he flipped back, his instincts appeared to have been correct. Though the folks—because that's who supported Buddy Roemer, "just us folks" types—strained to hear the radio or make out the totals flashing on the monitors in the three hotel ballrooms, they were boogying. If they had looked closely, however, as Roemer and all three major campaigns were doing in their green rooms, these partners would have noticed movement afoot in rural areas, Buddy's supposed stronghold. There, once-sleepy precincts were reporting snaking lines and record-breaking turnout, which translated into a surge of support for David Duke. Pollsters had predicted Duke would finish third in the gubernatorial, all-party primary with 12 percent and thus be eliminated.[10] Duke, a suburban Republican, came to national prominence in the 1990 US Senate race, doubling his final poll numbers and shaking the establishment until its collective knees knocked together.[11] That he was allegedly a former Nazi and KKK Grand Wizard should have kept Duke in the basement, considering a majority of those polled professed discomfort with the prospect of a neo-Nazi at the helm of state government.[12] As an outsider running against the Republican nominee, the Republican incumbent, and Democrat Edwin Edwards—a dominant force in Louisiana politics since the early seventies—Duke should not have had a shot at the November runoff, and with ten percent of the vote in and Roemer comfortably ahead, he didn't.

Later, the governor would claim he didn't see David Duke coming.

At about the same time Atlanta's Terry Pendleton grounded into a double play on WAFB, Roemer watched as another cluster of ballots streamed in to the public TV studios.[13] The corner of the screen now showed 14 percent counted. Roemer's maxed-out contributors, retirees/full-time volunteers, and campaign staff fell into a choking hush. Duke had vaulted into first place. *Impossible*, they told themselves. *It must be a suburban pocket.* Through the next half-hour, the race stayed tight, Roemer, Duke, and Edwards clinging to one-quarter of the vote each, with Edwards taking a narrow lead and not quite losing it. If the numbers held, Duke would end up missing the runoff by a few hundred votes, leaving Roemer to face the corrupt Edwards.[14] But then a flood of votes came in from Roemer's supposed stronghold of northern Louisiana and Democratic New Orleans, and the Sheraton plunged into silence, as if the pope had lifted a hand.

By eleven o'clock, the networks had called it. The live feed cut to the stately Pontchartrain Center ballroom in Kenner, Duke Country Central, where one thousand white working-class folks in striped button-downs slapped blue-and-white Duke stickers across their hearts and pumped their fists in the air.[15] One man, bearing tattoos of a swastika and the Confederate flag on either arm, was giving a TV interview and shouted above the din, "It don't mean nothing, my family's German." Another told a Texas reporter that he had switched his support from Roemer because the governor "borrowed a billion dollars to balance the budget—from the Jew banks."[16] The anti-Semite had to raise his voice to be heard over the operatic performance of "Dixie." There were few dry eyes among the assembled, and Duke stalwarts even placed their hands over their hearts for their preferred national anthem. "The Battle Hymn of the Republic," increasingly co-opted by white nationalists, followed and served as an introduction for a fiery-voiced pastor. This penultimate speaker gestured for silence and, with head bowed, asked the Lord for "a special blessing upon this assembly."[17]

When the network cut back to Roemer's rally, the governor took in the visual of his own supporters, faces blanched, mouths widening, and tears mixing with eyeliner. Had his numbers held, he had his shoes nearby and could have scampered out to the idling limo and been basking in the hosannas in minutes. Instead, the sitting governor said nothing and did not rise from the La-Z-Boy. He had gambled and lost cataclysmically, and the only consolation was that he missed nothing substantial during the World Series. The Twins preserved their lead with a scoreless ninth inning. Buddy did not want to dwell on surprise victories and stunning losses, either in his political career or following pointless athletic contests.

Roemer changed the channel swiftly enough to avoid witnessing David Duke in the role of beaming, prideful victor. The numbers were on his side now and proved his chances, as he'd warned the media for years, had been grossly underestimated. "He strikes a chord in people," said a woman from Morehouse Parish. "He has this populist appeal we haven't seen since Roosevelt."[18]

"With every minute, ladies and gentlemen," Duke intoned solemnly, "it appears that we will be in a runoff for the governorship of Louisiana." The roar drowned out the rest of his pronouncement.[19]

Waiting, soaking it up, and receiving their full attention again, Duke went on: "My thanks goes first to the force in my life, that's giving me strength, then helps me withstand a lot and continue to stand up for you, and that's Jesus Christ. Ladies and gentlemen, that's the force of my life—" Once more, the roars drowned him out. He spoke of the state's demons: illegal immigration and welfare queens. The attendees applauded his catchphrases, as if personally affected by these, the most important issues in the state.[20]

Roemer confidante Ray Strother spent the night drinking martinis and ignoring the news, convinced of defeat. In the morning, he bumped into the lame duck in the Governor's Mansion kitchen while stockpiling milk and cookies.

"You sure needed a better candidate," said Roemer.

"Buddy," Strother replied, "we just needed a better *plan*."[21]

Under hot lights, Roemer would subsequently tell reporters, "The voters said, 'Buddy, thanks, but you didn't do enough.' That's fair."[22]

The governor strongly hinted that he thought the employees who worked under him in the state government didn't deserve to worry about losing their jobs under a new administration. Strother averted his eyes; many of those staffers supported David Duke.

After his victory speech, Duke had another grey suit cut to his specifications; then he got to work. Over the next few weeks, he lined up the support of the state's conservative policymakers, including GOP careerists on Roemer's staff, making them offers they might refuse but would not.[23] As Republican strategist Eddie Mahe confessed to the *New York Times*, "I think we've got ourselves into a very difficult one."[24] One defector would spend the last month of the campaign pounding the phones for Duke; she and most others were unworried that their assistance might help a Nazi achieve political power. Rather, they expressed horror—not that Roemer had lost or that the conservative, conciliatory, and suddenly terribly real David Duke might get into the Governor's Mansion—but that Edwin Edwards, a known crook, might be back in charge. The governor's staffers weren't the only ones who thought a Duke victory in the runoff practically inevitable. Of Edwards, the incumbent said, "His negatives are so high he has little credibility." Fifty percent of voters reportedly disliked the Democrat.[25] Duke won more parishes, was only behind in the popular vote by about thirty thousand, and would no longer have to split votes among fellow Republicans.[26]

The rest of the country, however, ignited in an uproar. The anointment of David Duke ran counter to the narrative that the nation's civil rights struggles were dead and buried. Beth Rickey could have warned these people. The thirty-five-year-old Lafayette-born Ronald Reagan acolyte (when she was ten, the California governor dropped by her parents' house for a visit), who followed her construction magnate war hero father onto the Republican State Committee, had been trying to warn conservatives about Duke and his festering base for years. She had secretly co-founded the Louisiana Coalition against Racism and Nazism eighteen months earlier with a singular, specific mission statement: to crush political aspirant David Duke. With a ragtag handful of minor politicos, including a Baton Rouge clergyman, Rickey had been working—with minimal effect—behind the scenes to expose Duke's past associations with terrorists, a move that had earned her death threats from Duke supporters. Former Roemer campaign strategist Mark McKinnon watched in disbelief from Texas. "I thought Roemer was so talented that he could survive," he recalls, but Beth Rickey and her anti-racist cabal knew better.[27] And if people didn't realize the Duke campaign had become a virus, they were about to learn the hard way.

As Duke surged in the weeks leading up to the gubernatorial runoff, ex-governor Edwards trotted out old strategies in the hope lightning might strike for him for a *fourth* time, and Beth Rickey debated whether to go deeper into the muck. In many respects, her position after the primary became more tenuous. Had Duke been eliminated, it's likely she would have been embraced by Roemer's fragile coalition and possibly become a major political player. Instead, defeating Duke now meant repudiating the Republican candidate and implicitly supporting the Democratic Dragon. She wondered if it would be worth sacrificing her exalted position in the party, the one her family put her on track for and toward which she had been working as a post-grad. She could just let David Duke second-line into the Governor's Mansion and all her personal strife would go away. But Rickey believed "Duke's real aim is a white Christian nation of men and women of pure blood" and she couldn't stomach it.[28]

Before she decided, she wanted to peek again at David Duke's Pandora's box.[29] More than a dozen boxes, in fact, and all coincidentally housed at Rickey's school, Tulane University. On her initial pilgrimage two years earlier as a doctoral student in political science and under cover of anonymity, evidence of his skewed worldview had overwhelmed her. There were newsletters under Duke's byline warning of conspiratorial Jewish bankers and small-brained "Blacks [who] can see as well as Whites but can't think as well."[30] At the time, that material had seemed sufficient to tank Duke's State House candidacy, and she had stopped a few pages into her reading.

But when she rose to speak against Duke at a Republican state committee meeting, Rickey opened her mouth and found that her jaw trembled uncontrollably. Only a croak eked out. Rickey, an activist since age fifteen, imagined her monotone voice echoing through the riveted State House chamber and everyone staring at her homely face. A colleague—a man—spoke up instead. Regardless, only eight out of 128 committee members voted to censure the state senator, even after a tape recording emerged in which Duke could be heard blaming Jews for causing World War II and for an Alabama church bombing long believed to be KKK-related.[31] But how would the GOP feel now, with Duke presumably using the local race as a springboard for a run against the incumbent Republican president?

Rickey, alone in her Lower Garden District duplex, went through her papers again. Alone, again. A bunch of Polaroids, a few newspaper clippings, a monthly mailer to fellow travelers, notes in cursive on a speech about the "rising welfare underclass." When the telephone shrieked out in her silent apartment, Rickey signed a letter, "Yours, from the Twilight Zone," tossed her pen onto the pile and stood up.[32] The ringing phone had long been a source of unease for her, even before the threats.

On a walk around the block, holding an umbrella aloft, she went over the inventory in her head. Newspaper clippings? Blurry Polaroids? She couldn't go back to the state committee or the media with *that* third-grade book report. David Duke was her *party leader*. Realizing she was back in front of the gated entrance to her building, she glanced across Coliseum and Race Streets to see a smoker hovering near a park bench, his features obscured beneath matching umbrella and fingers to lips. He sported a plaid jacket, virtual suicide in New Orleans humidity, still somewhat inexplicable in autumn. Few people hung out in Coliseum Square Park; during the day, it served mostly as a jogging track or dog run and was always deserted at this hour.[33] Beth forced herself not to glare back but couldn't shake the suspicion that ignoring his presence would enrage him.

Turning back toward Third Street, she decided she needed outside help. Not just the anti-racist coalition and its Democrats and bishops or her fellow Never Duke Republicans. Beth might, God forbid, need to help Edwin Edwards help himself.

PART I

THE CROOK

CHAPTER 1

The Squeaker

In life, politics and hunting, I play by the rules, but I take all
the advantages the rules allow.

EDWIN EDWARDS

He couldn't help himself. Edwin Edwards could never stop blowing on the
dice and throwing it onto a craps table, or resist the urge to slap a stack of $100
bills atop the roulette's green turf, smirking as the croupier's eyes popped
out of their damn head.[1] Short of cash, he would gesture for more credit to
try to reroute his streak skyward. Edwin Washington Edwards was a gambler.
Sue him. (They wouldn't have dared.)

"Gambling is pretty well accepted in the French-Catholic tradition of
South Louisiana," said Rev. Michael Jarrell, associate pastor of Edwards'
original stomping grounds, the St. Michael's Catholic Church. "South
Louisiana is culturally different from the rest of the South."[2] It wasn't about
the money, though, or so he claimed. As a senior citizen, in the company
of his twenty-seven-year-old girlfriend, Edwards threw dice onto the craps
table and intoned, "This one's for mom and the kids."[3] Who did he think
he was fooling? Edwards did it all for personal glory, and regardless of who
objected.

Strongly told not to compete in his first congressional primary, he qualified for the race anyway and won. Told his name meant mud, he entered the
gubernatorial jungle primary for an unprecedented fourth term. Encouraged
to plead guilty to corruption charges in two criminal trials, he ignored the
advice of experts and took his case to the jury. In some ways, this inability
to stop himself made his career.

Life wasn't always so smooth for the slick "Fast Eddie," however. Edwin
Edwards descended from a family of French expats, who migrated from

Kentucky in the mid-nineteenth century and starting digging into the land in the parish that came to be called Avoyelles.[4] The nearest town, Marksville, smack-dab in the center of Louisiana, brewed a steady melting pot of Catholics and Evangelical Protestants, making the Edwardses among the original French Creoles.[5] Agnes Brouillette, Edwin's mother, was the French Catholic daughter of a blacksmith, surrounded by Protestants and their ilk.[6] Agnes zeroed in on Clarence "Boboy" Edwards, despite his background, lack of formal education, and comparative youth. Clarence was a third-grade dropout who had taken to laboring on a sharecropper farm after his father's death.[7] Described by Edwin and others as a quiet and hard father, Boboy was secretly very proud of everything his lawyer-turned-politician offspring accomplished, including Edwin's being named to the LSU Dean's List, and his legislative triumphs, even if Boboy preferred FDR's smooth style to the brash Long ways Edwin mimicked.[8]

The month Agnes bore Edwin in a town along the Red River in 1927, the Great Flood finally dissipated amid a summer heatwave. Between 250 and 300 million dollars-worth of damage had been done to the Mississippi Delta, especially in Arkansas, Mississippi, and Louisiana, but the federal government rode to the rescue and spent approximately one-third of the year's budget on cleanup, rescues, relocations, and whatever citizens needed.[9] The Edwards family, like most Southern sharecroppers, lived literally hand to mouth. "I know what it is to see people without food," he would say of that time. "I grew up in that type of environment. I don't want it to happen to anybody."[10] When he joined friends at the local bakery, he would skip ordering and instead sit waiting for discarded bread crusts to come his way.

Edwin was the middle of five children; Marion, the finance chair in Edwin's later campaigns, was less than a year younger, and Nolan, who also became a lawyer, was only two years younger than he. Together, the Edwards children spent their first through fourth grades in the nearby one-room schoolhouse, where each student sat through the same general knowledge lessons for four years running. "Air conditioning then was called windows," Edwin joked.[11]

"With his round, red cheeks, and clever eyes, the boy had the look of a Cajun Dennis the Menace, but it was impossible to stay mad at him," cousin Frenchy Brouillette wrote in a sensationalized autobiography. "In school, they used to say that little Edwin would flirt his way out of schoolwork, and even his dowdiest teachers would be competing with the young girls for his attention."[12]

When a repeat of the Great Flood threatened again less than a decade later, nine-year-old Edwin literally carried water on behalf of a paying Depression-era government program, helping hydrate the workers on the newly formed levees. As he noted in an apocryphal reminiscence years later, his weekly pay came in cash, tucked in an envelope.[13] That 1936 gig completed, he jumped on the rural electrification train. He told a TV interviewer eight decades later, "I got books out of the school library and got a basic education in wiring and wired my father's house. People in the area were amazed and wanted me to wire their houses," but, he added with a chuckle, "they wanted to wait a while to see if [ours] burned down."[14]

While not ashamed of the family's poverty, neither did Edwin intend to drift back into it. He and Marion picked cotton for their father—but got whipped when Boboy caught them stealing from his stockpile to pad theirs.[15] In another tale, he claimed to have impaled a finger during an adolescent fishing expedition, after which Boboy offered him two dollars to let him remove it, versus paying a doctor do it.

While Edwards could not recall much of the initial catastrophe, the recovery, and fallout, the Great Flood and Depression of the twenties and thirties must have left a deep personal impression on him. Watching neighbors lose their savings inspired Boboy and thus his sons to trust greenbacks and greenbacks only for the rest of their lives. The Great Flood of 1927, too, rejiggered Louisiana's political scene. A year after "a tragedy that made the state ripe for populist appeals to the have-nots," as one observer later noted, Huey Pierce Long became governor.[16]

The Edwards family rode a line of political neutrality, which isn't to say they were nonpartisan. The family kept out of political squabbles; the Civil War had scarred their ancestors, even though none had joined the fight. Edwin's paternal great-grandfather, William Edwards, died in a strange guerrilla action in June of 1862 in which he and his two sons confronted a Confederate splinter group that had orders to burn the area's cotton crop.[17] William, brandishing a rifle, marched to where a Federal marshal was being held for demanding a halt to the operation and asked for him to be released. The Confederates began firing, killing William instantly and wounding two others, including William's son.[18]

Edwin, while he too tried to find the neutral position in local politics, grew up in a parish that shined on colorful and somewhat unhinged politicians, brash women supporters and detractors, and a hard-drinking lifestyle. The prodigal son of Marksville, however, famously didn't indulge in liquor or beer and was often seen with a glass of juice. "My father was a very stern Presbyterian," Edwin would later say. "He disliked three things. Alcohol, tobacco and gambling. I gave him two out of three."[19] Why, observers wondered, did Edwards become a gambler but refrain from booze and smokes? One suspects that, for him, indulging in the latter two vices would lead to a loss of control, whereas when Edwards cradled dice in his palm, he controlled his destiny.

The second Kingfish of Louisiana got his start not at the card table or the union picket line but at the pulpit, circa age fourteen. The pulpit belonged to Marksville's Nazarene Church, the house of worship preferred by his mother. The minister would allow Edwin to serve as an unofficial youth preacher and to stand facing the congregation in his early teen years, whereupon the pious, fervent young man proselytized in a dry, stubborn way that didn't immediately resonate. He hesitated. He hemmed. The congregation fanned itself or waved listlessly at mosquitoes.[20] He was a reserved Cajun country teenager, a bit ashamed of his accent perhaps, or of his hesitancy switching from English to Cajun French and back again. "Cajun people were frowned upon by other sections of the state," he recalled. "We were a different category of people." After a few tired sermons, though, he found his tone. By the time he met Elaine, his future wife, Edwin Edwards had developed the style that would cause generations to swoon. He was short but affected a swagger that came to feel natural, and he mixed deadpan humor with a confidence that recalled one famous forebearer: Governor Huey Long. (They differed substantially in tone and oratorial volume, however.) "Every now and then," he reflected, "I like to say things to try and be funny and try and get attention."[21] That endeared him to parishioners, but not as much to conservative clergy with seniority.

"He's not relaxed like the normal Frenchman," his brother-in-law told the *New York Times* in an interview with Edwin's family. "Maybe that's because he's ambitious," his mother-in-law shot back. His father-in-law, the owner of the town's grocery store, explained, "He's not the type of politician that gets up and waves his arms and raises hell, like Huey and Earl Long."[22] Edwin did wave and raise his arms as a communicant, although eventually he patented a deadeye stare into the nothingness, one that somehow made his humor punchier, a Jack Benny–style comic.

Despite his early success and ability to wake up the drowsy faithful with dry wit, he was not destined to become a church leader. He had eaten too many bread crusts and not enough loaves. During the Depression, he watched as the church raked in cash week over week but could show no proof that it did anything to alleviate the parish's daily deprivations. Edwin was already girl crazy too. (He wanted to marry his high school sweetheart, Elaine, whom he'd met playing Spin the Bottle.[23]) Besides, he didn't have the temperament to behave not only on Sunday mornings but the other six days. The poor son of a sharecropper had told his mother mid-scolding that she would have to think twice about disciplining and yelling at him when he was governor. He was all of six at the time.[24]

To get there, he would need a lot more than pizzazz and a few ribald jokes. He had the looks, certainly, and the reputation to make the Crowley City Council, which he did after Louisiana State University's law school, an incomplete cadet training to fly yellow N3N-3 aircraft for the Navy, and several years as a lawyer.[25] He won that first race, he said, because "I had a good education and also spoke French, which helped in the early years."[26] He claimed he might have made a fortune (an even larger one) as a corporate attorney in rice-rich Crowley, but stuck with the political thing, knocked on doors, made telephone calls (his folks didn't own a phone), and shook hands within a wide radius of his firm en route to victory in 1954.[27] He would win every election for the next three decades.

American power isn't activated through legislative victories or name recognition. It's earned through campaigning. Edwin Edwards had seen this. In 1960, he watched as John F. Kennedy, a charismatic, tanned, youthful senator, edged out the number two man in the nation, Republican Richard M. Nixon, through television and powers of personal persuasion. In the fall of 1972, now president himself, Nixon, a hard-right Republican, would win a historic landslide reelection; the Democrats were about to have their worst campaign ever and Edwards had no coattails to ride on. And despite three terms in Congress and a prominent role prior to that as the outgoing governor's floor leader in the State Senate, Edwards had reason to expect defeat in his first gubernatorial try. He was caught not only between the warring factions on civil rights but also in the generation gap brought on by the controversy surrounding the Vietnam War. During President Nixon's first term, Edwards had publicly weighed in on an antiwar demonstration held in front of the White House that had descended into chaos: "Gunfire was not only justified but required," he was overheard telling DC police.[28] Not exactly a liberal Democrat, but then again Nixon, who had escalated the war by bombing Cambodia and Laos and launched himself to fame with a Communist witch hunt that kickstarted McCarthyism and harnessed right-wing anger, was headed for a two-thirds majority of Louisiana.[29]

By the late sixties, the Democrats had maintained a stranglehold on Louisiana politics for more than a century, since the post-Civil War Reconstruction era. Republicans were considered the party of the Yankees, their gloating betters in the War for Southern Independence. Republicans were the ones sending troops to try to quell mobs attacking black voter registrants or elected officials. Calvin Coolidge tried to block help for the areas battered by the Great Flood; the president, of course, belonged to the GOP.[30] They had been the party of big business interests, which, in 1940, nominated Wendell Willkie, most notable for suing to prevent the formation of the Tennessee Valley Authority, which, undeterred, ultimately gave mouth-to-mouth resuscitation to Southern states during the Depression.[31] The GOP, originally launched to crush the slave states in the 1850s and '60s presidential elections, had a muddled position on "the blacks" a century later. The Dixiecrat faction of the Democratic Party, personified by senators Richard B. Russell and Strom Thurmond, held filibusters and whipped up their voting base to stop anti-lynching, pro-voting, pro-civil rights bills in the Senate, but following the Civil Rights Act of 1964, Thurmond angrily jumped ship for the "super minority" GOP, giving them firmly one-third of Senate seats.[32] At the time, even the Republicans didn't seem to know what to make of this event, which proved to be an important bellwether in American political history.

Democrat Edwards, then in his first term in the US House of Representatives, held a salivated finger up to the wind. President Johnson expected their party's pro-black bills would cost the Democrats the South "for a generation" and Edwards represented a white district in a segregated state. Edwards abstained from voting on Johnson's 1966 civil rights bill, one of three Louisiana congressmen (all Democrats) to skip out.[33] The bill died in the Senate, dealing a blow to Johnson's standing in Congress and his chances at reelection.

Edwards, however, hadn't turned his back on marginalized black people. Growing up, he reflected, "everyone talked about fairness and equality but when it came to Negroes, no one talked about [that]. Farmers needing farm labor came in stake trucks to our side and drove them to the other side to work. But they were required to get them back before dark. Those of us who were poor whites got along with blacks but contact was limited to daylight hours and we did not go into each other's houses."[34]

His mother, Agnes, became a midwife during the Depression, delivering dozens or possibly hundreds of black babies.[35] Those kids were now grown and many remembered the Edwards family. Congresspersons could

appoint the local postmaster in their districts, and in 1969, when an opening cropped up in Palmetto, Louisiana, Edwin told confidantes he would
name Henry "Huey" Fontenot to the post—not remotely newsworthy,
even in a sleepy village like Palmetto, unless you factored in the color of
Fontenot's skin. Edwards quoted Fontenot, saying, "What am I going to
tell my three boys about going to school to better themselves, if every time
something comes up for them to have a chance, they're knocked down
because they're black?" Edwards' constituents wrote him pleading letters,
suggesting Fontenot would taint each parcel by his mere touch. The letters went mostly ignored.[36]

The fallout from Fontenot's hiring was immediate. The White Citizen's
Council threatened a boycott of the state's Cotton Festival if organizers
insisted on honoring Edwards. The letters about the "contaminated" mail
shifted; now, the same residents were threatening Edwards's life.[37] Tem-
pers were further inflamed when Edwards shooed away a mob of constituents up in almost-literal arms over a federal judge's recent ruling forcing
the integration of two local school systems. A gunshot ripped a hole in the
Crowley campaign office and almost killed a secretary.[38] A man carrying a
handgun, silencer, and three books about the Mafia, including *The Godfather*, was arrested at the Baton Rouge airport with Edwin Edwards' name
and hotel room number on a piece of paper tucked beneath the books.[39]
At the Louisiana Yambilee in Opelousas, an annual pageant, parade, and
epic festival held to celebrate—of all things—the sweet potato, Edwards and
bodyguards in matching gingham suits and sunglasses fanned out along the
parade route.[40] Edwards and his wife, Elaine, were all smiles, reaching out
for the offered hands of farmers, black women and children, white ladies in
horn-rimmed glasses and bonnets. Looming in the background, however,
were police deputies with sniper rifles, perched atop two-story department
stores and banks, enlisted for one reason: to protect civil rights Congressman Edwin Edwards.

Some also recalled his first racial controversy. The Crowley City Council
allowed predominantly-black Ross High School to send its marching band
to the local Christmas parade, but some of the city's leaders and parents
threatened to withdraw their white student marchers. Edwards told the kids
to decide for themselves. Here, walking the streets, was the man responsible for that grave offense. They recognized him not as the congressman
who had voted "nay" on Johnson's 1968 civil rights bill, but as the one who
voted "yea" on the 1966 renewal of the Voting Rights Act, among the few
Southern Democrats to do so, and for which some had sent death threats.[41]

Then, across a four-day span in April of 1970, bombs exploded at the Baton Rouge Country Club and the Louisiana State Senate. No one was killed, although the Senate president's desk and an air conditioner at the country club were rather unlucky. The timing of the attacks was suspicious— only non-white workers were present at either scene, no paying country club members or politicos. "A person of that nature has got to be a revolutionary or a man who is not completely sane—one or the other," growled Governor John McKeithen. Soon after, a bundle of dynamite turned up at the same country club. Then someone apparently shot a black arrow into the *State-Times* newspaper drop slot in Baton Rouge and warned that additional lynchings and injustices toward black people would be met by further action. Police, however, told the Shreveport *Times* an organized labor "crank" had likely framed the Black Panthers or a similar group to cover his tracks and that the bombings were retaliation for ongoing oil industry strikes. But, as with the Edwards votes, the horror ended up deeply embedded in voters' minds.[42]

Edwards believed the worst battles of segregation were behind Louisiana, that the "Negro question" had long been resolved. As his biographer Leo Honeycutt put it, the state had narrowly but firmly avoided the violence of Selma, Alabama, and Mississippi's Klan murders, and "Edwin took that as an indication his state led the new south and was ready for a colorblind leader."[43] While the civil rights debate is what many people connected to Edwards at the dawn of the seventies and was one of his biggest "drawbacks" in his first run for governor, in another sense, it served as a bona fide. He wouldn't get the segregationist bloc in a crowded primary anyway—there were far too many rabid right-wing competitors. The state had begun registering black voters, mainly Democrats, following the Civil Rights and Voting Rights Acts and, by 1970, the majority of Orleans Parish's voters were women, who tended to support integration in more substantial numbers.[44] The black vote could shift hard to Edwin Edwards, especially in New Orleans. It all depended on whether he could get the word out to them.

Edwards mulled all of this over and entered the most competitive clusterfuck of modern Southern politics: a seventeen-candidate slugfest for the Louisiana Governor's Mansion.[45] The cast of characters could give any voter a headache: Lieutenant Governor Taddy Aycock jumped into the race early, aiming to fill his term-limited boss's shoes. Two Longs—Gillis and Speedy, canceled each other out. Jimmie Davis, the two-term ex-governor and author of "You Are My Sunshine" for his previous campaign, returned after several terms out of the spotlight. John G. Schwegmann, owner of the eponymous grocery store chain, qualified for the primary, presumably hoping to capture the business kingpin vote. Bennett Johnson, an obscure state senator, threw his name into the proverbial hat and was not expected to make the general.[46] A. Roswell Thompson, an Imperial Wizard of his own made-up branch of the Ku Klux Klan, figured what the hell.[47] And then David Treen, an honest-to-God Republican, made the ballot. David C. Treen, a two-time loser from the New Orleans suburbs, had run against Hale Boggs, the US House majority whip, in 1968 and had come within four thousand votes of upsetting him, a near tie and one of the closest Louisiana elections on record. Amid this sea of competition, one dropout explained to Edwards: "Boy, you got to be crazy" to think an unknown Democratic congressman could fight Treen on the Right, and Jimmie Davis and two Longs on the Left.[48]

Davis, meanwhile, seemed "inevitable" based on his popularity in rural areas, statewide name recognition, and the acumen that made him a two-term governor in the first place. Louisiana State University dubbed him a true "man of the people"—white people. In his comeback race of 1959–60, Davis ran to the right of fellow segregationists and squeaked past them.[49] In 1968, he had almost been George Wallace's vice president on the American Independent Party ticket.[50] Davis, too, made moves in 1971. He pointed out that he and Edwards shared a commonality: "We're both the sons of sharecroppers," he said.[51] Of course, it was meant as a dig—*he's a hot shot lawyer in tailored suits, and I'm an "aw shucks" man of the people, and* still *the son of a sharecropper*. And, just to make sure Edwards couldn't win, Davis pinched Edmund Reggie. The state party strategist, instrumental in JFK breaking through to the Southern electorate and, most importantly, a close friend of Edwards, defected to Edwin's chief rival. Reggie saw the former two-time governor as a repeat favorite, and the betrayal severed the close personal relationship between the Edwardses and Reggies, who would not speak again for years.[52]

Jimmie Davis, however, had a chink in his armor, unnoticed by Reggie and all but a few, including Edwin Edwards, who remembered Davis spending several months of his first term—when Edwin was still at LSU Law—in California performing "You Are My Sunshine" and other hits for Hollywood musicals and "horse operas." Louisianans did not forgive that neglect. It left a berth for fresh blood—and someone who could capture newly registered voters.

Edwards needed to stand out somehow, but found himself lost in the seventeen-candidate shuffle, under criticism from all sides, including from the outgoing governor, John McKeithen, for whom he had once been floor leader in the State Senate before running for Congress. He fueled the fire by making cocky public pronouncements like, "Two out of ten women will go to bed with you, but you've got to ask the other eight."[53] A popular 1971 bumper sticker read: "Vote Against Edwards. The Wife You Save May Be Your Own."[54] Gubernatorial longshot Warren J. Moity, aka "Puggy," tried the opposite tactic, referring to Edwards as "Tweety Bird" in speeches and insinuating the congressman was a homosexual. At a debate, Edwards marched onto the stage and planted a kiss on Moity's cheek, stunning the crowd, which burst into applause and laughter.[55] *At least this Cajun congressman is entertaining*, his rivals grumbled.

As Davis slipped in the polls, Edwards stayed high. He had been proven right all along about the dynamics of the election. "The more that I got" into the race, he told Leo Honeycutt, "the better I felt. . . . I had a heavy, solid bloc of support [but] the more the votes in the rest of the state were diced by a number of candidates, the better chance I had to make the runoff."[56]

The attacks on Edwards backfired. On November 6, 1971, Jimmie Davis watched his reelection go down in flames. He and his wife tried to one-up each other in expressing their unbridled joy over his finishing fourth.[57]

That night, Elaine and Edwin watched local election reports on a bank of TVs in suite 1545 of "Louisiana's Hotel," the New Orleans Monteleone on Royal Street.[58] Surrounded by only their closest aides and family, the "party" took on the feel of defeat, or at least of campaigns of the pre-television and radio era. (Back then, candidates often turned in for the night and were awoken by telegram or, sometimes days later, by a horseback rider.) Elaine shook her head in wonder as the networks recycled footage of long lines and her husband waving to the flashbulbs. Johnston took the lead early on, with the northern, more conservative areas of the state reporting first, while the southern precincts, including New Orleans, took hours.

But that night, Edwin Edwards stunned the establishment. He came in first in the field of seventeen, leading J. Bennett Johnston and Gillis Long by five and nine points, respectively. "Louisiana voters, like the rest of the South, were looking for a new face and the new image for their state," said Edwards in his victory speech. Johnston, cocky in distant second, told reporters: "I don't regard it as an upset. . . . The political prognosticators weren't talking to the people."[59]

When the smoke cleared, the runoff began. Edwards had six more weeks till the general against Johnston and two more races to win to achieve his dream in 1972. Johnston made quick moves. The State Senator went after eighteen-year-olds newly allowed to register under a Federal constitutional amendment.[60] Crucially, he also earned Lieutenant Governor Aycock's support, shoring up the hard-right vote. It didn't help that Edwin's entreaties to "the blacks" and his refusal to promise to keep taxes low had the state's businessmen wary. Johnston, meanwhile, had opposed the busing program for integrating schools, which the voters of Shreveport would remember and reward him for.[61] In previous victories, Davis and McKeithen had gone hard after the white vote, all but literally drawing lines in the sand between themselves and the African American community—and the candidates promising to help it. This strategy typically paid off; their opponents often got *only* the black vote. Edwards was betting on breaking the cycle through rural outreach and pure magnetism. Getting ahead of himself, one Huey Long biographer wrote that "it appears the state is coming of age. Racism may well be dead in its traditional form in Louisiana."[62]

It was during the 1971 campaign, Edwards' cousin Frenchy Brouillette suggested, that Edwards realized the media and festival crowds would help him seduce the voting public. "It was just a high school popularity contest, and, as he did back in Marksville, Edwin used his style and wit to make himself the coolest bad boy in school. He knew that the ultimate candidate would be the man whom every woman wanted and every man wanted to be."[63]

Edwards, late in the race, struck back on a new front. "I would have to say that the major philosophical difference is in our awareness of the problems of the poor," he told a reporter. "I don't think he has been in contact with it. I think he's unsympathetic to it."[64] At their one and only debate, live on WDSU-TV in New Orleans, the Edwards campaign was blindsided by a new revelation. While Edwards had focused on the rural vote, Johnston had lined up endorsements by the Black Louisiana Action Committee, better known as BLAC, and BOLD, the Black Organization for Leadership Development. The damage was catastrophic. Edwin tried to spin it, saying there would be blowback for Johnston, seen as the more "white-friendly" candidate, but Congressman Edwards couldn't afford to hemorrhage even a few thousand runoff voters. He lined up black representative Dorothy Mae Taylor to try to draw Taylor's New Orleans support, but that couldn't compete with two black organizations and their get-out-the-vote operations for Johnston.[65] Edwards learned a pivotal lesson about who to cultivate for future races.

The runoff between Johnston and Edwards turned out nearly the same 1.18 million voters a week before Christmas as in the seventeen-candidate primary a month earlier. This time, the margin would be perilously thin, statistically one of the closest in Louisiana history, in fact. Edwards, parked in suite 1545 of the Monteleone with the same family members and cohorts from the primary, kept telling people a "coon-ass" governor was decades overdue, but truthfully, the early returns looked brutal. At ten p.m., Johnston took the lead and sat there for hours, at one point running up the score to a comfortable four-point margin. The black vote was seemingly divided; when votes from New Orleans came in, they were almost evenly split.[66]

Later, observers realized a new political organization had been working harder than anyone in the southeast. SOUL, or the Southern Organization for Unified Leadership, spent election day knocking on doors, passing out flyers at polling sites, and remaining visible for their endorsed candidate, Edwin Edwards. They were in New Orleans and, more importantly, they were from the African American community. With their bloc and landslide wins in little-noticed Terrebonne, Lafourche and St. Martin parishes, the candidates were running almost exactly 50/50.[67]

It lasted until the first minutes of December 19, 1971. Out of 1,164,036 votes cast, Edwards squeaked by with a four thousand vote margin, roughly one vote per precinct. Johnston increased his primary vote by nearly one-third, while Edwards increased his by barely one quarter. "For every parish Johnston carried in the north, Edwards matched it in the south," the Associated Press noted.[68] Edwards had overestimated his black turnout and Johnston won the cities, stunning even his own campaign, which had expected the black and more liberal votes to pick the civil rights congressman, but Edwin had outperformed his previous races in Acadia and other rural areas where farmers voted on economic ideas, not civil rights, and it proved decisive.[69]

Democrat Edwin Edwards crushed Republican Dave Treen in a general election matchup and moved on to his transition planning.[70] As governor, Edwards knew he could unite the African American community behind him. He could run the state as a liberal on taxes and a centrist on business interests, a civil rights leader, a populist comedian, and preacher-turned-politician, and get re-elected. All he had to do was pick up the dice, blow on them a little, say the lucky, magic words, and throw.

CHAPTER 2

Fast Eddie

In the civil rights years and throughout the early Edwards era, white Louisianans who stood against segregation were targets of the Ku Klux Klan. If a newspaper editorial board wrote an article blaming the KKK for a church bombing or for violently attacking peaceful protestors, that editorial board might itself become the target of terrorist attacks. In his posthumous memoir, *Bogalusa Daily News* editor Lou Major wrote of a 1960s boycott from John Birch Society members, as well as crosses burned on his lawn, tires slashed in his driveway, and threats against his family, none of which slowed him down. "The newspaper and Major personally were viciously insulted in the 'Midnight Mail,' the flyers published by the Klan and tossed late on Saturday nights onto the sidewalks and driveways of many Bogalusa homes."[1]

"They need to be exposed to the light of day and shamed for their heinous actions," Major explained to his newspaper readership. "But more than despised, these people need to be pitied. They have not kept up with civilization. They are throwbacks to a day when rash emotionalism ruled over reason."[2]

But when the Watts riots broke out in Los Angeles, Louisiana governor John McKeithen warned that he wouldn't tolerate such behavior in his state, no matter if the KKK had provoked it, and funneled money to white supremacists through the Louisiana State Sovereignty Commission, a detail that did not emerge until 2016.[3] Joe Biden, a soon-to-be Delaware senator, railed against busing black children into white-heavy school districts to undo some of the damage of segregation.[4] His fellow Democrats (and Republicans, as well as a majority of black people polled), including McKeithen, joined the fray on the anti-immigration front.

Not everyone tried to shoot the messenger or kill Klansmen with kindness. A league called Deacons for Defense and Justice armed themselves and saddled up to go after the KKK. They soon had their hands full. On August 30, 1971, shortly before Labor Day and the start of the school year in Pontiac, Michigan, when "a court-ordered plan to bus children across town to achieve racial Integration went into effect," Klansmen in Clint Eastwood and James Dean haircuts and white t-shirts set ten bombs on empty school buses.[5] Destroying the buses, in their minds, would halt the integration order and free white children of the tyranny of going to school with black kids. It didn't work. Five defendants were found guilty of conspiracy and of the bombings, thanks to a paid FBI informant, Jerome Lauinger, who had infiltrated the Rangers, what the *New York Times* called a "supermilitant" wing of the KKK. The anti-busing positions of McKeithen and other rightwing Democrats suddenly appeared tenuous.

But the Klan had tapped into something. When black and poor people rioted in Watts or were blamed for fires and violence mainly caused by police in Newark, the KKK could point to the headlines and say, "Told you so." Now the male white supremacists shifted their focus—they asked white moms to stand up. "The slender mother of three alternatively goaded, rallied, calmed and steadied her followers through a long morning of active protest against pupil busing," as a Michigan local wrote the following month. "Thousands of admirers—all of them white, most of them women, and all of them angry—followed Mrs. McCabe by protesting at the schools, chaining themselves to fences, blocking buses and defying arrest."[6]

Irene McCabe, the youthful, dyed-blond housewife, kept getting her face in the paper. It helped that she did not belong to the Klan. She had the Oakland County prosecutor on her team and palled around with cops and their spouses. She could've been in Ira Levin's book *The Stepford Wives*, only she would have *volunteered* to be replaced by a robot. Her beautiful blond face helped sell a Republican congressional campaign.[7] When the national news networks aimed cameras her way, McCabe would open her jacket and stick her chest forward, revealing her homemade t-shirt: "Bus Judges Not Children!" Mary Bacon, dubbed "the Klansman's Jane Fonda," also spoke on behalf of the KKK, introducing David Duke at a rally at the New Orleans Fair Grounds racecourse in the 1970s. "We are not just a bunch of illiterate Southern n***-killers," she said angrily. "We are good, white, Christian people working for a white America. When one of your wives or one of your sisters gets raped by a n***, maybe you'll get smart and join the Klan." In later elections, she would say, "How would you like your sister to be raped by one of them?," to which some might retort, *I wouldn't like it, regardless of who did the raping.*[8] "Women are the same as men in our organization," Duke told the *Times*. "We don't have any prohibitions or constitutional limitations regarding them. In fact, some of our best members are women."[9]

This is the melee that Edwin Edwards plunged headlong into in the spring of 1972, when he became Louisiana's fiftieth governor and the first from the southern part of the state since 1940.[10] Days before general election votes were cast, a "race riot" ended with a WBRZ-TV cameraman beaten and paralyzed by a reported mob. It threatened to overshadow the harmony of the first Edwards administration. Gone was the slick charmer who expressed confidence and affected unconcern about every new insult and degradation from the Democrats who were supposed to be rewarding him for his help. Before taking office, he went hard at McKeithen, his chief critic, for leaving a $30,000,000 deficit and not wanting "the new administration to do well" because "it'll make him look bad."[11] But the three elections had sapped his strength for the four-year fight ahead. It was as if, having achieved the office he'd dreamed of since he was barely old enough to talk, Edwin Edwards could no longer find the motivation.

In the spring of 1972, a gas tax he needed to fill a budget hole failed by six votes. Edwards' biographer wrote of the legislative battle over the tax, "Given enough alcohol, church-going lawmakers would agree to just about anything, which explained Louisiana's many bizarre, poorly written laws." As he watched control of the agenda slip away, Edwards uncharacteristically railed against his fellow politicians. "The problem is going to be resisting the temptation to increase the tax by two cents instead of one." Hint, hint.[12]

Edwards let the gas tax issue settle for a bit. He approached the predominantly black Louisiana Council on Human Relations, telling them that, under his administration, African Americans "have the right and obligation to push for the kind of involvement in government you are looking for." He soon announced the hiring of what was probably "the only black woman press secretary in any state government."[13] The *State-Times* interpreted this in a headline: "Edwards Vows to Reward Blacks for Their Support." The article that followed didn't help either. "He has also told black leaders that blacks had better qualify with civil service, 'because this is the only way anyone can obtain certain jobs.'"[14] Regardless of the accuracy of that incendiary quote, anyone reading it understood but one way to interpret it. *Reconstruction never ended*. Black people who supported him were considered qualified, while conservatives who hadn't suddenly found themselves out of the network. "There are three kinds of people to hire," Edwards later said. "Qualified friends, unqualified friends, and enemies. I've never exhausted the first category."

If it appeared that Edwards was implementing a corrupt scheme, his other actions seemed to balance it out for the public. Elaine had to spend the Edwards family's money on Mansion renovations—"I'd like to stay eight years to get my money's worth," she cracked—and hired an all-new kitchen staff: incarcerated men, a dozen of whom were convicted murderers.[15] Edwards also bucked conservatives and the oil industry on other fronts, helping the environment by signing eight bills further protecting it at roughly the same time the Feds were creating the Environmental Protection Agency. The environment didn't have a powerful voting bloc, although opponents of these bills did, so no one could say Edwards signed those bills because of some pay-to-play deal. Also—and crucially it would turn out—he signed an order repealing the last of the state's unenforced Jim Crow–era segregation laws. When Senator Alan J. Ellender died, Edwards and Nixon conferred about appointing a replacement for the three months prior to the next election. But the president couldn't come up with a name palatable to the Democrat governor. Edwards was surprised Nixon didn't immediately suggest a Republican moderate, perhaps even Treen, someone who could then pivot to running for the seat properly, but perhaps Nixon saw the same red flags he did. When a governor appointed someone, a dozen rivals, enemies, and even supporters would lash out at him for not naming *them*. In the end, Edwin Edwards went with the most surprising but perhaps the simplest pick: he chose Elaine Edwards.[16]

With everyone talking about the surprise new US senator, Edwards had an inspiration, this time with his strategy of "wait for them to forget." After months of stalling, the legislature revisited the gasoline tax and passed it by large margins. He followed this crucial victory by appointing a black woman to the judge's bench for the first time in state history, balanced the budget, eliminated state agencies, and revised the old-school patronage system that would've required him to personally select hundreds or thousands of often total strangers for obscure state positions. He presided over a constitutional convention and new constitution that is still in effect today, stayed out of the five-way race to fill the seat of missing and presumed dead plane-crash victim Hale Boggs, the House Majority Leader, and, as if anyone thought Edwards did it all for power, started a rumor he wouldn't run again in 1975.[17]

Of course, he did run. He'd scratched and kicked his way to his dream job—there was no plausible scenario in which he wouldn't be a candidate. Perhaps unsurprisingly, it ended up being the biggest cakewalk of his career.[18] Running on the coattails of a nine-figure budget surplus, Edwards pummeled five other Democrats, including Addison Roswell Thompson, the self-proclaimed one-man Klan, in the primary, and ran unopposed in the general. Two opposing candidates were so humiliated, they promptly switched to the Republican Party, perhaps hoping the state would be not only sick of Edwards by the time his term expired but of Democrats in general. Although these moves and Edwards' commanding 62 percent of the vote caused much guffawing at the time, it's clear now that the 1975 election was a major turning point in Southern and national politics. In some ways, the years immediately after Watergate and Nixon's resignation brought in liberal reformers, many of whom, like Jimmy Carter, were more interested in morality and good government than effecting good legislative and campaign strategies, which opened the door for ambitious, big-business conservatives. The national Democrats needed go-getter populists like Edwin Edwards. Instead, from then on, they dug trenches and played defense.[19]

It may be difficult to imagine, but the Mafia had a stranglehold in the Louisiana business world and politics from the post-WWII years until the 1990s.[20] Gangster Carlos Marcello allegedly ran a criminal enterprise on behalf of Frank Costello and the Genovese family of New York, bringing slot machines to New Orleans. Marcello is best known for bragging about "masterminding" the Kennedy assassination on his deathbed, although his confession followed a series of strokes.[21] There is no question, however, that he was involved in criminal activities, allegedly as Edwin's "official political fixer," funneling bribes from business leaders to the governor's brother Nolan, a lawyer. Marcello was the culprit in a major scandal during the second Edwards administration, which went undetected for several years. It involved a political player named Charles E. Roemer II, a.k.a. "Budgie."[22]

Charlie Roemer didn't start out as some small-time hood or a corrupt friend of some politicians. Despite his white skin, he helped lead outreach to the black community for Edwards' first gubernatorial run. Along with his son, nicknamed "Buddy" to distinguish him from his towering father, Budgie Roemer directed an innovative computer firm and developed its key software program, the likes of which few had seen in the 1970s, to crunch numbers for the Edwards campaign.[23] Innovative Data Systems' software zeroed in on key issues, voters, and political figures as tipping points that could turn the tide for Edwin Edwards. The Roemers later boasted that their software polled issues in real time and sent potentially persuadable voters telegrams two days before an election. Having proved the system worked, Charlie was rewarded with the job of Commissioner of Administration under Governor Edwards, a high-echelon position similar to that of a budget director.[24] But Roemer wasn't content with that title—or its salary, apparently.

Carlos Marcello and four other men, including Charlie Roemer, were hit with racketeering, bribery, and fraud charges after a sting where "undercover FBI agents posed as crooked insurance executives . . . taking part in a scheme to win a multimillion-dollar state group insurance contract through bribery."[25] Roemer and Marcello each did several years in prison, although their convictions were later overturned on a technicality.[26] By then, Budgie Roemer's son Buddy had taken office as Louisiana's fifty-second governor.

Although he emerged relatively unscathed from Charles Roemer's Mafia scandal, Edwin Edwards unquestionably came out tainted from "Koreagate." North Korean-born lobbyist Tongsun Park was a true rags to riches to story, even earning the moniker "the Asian Great Gatsby."[27] But his true career path seemed to be buying influence for the South Koreans and keeping their country in rice money. He admitted to bribing ten congressmen in order to keep rice exports. Also, he just so happened to be working as an agent with South Korean Central Intelligence.[28] Once he received immunity, Park saw little risk in exposing everyone involved. The *Washington Post* snarled about Park's "charmed life in the scandal, his affection for big bucks, and his proclivity for American ways."[29] He paid no attention, and the biggest scandal to hit DC since the Watergate burglary was underway. Louisiana's Democratic congressman Otto Passman, the chairman of the House Appropriations Committee, stood trial on charges he'd received hundreds of thousands of dollars from Park, tax evasion, and that he'd engineered rice deals between the two countries. Park claimed to have given Passman $5,000 on a 1972 Hong Kong junket and told him there was more where that came from.[30] Also on a junket to meet with Koreans that year? Edwin W. Edwards.

Shockingly, Edwards confessed. Only he didn't call it a bribe and he didn't say he'd accepted it. On October 25, 1976, not even a year into his second term, Edwards held a news conference and said that he hadn't taken "one nickel from any agent of any foreign country" but that his wife, Elaine, had accepted an envelope with $10,000 as a gift from a harmless family friend. This could not have helped the Edwards' marriage, which was strained already.[31] But what Edwards said next defies explanation.

"Will it make you feel better if I told you what happened?

"All right. When I was running for governor, Park visited me in New Orleans and that was the time we had a conversation in which I got the impression he was going to make me an offer of a contribution.

"I was concerned about accepting it because I was a member of Congress. I told him, 'No, my campaign is going well' even though he never specifically said he wanted to contribute.

"He went downstairs and had coffee with Elaine, who has been a friend of his, just like my children have been friends of his, since going back to 1969 or 1968.

"In the course of the conversation—and this all was developed in I.R.S. hearings—he said: 'Look, it doesn't look like Edwin wants to accept any help from me in the campaign, and I understand that, but I want to do something for you and Vicki and Anna,' and he gave her an envelope and said, 'Take this and spend it for you and your daughters but don't tell Edwin about it because I don't think he would let you keep it.' So, my wife, being prudent as she is, did exactly what he told her."[32]

When this quote appeared in the *New York Times*, Edwards came under heavy fire. But although his approval rating plummeted, miraculously, he did not even have to appear before the grand jury in the Koreagate trial. Elaine wasn't charged, either, perhaps because the gift had been accepted prior to her Senate tenure. There were other financial scandals or at least hints of impropriety in the press, such as the time a reporter dug through a trash can and discovered notes from a meeting at which "Edwards sold powerful state jobs for campaign contributions. Edwards said he made promises and took $130,000 to keep the money from going to other candidates, but never meant to keep the promises and returned the money after the election."[33] After Edwards' former bodyguard Clyde Vidrine told the press the meeting notes were accurate and that Edwards had indeed sold state jobs for contributions, a two-year investigation began. A federal grand jury discovered "that a quasi-governmental organization called the Family Health Foundation gave Edwards airplane trips and campaign contributions," but didn't prosecute the governor. Instead, Edwards' old State Highway Board chairman, Lewis Johnson, ended up in the penitentiary for making illegal contributions to the 1971 Edwards campaign. "Edwards says that although it was illegal for Johnson to make the contributions, it was legal for him to accept them."[34]

While all of this built up, the governor's old friend Clyde Vidrine put the finishing touches on a book. *Just Takin' Orders*, published in 1977 and reprinted in a substantially expanded edition in 1985, torpedoed Edwards' presidential or vice presidential prospects. With salacious revelations on every page, should the reader believe them, *Just Takin' Orders* is a wild, erratic read. Vidrine, the tanned, blond, double-chinned bodyguard who called himself Edwards' right hand, had been a rice farmer in Ville Platte when he began palling around with the young congressman.[35] Vidrine reportedly arranged for a mortgage for his farm to fund the first Edwards gubernatorial campaign. He spirited the candidate between events in a black car and stood between his boy and fawning women or nosy reporters and their microphones. In the book, Edwards comes off as a double-dealer, publicly boosting black workers while secretly meeting with the Klan to tell them he won't particularly shine on minorities. Edwards apparently slept with up to five girls per night on twice-per-month trips to Las Vegas, sometimes bringing each to Vidrine's door to prove his own "durability."[36] The governor would, according to *Just Takin' Orders*, set aside several thousand dollars to be left behind before each Vegas jaunt, so he could present it to Elaine as proof of his success at the craps tables. Significantly, the tell-all also revealed Edwards to have allegedly built up a $500,000 slush fund with "campaign contributions" from which he siphoned to cover gambling debts in Las Vegas.[37]

Louisianans cackled about the allegations and gave their governor a new nickname: "Fast Eddie," a reference to the pool shark character in the book and movie "The Hustler."[38] ("I deserved it," he would later admit.) And while few actually read the gossipy memoir itself, its revelations would dog Edwards in the newspapers until well after he left office.[39]

Why did Edwards try to appear straight until he became governor, after which it all quickly seemed to fall apart? Perhaps it was there all along, only he didn't start getting caught for alleged crimes until then. Maybe he genuinely behaved with dignity and ethical considerations in mind until he inadvertently blew a chunk of his pathetic annual salary on a gambling junket and then needed to take bribes to cover his debts. But it's more likely there were two facets to Edwin Washington Edwards: the ambitious politico with the strategic instincts to check his impulses to gamble and philander, and the Edwards who couldn't resist temptation.

"If you want to give me the opportunity," Edwards told a reporter, "I can be just as sinful in Baton Rouge as any place else in the world. It's a lot easier. I know more people here. Whatever my faults are, I'm not a hypocrite."[40] No, he wasn't. For the first time in what would be a storied career of doing so, he embraced the infamy.

Edwards was term-limited in the 1979 gubernatorial election. A decade and a half after president Lyndon Johnson predicted the Democrats would lose the South for "a generation" over civil rights, it is here that cracks began to appear in Louisiana.[41]

Much of what happened can be traced back to the inevitable letdown and resulting anger from African Americans, who saw that the party talked tough on civil rights but neglected them or took their support for granted. When white students or veterans protested the Vietnam War, which finally ended in 1975, the media treated it as a "movement." When black people tried to point out discrimination in housing, school administration, and the workforce, they were met with unequal force, including by Democratic officials.

On November 16, 1972, two black Southern University students were killed by police in Baton Rouge. In protest of "a racist curriculum," which included poor living and working conditions for SUNO employees, an estimated one thousand students had taken over the administration building on campus. That night, they allegedly ignored a demand to vacate immediately. Whether they refused to comply, could not hear the order, or simply did not have enough time to leave has been subject to decades of debate. In the resulting riot, two students were killed "either by buckshot or by shrapnel from exploding grenades or bombs." The deputy sheriff confirmed his men used hand-grenade simulators, shotguns, and riot guns. In a statement following the violence, the protestors claimed, "the progressive forces of Jackson State, Kent State, Attica, and now Southern University have seen their basic right to life snuffed out by a racist political structure." The students met Governor Edwards with a raucous reception, and not in a good way. When he left campus, having implored them to stand down, the students cracked wise. One said the governor had "the brains of a gnat" and suggested campaigning to make sure his first term would be the only one "for the little Cajun."

Dr. Clyde Smith, a SUNO professor, told the media that there had been "atrocities and barbarous acts perpetrated on black students," and called Edwards responsible for the violence.[42] Critics believed that the governor had used the events to his advantage and suggested that Edwards needed to look like he wasn't letting black people get away with "violent crimes" for the racist white electorate.[43]

In response, Edwards shut down the campus. His action, as well as ordering a reported one hundred National Guardsmen to SUNO, with several hundreds on call at a nearby Air Force base, riled up the students again. They set fire to the school cafeteria, causing a reported $50,000 worth of damage. There was a rumor a faction had formed with the express purpose of assassinating the governor. "The students spoke in very vile language and said they would not move," Edwards told a reporter.[44] He claimed that he'd been attacked from the Right for letting the student takeover happen without using force, and he pointed out the "damned if you do" irony of the situation. As for the murder plot, he claimed such threats were on the regular for him. (Of course, he didn't mention that they used to come almost exclusively from white racists.)

In response, a Black Panther and ex-Navy man gunned down two New Orleans police officers, one an African American cadet, on New Year's Eve. A week later, he wounded the white owner of a grocery store in a predominantly black neighborhood, broke into the downtown Howard Johnson hotel through a fire exit, and told a terrified employee, "Don't worry, sister. We're only shooting whites today." He executed two Virginia honeymooners in their suite, then gunned down a pair of high-level hotel employees, including the general manager, and three police officers responding to the distress call. With the murderer now sniping on the hotel's roof and cops pinned down on surrounding rooftops, a lieutenant colonel in the Marines piloted a helicopter without clearance and he and several other Marines exchanged gunfire with the sniper for several straight hours. The tide seemed to turn in the serial killer's favor, however, when he hit the helicopter's transmission, threatening to cause a secondary, afternoon-rush-hour catastrophe. Instead, the sniper got cocky and, as he climbed out of hiding to hit the helicopter again, he was hit over two hundred times by bullets from the Marines and police snipers.[45]

The prospect of black student takeovers and riots, sniper killings, and mob violence led to increased Klan membership in the 1970s. In Dearborn, Michigan, a Klan offshoot casually suggested doing "some killing [to] cut off, root and branch, the satanic Jews and all their lackeys who are stirring up the n***s against us."[46] In his 1982 memoir, *My Life in the Klan*, former undercover FBI agent Jerry Thompson detailed the rise of KKK activity, including Klan presence on campuses in Los Angeles, Nashville, and Chapel Hill, which in 1975 booked the twenty-four-year-old David Duke to speak.[47] Historian John Drabble wrote that there were more Nazis in America in the seventies than at any point since World War II, and that the FBI suspected a tidal wave was coming, but they were stretched thin with attacks and hateful rhetoric in every corner of the country.[48]

They certainly didn't seem prepared on November 3, 1979, when the KKK and purported Nazis joined forces to break up a left-wing worker's march in Greensboro, North Carolina. The Greensboro Police Department knew what was coming but neglected to inform the FBI or the targets of the planned violence. When the march started out from one of the city's predominantly black housing projects, organizers spotted sneering white men in plaid shirts and blue jean jackets tailing them. Insults were exchanged and the Klansmen and Nazis bounded out of their vehicles with shotguns and clubs. The protestors scattered but their pursuers laid down fire into the throngs. The melee, which lasted under ninety seconds, claimed the lives of five protestors, several shotgunned to death. Among the wounded—a kindergartner.[49]

Both the funerals of the victims and trials of the perpetrators were picketed by right-wing reactionaries who displayed anticommunist cardboard signs, and a marcher's widow attended her husband's service gripping a rifle and surrounded by comrades with M-16s.[50] Surprisingly, the violence dissipated despite two not-guilty verdicts in separate criminal state and federal civil rights trials.[51] (The men responsible were all slapped with a $48,000,000 civil suit, later settled for a mere $351,000.[52]) One outlet later called it "The Massacre That Spawned the Alt Right."[53]

At the time of the shootings, Louis Lambert, Edwin Edwards' hand-picked successor, had narrowly edged out the competition in the 1979 Louisiana gubernatorial primary. Lambert's candidacy kept getting tied to Edwards, which held him to a low approval rating, but Edwards saw a presumptive Lambert victory as a double-edged sword—for Edwards' rivals. Though term-limited this round, nothing could stop Edwards from running again in 1983, even the fact that he would have to oust his own protege to do so. Should 1979 Republican nominee Dave Treen pull off a miracle, he would be a Republican running for reelection in a state where only one in every twenty registrants was affiliated with the GOP. Why would anyone support *his* re-election over the larger-than-life figure known as the Cajun Prince?

On December 8, 1979, Louisianans cast ballots in yet another election for the record books. Dave Treen received 690,691 votes for governor to Louis Lambert's 680,134, a difference of just over ten thousand votes, yet another one of the narrowest statewide general elections in history.[54] Treen became Louisiana's first Republican governor since the post–Civil War Reconstruction era, a gap of 122 years. He inherited a strong, growing, oil-based economy, and a mandate to reform government and root out corruption. His substantial, underestimated base had come through for him, and their hatred of Edwin Edwards and his miniature Watergates, which had made their beloved state a laughingstock in the national papers, would be addressed in due time, by government investigation if necessary.

As he left office for the political wilderness for the first time since announcing for the Crowley City Council, Fast Eddie made a few moves to reward friends and family. He had pardoned over 1,100 people during his terms, including twenty-six-year-old Rodney Wingate Jr., a drug convict who happened to be a friend and client of one Nolan Edwards, the governor's younger brother.[55] This decision would have horrifying implications beyond the world of politics in just a few years, but for now, it seemed to be another quid pro quo for the press to feast on as they welcomed another "good government conservative" into power.

Edwin Edwards had indeed lost his grip on state government, his closest confidantes, including his friend and bodyguard, Clyde Vidrine, his wife, Elaine, and his grown-up children, all of whom cringed when he immediately confirmed he would be mounting a comeback campaign in 1983. But a lot can happen in one gubernatorial term, and, as Edwin Edwards had experienced firsthand, the people can turn on you in a heartbeat.

PART II

THE WIZARD

CHAPTER 3

Aryan Youth

I am a National Socialist. You can call me a Nazi if you want.

DAVID DUKE

A mob received candidate David Duke at the doors to the VFW Hall.[1] Flashbulbs practically blinded the candidate on the way in, where he was met with beer-swilling, howling, practically euphoric supporters. After days of combative national and international TV and newspaper interviews, he had almost forgotten the enthusiasm he could muster from members of his own race and class. "Sometimes at night," he told biographer Michael Zatarain, "after a particularly vicious attack and the campaigning was done, I would take a long, steamy shower and let the pain slowly fall away with the tears."[2] Voter turnout for the 1989 State House runoff, between Duke and John Treen, had been a reported 78 percent, nearly a record, and Duke expected high turnout would favor him. This, and all the yard signs he'd seen on his way over to the Victory Party, had him practically bouncing in place, unable to stop grinning.

"Duke looked every bit the friendly, reasonable boy-next-door: campaigning for a seat in the state legislature as a conservative Republican in a mostly white district, he appealed to voters who agreed with his finely-tuned platform of tax relief, welfare reform, and an end to affirmative action programs," wrote one researcher.[3] ABC News reporter Mike von Freund, standing within reach, marveled that Duke, with this kind of welcome, might have the support for a US Senate run in 1990, if only his background wouldn't disqualify him for so many. Duke smirked but said nothing. The more von Freund watched, however, the wider his mouth grew. "No, I think you could win anyway!" he said.[4] A supporter said, "When you saw Mr. Treen on television, he looked like he was around Metairie Country Club all the time. . . . I really didn't think he had my best interest [*sic*] at heart."⁵ Members of the gathered crowd, who had been waiting on Duke and seemed emboldened by his arrival, turned their gaze on the roped-off press section.

They taunted UPI reporter Steven Watsky, whose last name gave off hints of a certain ethnicity, with one man hissing, "We missed one of you in the gas chambers."⁶

"Shit," said a nearby (black) cameraman, "we gotta get out of here before they lynch us."

Someone punched the reporter in the chest. As Watsky lunged to return fire, a photographer grabbed and hauled him away, lest the presumed lynching actually occur.⁷

This was Duke Country. It existed not only on a geographic map but in a kind of spirit inhabited by a large group, finally able to vent their frustrations and political views they had been told to keep to themselves lest they "offend" someone.⁸ They were Jefferson Parish residents who searched for a candidate to channel their pain over the 1980s economic downturn, during which wages and salaries had plummeted over 6 percent in five years. They were the ones who had told the pollsters they either supported Duke or claimed "no preference" when contacted, leading to undercounting for Duke.⁹ They were the ones who had blindsided President Ronald Reagan and his successor George H. W. Bush, and Bush's campaign team, led by strategist Lee Atwater.¹⁰ Despite conceiving the racially charged Willie Horton ad that turned the tide for his boss in the presidential election mere months earlier, Atwater (and Bush) had expressed horror to learn that John Treen, State Central Committee member, home construction professional, and brother of a former governor, had to face this "Republican" in the runoff for the Louisiana legislature. Worse for the Republican National Committee, only diehards turn out for run-offs, and John Treen didn't know any of them.

In a speech after the Greensboro Massacre, antiracist activist Anne Braden had warned, "The real danger today comes from the people in high places, from the halls of Congress to the boardrooms . . . telling the white people that if their taxes are eating up their paychecks, it's . . . because of government programs that benefit black people . . . because blacks are getting all the jobs."¹¹ She added that she worried that the Klan would thrive in that kind of political environment, to the point it could create "a fascist movement in the 1980s in America." In a letter to *The Advocate* decades after the runoff, a Duke voter explained that the reason so many supported a former "also-ran yahoo" in 1989 was not their candidate's racist or fascistic tendencies but rather that "Treen wanted to get rid of the $75,000 homestead exemption on property taxes so that there would be that much more money for the pork barrel" and Duke promised to make the rebate permanent.[12] On February 18, 1989, hundreds of vocal homeowners voted in drizzly and unusually chilly fifty-degree conditions and, after nightfall, turned out to the VFW.[13] Duke burst into the hall to a cascade of cheers. Grinning uninhibitedly, he let the faithful shriek themselves hoarse, and at last a breathless hush fell over the room. The press had front row seats for what subsequently transpired.

Duke, mouth close to the microphone, voice gentle and just this side of inaudible, said firmly, "I've just been to the county clerk's office and I have an announcement to make." He didn't let them wait long in this solemn silence. Breaking into his trademark megawatt smile, he shouted: "We won!" Out of 16,691 cast, Duke slipped through by a heart-stopping 227 votes. The hall broke into an ear-splitting roar and spontaneous chants of "Duke! Duke! Duke!" It was, as the candidate would later say, a "new day for America."[14]

At the Howard Johnson across town, a defeated John Treen wept. Republican State Central Committee member Beth Rickey stood nearby, nearly frothing with contempt. She had urged Treen to knock on doors or at least do *something* to counter Duke. "Campaigning is just not something John likes to do," she said. "I went with him one day in his home precinct and he was miserable the entire time."[15] Her idol, Ronald Reagan, having left office hours prior, had written a letter and recorded a radio spot in support of Treen.[16] Edwin Edwards blamed President Reagan, specifically, for Duke's victory: "Everybody in Louisiana knows Reagan didn't know John Treen."[17] Rickey went home, as gut-punched as if it had been her name on the ballot.

"I think David has come into his own," said Don Black, Duke's former associate with the KKK, who had recently spoke of "taking this country back" through the electoral process. "He has the potential for great leadership. . . . he's the Jesse Jackson of white rights in America," Black added, referring to the 1988 Democratic presidential candidate. "We'll be hearing a lot from him."[18]

A majority of Duke's voters had had zero college experience, almost half made under $35,000 per year, and his victory came thanks to winning the Democratic electorate in the district, especially the same people who had supported Edwards in his run for governor in '83.[19] Satisfied to achieve *any* victory with *any* coalition, State Representative–Elect Duke (R-Jefferson

Parish) leaned back to take it all in, just as a sign reading "Duke for Governor" appeared above the assemblage.

When discussing David Duke, one of the first points observers make is that he grew up in an "all-white" neighborhood close to the one he would grow up to represent in the State House.[20] More importantly and perhaps fatefully, it was in the New Orleans suburbs where he would one day set up shop and run for office. But Duke wasn't actually born in New Orleans. He came into the world via a hospital in Tulsa, Oklahoma, in 1950, making him all of thirty-eight when he won a local political contest and became a household name nationally.[21] New Orleanians don't take kindly to carpetbaggers, but because of Duke's right-wing views and his wisdom in refraining from telling locals how "we did it differently in *my* hometown," he never faced any serious criticism for not being from the state he presumed to lead. In fact, for much of his meteoric rise, Duke rarely encountered severe criticism from Louisianans. Even as an undergrad at Louisiana State University, using the campus's "Free Speech Alley" to rant about right-wing planks like affirmative action and welfare, he only started to draw substantial crowds when hippies, Vietnam vets, civil rights activists, amused students, and left-wing do-gooders started to spread the word about "this racist student."[22] Many students attended their first-ever political rallies to hear what the fuss was all about; some left naively assuming he spoke to them. The *Los Angeles Times* later described Duke's printed materials as focused on helping the white race, specifically, and expressing support for the Nazi Party.[23] James Reddoch, LSU's vice president for Student Affairs during Duke's heyday, explained that the Hitler worship received the loudest boos of all, but "hecklers are part of the Free Speech Alley tradition and he handled them well. He was always well-spoken and polite."[24]

Today, we can surmise why Edwards wanted to be governor. The Silver Fox sought power from a young age because, cliché or no cliché, he believed he had been blessed with a destiny: to be governor and then to be governor for as long as he could hold on, for the periods of his life when he would not be governor were nothing, forgettable, embarrassingly useless. Duke, however, baffled many, especially moderates, Leftists, and even members of his campaigns, who didn't pry but accepted his superficial explanations for seeking office. It's simplistic to conclude these offices were stepping stones to the presidency, as that doesn't cover why he wanted to run the country either. (Beth Rickey believed Duke saw "things in terms of power and survival, not the struggle for what is right and wrong."[25] In 1970, Duke wrote, "Politics is simply a struggle for power. Power will be in the hands of people who support white interests, or . . . in the hands of those who serve non-white interests."[26]) Nixon essentially thought the presidency a gift to his devoted mother for her faith in him; Jimmy Carter believed the demoralized country needed a genuine man of the people to course correct after the Watergate years; Lyndon Johnson wanted to be president to overcome his family's humiliation at his daddy having been run out of office in Texas over some silly "principles."[27]

David Duke's father, David Hedger Duke, was born in 1912 in Marshall County, Kansas, and his namesake and only son followed thirty-eight years later in Tulsa. Duke Sr.'s grandfather had been a Union soldier captured at Gettysburg, and, according to family lore, was rescued from drowning by a Confederate. The Confederate solider later co-founded a white nationalist organization, the Ku Klux Klan.[28] When David was a high school freshman, David Sr. told his family they were a Goldwater clan, but, as he later swore to *Newsweek*, he himself never espoused racist views.[29] "I tried to guide him in the right direction like any father does," David Sr. said in 1991. "It's just too bad about all the black violence. It's too bad we can't do something about it."[30] Duke looked back that same way, saying now that he'd become a parent, he could see that his own actions had probably freaked his father out. But, he explained, momentum had already taken hold.[31]

At the peak of the Vietnam War, Duke's world fell apart. In 1966, as Democrats in his childhood New Orleans neighborhood started grumbling about the US involvement overseas, Duke's father received orders from the State Department to set up an engineering operation in Laos.[32] After his older sister married and moved away, David was left with his mother, rumored to be a heavy drinker.[33] David rapidly lost interest in making friends and started bashing Communism and expressing pro-war views. In eighth grade at an ultra-conservative Christian academy, Duke received an assignment to take the "pro" side of a segregation argument for an essay. He ended up at the White Citizen's Council office in the Central Business District for research.

The Council, established a decade earlier in response to *Brown v. Board of Education*, the Supreme Court decision ostensibly eliminating school segregation, couldn't have been more welcoming to the temporarily fatherless teenage boy. The informative, dedicated group had come together to warn about integration-related threats to the community either seen or heard rumored and, like Duke's neighbors, were mostly Caucasians. "To all white citizens of the south, greetings," their posters began. "Stop buying Ford cars and trucks and other Ford products. MILLIONS and MILLIONS

and MILLIONS of dollars of Ford profits have been distributed to integration and civil rights organizations to fight the white people of the SOUTH,
by forcing them to associate with negroes [*sic*]." Another read: "Help Save
the Youth of America . . . Don't Let Your Children Buy, or Listen to These
Negro Records."[34] Duke enthusiastically wrote his paper and apparently
won the "debate."[35]

He soon became a hardened separatist on issues of segregation. In the
eighties, he explained, "Well, once I became convinced that the race issue
[was] what I consider to be the crisis facing Western man, I became convinced that one could simply not sit on the sidelines and learn about things,
especially something of such critical importance, without acting. And so I
looked around as a young person, and the only organization I saw that was
really doing anything completely honest on the racial issue was the Knights
of the Ku Klux Klan, led by Jim Lindsay. . . . I was seventeen-and-a-half."[36]

He read about the Klan, an organization that was birthed to disrupt any
racial harmony resulting from Reconstruction and that peaked with the
revisionist movie *Birth of a Nation*, a film released when Duke Sr. had been
a toddler. Duke claimed the Klan "defended our rights and heritage," was
Christian in nature, and served as a guiding light for him in the turbulent
sixties.[37] His reading convinced him that the Civil War hadn't been a racist
enterprise but a battle for "independence and not slavery."[38] Yet witnesses
claimed to have seen weapons, as well as Nazi helmets, in Duke's house
when he was still a teenager.

Soon after, like many hard-right Americans, Duke gaped in bewildered
joy at American Nazi Party founder George Lincoln Rockwell. In 1961, the
year Duke turned eleven, Rockwell made national headlines when he and
nine fellow neo-Nazis picketed an NAACP charity screening of the Paul
Newman movie "Exodus," about the founding of Israel, in New Orleans.[39]
For Rockwell, a celebration of Jews or a fundraiser for black people meant
veiled support for race mixing or the Communist menace or both. The
men carried signs reading "Gas Chamber for Traitors" and other incendiary slogans. They were shooed away from the event, and were threatened
with a charge of "alarm[ing] the public." The following month, Nazis surprised outsiders when they turned up at a speech by Malcolm X in Washington, DC, Rockwell's base of operations at the time. After donating $20
to the Nation of Islam, of which Malcolm X was then a member, Rockwell
fondly referred to the group's public face, Elijah Muhammad, as "Black
Hitler" and praised him for the miraculous rescue of "millions of the dirty,
immoral, drunken, filthy-mouthed, lazy and repulsive people sneeringly

called 'n***s' and inspir[ing] them to the point where they are clean, sober, honest, hard working, dignified, dedicated and admirable human beings in spite of their color."[40] He also said that he and Muhammad agreed that interracial mixing was "a fraud" perpetuated by Jewish interests. That, Duke decided, was where he stood too. He didn't hate black people, he despised powerful minorities who kept *everybody* down. He decided to read up as much as he could on this Rockwell fellow.

At LSU, Duke made a name for himself among the protestors and anti-government rebels, especially after Nixon's ascension to the presidency. At the time, students had to have their heads shaved before freshman year and women couldn't wear pants. "There they were, wearing brown shirts and armbands. Duke walked out, looking as much like Hitler as he could—the little mustache, hair combed the same way," said then-student Michael Connelly, describing a scene he witnessed on campus in 1971. "They were singing Nazi songs and doing the salute."[41] Duke denied being a Nazi but admitted to wishing he could join the National Socialist Party, which no longer existed.[42] Twenty years later, Kenneth Stern of the American Jewish Committee claimed Duke kept evading the question of Nazism by saying "he is against totalitarianism of any kind." Off the record, though, according to Stern, Duke would say things like "Eichmann got a raw deal" from the Nuremberg Trials that sentenced him to die for perpetrating the Holocaust and that "there were no extermination camps."[43]

LSU's Free Speech Alley, initially an actual alley with a podium planted in it, proved a fertile breeding ground for the young right-winger.[44] Duke's voice had an "aw shucks," high-pitched quality that was both disarming and endearing, if not classically statesmanlike. It helped tamp down the outrage—he didn't sound like a bitter, nasty old white man, frothing all the way back to the nineteenth century. He raised his voice over the boos to rail against inferior black genetics and an international Jewish conspiracy to weaken America's standing to pave the way for Communism.[45] The more his fellow students heckled, the bigger the crowd would be the next time he took over the podium. Duke, rarely nostalgic, later reflected on that time with admiration for the black LSU students who helped him improve his debating tactics because their superior numbers and passion always outweighed his. "Debating the enemy," he claimed, was perhaps the most memorable part of his college experience.[46] When he returned to the Alley at the peak of his campaign for governor, left-wingers turned out by the dozens. They screamed, they waved signs reading "David Duke: Nazi for the '90s." The only thing that seemed to change was the specifics of Duke's message; as a politician, Duke addressed "thought crimes" and the declining fortunes of the middle class, subjects somewhat over the heads of the grunge-loving poor kids on scholarship or the slumming rich WASPs. "I'm the only candidate with no skeletons in my closet." "Skeletons? Man, you got dinosaurs," a black student called out. "Man, you got museum pieces." Duke smirked. Like Edwin Edwards, Duke prided himself on his sense of humor.

In his 1990s campaigns, opponents circulated an image of Duke in a Hitler Youth uniform and picketing a 1970 speech by left-wing Jewish attorney William Kunstler outside Tulane University's McAlister Auditorium, and holding a sign with "Kunstler is a Communist Jew" on one side and "Gas the Chicago 7" on the other.[47] (The *C* in *Chicago*, it should be noted, was rendered as the Communist sigil.) Two decades on, Duke explained all this as "guerrilla theater" designed to get his name in the press, "youthful folly," and a satirical "spoof." He never belonged to Hitler's movement, he said.[48]

While everyone knew David Duke's name on campus, once he graduated, nobody particularly cared about some Baton Rouge Nazi. Without a captive, enraged audience to feed off of, his writings and musings had the air of the town crank. While visiting his father for a summer in Laos, during which he taught English to members of the Laotian officers' corps, he returned to the New Orleans area and was promptly arrested for inciting a riot in front of the city's Robert E. Lee statue.[49] Addison Roswell Thompson, Edwards' white supremacist opponent for the Governor's Mansion, attended in Klan robes and laid a Confederate flag at Lee's feet. Thompson also allegedly antagonized passersby with cracks about black people.[50]

During Duke's night in the infamous O.P.P. (Orleans Parish Prison), rumors spread that a black-hating Nazi blond boy had gotten himself locked up. Duke claimed that militant Leftists in the neighboring cells knew who he was. He claimed he spent the whole night waiting for them to bust in and murder him. The charges were quickly dropped, however.[51] Later that year, Duke worked as a fundraiser for Alabama governor George Wallace's presidential campaign, but Duke's tenure ended abruptly, when the campaign accused him of embezzlement. After Wallace's paralyzation and near-fatal shooting, the candidate quit and the charges against Duke were once again dropped.[52]

Duke flailed for several years. He committed to enlisting right-wing candidates to run in local elections throughout the US, but his efforts gained little traction. In 1975, he made his first move to launch the "David Duke" brand. "I kind of thought the Klan wasn't sophisticated enough," he told student interviewer Evelyn Rich, but he detected room to grow the KKK into a national brand out of its low-key, rinky-dink "homegrown" beginnings, and that "it had a lot of potential for making some great changes in this country. They had a fantastic heritage behind it. The truth is that a lot of the different Klan groups, I thought, were quite muddled up."

Jim Lindsay, though, could do no wrong. "He was almost like a dad to me—a real fine gentleman,"[53] he said of the Grand Wizard who listened to criticism of the Klan's low membership numbers and recruited Duke to become the organization's National Information Director. Duke said at the time he joined, the Klan had no traction or buzz, so he created a newsletter, *The Crusader*, and a PR campaign, lining up a stream of combative radio and television interviews. Then, at about the time Duke replaced Jim Lindsay as Grand Wizard in the local Klan, tragedy struck. Lindsay was murdered.

Lindsay's 1975 demise occurred under muddled circumstances, allegedly after either a marital dispute or a mugging gone bad, depending on whose version of events one believes, in broad daylight, in front of his New Orleans home.[54] Duke said Lindsay's demise, which cleared the path for Duke to remake the Klan for a new, post-Jim Crow era, was a coincidence and that Lindsay had stepped down beforehand. Regardless of the circumstances, Duke became the youngest ever Grand Wizard of the century-old organization. No more would he wear Nazi uniforms or Klan robes except for cross-burnings and other ceremonial rites; instead, as an anti-racist activist put it, Duke invented the "three-piece suit Klan," singlehandedly launching a rebrand that set the organization on a path to power.[55] Perhaps the elitist businessman image turned off some moderate and left-wing working stiffs, but Duke had factored that in. He figured a pro-capitalist, small-business-friendly figurehead would lure in those put off by the KKK's notoriety, signaling that they weren't a racist guerrilla band but a legitimate political party, and the Commie Democrats and big business Republicans were on notice. "We hoped to bring enough people together to form a political power base," he explained a decade later. "We wanted a new social order, so to speak . . . to bring more people into the organization—create almost a separate type of community and make it larger and larger until we could influence dramatically elections and the political process in the United States." He said it would be dedicated to the preservation of "white rights."[56]

The only fighting he encouraged seemed to involve black people beating the hell out of white people. In a pseudonymous self-published book, *African Atto*, author "Muhammad X" tried to stir up a race war.[57] One print advertisement for the book asked "When was the last time whitey called you N***?" Below that, a cartoonish Afro-sporting black man kicked a mullet-sporting white man in the jaw. "Black Power = Sex Power. Fear No Man, Black or White. For a very limited time the cost of the entire African Atto course is only $9.95."[58]

Few ordered the street fighting manual, and Duke had to hurriedly find another way to make money. As he considered entering electoral politics, the Wizard hesitated at the possibility of becoming a public figure, a divisive one at that. The fame, he imagined, was partly what drew the crazies on both sides to a candidate. George Wallace hadn't even been shot for a real reason—just some nut job trying to alter the course of history. And George Lincoln Rockwell? Well, a young David Duke shuddered to think about what happened to his idol.

CHAPTER 4

Klansman, Unhooded

On August 25, 1967, American Nazi Party leader George Lincoln Rockwell, stern-faced, and humorless but arresting speaker and international figure, slid a handful of coins into the slots at a washing machine in his local Arlington, Virginia, laundromat and shopping mall. He stepped out and climbed into his blue-and-white Chevy and put the vehicle into reverse. John Patler, who had legally altered his birth name to mimic "Hitler," and whose domineering father had murdered Patler's mother, watched the vehicle from the shopping center's roof. In a letter just days earlier to Rockwell, his former "commander" in the Nazi movement, Patler wrote: "I don't think there are two people on earth who think and feel the same as we do. . . . You are a very important part of my life. I need you as much as you need me. Without you there is no future."[1] Patler lifted a German semi-automatic pistol and fired twice. Rockwell was hit by both shots, once in the chest and, as he tried to dive out of the way, a second time by a bullet that slammed into his head, killing him instantly. The American Nazi Party continued on, calling the unhinged murderer a former party member who had been expelled for being a Bolshevik.[2]

A teenage David Duke, just becoming a Rockwell acolyte, couldn't believe it. Although he had not yet endorsed "white power" (a term Rockwell is credited with coining), he had already come to think of Rockwell as his idol.[3] Following the Nazi commander's death, David Duke committed wholeheartedly to Rockwell's hatred for Jews and denial of black humanity.

Duke, ahead of his time again in the early seventies, also tried to do something about non-white migrants. He had gone to the border in the footsteps of the Klan, which had served as a source for the first official Border Patrol, with a group of other concerned citizens to prevent illegal immigration. They brought stacks of flyers with caricatures of an old Jewish man, an Afro-sporting black male, and a Mexican bandit, headed "Beware! We want your jobs - we want your homes - we want your country."[4] The Border Watch included half a dozen Klansman and set up shop near Brownsville, Texas, in "Klan Border Watch" cars with KKK symbols on each door; they patrolled at night when they assumed the US government would not have the manpower to stem the tide of illegal aliens slipping into the country.[5] The men, Duke said, reported in via CB radios. Of course, they rarely needed to, as local media followed them out there with spotlights and cameras, scaring off any potential crossers. Besides, since there were no black people sneaking into the US through Mexico, stunts like these didn't endear him to his new membership. Why so much about the Jews? Former Klan strategist Tom Metzger, who attended the Border Watch stunt, speculated, "He got enthralled with the [Nazi] idea." Metzger claimed Duke let the privileges of power get to his head, including when it came to women.[6] At a San Diego rally to recruit more patrolmen for the border, he was unprotected by his thin membership. Protestors pelted Duke and a dozen others with eggs and smashed a car window.[7]

Although Duke had married an LSU student, Chloê Eleanor Hardin, whom he'd met through a group called the White Youth Alliance, rumors of promiscuity dogged him throughout his tenure with the KKK. Metzger left to start a splinter group, California's White Aryan Resistance. Later, he turned against Duke over what he called embarrassing adultery. Duke ignored the allegations and focused on his plan to remake the Klan for the new era. While many Nazis and Klan members began to push a more confrontational, even terroristic approach, Duke resisted but didn't condemn or condone anyone's actions. He renewed his pledge not to use violent tactics, possibly due to a fear of infiltration by undercover government agents or left-wingers. There were consequences for him years down the road regardless. Meanwhile, he kept up a snarky tone in his writing and strategizing, including an infamous greeting card sent to supporters one holiday season expressing hopes for a "White Christmas."[8]

Observers had long expected Duke to launch a campaign for public office in Louisiana, although they uniformly predicted he would be crushed. The Jim Crow era had fizzled by 1975, and so had the incendiary debate about busing black students and other racially charged issues. Local journalist John Maginnis said these issues weren't quite so galvanizing, especially with a growing economy under Governor Edwards. After the Long family used black people to solidify their base and white business leaders hired black workers for trade jobs and manual labor, a strange kind of harmony settled over Louisiana.[9] Sure, there were racist politicos, including Judge Leander Perez of Plaquemines Parish, who made a name for himself by trying to block the local school system's integration plan and getting himself excommunicated by the local archbishop, but race and racism were no longer *the* hot button issues.[10] Most Louisianans were therefore blindsided by Duke's emergence, if they even learned of it at the time.

After entering the 1975 16th District State Senate primary, Duke made headlines in the *New York Times* and elsewhere, insisting he had cleaned up the Klan and did not have racist tendencies.[11] In a radio advertisement for a KKK rally the month of the election, however, the script he approved referred to him as "of the Klan," claimed white people bore the brunt of discrimination, and invited interested parties to stick around for a glorious cross-burning. "Give the majority a real voice," he said on the stump, never mentioning his role as a Grand Wizard of the KKK in his speeches.[12]

The 16th was a very conservative district, although it encompassed the LSU campus, where Duke thought he could dominate as a handsome twenty-five-year-old alumnus. He may have appealed to some students but more as a curiosity than a serious candidate, however. The incumbent's campaign settled on a very simple strategy: ignore the challenger. Against an anti-busing incumbent, Duke mustered a respectable but clearly non-threatening 33 percent of the vote, and then fared worse in a far busier race for District 10 four years later, bottoming out with barely one-quarter of the vote, while the incumbent, fellow Democrat Marcel Joseph Tiemann, snagged well over half of it.[13] Meanwhile, he had better luck with recruiting, increasing the Klan's membership in the seventies from an estimated 1,500 to 5,000 in 1973 to over 10,000 in 1981.[14]

He also fought his most famous court battles during this time. After losing the 1975 election, Duke held a Klan rally on a chilly November Saturday inside an East Baton Rouge high school gymnasium—or meant to, if the US Department of Health, Education and Welfare's Civil Rights branch hadn't interfered. After the department threatened the district with severing all federal funding, the school board withdrew permission for the event. Duke sued and was represented by a lawyer he found through the American Civil Liberties Union.[15] The US Supreme Court had overturned a Klansman's arrest and conviction in a 1969 case, saying that the First Amendment protected offensive groups and controversial speech unless it incited or produced "imminent lawless action."[16] Duke's case didn't even *involve* incendiary speech, he noted, as the event had not been allowed to go forward in the first place. He had an excellent case, he and the ACLU agreed, particularly on constitutional grounds and precedent. *Knights of the Ku Klux Klan, Realm of Louisiana v. East Baton Rouge Parish School Board* raged for years, then went to a state court, which dismissed the case almost instantly and without comment, pawning the incendiary matter off on an appeals court.[17]

Meanwhile, Duke developed more legal problems, this time on the criminal front. After a white nationalist gathering in New Orleans, dubbed the 1976 World Nationalist Conference, a group of Klansmen became incensed at undercover cops taking pictures of them and their license plates, like they were attending a Corleone wedding in *The Godfather*. Duke leapt up onto a truck bed to try to get the Klansmen's attention before they started throwing punches with cops, and the crowd dispersed without violence. However, later that evening, Duke received a phone call telling him he had been slapped with a warrant. His lawyer, unconnected to the Klan, got the initial rioting charge reduced to a misdemeanor, which Duke would later be convicted of. In a strange quirk, he became a convicted criminal years before Edwin Edwards first faced a judge.[18]

These bumps didn't slow down the Duke family. In the 1970s, David and Chloê became parents to two girls, Erika and Kirstin, and bought a house in a working-class section of Metairie, the New Orleans suburb just over the Jefferson Parish line. A gated two-story home with an off-street carport, the house on Cypress Street would be a base of operations for not only Duke but Louisiana's Klan operations for years to come.[19] There were three core neighborhoods in Metairie; one, an old-money enclave with the elite white collar workers; another, working-class folks who had hustled their way up in the world; and the up-and-coming one, also predominately white.

Joining him on Cypress Street, at least on official business at first, were confidantes Don Black and Tom Metzger. Metzger would shave his head and become a fearsome figure in both appearance and on paper as Grand Dragon for all KKK operations in California, and in 1980, eked out a win in the Democratic primary for Congress.[20] All three "hoped to make America great again" in their own way, mainly through restrictive immigration policies.[21] "Our clear goal," Duke wrote, "must be the advancement of the white race and separation of the white and black races. This goal must include freeing of the American media and government from subservient Jewish interests."[22] Metzger came to Duke's aid in a horrifying moment at the California military base Fort Pendleton, following a white supremacist rally there. During a melee, someone whacked Duke on the back of the head with a blunt instrument, nearly killing him. Metzger pulled Duke to safety, earning his Grand Dragon designation in spades.

That year, after the Fifth Circuit Court of Appeals remanded the dismissed lawsuit against the East Baton Rouge Parish School Board back to the lower court, which ruled in the school's favor, the Knights of the Ku Klux Klan appealed all the way to the US Supreme Court. The judges ruled the Klan had the right to hold a contracted rally without cancellation under constitutional grounds. The East Baton Rouge school district appealed this, too, but the Court of Appeals denied the motion and awarded the Klan $35,000 in attorney's fees. Although Duke and the Klan received a paltry $2,500 judgment, Duke realized that his first moment in the national spotlight had arrived at last.

With all his legal problems and—more importantly—the resultant costs, Duke hit the road for a coast-to-coast speaking blitz. Several schools canceled or protested, but for Duke, there was an upside to everything. Should the speech be received without incident, it would likely still make the action-starved local papers, and between contributions from inspired new supporters and the fee from the university, Duke could make an adequate living. Of course, a truncated event, one that turned into a shouting match, riot, or a train wreck, or even one that was completely canceled might lead to even more contributions, as aggrieved white citizens would send in cash or checks to the Duke organization in Louisiana in support of free speech. An infamous booking at UNC Chapel Hill turned into the latter. Protestors invaded Memorial Auditorium before Duke could get going and screamed "Go to hell, Duke!" and "Power to the people!," forcing Duke off the stage and prompting the dean of Students Affairs to take the microphone and try to appeal to students, mostly black, to "let the man speak." The protestors chanted on for several more minutes until Duke went back to his hotel and the triumphant students cheered the news.[23]

Duke used the incident to garner national publicity, which he fueled by submitting a letter to the editor of the student newspaper decrying his treatment. In the widely reported, handwritten rant, he blamed "certain Marxists and blacks" for suppressing his freedom of speech and asked how "they know what I say is nothing of value if they don't hear what I have to say."[24] Duke suddenly found himself in demand nationally and internationally.

The National Front, a neo-Nazi organization in the UK, beckoned, and Duke appeared in a primetime BBC interview and in his Klan robes outside Parliament, where inside a debate raged about ejecting him from the kingdom. "Why is it," he asked, "that the government allows great numbers of non-British into the country who spit on the flag and will never assimilate into society? It is too bad that Europeans adopt the worst aspects of America—like fast food and integration."[25] The visit, which the British newspapers recapped from the perspective of the "bobbies" trying to arrest and expel him, proved the starting gun in a new English Far Right wave that picked up where Holocaust deniers left off.[26]

When Duke returned from his whirlwind tour, he realized his mistake in leaving at all. The first blow came from his wife, Chloê. The house on Cypress Street was nearly empty when Duke walked in. His spouse had taken their two young girls to live with their maternal grandparents in Florida. "Working with the Klan put too much pressure on her," Duke later admitted. "My being gone, it got too hectic for her."[27] Indeed, Chloê had been answering phones for the KKK, taking care of her two girls, and helping her husband advance his political and public speaking career, the family's only source of income.[28] But Chloê wouldn't be leaving Duke's orbit or even the Klan.[29] Though she later said she did "not agree with extremist or racially prejudiced views," she continued to praise her ex, calling him "the Jesse Jackson of white rights in America." She and David wouldn't divorce for several more years, and that would be mainly so she could marry another white supremacist, Don Black.[30]

After his breakup and the drubbing he took in the 1979 state Senate race, Duke reached a low point that would last a decade. The first major change he made was to quit the Ku Klux Klan. "I've done things in my life I'd take back," he would one day tell angry students protesting him. When challenged to provide evidence of his allegations or to explain why he tempered his inflammatory views, Duke shrugged. "We all grow up," he said. The change took years or perhaps truthfully was never completed, however. In the late seventies, he'd become "less obsessed 'with Zionist issues,'" as he told his biographer, and the Klan, eager to move on from issues resolved by Allied victories in World War II, and which concerned itself far less with light-skinned European Jews anyway, seemed eager to marshal its scattered forces. To that end, as Duke left, he set his friend Don Black up with the leadership of the KKK and then, in one of the most disputed incidents of his career, attempted to sell the group's membership list to Alabama's Invisible Empire and its self-proclaimed Imperial Wizard, Bill Wilkinson.[31]

Duke's asking price, coordinated with Black, would be $35,000 to fold the Knights of the Ku Klux Klan into the Invisible Empire and balloon white supremacy's Southern network. But Wilkinson did not like Duke, and at their farmhouse showdown, hid television reporters and their cameras in a barn near the private signing ceremony; they ambushed Duke with microphones and lenses the moment he took up his pen. Wilkinson figured once Duke left the Klan in disgrace, membership would collapse and he could poach them for nothing. After the deal collapsed, Black took over the Klan and struggled to keep it going into the 1980s.[32]

Unbeknownst to anyone else involved in either organization, Bill Wilkinson had been an FBI informant since 1974.[33] When that story broke months after the failed mailing list deal, Wilkinson denied everything and dropped out of sight, but not before publicly accusing Duke of auctioning off the Klan membership and thus the closely guarded names of sympathizers. Duke, having accomplished little except to make himself internationally notorious, sank even further in the eyes of the public—including within the white supremacy movement. He formed two new organizations— Americana Books, a publishing company dedicated to propagating "all sides" of the political spectrum, and the National Association for the Advancement of White People with Don Black, spoofing the NAACP and through which, crucially, Duke could fundraise during his dormant years.[34]

Don Black immediately got busy. The following year, the new Klan leader and five others attempted to overthrow the left-wing government of Dominica, a sovereign Caribbean nation, by boat and by force, part of a "Nazification of the Klan" that advocated for US government overthrow.[35] "We always thought Duke was involved in some way," then-prosecutor Lindsay Larson said. But despite testifying in front of a grand jury and telling the Associated Press he had helped Black plan the invasion—then later denying it—Duke escaped without charge. Regardless of his help or non-involvement, with Duke apparently out of the way, the white supremacy movement embraced violent revolution in the 1980s.[36]

In 1981, the head of Alabama's Klan group, upset that a jury had been unable to convict a black person for the murder of a white cop, told the media: "If a Black man can get away with killing a White man, we ought to be able to get away with killing a Black man." The Klansman's son Henry Hays soon tested this theory out, lynching a black teenager in Mobile. After the police claimed it was a business dispute (drugs being the business), the FBI stepped in. Hays was convicted, sentenced to death, and became the first white person executed for killing a black person in eighty-four years.

The hits kept on coming, as the Alabama Klan had to be disbanded after losing a $7,000,000 wrongful death suit over the killing.[37]

Around this time, an eleven-member group formed, calling itself the Order, and put a talk show host on its kill list. Alan Berg, fifty, Jewish, with a Beatles haircut and shaggy beard, had a popular Denver radio show—more importantly to the Klan and its ilk, however, Berg taunted right-wing callers on-air. An early shock jock prototype, Berg would often argue from comically obtuse positions with a straight face and abruptly hang up on anyone who irritated him, no matter their political affiliation. In 1984, mere months after its formation, the Order green-lit the execution-style murder of Berg. Berg's biographer Stephen Singular said that the Order's subsequent goal would be to wipe Jews, black people, feminists, and anyone who stood in their way off the planet, one at a time.[38]

On June 18, Berg stepped out of his VW Beetle in his townhouse driveway and was struck twelve times by automatic gunfire. The murderer fled. Weeks later, the FBI raided a Klan warehouse and found what they claimed was the murder weapon, a modified MAC-10. One suspect burned to death the following December when the Feds showed up at his home, while two others were captured and sentenced to a combined 442 years in prison for civil rights violations.[39] One of these, David Lane, had been a member of the Klan and, although he never admitted to guilt in the Berg killing, he did refer to it once in an interview, saying, "He has not mouthed his hate-whitey propaganda from his 50,000-watt Zionist pulpit for quite a few years."[40] Lane and his fellow travelers had all been inspired by an incendiary anti-Semitic book called *The Turner Diaries*, which would soon turn up in David Duke's Metairie headquarters and cause far more damage than anyone could have predicted.[41]

Taking Duke at his word that he left the Klan in 1980, it's difficult to imagine a rationale. He still espoused white supremacist views such as the belief that black civil rights leaders were Communist saboteurs, and he didn't make any serious efforts to run for office during this period. A decade later, he would tell biographer Michael Zatarain, "I know that for me to be able to promote the ideals that I felt were crucial to the survival of the white race, I would have to find a new avenue . . . to get my message across to those people I couldn't reach through the Klan." He also reflected, "I came to the belief that the Klan wasn't the best path to victory. Under those circumstances, the only honorable course of action I can take is to step aside in my leadership role. On a personal level I remain committed as ever to the white cause."[42]

Throughout much of the eighties, Duke struggled to find that avenue and those unreachable, non-KKK members. Meanwhile, the documentary *Blood in the Face* spotlighted Don Black and showed that the national movement had grown under his leadership (in the film, proud neo-Nazis pontificate on shooting everyone who isn't white "on sight").[43] Increasingly self-isolated on Cypress Street, Duke worked on a newsletter read by perhaps several thousand people per month and sold books through mail order, including *The Turner Diaries*.[44] He established a routine of whacking golf balls around the public course in City Park several days per week, unable to muster the motivation to put himself back into the spotlight.[45]

Then came Forsyth.

On a biting cold Saturday in January 1987, thousands of people of all backgrounds were due at a march meant to welcome black people back to Forsyth County, Georgia, where few African Americans had lived since a series of lynchings three quarters of a century earlier. The inspiration for Duke's involvement is the subject of a long-running dispute. *Slate* claimed Duke, hearing rumors of violent attacks by white counterprotestors attending an earlier pro-integration march, didn't want to miss out a second time on the publicity, while other sources suggest panicked opponents of a plan to build public housing for low-income folks (read: black people) decided to invite Duke.[46] Regardless, concerned white citizens formed a group called, of course, Keep Forsyth White. Either way, Duke explained that he accepted the invitation to speak at a counterprotest to promote his message: "Today, we declare that we have the right to associate with whom we desire, the right to preserve our culture and heritage, the right of our children to an education, and the right of all people, young and old, men and women, to live in communities without the black plague of crime, murder, and terror of our citizens."[47]

Despite the presence of tens of thousands of expected peace marchers wading across snow-soaked streets and overpasses, including Democratic presidential contender Gary Hart and Martin Luther King III, son of the slain civil rights leader, the news cameras, tape recorders, former segregationist governor Lester Maddox, and the eyes of gawkers were fixated on one image: that of a mustachioed thirty-six-year-old blond man from Louisiana, with no political clout or elective office.[48]

White Forsyth County citizens, he went on, weren't picketing out of a racist hatred for black people. No, they were simply worried that Forsyth, Georgia, and the United States would collapse like so many "non-white" societies. "The awakening had been long coming," he said, "but the sleepy white giant, the founder and the backbone of America, is finally stirring. You and I are going to make it all possible. We will be blessed to live in the most threatening and also most exciting time in the long history of our people."[49]

Setting out, the counterprotest march almost instantly descended into the kind of chaos Duke both secretly wanted and publicly proclaimed to be doing everything to avoid. Several alleged Klansmen were arrested for possession of firearms at the "peaceful" protest. As darkness fell, cloaking them, the counterdemonstrators grew emboldened. "No n***s in Forsyth! "N***s go home!" went one chant, which Duke would then attempt to drown out, shrieking through a bullhorn: "The worst thing we can do for the cause is to break the law!"[50] The picketers stomped through the slush, filing alongside the protestors, riled up rather than inspired by Duke's speech. They glared. The cops shifted their belts nervously. Duke stayed on a highway shoulder, amid the piled-up snow, sensing trouble. The Georgia Bureau of Investigation, in charge of monitoring the two marches, conferred and decided to wave Duke over. When the ex-Klansman, grinning amiably, walked up to them, Don Black at his side, to perhaps see if they had an alternate route plan, agents sprang into action.

Duke, Black, and more than sixty other counter-marchers were arrested. The official charge, parading without a permit, incensed Duke particularly. The local sheriff's department had given him the a-OK to march without one. Duke's hands were cuffed behind his back and he was left standing on the side of the road for what he would later claim was eight hours without food or water. "Unbelievable," he said. "They had us up to our ankles in cold water."[51]

The authorities were possibly discouraged from leveling more serious inciting charges and other felonies after Duke made the six o'clock news announcing the "beginning of the white civil rights movement."[52] *Newsweek* would claim that Duke built up a five-figure nest egg through the legal defense fund, which he barely had to touch to get his penalties dropped down to a $50 fine. Crucially, Forsyth put the fight back in Duke. With widespread press coverage and growing sympathy not only for his pet causes but conservatism in general, primetime programming finally sought out Duke Country, and its progenitor aimed to capitalize on it. In *NAAWP News* number 43, he said, "Historians will look at Saturday, January 23, 1987, as the apex of the Black movement in the United States and the genesis of an entirely new civil rights movement in America, a powerful mass movement for the survival and advancement of the White race on this continent."[53]

Jesse Jackson, the black reverend and confidante of the late Dr. King, had already announced he would run for the Democratic nomination for president in 1988, and Duke decided he could piggyback on this development for further headlines by doing the same. "Black civil rights champion versus ex-KKK leader" had Joe Louis-Max Schmeling vibes from the get-go, and Duke did have some early momentum, including initial donations totaling in the hundreds of thousands of dollars. But the Democratic Party apparatus seemed more determined to defeat him than his actual primary opponents. The DNC wouldn't let him in debates, told their voters not to vote for him, and asked candidates to ignore him. "If we let all the nuts who wanted to run for president participate in every debate," said one staffer, "we'd have to hold them in football stadiums."[54]

Holding him back, too, were demographics. Despite boasting of an instant base of five hundred thousand Klan members and supporters, the reality was that this small overall percentage of the population was spread throughout the fifty states and DC, and certainly thinned out further when one crunched the numbers of early primary states. Although he focused his sights on California's right-wing pockets and Georgia's growing support base, he simply didn't have room to maneuver in a generally liberal party's primary. In his campaign announcement, Duke referenced segregationist George Wallace, a Democrat who ran in 1968 and 1972, but Wallace Democrats had joined him in a third party during his latter run.[55] The Democrats in the first-in-the-nation New Hampshire primary *were* Democrats, unlike in Louisiana where conservatives kept their longtime registrations mostly out of habit. New Hampshire, though a crushing defeat on one level, hadn't all been bad news; Duke won the little-noticed vice presidential vote with six out of every ten voters in support. Although he switched to the Populist Party for the general election and mustered a mere 150,000 votes, Duke sustained the momentum brewing after Forsyth.

He also could return home to an interesting political situation in Louisiana, where a Democratic governor was under siege from conservatives. Duke watched quietly from the sidelines as Buddy Roemer tried proposal after proposal, including tax increases, with a mixture of dread for his state and a cheetah's lip-licking giddiness at watching wounded prey flail. Duke thought, too, of the 1988 presidential debate at Tulane University's McAlister Auditorium, site of his famous 1970s one-man protest of William Kunstler. The Democrats had had a party in *his* city and had prevented him from appearing? Duke knew he wouldn't have made a scene or said anything that embarrassed the party at its core. Outside, he drew the media to him, as in Forsyth, and made his pitch for the presidency. Then, shouted down by protestors, including a young student named Tim Wise, Duke stepped away from the microphone bank and engaged in a measured exchange with the kids for almost an hour.

"'You're not going to believe this,'" said Wise, quoting a friend. "'David Duke is down there! Wanna fuck with him?'" Wise said he demurred at first, remembering Duke as a Klansman and the Klan as the organization that bombed the elementary school he'd attended in Nashville.[56] Soon, however, he found himself wandering down to the auditorium's front steps to gawk at the man he'd seen and been mesmerized by in his appearances on *Donahue*. There were several students giving Duke grief, interrupting him, challenging the purported Nazi, but to Wise, "it just seemed so cartoonish."[57] He didn't think much of Duke again until a few months later, when the now-defeated presidential candidate made his next move.

After the 1988 election elevated Republican George Bush to the Oval Office, Duke slunk back to Cypress Street, cringing at the idea of having to crank out fundraising solicitations and worry incessantly about where the next infinitesimal donation might come from. A friend dropped by to cheer him up, hoping to fill Duke in on recent political gossip. With Duke mainly spaced out, the pal mentioned that a state representative had accepted a judgeship, creating a vacancy in his current legislative seat and thus necessitating a special election.[58] The seat encompassed nearly all of Metairie and terminated just two blocks from Duke's house.

Duke had to ask himself: did he want to fight another bruising battle, defending his reputation in interviews and while shaking hands outside Schwegmann's? All that and tons of money and energy wasted over maybe ten, twelve thousand votes in a general election? He decided he'd at least attempt to qualify, which wouldn't take much, and not commit to sticking it out if his heart wasn't in it.

The first thing he told his campaign manager: *Get me a Change of Voter Registration form, stat.*

CHAPTER 5

What Beth Rickey Found

Deep within the Tulane University archives, buried at the bottom of box 11, at the back of folder 27, there is an advertisement. The ad, tucked into a newsletter for David Duke's NAAWP, lists ninety-one book titles available for sale from a Louisiana bookstore, which happens to be David Duke's and tucked in his basement.[1] The *Wall Street Journal* noted, "25 appear to be about Jews, Hitler or Germany," and they weren't about how devastating the Holocaust was for Jews. Among them? *The Turner Diaries*. Discovered by Beth Rickey and her team in the late 1980s, the sheet of newsprint altered the course of American politics. There would be a reckoning, and a line in the sand would be drawn, with win-at-all-costs conservatives on one side, willing to forgive every transgression by any Republican; on the other side, the rest of the country. "You're either with us," President Bush's son would say during his own White House tenure, "or against us."

When she started out in politics, Rickey was a diehard Republican, definitely "with" them. In a blog post about Rickey's death, her associate Jeff Sadow described her as possibly the only political science post-grad at the University of New Orleans with conservative views other than himself.[2] Born in 1956, to a family best-known for her uncle, Branch, who signed baseball's first black player, Jackie Robinson, to the Brooklyn Dodgers, Rickey had long had a sense of purpose and racial justice instilled in her. Her father, who founded a Presbyterian church in Lafayette, had worked for General Patton, whom David Duke, Sr. claimed to have delivered messages to from Eisenhower, and, with the crucial caveat that, while fixing railroads in Europe during WWII, Horace Rickey had also liberated a concentration camp.[3] "My great great-grandfather was once one of Louisiana's largest slaveholders," she would later write. His son, a policeman in the nineteenth century, "stood up to the Klan as sheriff of St. Helena Parish" and hid a black man accused of raping a white woman until the true culprit could be charged. Rickey was on the latter side.[4] She fell hard for presidential prospect Ronald Reagan as an adolescent, when the then-governor paid a visit to Rickey's parents.[5] She missed or ignored Ronald Reagan's coded messages to white supremacists in the 80s (*I will not say anything bad about black people, but nor will I do anything to earn their support*), although she "squirmed" when the KKK endorsed him.[6] Nonetheless, she was an alternate convention delegate for Reagan in both of his successful races. When Rickey ran for a Republican State Central Committee spot, she campaigned hard in the Garden District, where she resided, and friend Jeff Sadow worked his neighbors in the French Quarter, which overlapped with the contested district.[7] Rickey won by three votes.[8] Horace B. Rickey Jr., who had once held a spot on the same State Committee but had passed away over a decade earlier, would've beamed with pride at his thirty-two-year-old daughter's first foray into elective politics.[9]

With her newfound power—little though it may have been in the scheme of things—Rickey immediately set out to make her mark on the state GOP. With the 1988 Republican National Convention set to take place in New Orleans, she found herself in a position to match major elected officials, including senators, to local Louisianan hosts, such as Sadow.[10] She blessed her friend with the Indiana delegation, which became crucial in Bush's nomination the following day when Sadow's guest, Dan Quayle, was named the vice-presidential nominee. The state and national Republican Party noticed Beth and officials reached out to offer her assistance in her career, but she declined to run or accept roles on campaigns, citing her graduate school studies. She held firm until John Treen called with an offer she couldn't refuse.

All systems seemed a "go" for Republicans in the 1989 special election. Democratic governor Buddy Roemer even acceded to the GOP's request to have the election forthwith in order to keep David Vitter, a young Ivy League grad, from qualifying and to pave the way for their buddy, John Treen.[11] Treen recruited his brother, Dave, the former governor, to head up his team. Several other candidates jumped in, but Treen felt confident he could get more than 50 percent of the vote regardless. The demographics—seven Republican registrants for every dozen Democrats—worked in Treen's favor, or so folks thought.[12] Unnoticed by the press, David Duke had quietly switched his registration to the Republican Party.

Duke's announcement threw the rival campaigns into turmoil. Opponent Delton Charles refused calls to attack Duke, lest he need the state representative's support in the general election. Sheriff Harry Lee, an influential "whip" for huge swaths of the New Orleans-area electorate, ostensibly supported Democrat Budd Olister; however, Lee, of Chinese descent, had instituted a racial profiling program in Metairie that Duke trumpeted as the way of the future in Louisiana. His supporters were either in favor of it as well, or signed up for his campaign because of his support for the homestead exemption, the $75,000 savings homeowners would lose if Governor Roemer's plan passed. Duke's two campaign themes caused his crowds to double in just days. Treen, sifting through this news, realized that the other candidates were canceling themselves out—he would have to go against Duke alone. In a moment of inspiration, he turned to Beth Rickey and asked her if she might come to work for him on some light opposition research.

Meanwhile, Treen and the state GOP plotted to keep Duke out of contention for the official Republican Party nomination. Duke spoke at the party's private nomination meeting and received deafening applause, but officials assumed that would be the last of it. Later that evening, when Duke came in third in balloting, the party realized he had dragged down Treen's total and kept him from winning outright. Without informing Duke's campaign, Treen pushed the GOP to hold a second, unannounced gathering of party leaders, at which Treen won the nomination on the first ballot.[13] After being shut out, the other candidates vowed to get even with Treen, someday, somehow.[14]

Rickey and Treen would later privately admit that Duke had outplayed them again, even in defeat. By forcing the Party to vote clandestinely, they gave voters the impression of a rigged election, or at least one in which politicians, not citizens, had done the voting. On top of that, they missed a pivotal opportunity to disqualify Duke on residency grounds, perhaps due to the belief—shared by each of the half-dozen candidates—that Duke pulled votes from their opponents, but not from them.[15]

One reason for their disinterest in taking legal action: Duke polled in the single digits. In the first instance of what would become a running theme, the campaigns didn't truly analyze their numbers until the post-election decompression sessions. Duke, they would learn, *always* outperformed his projections. There were indicators entirely missed by the strategists all along; however, casual observers who might have counted his yard signs (Duke's vastly outnumbered Treen's before the primary), viewed the screaming crowds at his rallies, and read the press coverage that ignored all but the challenger and anointed one could have picked up on them. Moreover, endorsements from "Democrats for Better Government," although more or less a front for the Duke campaign, and Businesses in Government (B.I.G.) looked great in Duke's campaign literature.[16] He also had the advantage—after a decade and a half of being ahead of his time—of finally finding the right election with the right opponents in the right district at the right moment.

Rather than fading, Duke's prospects miraculously improved immeasurably after being denied the GOP nomination. At the end of 1988, the New Orleans murder rate shot up to record-breaking levels, becoming the fourth highest overall in the United States. Twenty-eight people were killed in January 1989, the month of the primary.[17] White flight to Metairie increased and its residents, reading of terrifying gang bloodshed on a near-daily basis, doubled down in their support for the sheriff's initiative to stop and question any unfamiliar black teenager or adult wandering suburban neighborhoods. Then the imaginary black on white violence voters feared became real.

At a parade lead by Governor Buddy Roemer on Canal Street in New Orleans on Martin Luther King Jr.'s birthday, black marchers reportedly broke ranks and charged at several white spectators, punching and kicking them.[18] Someone started a chant: "Whites off!"[19] The evening news repeated footage of one white pregnant woman cowering in a retail store.[20] While it has never been definitively established whether something set paraders off or whether theirs was an unprovoked, race-based attack, regardless, the timing boosted Duke's underdog campaign. "I wouldn't put it past David Duke to pay some black kids to start a riot," said William Hess of the Anti-Defamation League without evidence.[21] Ed Renwick of Loyola University's Institute of Politics told the *Chicago Tribune*, "For a person running his type of campaign, the news couldn't be better."[22] Indeed, candidate Delton Charles grumbled, sarcastically, "This is all we need."[23] Duke shrugged. He blamed the state for giving away too much of its budget to welfare recipients and not enough to local police departments like Lee's.[24]

Although few insiders were predicting a Duke win, even the week before the primary, all the warning signs were there. Members of the radical Jewish Defense Organization were so concerned, in fact, that they sent their controversial founder to New Orleans. Mordechai Levy, who had celebrated the bombing of the American Arab Anti-Discrimination Committee in Los Angeles four years earlier and was later described as a "chaos agent" by right-wing fringe candidate Lyndon LaRouche's inner circle, first tried to visit Louisiana in January, shortly before the primary, but the temple hosting his event canceled on him.[25] Its rabbi called the situation a catch-22 in a press statement—if they were to show Louisiana how toxic Duke's views were, that would only increase his support from racists, but were they to remain silent in the face of Nazism, Duke might win anyway.[26] Jane Buchsbaum, head of the New Orleans Jewish Federation, didn't want Levy stirring up white fears. She called Levy and told him, "I'm sure you have a good heart, but the more you speak on this and the more you say you're a Yankee from New York, the more people here in Louisiana hate you. You're trying to stop David Duke and you're getting people to like him and hate you."[27] Levy spoke anyway.

"AMERICAN JEWS IT'S TIME TO FIGHT BACK OR GET OUT!" the event flyer said. Also in all caps, his screed read,

> Dark clouds are coming for American Jews. Today we see a rise in anti-Semitism that our movement predicted . . . we warned the day would come when Nazis would start winning elections. It will come with the state election of David Duke in Louisiana. . . . It is no longer just a question of anti-Semitic feelings but of a powder keg with enough of a volatile mixture that when the spark finally comes . . . the Jew will be caught in its fierce explosion.[28]

Levy went on to warn of a "repeat of history" with the Third Reich and of Jewish leaders, unconcerned about or too willing to meekly compromise with far-right governments, ceding the way for the Final Solution to the Jewish problem. In a hot mic moment, he allegedly called the area's voters "asshole-idiot white devils."[29]

Initially, some New Orleans-area Jews welcomed Levy, suggesting he might light a fire under the sleepy electorate or help with organizing. As one attendee reflected a quarter century later, "He really raised the ire against Duke and helped us organize. . . . He did a lot of good and raised a lot of awareness."[30] But the idea of Yankees coming to Louisiana and demanding people vote a certain way or face possibly violent repercussions offended more people than Duke's cross burnings. Buchsbaum believed the negative PR from Levy's visit boosted rather than stalled Duke's campaign.[31]

"I thought I was running for office in a race nobody'd heard of," John Treen raged. "Now I've got to win. And to tell you the truth, I don't know that I'm going to."[32] For once, Treen's political instincts would prove correct. Four days after MLK Day, Duke garnered nearly four thousand votes and ended up with a runoff lead of fourteen points. In their head-to-head matchup a few weeks later, Duke would outpace Treen one more crucial time.

Rickey, who did not feel comfortable going after Duke directly, believing him too popular and herself a total unknown, may have been the state

Central Committee member who told the *LA Times*, "I think it's a disgrace to the Republican party that there were such appeals to bigotry. There should be no place for that in this party. We've been set back years in our hope to appeal to minorities."[33] Duke haters suspected the newly elected House member would immediately pivot to the 1990 US Senate race, and they needed to act quickly to gather as much damaging material as they could, whatever that might be.

Beth Rickey had seen several moves ahead, however. Throughout the 1989 campaign and runoff, she had tried, quietly and behind the scenes, to warn the state Republican Party, the media, and, in a roundabout way, the voters about what they were about to do. She saw it as her destiny. She had served as a "Treen Queen" in the 1972 general matchup between Dave Treen and Edwin Edwards; she cried when Nixon resigned in her eighteenth year and blindly supported Ronald Reagan, her personal hero, as well as the Republican Party apparatus and its candidates generally; but through her merciless pursuit of Duke, Rickey, then a thirty-one-year-old doctoral student, served as an anti-racist advocate Wise and Louisiana liberals could relate to.[34] It helped, too, that she was "implacably horrified by Nazism," as fellow anti-Duker Tim Wise put it.

As she dipped a toe into the cesspool of Duke's past, Beth kept encountering conservatives who expressed concern about Duke but, according to Wise, would say things like, "I sort of like what he said about welfare [and] affirmative action."[35] Wise, as well as Tulane professor Lawrence Powell and his graduate student Lance Hill, crossed paths with Rickey when she first started investigating Duke's archives, some of which had been donated by the state representative himself to the Tulane library. Hill excitedly told the others about how Pulaski, Tennessee, sick of the KKK's presence in their town, collectively created orange banners slamming the prejudicial group and paraded through the streets to reclaim their town as a welcoming community.[36] But such anecdotes were not going to be enough to inspire turnout to defeat Duke, as Hill, Rickey, and Powell's new group knew, especially in a major statewide race. Rickey believed Duke skirted media potshots at his Klan leadership role by saying that had all happened years prior, but, said Rickey, "we knew he would be vulnerable on the Nazi issue."[37]

In the Senate race, the anti-Duke coalition tried to remain sensitive to Republican members like Beth by not endorsing the Democratic incumbent, Bennett Johnston. Group leaders decided that the way to defeat Duke would be to hit him from the right on his fictional account of military volunteerism. The coalition spread the story that Duke had not conducted rice drops in Vietnam, as he'd boasted, but actually hung out with his father for a summer, teaching English to Laotian officers. The *New Orleans Times-Picayune* reported it had found proof Duke had paid his personal income taxes late and had written a how-to sex guide. "We thought, 'So what? The guy's a Nazi!'" Tim Wise recalled. "Who cares? His paying his taxes late and [not] actually going to 'Nam wasn't the problem."[38]

Other members of the "Stop Duke" group, which became the Louisiana Coalition Against Racism and Nazism (LCARN), agreed the best way to blunt Duke's momentum would be to uncover hard evidence of Duke's Nazi leanings and other "moral" failings. "This is the Fourth Reich," Tulane professor Larry Powell said at a meeting, apoplectic.[39] (Powell may have been upset about the pair of death threats he reported receiving during this time, likely due to his speaking out in favor of demolishing the New Orleans Liberty Place monument, a paean to an 1874 white supremacist coup attempt.) Mitch Landrieu, then a state representative from New Orleans, agreed that Duke's Achilles heel might be his Nazi leanings and goal of white supremacy.[40] While uptown New Orleans conservatives were funding their efforts through cocktail parties, LCARN's members quietly worked after hours building a portfolio on Duke's racist past. Their principal source, despite her political persuasion, was Beth Rickey.

The first test of the Coalition came quickly. The Populist Party, founded by the Klan and neo-Nazis, announced a convention to pat itself on the back for, liberals presumed, helping David Duke get elected in a Louisiana House race. Although Duke's name did not appear on the list of speakers or attendees at the Chicago, Illinois, meeting, the ex-Klansman had been the Populist candidate for president only a year earlier; he had disowned his racist past but, Rickey knew, Duke wouldn't possess the cojones to snub an organization that contributed heavily to his campaign of only two weeks prior. Rickey volunteered to fly up to Illinois, intending to tape-record Duke's presumptive speech. The Coalition didn't advise her to tail Duke to Chicago, but she couldn't resist.

The Populist Party jamboree was held in a large ballroom, heavily guarded by a security squad. Uniformed Nazis were everywhere, clicking their heels together and Heil Hitler-ing. Rickey had enlisted a female friend to accompany her, and together they stopped midway through the ballroom, eying the brown shirts, swastika armbands, and Klan robes.[41] With her recorder tucked in her skirt, Rickey silently prayed, tried to smile, and drifted sluggishly toward the ballroom doors. She was stopped immediately by security, however.

Duke, it turned out, had indeed been cajoled into speaking, apparently by Willis Carto, leader of the anti-Semitic Liberty Lobby group. The state representative from Louisiana couldn't reject Carto's Populists outright, but nor could he overtly support their racist platform and fascist-leaning membership. After Carto agreed to prevent the media from accessing the speech, Duke confirmed his attendance. Rickey, though, had received approval for the convention under a phony media affiliation.

"Oh, I'm a Populist too," she said before the volunteer security guard could inquire about her press designation. "How are you? Haven't seen you in a while."[42]

The two women miraculously found a pair of unoccupied seats in the front row—essential for capturing the exact content of Duke's speech, terrifying from a safety perspective. The recording device, though, was the size of a porterhouse and significantly heavier. Rickey had to resist the temptation to reach beneath the hem, yank the recorder out, and get her unmasking over with. Rickey tried not to glance over at the man in the brown shirt seated next to her, his arms folded in haughty silence, because she was pretty sure she knew what was on his armband.

The first speaker glared at Rickey, as if somehow recognizing her. He then railed about the press and presumed Jewish infiltrators, and pointed straight at Rickey. Her heart stopped for an instant before she realized the speaker was actually gesturing at the brown shirt, who had a shaved head. Such "skinheads," the speaker suggested, would take care of any uninvited spies. As the applause thundered, Beth let out the air ballooning her lungs. "The speakers were all angry," she reported, "angry about minorities, angry about the media, just plain angry."[43]

Forty minutes passed. Rickey had barely calmed herself when she heard a loud "click." With the speaker taking a breath between sentences, the silence appeared to have been shattered by the sound. The recorder, Beth suspected, had run out. Worse, the mechanical stop had dislodged the device from its place up her skirt. As the machine started to slide down her leg, threatening to become visible and clatter to the auditorium floor at any moment, Beth scurried out of the room. Luckily, at just that moment, Rickey's friend coincidentally leapt to her feet and proclaimed, "I've heard enough" and stormed out.[44]

By the time Rickey completed her readjustments and returned alone, David Duke had taken the stage. "We did it!" he exclaimed to howls of joy. "My victory in Louisiana was a victory for the white majority movement in this country," he explained.

"The Republican Party of Louisiana is in our camp. I had to run within that process because, well, that's where our people are.

"Republicans in my district are like us, and I can bring them into our fold," he said. "I'm a Republican now, but I'll always be a *Populist* Republican."

The man beside Beth cocked his head to study her. On a hunch, she blurted out a "Duke! Duke!" that got everyone chanting the politician's name.[45]

On the verge of vomiting from nerves and from Duke's references to Zionists, the Black Caucus, and an "illegitimate underclass"—the worshipful audience reaction didn't help— Rickey pushed open the auditorium doors and nearly collided with American Nazi Party vice chairman Art Jones. On a hunch, she shuffled to the opposite side of the room, creating a vantage point for herself but remaining almost out of sight. (She believed that Duke either didn't know who she was or at least wouldn't recognize her.) When the state rep emerged, glowing with victoriousness, Jones approached. Rickey gaped as Duke firmly shook Jones's hand. As if on cue, a flashbulb went off and the pair were jarred back to political reality. Jones turned, practically lunged at the cameraman, and had to be held back.[46]

Rickey always swore she did not arrange for a photographer to capture the moment. She hadn't known whether Duke and Jones had met previously. When the story hit the wire services, Jones, in a replica Nazi SS uniform, denied any relationship, and Duke called the neo-Nazi a fringe character. When questioned further about Jones's affiliation, Duke claimed he didn't know anything about it, and that he didn't affiliate with Nazis or support their beliefs. When Rickey released the tape recording of his speech, the media had trouble churning out bite-sized portions and seemed to accept that Duke had to speak to the Populist membership to thank them for their support. Duke hadn't said anything, reporters claimed, that "proved" he had lied about his beliefs. The whole thing seemed to fizzle out in a matter of days, with the exception that when undecided voters were questioned about it in the coming campaign, those who were on the fence about Duke might bring up the Nazi affiliation as a reason for their hesitation.[47]

Beth Rickey had run out of slam-dunks in her war against David Duke. And when the rumor that the representative would piggyback on his local victory to launch a US Senate campaign proved true, Rickey verged on a full-blown panic attack. Yet most insiders agreed Duke had no chance against Democratic Senator Bennett Johnston, who said he thought Duke's entry would merely "make it more fun."[48] In the coming eighteen months, Duke, "a charlatan and a phony" to party leaders, would be repeatedly dismissed by experts, who said, *This guy is a fringe candidate and incapable of building a coalition to win statewide or national elections.*[49] However, Beth Rickey had learned from 1989, when she researched Duke's past on behalf of his runoff opponent, not to turn her back on the electorate for even a second.

Between classes and papers for her doctoral degree, as well as her commitments to the Republican Party apparatus in Baton Rouge, Rickey spent days in the Tulane University library, reading the infinitesimal print in David Duke's newsletters, campaign filings, and advertising, and the books produced under his own name, of which there seemed to be suspiciously few for a so-called writer. Maybe, she wondered, there were other publications she couldn't find.

In December 1988, Duke released a series of cassette tapes discussing "the race issue" for the benefit of "White racialists," as his advertisements put it.[50] For $30, anyone could receive a forty-five-minute videocassette of the former Grand Wizard expounding on "the true nature of affirmative action, the effects of integration and forced busing, the common crisis of massive non-White immigration and high non-White birthrates." The other, more affordable advertised VHS tapes suggested a similar theme: "David Duke on Race," "The Jewish Question (Parts I and II)," and "Duke Speaks at U of Montana (Parts 1 and 2)," ostensibly documenting a talk in which he "[won] the audience over to a basic racial understanding."[51]

Some of the newsletters, too, were filled with explosive passages. "The media is dominated by Jews . . . these Jews are not Good Americans . . . racial mixture leads to many physiological anomalies that can be very damaging," and "if general [race] mixing is allowed, there is always degradation in the population," one newsletter read.[52] "Bolsheviks, Jews, and Negroes": all three were bogeyman in World War II-era fascist Italy, and all were attacked at one time or another in Duke's NAAWP writings.[53] Duke, Rickey realized, had "left a paper trail that was twenty years long" pointing to Nazism and racism up until nearly the present day. "His claim that this was all in his 'past' was blatantly untrue," she decided.[54]

Rickey left the library convinced Duke had always been a "professional racist." She presented her opposition research dossier, which contained some of the above, to Treen, then still in the race. Rickey later reflected:

> The collection of flesh beneath John Treen's eyes belied a deeper frustration. He was getting obscene phone calls at home, thanks to a rumor spread by Duke forces that he was a child molester. . . .
> I asked why he hadn't made more of Duke's Nazi ties.
> "We're depending on you folks in the media to get that news out."

"Don't hold your breath. They're waiting for you to do it. . . . You need more than that," I said. "Call a press conference with some World War II veterans in your district. . . . Tell people that y'all fought the Nazis to preserve democracy so even people like Duke can run for office."[55]

Treen hadn't thought Duke had a chance and Rickey, at least early on, tended to agree. By the time of the runoff, the release of the dossier would have taken on the feel of a phony smear campaign and been dismissed. Rickey instead took her laundry list of Duke's past actions to her cohorts in the Republican State Committee. "They turned their heads and said, 'So what?'" she wrote.[56]

Coalition executive director Lance Hill, upon seeing these passages, recognized similar themes from *Mein Kampf*, Adolf Hitler's anti-Semitic treatise. Later, for the dossier, he would match passages from the NAAWP newsletter Duke produced—"I believe that in fact nationality comes from genes"—to the Nazi dictator—"nationality or rather race does not happen to lie in language but in blood." (Duke claimed his quotes were taken out of context, including those about Hitler, and insisted he never agreed with Hitler on race issues.[57]) So incensed was Hill that he agreed to accompany Rickey on a visit to NAAWP headquarters and Americana Books and see if they were offering more racist propaganda. He explained that, were they to find Nazi and racist books for sale in Duke's legislative headquarters, it would shut down arguments from Duke apologists that their man had changed. When they called the listed NAAWP contact number to confirm they had the right address, they were met with a surprising greeting: "David Duke, district eighty-one."

Recovering swiftly, Hill realized a receptionist had answered. He told them he wanted to buy *The Turner Diaries*, a novel about heroic white people who attack the Capitol with mortar fire, lynch politicians, and, through a race war, commit ethnic cleansing. Terrorists, including the group that had murdered Alan Berg, swore by the book as a biblical work or how-to guide. The receptionist confirmed they carried the book. Hill decided not to go after all, worried he would run into Duke, who might recognize him. Rickey, fearing not only an uncomfortable chance encounter with the state representative—or one that set Duke off on an enraged rant—but also being recognized by legislative staff, asked a friend to accompany her.

On their visit, Rickey's friend took the lead, purchasing a copy of *The Turner Diaries*. Just as the receptionist squinted at them, perhaps about to ask who they were, they scurried back out. In fact, they left so quickly, they didn't have time to browse. But by showing up at 3603 Cypress Street, Rickey and Hill confirmed that the 81st district legislative office, the National Association for the Advancement of White People headquarters, and Americana Books were all housed in a basement—David Duke's basement.

Surely this would inspire her legislative colleagues to action. Just in case, however, and to get a better sense of Americana's inventory, Beth then sent more undercover operatives to Cypress Street, this time with a list that included *The Myth of the Six Million*, *Hitler Was My Friend*, and *The New Mythology of Equality*. She also wanted a pair of what she suspected were damning audio cassettes, including one about George Lincoln Rockwell. If the book titles didn't disturb Committee members, maybe audio recordings of the American Nazi Party founder would. Unfortunately, a staffer at Duke headquarters noticed the first undercover operative and watched her like a hawk. She pretended to be interested in the bizarre presence of a washer and dryer and carefully ignored NAAWP t-shirts folded and displayed on shelving. The staffer told her that they were out of *Hitler Was My Friend* and tried to get her to take a copy of *Mein Kampf* instead. He eventually convinced the nervous researcher to take Hitler's manifesto, as well as some NAAWP newsletters. But she must've still seemed suspicious to him, for she reported back to Rickey that, as she got in her car, she noticed him in her rearview mirror, eying her vehicle and scribbling something on a piece of paper.[58]

Meanwhile, events were spinning out of control for both Duke and Rickey. A group of Louisiana-based holocaust survivors attended the opening of a holocaust exhibit in the Capitol rotunda.[59] As Buddy Roemer spoke at the unveiling, Duke stepped out of the legislative chamber. He was immediately recognized by a Lodz and Warsaw ghettos survivor. As Anne Levy squinted at him from across the room, Duke strolled the gallery, ignoring the press, cameras, interested members of the public, and the politicians speaking in front of all the visitors. Hands behind his back, he peered silently at the still images lining the panels with a look of polite curiosity on his face. Levy charged over to the man who, she claimed, denied her experience. What the hell, Levy wanted to know, did David Duke, attendee of Holocaust-revisionism conferences, mean by coming here to gape at a terrible tragedy he didn't believe even happened?[60]

"I didn't say it didn't happen," he said measuredly. "I said it was *exaggerated*."[61]

Noticing the cameras 180-ing to cover him, Duke walked away. Levy, shaking, gulped, and lit out in pursuit. The media snatched cameras off tripods and followed at a clip. Duke, remaining mum, darted around the room while pursuers nipped at his heels in a comical chase, until he finally gave up and sped out of the rotunda. The incident made the news that night, with Duke calling the confrontation "a Zionist conspiracy," according to Anne Levy.[62]

Rickey had to make a snap decision. The Republican State Central Committee had its next meeting in only a week, and she could make a motion to have Duke censured by the state party. "We have a moral responsibility to speak out," she told a reporter privately. "We have a Nazi in our midst. If Duke is not confronted, he'll go on and gain legitimacy. He is blurring the line between racists and conservatives."[63]

There were many more reasons *not* to do it. When Rickey got in touch with Lee Atwater, the head of the Republican National Committee, he agreed that censure—and more elaborate methods—were needed before Duke dragged down the entire Republican Party.[64] But Billy Nungesser, chairman of the state party, firmly rejected this, claiming that he worried attacking Duke would stir up his vile base and that it would affect turnout in 1990–91.[65] Already, there had been an avalanche of outraged letters. "I have decided to withhold my support of the Republican Party until such time as this position [censure] is reconsidered and reversed," one note read.[66] Atwater changed his mind, as well, claiming to have adopted a wait-and-see approach regarding Duke's popularity within the GOP and to avoid feeding the beast in the interim.[67] Rickey, ever the faithful part of the "party faithful" cliché, understood. They reached a compromise where Rickey would be allowed to distribute her brief dossier among Committee members behind the scenes. She told herself this wasn't chickening out in the face of Nungesser's vehemence. Surely, she thought, her colleagues would rally behind her cause and vote to reprimand Duke.[68] She figured censure would have no effect, but couldn't stomach not at least *trying* to realign justice and the universe. Beth "took very seriously the fact that many of her Republican colleagues were not as appalled by what Duke stood for as she was," said friend Kenneth Stern. "You always have to respect somebody who sees somebody inside their political tent who is not standing up to bigotry within their community because either they do a political calculus or they're more loyal outside than inside. Beth had a consistent principle about bigotry no matter where it came from, that moral sense exuded from her being. She was proud of the connection to Branch Rickey [who signed Jackie Robinson.] All of that informed who she was."[69]

"I started dragging my feet," Rickey admitted, "and I was a little afraid of Duke as well. But then I thought if Anne Levy has got the guts to walk up to the man and ask him why he said the Holocaust never happened, I certainly could summon the courage to expose his Nazi-books-selling operation."[70]

Years later, she wrote, "Anne Levy needed backup from someone who was non-Jewish and, being a Reagan Republican, I couldn't be accused of being just another liberal opposed to Duke."[71] In an interview, she called Duke a "philosophical Nazi" and put him on the defensive.[72] In response to the scandal breaking in June of 1989, Duke said, "I want to get rid of anything that distracts from my agenda."[73]

As Rickey, head down, scampering in heels, made her way around the Committee meeting in the Capitol, State Rep. David Duke swooped in, his hand out to introduce himself. Attached to Duke's left hip was a blond he introduced as his new girlfriend. Before Rickey could say anything, however (not that she could muster the words —where to start? "Out of curiosity, are you a Nazi?") Treen swooped in, stepping into Duke's personal space.

"You are a lying, character-assassinating son of a bitch," barked Treen.[74]

And they were off. Rickey left her vanquished former boss and the ex/current Nazi in a back-and-forth over statements Duke allegedly made in the campaign about Treen and his sexual proclivities. Later, Rickey could sense someone watching her and turned, peering around the room. She spotted Duke, still holding hands with his girlfriend, studying Rickey intently. That's Beth Rickey, he told a lobbyist, smiling wryly, "my sworn enemy."[75]

With a vote on her potential motion delayed, Beth sat in the back of the room and rubbed her temples. Lobbying legislatures about Holocaust denialism and African American genetics didn't sit right with her. She shouldn't *have* to go it alone, shouldn't have had to put herself out there at all. She was a student, for God's sake, in a basically powerless party position with no ability to vote on state laws or make fundamental changes to the political process. All she could do was talk.

And so when David Duke seated himself next to her on the bench, slid his arm behind her seat, and started yakking, she didn't freeze up. Instead, she went straight to her challenges in her trademark monotone voice that could alternately seem judicial and disarmingly emotionless. After all, he caught her lobbying against him with his own eyes. She couldn't deny being the enemy. She demanded to know if he really believed that nonsense in his newsletters about Jews running the world and race mixing being responsible for the collapse of civilizations. He replied, "It's a religion to me."

Rickey insisted on a confirmation or refutation of the rumor that Duke had been involved with the death of then Grand Wizard Jim Lindsay. His mentor's demise, she pointed out, cleared a path for Duke to take over his leadership position. Duke offered a non-denial denial. "Yes, some people think I killed him," he said.[76] Before Rickey could so much as gulp, the meeting ended and she lost Duke in the shuffle.

"We must declare Duke's philosophy as beyond the bounds of decency," Rickey wrote. "Just because a person comes along and articulates certain positions doesn't mean that we should blindly accept him. We need to call Duke what he is: a racist, a bigot, and a divisive and negative influence on the electoral system."[77] She pointed out that "kook" Lyndon LaRouche coasted to victory in an Illinois primary after the Democrats thought it wiser to ignore him than fight.[78]

Around this time, the future core of the Louisiana Coalition Against Racism and Nazism entered Rickey and Hill's orbit. Beth asked her friend Ken Stern of the Jewish Action Committee in New York for help with the group's name; "she wanted to know if I thought it should have the word 'Nazi' in it," he recalled.[79] "When I couldn't find any republicans to take a public stand with me," she wrote, "I helped form a coalition of like-minded people to disseminate information." She recalled Quin Hillyer, a New Orleans–born conservative eight years her junior, a Young Reagan delegate to the 1980 National Convention and someone she had collaborated with in the eighties as Beth made her way up the political ladder in Lafayette.[80] Hillyer had entered the working world via the *Times-Picayune*, initially as a sports columnist. In 1989, his RNC-member father had warned him everyone was underestimating Duke's potential in a little-noticed State House race. Quin pored through the *Times-Picayune*'s archives, "appalled" at the biographical information and past statements Duke had made on the record. When he approached the paper about looking into Duke or at least doing a brief exposé on his activities ahead of the House primary, however, Hillyer ran into apathetic members of the elite class, the first of many such people the Coalition was to encounter. "They told me don't worry about it, he doesn't have a chance." Hillyer was so outraged by the material and miffed at potential donors who wouldn't step up, he took a dossier to John Treen's Metairie office after business hours, where he found the candidate working late.

"Oh, I already have someone on it," Treen said with a sigh. He nodded to the backroom. "Go ask if she's seen your material yet."[81]

The "she" working on the anti-Duke research was, of course, Beth Rickey. After reigniting their friendship, the two hatched a plan to collaborate on any anti-Duke advertising and press releases for the Treen campaign and, assuming Duke would be defeated without a runoff, wrap up their work in a couple of weeks. But after Duke's stunning victory and amid increasing indicators he would pivot to running for the US Senate, their research resumed

in earnest.[82] After Rickey's discovery of the Nazi books and the failed censure motion, Hillyer lent his writing talent to craft tight, eye-catching press
releases and other documents for the anti-Duke movement.

Back in New Orleans proper, Lance Hill created a press release announcing his and Beth's discoveries, to the grumbling of Billy Nungesser, the head
of the state GOP.[83] But Nungesser couldn't stop Hill, who didn't give a damn
what the Louisiana Republicans wanted. Beth, admitting that her efforts to
get the word out through backdoor channels had failed, agreed to return to
the State House and speak to any press who cared to cover the story. Duke,
in the House Committee room at the time, seemed oblivious to the hub-
bub building in the hallway. Hill's efforts had at least been rewarded with
a small swarm of reporters and cameras, and Rickey was literally under the
hot lights before she could mentally prepare for her face to lead the evening news. She cleared her throat and decided that, instead of a prepared
speech, she would hand out copies of the dossier on Duke to the media first.
As she spontaneously described what she had found, Duke emerged from
the House chamber to shrieks of pleasure. Fans having made the trip in
hopes of encountering the good-looking blond man refused to leave without
personalized autographs. A reporter from WVUE-TV, wasting not a second,
snatched up the LCARN copy of *Six Million* and sped toward the State Rep.[84]

"Are you selling this out of your state office?" asked the reporter, shaking the book.

Duke demanded to know whose copy it was. Before Rickey could cower,
the reporter turned and pointed wordlessly at her. Upon seeing his "enemy,"
Duke visibly reddened and raised his voice: "You're treating me like Salman
Rushdie!" he said, and stormed away, back into the legislative chamber where,
Rickey realized, he would be off-limits to non-elected officials.[85]

Soon after, Rickey received an anonymous call; the caller told her if she
pushed forward with her motion to censure Duke, she'd get one between
the eyes.[86] Hearing about the call changed Nungesser's tune, or seemed to
in the moment. The Republican chairman agreed to bring the motion to a
vote but wanted some neutral party, not Rickey, considered too emotionally invested, to introduce it. By the next meeting, however, Rickey knew
all the chaos hadn't actually improved her chances. Deciding to acquiesce
to Nungesser and not make a fuss, Rickey stood silently while someone
else presented her case. But State Senator Ben Bagert, running for the US
Senate, toed the chairman's line. Duke, he said, should face censure, but
in the voting booth, not at a closed committee meeting. "Let's point out
the differences at the polls," Bagert told the group. "Let's show we're the

party of Reagan, not Hitler."[87] This didn't sit well with Quin Hillyer, who had resigned from the *Times-Picayune* to help Bagert's campaign. But Bagert shrugged off Hillyer's pleas to at least not underestimate Duke's polling as Treen had done the year before.

Hillyer met Rickey for a friendly catch-up lunch in late 1989. "We talked on the phone six or seven times during that year, comparing notes on Duke," he recalled, "but now she said she had helped start this not-yet named organization." Rickey leveled with Hillyer. "Look," she said, "I actually needed to see you today because the anti-Duke coalition is having its second meeting tonight at the Metairie Jewish Community Center." Rickey, one of the co-founders, couldn't attend and needed someone to represent "her interests" as the conservative outlier.

November 20, 1989, was a bitterly cold, moonless, rainy night. Weary from the suspicion that Bagert and Johnston were not going to be so welcoming, the unnamed anti-Duke group's secret meeting seemed suitably battered and tired already. They tried out several names, including the Nuke Duke Committee and TRUTH—The Real Unmasking of Terrorism Hidden. But after putting the label Louisiana Coalition Against Racism and Nazism on the header of a press release, the group gradually understood that it had inadvertently already picked the name and an un-catchy acronym, LCARN.[88] What did get officially decided was the ten-person board, which included Beth Rickey and, simply for filling in and being committed to stopping the ascendancy of David Duke, Hillyer. Elated, Quin set out to find another job, at first intending to stick to sports journalism to avoid a conflict of interest with the board of LCARN. But when he landed a long-sought-after offer from the *Gambit*, a free weekly New Orleans paper, he found his employer needed someone to cover local politics. Eyes averted, Hillyer attended the third meeting "and told them I already had to leave the board. 'It'll probably be better this way because I can help the cause more this way anyway,'" he offered.[89] He regretted having to leave Beth in a nascent group with so many liberals and other people with whom the two did not agree except on their disdain for David Duke.

Before he left, Lance Hill, Larry Powell, Jane Buchsbaun, and Hillyer put together a kind of manifesto on which they would fall back during the coming campaigns. They decided at the second and third meetings how they wanted to attack Duke in 1990, although there was still some internal debate and external pressure over what to focus funds on: attacks regarding the representative's military service record and taxes or attacks on his Klan and Nazi leanings. An internal LCARN memo read, "Focus on what makes

Duke different than others who are conservative. It's not his stands on welfare, etc. that will defeat him. He deals in half-truths and outright lies. He
cleverly avoids accusations about his past and switches to more popular-
appealing current issues. TRUTH is our best weapon. Don't be side-tracked!
Focus entirely on his Nazi and Ku Klux Klan philosophy. Confront him at
every opportunity on those two points. Educate our audiences entirely on
those two points."[90]

Having failed to censure Duke or truly blow the lid off his life story,
Rickey sat in her New Orleans apartment, sighing over coffee and the situation with other members of the "plot," as Rickey called it, to foster "the
political demise of David Duke": Hill, future LCARN chairman Reverend
James Stovall, and LSU professor Paul Sanzenbach were there, as was Larry
Powell, soon to be voted co-vice chair of LCARN with Rickey.[91] The movement needed more ordinary people, they realized. More women. More writ-
ers like Jason Berry, willing to dig into Duke's past. Rickey's diary from this
time noted her "general mood: I am feeling very frustrated and dissatisfied
with this whole thing. I don't know why—I feel that I am expected to set an
agenda and carry out everything."[92] She admitted everyone was helping her,
though, and couldn't say why she felt that way about the endeavor.

Stovall showed everyone a Shreveport *Journal* article on Duke's rally in
that city: another thousand rabid Dukesters had turned out. "Duke is becoming more outspoken and freer in his comments, too," Stovall pointed out.
Beth said she had been in touch with the Republican Senate Committee,
which had volunteered to draw up all necessary paperwork for the group's
501(c)4. Then, in Rickey's telling, at ten o'clock, as the meeting seemed in
danger of petering out without resolutions, Beth's phone rang. Something
politely told her not to answer it, to instead focus on her guests, but she
picked it up anyway.

"Beth?"

"Yes."

"Beth, hi, this is David Duke."[93]

Rickey nearly dropped the phone on the floor. It was definitely not a
prank, she realized instantly. The voice was unmistakable. *The Devil*.

CHAPTER 6

Vox Populist

"Hello David," Beth said coldly, cocking her head around to meet the widening eyes of the anti-Duke coalition. Mouths opened in horror. "I've got company at the moment, do you mind calling back another time?"[1]

Elizabeth A. Rickey of New Orleans had the attention of the most talked-about man in the country, and she would immediately have cause to regret it. After clearing everyone out of her apartment (*You sure you want to be alone with him*, they asked, *even if he's not actually in the room?*), Rickey got down to brass tacks with the state rep. He told her he didn't condone Nazism "or Totalitarianism of any kind." Rickey began nodding off due to the late hour, but when she awoke with a start, Duke was telling her his life story, with the Mike + the Mechanics hit "Silent Running" looped in the background. (The song had a chorus Duke surely wanted to serve as a subliminal message: "Can you hear me running?" it went. However, the lyrics detail a future world in which a civil war has wiped out most of society and a Big Brother-style government emerges forcing people to, for starters, salute the flag or face severe repercussions.) But once she turned on her tape recorder and listened to him roll on, the real purpose of his call started to eke out. Duke, in his rambling, mentioned, according to Rickey's scribbled notes, "race, eugenics, poetry, Aryans, etc." kept referring to "the Jewish question," claimed there were diseases only Jews carried, and would bring up race mixing as something that, by achieving higher office, he might be able to put a stop to.[2] She was mesmerized by his piling on the "facts." "You get kind of goofy and start identifying with your captor, so to speak. And I would call people [afterward] and say, 'Look, deprogram me. You know, I've gotten all this stuff in my head.'"[3]

"He's the ultimate con man," she said. "He's not telling the truth. And the truth is that he is a great admirer of National Socialism. He's a great admirer of Adolf Hitler. And he still believes . . . in the beliefs of racial superiority . . . that the white Aryans are superior, and that Jews are evil." Later, she said, "He's a racial ideologue of a type that I have yet to encounter in my entire lifetime."[4]

Ultimately, Rickey piled up forty-eight hours of tapes from calls and in-person meetings with Duke over several weeks. The politician tried to come across as a changed or reborn man, a harmless weirdo who made boneheaded decisions after becoming captivated with right-wing movements and the powerful figures who tried to change the world and rid it of communists, money grabbers, and genetically inferior races.[5] She found herself strangely drawn to the state rep., despite the subjects of conversation, and despite the fact that she was physically repelled by the cosmetic surgery he'd apparently undergone to alter his appearance, thinning out his long, wide nose and giving himself a facelift. *Sojourners* claimed "Duke went to a plastic surgeon and had his face Aryanized with a nose and chin job. He has tried to do the same with his ideology. But he is still just a fascist with a facelift."[6] Anna Quindlen's takedown of Duke in a nationally syndicated column began, "Some people wonder why so much has been made of David Duke's plastic surgery. The answer is simple. David Duke's new face is a symbol of what he seeks to do: turn back the clock and pretend to be something he is not."[7] Rickey could not have agreed more: the cover-up encompassed aesthetic and political fronts.

When she bluntly inquired about his reasons, Duke told her he highly recommended cosmetic touch-ups for almost anyone.[8] Regardless of Duke's rationale, his surgeries divided the masses. More young women signed up for the campaign, passed Duke their phone numbers, or outright kissed him in bars or along the campaign trail. Liberal-leaning men and those already repelled by his politics took to making fun of him, even to his face. ("Nose Job Nazi" became a popular anti-Duke sign.) One woman heckler called his appearance "terrible."[9] Uptown New Orleanians reportedly boycotted the responsible plastic surgeon because of his association with the ex-Klansman.[10] When Duke suggested they meet for lunch, Rickey had to remember not to stare too hard at that *schnoz*.

She found herself strangely compelled to meet with Duke; she told herself it was because Duke might blurt out something particularly controversial about black people or Jews while Beth clandestinely recorded, but the appeal may have gone beyond that. Certainly, Duke was an attractive man, charismatic and persistent without losing his charm. "There was something about Duke that even the most repulsed among us could not deny," Rickey wrote.[11] She later suggested "he radiated a sensual intensity," adding that Duke developed into "the most spectacular politician in these latitudes since former governor Edwin Edwards."[12]

"I want to make clear," Hillyer said decades later, "theirs was not a romantic relationship."[13] Instead, Duke's charm offensive had entirely political dimensions. "David considers himself an intellectual and couldn't bear the idea that conservative intellectuals would not agree with him, so he kept trying to corner me at an event," said Hillyer, "but obviously, he became more obsessed with her. She told all her friends, 'I can't believe this guy's calling me, babbling on about how Jews are child molesters.'" She told Hillyer all the bizarre details, including describing the two of them driving down Interstate 10 in New Orleans in Duke's convertible with the top down, with Rickey trying to play oldies ("Negro music," Duke said, punching the next station[14]) and the representative singing the *Man of La Mancha* tune "The Impossible Dream" while his kids, visiting from Florida, blinked uncertainly in the backseat. When Duke referenced dressing Erika in Klan robes as a toddler, she exclaimed, "Dad!"[15]

The kids wanted pizza, but Duke took them to a bar with raw oysters, then tried to convince everyone to visit Baskin-Robbins near the Tulane campus instead of Zack's, a locally owned frozen yogurt spot, presumably because college students would flock to him at the former. After convincing Duke to choose the latter, Rickey sensed Duke was reluctant to get out of the car. "I felt very strange walking in there with him and being surrounded by blacks," she noted. "He kept talking about how we were going to get mugged."

Over several encounters, Duke wore down Rickey's resistance through his soft-spoken children, to whom she gave quarters for video games. Duke, meanwhile, bored the kids to sleep by refusing to engage in even cursory small talk about something other than politics.[16] Even when Rickey tried to get him to explain why he called African Americans "Negroes" in private and "blacks" in public, Duke would change the subject to Jewish people. He periodically asked her to stop telling everyone about the Nazi books in his legislative office, as she had "stirred up the Jews" and earned him death threats.[17] After all, he said, he had gotten rid of all the offensive materials. (Reporter Jason Berry visited Duke's office and confirmed that a poster of Klan founder Nathan Bedford Forrest and a confederate flag had been removed from the walls after the book-buying story broke.[18]) Despite this, Rickey found herself compelled both by his relentless interest in hanging out with her and by her own instincts, which told her to get as much damaging material as possible, her personal safety and sanity be damned. She started showing up at the houses of Duke associates, including that of his black childhood nanny, looking for damaging information.[19]

At their lunches and dinners, which continued despite her best judgment, Rickey recalled Duke praising notorious members of the Third Reich, including Adolf Eichmann, architect of the Holocaust, whom the state rep. suggested got a bum rap at the Nuremberg Trials.[20] But nothing bothered Rickey more during Duke's charm offensive than a monologue about Dr. Josef Mengele at a lunch at Ming Palace in Metairie.

Would David Duke really profess admiration for genetic research conducted by a Nazi doctor, who conducted abominable experiments on children, healthy Jews, and persons with disabilities, people who had testified against him by the dozens? *That* Mengele? "Beth, the man had a PhD," Duke said. "Do you think he would have jeopardized his career with so many witnesses? Come on."[21]

Rickey at first felt sorry about this pathetic demonstration from this single, friendless man on top of the world.[22] She viewed him as a bullied junior high school kid who craved acceptance and, once he figured out a way to get it, stuck to that path. Duke could have improvised a one-liner in class, brought the (school) house down, and decided to try standup comedy. Instead, his audience became the prejudiced, the misled and aggrieved, nostalgic and privileged, who hadn't achieved their dreams or received the free ride they'd been instructed to expect, and who now heard a popular figure casting blame on a swath of outsiders, who were speeding by without picking them up along the way. Duke Country residents wanted out of their staid lives, and its leader dangled what amounted to economic and cultural promissory notes. *Elect me*, they might've read, *and I'll right the wrongs against our race and way of life.* In the end, as Rickey noted, "Duke was both more sinister than ordinary redneck racists and far more politically savvy."[23]

Rickey claimed she stopped speaking to Duke when he tried to get in touch after their "holocaust" lunch in Metairie. He had suggested the genocide had been exaggerated and that Hitler wouldn't have shipped people to Poland if he would simply exterminate them upon arrival.[24] She thought of her father, who had liberated camps as part of Patton's staff. She outed herself in the press as having secretly recorded Duke, finally convinced that he meant what he said in their initial calls and conversations. What was the purpose of all of this? What exactly did he want from this relationship?

"I want you to hold a press conference and say you were wrong about me," he told Beth. When she pointed out that Duke hadn't disproven any of her hunches about his views, Rickey said he practically sneered. "Well, Beth," he said. "Remember, I haven't attacked you—yet."[25]

Since announcing for the 1989 House election, David Duke *had* changed, though. It wasn't just his views on current political issues or race (or so he claimed.) After a decade in the political and cultural wilderness, where his racially charged organizations received little press, few donations, or any room at the table, he'd become a state representative and a genuine political force in Louisiana. With that cachet came autograph seekers, book sales, speaking engagements, donations to his campaign chest (assuming he would run again for something someday somewhere), and interactions with his public. For years, Edwin Edwards, now practically a senior citizen, had received kisses from beautiful blondes and hugs from children and the elderly. Now, after hearing him rail against entitlements and government budgets, seniors collecting social security checks shook Duke's hand and thanked him for fighting "takers" of more than "their fair share" of welfare and other socialist programs. He slept with a different young blond woman every night, or at least suggested he could. He would be invited back on Phil Donahue's massively popular syndicated TV show. He went on *Nightline* and *Larry King Live* and was interviewed by every major newspaper in the US. But most importantly, his message was getting out there, and it was showing up in the polls.[26]

It hadn't always been that way, of course, not even for much of 1989. The month of the State House primary, he sat at seven percent in polls. He had gone on to humiliate the elites—party leaders, the rich donors, the media— and the voters who didn't support him because they saw his poll numbers and thought, *It's not worth the effort to go out there, Treen's gonna win.* Duke finished first in the primary by more than a third and was the winner and representative-elect by a hair in the runoff. To Duke, it didn't matter how he had done it, it's that he had.

Although he might not want to relive it, to look back and cringe at those early days, they are quite remarkable when one compares them to the payoff at the end. Duke's 1989 kickoff event had been staffed by a mere three volunteers. But when he knocked on doors in the middle-class sections of town, the reception seemed overwhelmingly positive, or at least enough to keep him motivated, day after day, to buck the system that seemed to be rigged in John Treen's favor. One woman told a reporter, "He's honest, and he's not trying to hide any of his past . . . and he just makes you like him. . . . That affirmative action, he wants to get rid of it. . . . If blacks are not qualified for anything, why should they be given a better chance?"[27]

One young teacher said: "I'm more interested in what he'll do than what he's done in the past," confirming that the race would be one of issues instead of character or track record. "Because of his youth, he'll have more energy. It's fresh blood. . . . It wouldn't influence me one bit what he did in the past," she said.[28] Others would tell Duke he earned their vote by opposing taxes on individuals or to help defeat the Democratic governor's costly ballot initiatives.

After leading in the primary and beating John Treen one-on-one in the runoff, Duke made good on his anti-tax promises. When Duke took his spot in the legislature, he received a standing ovation from his colleagues and, from the gallery, thunderous applause that convinced him that voters beyond District 81 were learning about his message and were jazzed about his next move.[29] He immediately pivoted to campaigning against a billion-dollar Roemer tax proposal, which served two purposes: prove to the state GOP that he was an invincible, praiseworthy political force, and to shore up support in other parishes for his next move.

Although it had eked through the legislature, Roemer's reform bill, his first success after a pair of defeats, needed to be put to a referendum before becoming a constitutional amendment. The proposal, a fairly basic one that would raise income taxes and gas prices by less than one cent per gallon and pay for any shortages through a cut of mineral sales, also came balanced with sales tax cuts, which helped sell it to voters. But the public didn't know if it should *have* to pay more for highway, hospital, and airport improvements, and the referendum could be as close as a coin toss.

Duke had mere weeks to turn voters against the referendum before the April vote. "I think the people of this state are much wiser than the politicians who are trying to rule us," he said.[30] In all-day meetings, Governor Roemer, up for reelection in 1991, would warn people that the alternative would be severe job cuts and maybe hospital and university closures.[31] That didn't motivate voters, though. They figured Buddy Roemer was throwing another tantrum. Instead, the crowds turned out by the hundreds for Duke's barnstorming rallies around Louisiana, during which he would rail against Roemer, his tax plan, and his backers.

When the polls closed, it became immediately clear Duke would win the unofficial battle with Roemer. The tax proposal went down in flames by ten points. Once more, either the polls had been wrong about Duke's appeal the whole time or his final blitz had turned the tide, perhaps both. The Louisiana Coalition Against Racism and Nazism collectively gaped in horror as they watched Duke in local news highlight reels, waving to supporters on parade routes and from a podium. Lurking in the background, as usual, that handmade sign: "Duke For Governor."[32]

Duke, however, had another race in mind. In 1990, centrist Democrat J. Bennett Johnston faced a tough Senate reelection fight against a resurgent Republican Party. State Senator Bernard J. "Ben" Bagert, who had recently made the jump to the Republicans, had been nudged into the contest by the GOP for his combative nature in the legislature, never letting anyone get away with vote-switching or bullshitting the Senate about a bill. He also prided himself on being a dealmaker, serving as the last senator Governor Roemer needed to shore up a razor-thin vote; of course, he would exact a price for each of these tide-turning thumbs-up, and his price might be steep. If Bagert needed Roemer to endorse him or at least remain silent in the US Senate race, Ben Bagert wouldn't ask—Roemer knew better than that. And while Bagert wasn't very well-known, he did have a broad if small base, including businessmen and black churchgoers, each of which would prove crucial, in the party's thinking, when it came to a head-to-head with Johnston.[33]

Bagert's campaign roared to life in the party's nominating process, with the state senator having shored up bureaucratic support well in advance and hiring strategists to get out the vote in the parishes, each of which had one vote in the nominating process. By lining up all the significant endorsements, Bagert made a case for his opponents dropping out, which they mostly did. One name that stayed on the ballot was David Duke's.

Bagert hated Duke and the feeling may have been mutual. The state senator called the state rep. a "maggot" and suggested Duke was still a closet racist. "He doesn't talk about blacks anymore," Bagert said. "It's just a wink and a nod; everyone knows what he means."[34] Duke and Bagert had met in 1976 on the day a bust of P. B. S. Pinchback, the state's first black governor, was unveiled in the State House. Duke crashed the event with an unidentified companion in blackface and a sign around his neck with the honored governor's name on it. Bagert allegedly had to be held back from punching Duke and threatened him with a pounding if he didn't leave immediately.[35]

In the fall of 1989, party crashing uptown, where he miraculously didn't run into Beth Rickey, Duke instead bumped into New Orleans mayor Dutch

Morial. One would imagine that of all the dozens of politically connected Republicans, conservative Democrats, and even the catering staff, Duke would have had the most trouble connecting with the city's first black leader and a lion of the Democratic Party. Instead, Morial, grinning broadly as only the most experienced and effective politicians can in close proximity to a supposed nemesis, swung across the living room and into the foyer to greet Duke. "Mr. State Representative," he said, "we have something in common."

"Oh? And what's that?"

"We're both running against J. Bennett Johnston for that Senate seat next year."[36]

Now, Morial had the old Klansman beaming. The mayor, Duke knew, had seen two steps ahead. With a popular black candidate in the race, Johnston didn't have a prayer of winning the Democrats' main base in Louisiana, depriving him of a majority. With ex-Grand Wizard David Duke in the race, Johnston wouldn't be able to make up the difference by pulling in all the conservatives repelled by "that black mayor."

Johnston, a friend of big business, was an easy target for the state rep. Duke could emphasize his outsider status with the rural and middle-class voters, as well as conservative Democrats. That left Bagert to pull up the rear and, with seven percent in the first poll, the state senator might do just that. But since Johnston clobbered Duke in head-to-head polling, insiders didn't scrutinize the numbers and missed a crucial detail. Older voters, it turned out, refused to respond to polls at alarming rates, an indicator they were embarrassed to admit their preferences. The incumbent listened to conventional wisdom, which suggested he ignore the ex-Klansman and coast on his record as the chairman of the Energy Committee and the water and development subcommittee. He should've been impervious to right-wing attacks in an oil-driven state, but with job losses increasing each year in the industry, he could no longer coast to reelection as a petroleum man. Worse, social issues were overtaking economics as voters' main concern. It would only be a matter of an election cycle or two before the GOP fielded a major threat. Ben Bagert, though, wasn't it.

Bagert, in fact, boosted Duke by pulling Johnston below the margin he needed to avoid a runoff, and Bagert didn't have a hope in hell of making the runoff.[37] The media, party officials, and even the candidates themselves, however, continued to downplay Duke's chances in the race. As the primary neared, both Bagert and Johnston were still referencing the third combatant, described as an albatross hanging over the Republican Party, in vague allusions.[38] Worried, though, about a vicious runoff, Johnston finally heeded the call of LCARN and vocally addressed Duke.

"The National Association for the Advance of White People is the Klan without bedsheets. Did you all read about the sex book he wrote? If I had done one-tenth of what David Duke has done, one-tenth . . . why, they'd ride me out of town on a rail. Why, this man has celebrated Adolf Hitler's birthday every year!"[39]

The US senator's campaign mailer soon read "K-K-Kan [*sic*] You Believe Duke???"[40] Johnston had put Bagert on the spot. Bagert now had to decide whether to stick with his strategy of leaving Duke alone in case he needed the neo-Nazi's voters in the runoff or look tough bucking his opponent.

The disappointments for the Duke campaign soon arrived and in waves. Dutch Morial passed away suddenly, terminating Morial and Duke's conspiratorial strategy to end up in the runoff. In New Orleans, with Duke speaking first at a forum, Bagert invaded the stage and confronted Duke, getting into a heated argument that startled the audience out of its doldrums. Duke, trying to resume his prepared remarks, attacked Bagert for calling him "a Nazi, a bigot and a maggot."

"I never called you a bigot," deadpanned Bagert, to cackling laughter.

"How about 'maggot?'" Duke asked, his face reddening. This wasn't political theater; Bagert, everyone saw, had got to him.

"I did say that we in the Republican Party were turning a maggot into a martyr, but I never called you a Nazi," said Bagert. "Everybody knows about your Nazi activities."[41]

They did, although it didn't stop Louisianans from packing Duke events. From day one, the campaign stunned insiders, who must've somehow missed Duke's upset win the year before. At the January 20, 1990, kickoff event, volunteers kept adding chairs to the Monroe Holiday Inn meeting room as they watched the parking lot clog up with cars. Five hundred attendees ultimately lined up. Duke outdid himself in Crowley, the Edwin Edwards stronghold, drawing six hundred. And at a Bossier City rally a few weeks after the kickoff, Duke, publicly optimistic and quietly anxiety ridden from his years as an also-ran, asked his team to remove several dozen folding chairs on a hunch the event would be a bust. Instead, before he spoke, an estimated one thousand supporters had jammed themselves inside. The crowd cheered warm-up acts from within the campaign who hit upon each of the four Ps, as supporter and ex-congressman John Rarick called them: "perverts, pinkos, and the political prostitutes."[42] Duke hit on the flat tax (pro), spending (slash it), and pornography, abortion, and other staples of the religious Right (ban it all). He riled up the masses by calling Johnston a liberal and saying he would "force [the Senator] to go to the blacks and then I'll Atwater him!"[43] But his biggest ovation came toward the end, when he quoted a Tom Petty lyric and suggested that, in victory or defeat, he wouldn't back down for anyone. His campaign coordinator had never seen such enthusiasm for a local candidate. The staff started telling everyone: *Duke could go all the way.*[44]

Although Johnston lead by two dozen points, the rally numbers didn't lie, and neither did the focus groups. LCARN hired pollsters, including Mark Penn, future player in presidential politics, to field-test possible messages against Duke.[45] How to turn conservatives against him? Taxes, lying about his military service, Nazism, the Klan, or something else? Penn asked what effect Duke's being a Klansman (or ex-KKK Grand Wizard) had on the group. The data came back and stunned the coalition. The Klan revelations didn't nudge Duke's support, which they suspected might be the case, given that many white Louisianans had KKK members in their family trees, but the Nazi connection and pro-Hitler book sales didn't make the focus group squirm either.[46] Some people weren't even bothered by a shocking transcript from a Duke interview, released after its discovery by Beth Rickey on a research trip to Boston.[47] "Did you ever notice how many [Holocaust] survivors they have? 15,000 meet here, 400 survivors convention there," he cracked. "Nazis sure were inefficient, weren't they? Boy, boy boy! You have almost no survivors that ever say they saw a gas chamber."[48]

Duke's exaggerated military service, however, seemed to resonate; his positives went down when Penn pressed the matter. Meanwhile, follow-up questions about the book sales, like "What if you knew that David's response to this was: 'I'm a bookseller, but that doesn't make me B. Dalton,'" brought Duke's numbers back up. "See?" said right-wing anti-Dukes, to liberal LCARN members' chagrin, "the military attack line keeps the negatives high." A conservative anti-Duke woman on the board said, "You can't talk about Nazi stuff" without wasting her donation on an attack ad that wouldn't hurt Duke. But, Tim Wise argued, that's not really what the numbers said. He also pointed out that Penn hadn't field tested a rebuttal to *Duke's* rebuttal, something along the lines of, "Well, actually, the *only* books he sold were Nazi books."[49]

Rickey suggested Duke had to be publicly opposed by a united community. "He counts on people being nice and backing off," she explained at a LCARN meeting, but at the same time attacking him could turn into a catch-22, rendering him a martyr.[50] Regardless of attacks on Duke's affirmative action message, it seemed to resonate. In a 1990 poll, eight in ten adults said they opposed preferential hiring for black people, and more than seven out of ten had the same disdain for minority set-asides in college admissions.[51]

While LCARN fought internally, Duke built up his campaign team for the war ahead. Duke had two ex-cops in powerful roles, both of whom had been kicked off the force.[52] Howie Farrell said he'd been dismissed for trying to organize a police union, but *Times-Picayune* reporter Tyler Bridges found evidence that Farrell had been let go after intimidating and then unlawfully arresting a teenager whom he'd stopped for "speeding"; Farrell, it seemed, never turned on his radar gun. Meanwhile, Kenny Knight, Duke's volunteer coordinator, had been busted for pilfering construction site lumber in 1973.[53] More problematic characters turned up on the payroll. Willard Barbour "Babs" Minhinnette became the head of the NAAWP after Duke left to run for the House; during the campaign, Babs was in charge of the Duke campaign's Baton Rouge outpost.[54] Lawyer Jim McPherson, though, said Duke's campaign "was a one-man show" with the candidate calling the shots—all the shots. "It was the best thing for him. It was simpler." Duke, he said, knew what to do and how to whip up his base. With "pandemonium" at every stop on the trail, as *Esquire* termed it, why fix what ain't broke?[55]

To cover more ground, Duke sat in the passenger seat of a van most of the day with a staffer at the wheel and covered as many markets, concerts, and festivals as he could in a waking day. "Need your support," he would call out. "You got it," they would holler back, waving. "You're the monkey wrench we need to stop the machine," one supporter shouted. "A lot of people are afraid to stand up in public and say it," a Lake Charles resident explained. "But when they get behind that curtain, they're gonna vote for him, even though he's as radical as he is."[56]

Some would try to hand him cash or other valuables, which he had a hard time refusing. The *Wall Street Journal* noted that because so many contributions were under $200, Duke didn't have to list them all, particularly all those $1s and $5s stuffed into his hands. At a Bossier City rally, volunteer Linda Melton said she gathered $10,000 in cash from 1,500 attendees, all of which she "stuffed into a garbage bag at the end of the night" and which she claimed was "never properly counted." Melton added, "'Duke took the money upstairs himself."[57] Senator Johnston expected that his $2,500,000 war chest would be enough to crush his opponents, but he hadn't counted on Duke's grassroots support.[58] By collecting fistfuls of cash as he worked autograph lines, the Metairie representative built a war chest of his own, and by Election Day, he would stun the political establishment by netting roughly $2,400,000.[59]

Duke inadvertently made it easier on himself by causing problems for the Republicans in state government. A key moment in our national politics came in a fight over a discrimination bill in the legislature. Duke's affirmative action bill, though sliced to bits, emerged from committee and made it to the House floor. In a stunning turn of events, the yays had it by thirty-eight votes, an overwhelming margin. Rep. Charles Jones of the House black caucus singled out Duke for blame, seething that the bill showed it was "all right to be a former member of the Ku Klux Klan" and still become a legislator in Louisiana. "You can camouflage things but racism is racism," Jones grumbled. Duke took offense to being called a racist, saying his bill actually *outlawed* racist quotas. "This bill simply prohibits racial discrimination in hiring, promotion, scholarships," he said. "There is no justification to discriminate against someone who works hard, who is qualified for a job."[60]

As it sunk in that Duke had not only won office, he'd won passage of a racist bill, a lot of the fight went out of the old guard. Rep. Joseph Accardo lamented, "I've not seen this kind of turmoil before. Before, there was more good will."[61] John Treen just chalked it all up to one more sneak attack by the "master of deception." Previously, this kind of "turmoil" could mainly be found in the *Federal* government, where senators occasionally caned one another within an inch of their lives over slavery.

Around this same time, another little-noticed event occurred that should have been a clue for Democrats running against racists or former racists: the hiring by the Duke campaign of Rusty Cantelli. The campaign strategist and former Treen supporter, a friend of Dr. Martin Luther King's, hailed Duke as "an outsider, a grass-roots type," who was "vainly trying to discuss ideas" while others shouted him down for a past he disowned.[62] Cantelli, a District 81 resident, had switched his 1989 runoff vote to David Duke and jumped aboard the 1990 Senate campaign. Duke suddenly had an experienced and effective teammate, rather than just a group of problematic yes men. Cantelli got to work, cranking out multiple thirty-minute spots that ran in primetime and featured Duke, at ease and responding to scripted softballs from a comely interviewer. Those and other ads featured Duke at times speaking directly to voters in a calm voice about "reverse discrimination," certainly, but also about the fear in the streets, especially in inner cities, as crime continued to rise. "Don't just send them a message," his campaign tagline went, "send them a senator."[63]

It worked. In only a few weeks, Duke racked up tens of thousands of dollars through his on-screen 1-900 number, en route to a predicted $200,000 in the final weeks of the race. Then the phone company pulled the plug. South Central Bell said that company policy clearly stated that Duke could not use a 1-900 hotline to solicit political donations.[64] He never received any of the funds, even after filing a lawsuit.[65]

Meanwhile, Johnston, seeing Duke's FEC reports, pivoted to raising money from out-of-state, ironically an old Duke tactic. As a conservative Democrat, the incumbent, however, could call on powerful friends from Congress and beyond, including the National Rifle Association, especially its leader, James Jay Baker. His letter to voters called Johnston an NRA member for life and a grand "friend of law-abiding gun owners and sportsmen." Surprisingly, the fundraising plea goes on to describe that, on the Energy Committee, the senator "helped preserve over 120,000 acres of Louisiana wetlands." Former Nixon advisor and fresh Democratic senator Daniel Patrick Moynihan, a foe to welfare reform, sent a similar plea for Johnston using Duke's own statements. "I question whether 6 million Jews actually died in Nazi death camps," the letter quoted him, pulling from the August 1982 *NAAWP News*. Moynihan called out Duke for pretending to repudiate Nazism and the KKK because he "has learned from years in the Ku Klux Klan that overt racism and obvious rabble-rousing won't win him widespread public support."[66] With a mailing list that included New York City's Jewish enclaves, Moynihan noted that his colleague had been a committed friend to Israel and, with Johnston a powerful senior Democrat in top committee posts, his defeat would be Israel's, as well. The letter kept hammering away over several pages, pointing out that Duke had earned donations from every state in the Union by the end of 1989.[67]

With Johnston increasingly desperate to outraise and outspend Duke, an internal analysis by his campaign found that there were few "ticket-splitters" out there, meaning conservatives who might recoil from Duke and vote for a Democrat instead. The pollsters found that most of Louisiana's "persuadables" were "in staunch Republican areas" and that while Johnston may not win them, he needed to go hard after them in concert with Democratic strongholds or lose almost solely via low turnout.[68] It wasn't entirely Johnston himself that had dragged down his campaign. The map had started to turn against Democrats in 1986, when John Breaux won reelection to the US Senate. His seemingly comfortable five-point victory in the runoff overshadowed the primary, in which a Republican finished first and a close read of the final tally showed Breaux received only forty-five to fifty-five percent in almost half of all parishes. Johnston, therefore, was in the fight of his life and didn't realize it.

The Louisiana Coalition, meanwhile, still hadn't fully committed to helping the Democrat defeat Duke. Lance Hill, a political enigma who supported the Second Amendment and the civil rights movement in equal measure, built a dossier, starting with a NAAWP map he uncovered purportedly dividing the country into ethnic zones. Hill's growing archive contained evidence of Duke's affiliation with racists and racist organizations in the 1980s, after supposedly quitting the Klan. Among Duke's casually donated papers, there was an interview with a Tulane student, who had been given questions from a gleeful, pranksterish Hill, and in Evelyn Rich's transcripts, Duke attacking President Roosevelt for allowing Pearl Harbor, suggesting the country should've stayed neutral in World War II, musing on a future eugenics program that would fund white adults with high IQs reluctant to produce Aryan offspring, suggested there were "atrocities committed by the free-born Negroes" and, perhaps mostly damningly, said of Populist Party leader Willis Carto (whom he claimed to not know three years later), "I've been on good terms with all of those people for years."[69] He also called Carto "the most important publisher of anti-Jewish material."[70] The Jews, he claimed, were "trying to exterminate our race. I think, probably in a moral sense, the Jewish people have been a blight. I mean as a whole, not every Jew. And they probably deserve to go into the ashbin of history. But saying that and actually shooting or killing people in masses, are two different things. I'm not advocating extermination. I think the best thing is to resettle them in someplace where they can't exploit others."[71]

In a March 1985 interview with Rich, he suggested that black people were more likely to commit crimes as a near-genetic imperative, a point he continued to insist on for years.[72] Meanwhile, Rickey hit another motherlode of 1985–86 transcripts in which Duke, talking to white supremacists, said that while the Holocaust was real, Jews and Christians were *both* targeted. LCARN Chairman Rev. Stovall told a reporter, "We made up our minds early to not try to defeat Duke" on his philandering or any other character flaw.[73] That eliminated the softcore porn book, a faux-sex manual Duke had written under an alias.[74] The press largely dismissed Hill's dossier, at least before the 1990 campaign concluded.[75] Johnston was of the same mind, sitting on another stockpile while his verbal attacks on the state rep. took effect and doing his best not to rock the boat in a close race. Rickey, of course, knew better than to think letting David Duke play on even ground could result in anything other than a victory—for Duke.

Meanwhile, Duke's fans got the memo about keeping their racism and anti-Semitism low-key and left his name off flyers supporting the cause. In November, the National Socialist Youth Movement apparently distributed a two-paragraph call to action at Lakeside Mall, Metairie's shopping hub, with a mysterious PO box and phone number belonging to something called LON and instructing members of the white race to get in touch to help the Nazi youth achieve equality and save Caucasian heritage. "Are you sick and tired of illegale [*sic*] drugs on OUR streets, rampant crime, murder and rape in OUR cities and neighborhoods? Reverse discrimination in the workplace and on campus? Jews control OUR banks and media. Blacks control OUR streets. End this horror!"[76]

Finally, the stalemate broke. After weeks of attacks on Duke and a seemingly reenergized campaign, Ben Bagert—remember him?—had only clawed his way to eight percent of the vote, about where he had been when he announced months prior. He announced he was quitting. "As my campaign finally began to get on track in the last couple of weeks, it became more and more apparent, that instead of forcing a runoff between myself and Bennett Johnston, I might very well be forcing a runoff between somebody else and Bennett Johnston." That somebody else meant a certain ex-KKK Grand Wizard, of course. "The way to look at it is that we are doing our best to insure the defeat of extremism and bigotry," said Charles Black of the Republican National Committee. With Bagert out of the race, the national party would continue to "oppose David Duke no matter who's running against him."[77]

That was about as close to an endorsement as one of the most powerful Democrats in the country could hope to get from an RNC spokesperson. The *New York Times* all but certified Johnston's victory on the spot, agreeing with two New Orleans pollsters that Duke wouldn't get anywhere near victory in that weekend's voting. With Duke still polling with less than half the support he needed for a majority and a united coalition of Republican and Democratic senators endorsing his opponent and condemning Duke, Tyler Bridges reported that Duke fell into a deep funk. He did have one idea, which he wasn't sure could turn things around. "The fix is [in], and people won't buy it," said his spokesman. "People are really fed up with the political establishment and the establishment media. With the establishment aligning itself against David Duke, they send a lot of voters our way."[78]

The word went out: a shady deal between Johnston and Bagert had lined up the latter's eleventh-hour lightning strike to deny Duke victory. Johnston hadn't motivated Democrats, but Bagert had unintentionally motivated conservatives. While Duke changed tactics, holding a series of woe-is-me rallies attacking *both* candidates, Johnston traveled by plane to his few remaining campaign events, scribbling a prediction on a napkin: *I will win by a 30-point landslide.*[79]

By dropping out four days before the vote, Bagert would remain on the ballot and his votes would not be counted. Johnston tried to convince Bagert's people to switch their support, lest their votes be for nothing, but he didn't present the greatest argument. "I'm very much hoping that the Bagert vote, which has been about eight percent, would come to me,"[80] he said, an unsure prom king contestant working the slow dancers.

It didn't work, but it didn't matter. Johnston prevailed but by a harrowing margin: barely ten percent. As the total rolled in, the *Times* analysis sent a shudder through Beth Rickey: "David Duke may have lost the vote count last Saturday, but in all other respects his Louisiana senate campaign was victorious. In accordance with his long-term strategy, Mr. Duke has taken another giant step toward moving white supremacy off the margin and into the mainstream of American politics."[81] Duke's supporters didn't see it quite that way at first; one lashed out at a CNN correspondent for calling Duke's base "neo-Nazi sympathizers."[82] And although Duke came up far short mathematically, "it would be a mistake to measure David Duke by conventional political standards," the *Times* wrote.[83] He doubled his numbers from the final poll, an astonishing feat, and stunned the nation with a six hundred thousand vote total. John Maginnis wrote, "The pollsters who focused on Duke's negatives overlooked the fact that many voters felt more negatively about Johnston." Most tellingly, Duke captured fifty-five percent of the white vote. The undecideds or Bagert fans, it appeared, had broken for Duke or simply shrugged off the race as not being close enough to care about.[84]

Rev. Stovall, at LCARN's election watch party at the New Orleans Sheraton, almost couldn't speak. "We got beat," he said. "Duke won. He carried a majority of the white vote."[85] He considered it the Coalition's third consecutive loss, including the two state representative votes. Stovall's own Baton Rouge neighborhood awarded Duke a majority of their vote. Hill, in a stew as well, suggested that their meager ad spend meant they hadn't hit Duke hard enough.[86] Rickey was torn between feeling positive about the effort to worrying that it could've ultimately helped turn out racists who didn't know about the Republican. "I don't agree with the argument that one should not speak out because it gives the subject more visibility. At times, though," she admitted, "we probably helped to fuel him."[87] Polls confirmed that Duke's support surged in the final weeks. Duke hadn't been dented by the attacks against him; in fact, he seemed to only grow stronger, outrunning his polls and collecting a war chest for a possible run for governor in a year. LCARN knew it had an even nastier fight ahead. Buddy Roemer, the incumbent, had repeatedly alienated his coalition by vetoing anti-abortion bills and failing to turn around the state's financial situation.[88] Edwin Edwards had so many problems, LCARN didn't even want to mention his name, which was mud. If Duke got into a runoff with either of them, Louisiana would be in deep shit, the group decided. They seized on a sliver of good news from the 1990 exit polling: more than three-quarters of respondents thought Duke's Klan days were behind him. Might that sliver of hope provide an opening for Powell, Hill, Stovall, and Rickey and *their* campaign?

They initially focused on the tens of thousands of dollars in debts their nonprofit had accumulated and brainstormed how the hell they would eliminate it, and the question of whether to endorse someone in 1991 and, if so, who. Did they refocus their efforts on branding Duke a Nazi or compromise with the organization's backers and hit him on taxes and his fib about serving in the military? Deliberations ramped up in the spring of 1991 after David Duke appeared on national television, holding a press conference in primetime.

"I'm hitting the ground running," he said. "We've got a great chance to win" the governor's race.[89] Ignoring polls that ranked him a major underdog in the governor's race, he added resolutely, "I'll be there to the end." Fellow underdog Kathleen Blanco said she didn't think Duke and the other tiresome men had a shot. "I think I have a dimension of stability. I think Louisiana is ready for some peace and some harmony."[90]

To the contrary, said Louisianans, we're ready for *David Duke*.

PART III

THE GRAND OLD PARTISANS

CHAPTER 7

The Murder

The Chinese have a saying that if you wait on the riverbank long enough,
the bodies of your enemies will float by.

EDWIN EDWARDS

"Dave Treen is so slow," said Edwin Edwards, "it takes him an hour and a
half to watch '60 Minutes.'"[1]

The crowd roared. After a four-year absence of a light liveliness in their
politics, Louisiana finally had something to chuckle about. For an entire
gubernatorial term, the middle class had been hearing nothing but worst-
case scenarios and apologies as state government squeezed them into a
vise. Finally, here came the former governor, the slickest of the slippery
politicians, back to remind everyone politics didn't have to be all oil cri-
ses and economic downturns. They remembered the 1970s as the Edwards
years—the oil boom, social progress, some colorful politicians, thank God.
Now, he was back, with $80 satin jumpsuits crafted for each worker on the
1983 campaign just to wear for softball games, only a blip in a $13,000,0000
campaign budget, the most colorful living political figure in the nation.[2]
He would pizzazz the hell out of them for this, the costliest local election
in American history.[3]

Edwin Edwards had not enjoyed his exile either. He left office with a
half-billion-dollar surplus, but the Tongsun Park scandal, the Mafia scandal,
the gambling stories and the muckraking, the infidelity rumors, the grand
juries, and Republican attacks all dogged him. Marion, his brother and campaign finance manager, narrowly escaped an indictment in an investigation
over a state land deal he brokered in his real estate practice. Another brother,
Nolan, a lawyer in New Orleans, lobbied the state on behalf of criminals in

the prison system, hoping to earn them pardons.[4] Those inmates became several of the more than one thousand people who received state pardons from Governor Edwards, but this didn't seem to be enough evidence of corruption for a judge. Edwin would be named in yet another court battle, this time in the Gulf Oil Corp. case, during which an oil lobbyist testified that Edwards, Senator Russell Long, and other Louisiana politicians had accepted under-the-radar campaign donations. Edwards denied the accusation. When asked about his plans for the future as he was departing office, Governor Edwards quipped, "Try not to get indicted."[5] Edwards got the credit when the Superdome opened in the mid-seventies, and he would get blamed when the New Orleans Jazz NBA basketball team left for Salt Lake City at the end of his term. Worse, black 'Dome managers threatened a walkout and boycott of the building their patron had built if the next-door Hyatt Hotel took over management of the entire property. What would his former base think of him in 1983, now that his name was back on the ballot after his first gap in decades?

Many had switched their support to the Republican Party to make history with Dave Treen. Edwards, supposedly the education governor, hadn't been able to pass teacher pay increases; Treen from the anti-government, anti-public school GOP, muscled through a $90,000,000 appropriation to give teachers multi-thousand-dollar bonuses for "professional training" after hours. The populist Edwards watched in annoyance as Treen worked with the legislature to slash taxes on "the little people," the ones who had never voted for a Republican, not even Ronald Reagan. But that half-billion dollar surplus? Treen had squandered it. By 1984, the state would have a deficit of a *quarter billion bucks*. During Treen's term, eighty thousand oil workers moved to Louisiana for the job; by the end of it, one quarter of them would have moved out of state.[6]

Clyde Vidrine's book and its allegations of infidelity, gambling, and cash debts dogged Edwards as he prepared to run again in 1983. The subject of the book read aloud from a particularly salacious passage at a dinner banquet for journalists. Vidrine had detailed a night in Vegas when Edwards had bedded five women in a row. "Elaine knows that's not true," Edwards said, flipping pages, "because I'm only good for four-and-a-half times."[7] He quipped to the *Washington Post*: "I wish it were all true. . . . If they don't stop spreading all these false rumors about me, I'm going to have to spread some true rumors that are worse."[8] And later, on the allegation of womanizing: "It damaged me with some of my girlfriends." When Edwards confirmed he would challenge Treen for a record-tying third term, his wife,

Elaine, said that was all fine and dandy but she would refuse to move back into the governor's mansion with him.[9]

The ex-governor stayed at the incumbent's heels for four years without let-up. He was running, Edwards said, and "only death alone can separate me from this. . . . We are being led by a governor whose only answer to unemployment is to buy a $350,000 jet."[10] He hit Treen for having been a segregationist, a Dixiecrat before joining the GOP, and for hiring all of the Democrats who were eliminated from the runoff (and who had endorsed Treen), accusations Edwards critics called a "smoke screen" for the Democrat's own corruption.[11] Edwards, undeterred, moved on to asking about "his" surplus, or why the state budget had risen dramatically. He materialized at the LSU Tiger NCCA playoffs and was pooh-poohed as a media whore, but Edwards got his face on television during those games and Treen was nowhere in sight. Treen struck back, muscling through a bill to require every candidate to share their tax information and net worth; the press correctly saw this as a way to get even with Edwards, who may have been wealthier than his rural supporters imagined. As the war of words heated up, a crop duster flew over the unveiling of the Luling Bridge, dragging a banner reading "Edwin did it!"[12] When Treen staked his reelection on the passage of CWEL, the acronym for a complicated oil tax bill, Edwards returned to the State House floor to castigate it and warn lawmakers: *if this passes, I'm going to blame you for it in '83.* Perhaps unsurprisingly, fundraising came significantly easier for the challenger. Edwards claimed some of his biggest contributors were ex-Treen men who couldn't get the governor on the horn. "To Treen's credit, many of these people never supported a winner before, and they expected more in the way of service and involvement than he could deliver." He joked, "Governor Treen is my best campaign manager."[13]

Edwards later told a rapt press, "I don't think he has the temperament for the job and I do. I understand the challenges and I'm concerned the gains made during the 70s are being evaporated. It's true I don't need to be governor again, but I like Louisiana and the executive branch."[14] Treen continued to struggle. "Don't feed me that line of bullshit," a woman reporter once said to Treen. "I'm not used to that kind of language from a lady!" said the governor. "I'm not used to that kind of bullshit from a governor," the reporter snapped.[15]

At a speech following a parade in Metairie, at which Edwards doled out flowers and kisses, he said of Treen's neighborhood, "Why, I bet he couldn't get twenty people in my backyard," and chuckled. "Some politicians like to kiss babies. I like to kiss the baby's mommas."[16] And then he was off to another event, one of ninety in sixty parishes in only a few weeks. The blitz was necessary, internal sources said, because Edwards had slipped eight points in polling after Treen started an ad campaign attacking Edwards on crime and the hundreds of pardons he'd signed in office, including several for his lawyer brother Nolan's clients.

As Edwards got going, he increasingly relied on his brothers, especially Marion, who fell ill in the spring of 1982. "He's got liver cancer," Edwin announced privately. "Sure makes all this seem unimportant."[17] Years later, the news still affected Edwin. Marion had been the guiding force of many an Edwards campaign, the secret weapon behind the initial gubernatorial run, putting them over the top with strong fundraising. They both spoke French, wowing Cajuns on the campaign trail. They had the same eyes, about the only thing that seemed to prove their blood relation; as reporter John Maginnis noted, the next closest thing was their loyalty to each other. Through thirteen elections and thirteen wins, Marion had fundraised for slightly older brother Edwin all the way. "Fundraising is the most disagreeable part of politics," Edwin said. "You are torn between two principles: there are people who don't want to fool with politics and there are those who would be offended if you don't let them make a contribution."[18] Edwin's rule—*Don't ask for contributions; let them come to you*—applied only so far as meetings with the candidate went. One-on-one with marks, Marion would get tens of thousands from a single donor, making the contributor feel that the entire campaign rested on one check by sharing the stories of the boys' poverty-stricken childhood. The susceptible listener would be "reaching for his checkbook and his handkerchief at the same time," one observer joked.[19]

The possibility that Edwin would lose Marion, his closest relation, shook him. Luckily, after three months in Houston undergoing chemotherapy, his brother felt revitalized enough to tell the candidate to count on him for the bruising battle ahead.

On August 18, 1983, a quiet Thursday in an otherwise overheated, relentless campaign, Edwin Edwards sat in his New Orleans townhouse and discussed the campaign plan for the rest of the day. The general consensus seemed to be that the Republicans were getting crazier. Everyone chuckled nervously about an incident the night before outside the Alexandria Civic Center; while Edwin was inside speaking, a campaign staffer noticed that most of the cars in the parking lot were affixed with sheets of paper—copyright-infringing photocopies from Vidrine's book. As the staffer instructed volunteers to snatch up all the pages before the rally let out, a car pulled up and someone yelled at the staffer to leave the papers where they were. When a police officer approached to investigate the commotion, the driver sped off. Moments later, he was arrested for possession of a sawed-off shotgun.[20]

Back in Crowley, attorney Nolan Edwards opened up his law office that August morning at about eight o'clock and had met with multiple clients before problematic character Rodney Wingate arrived at roughly eight thirty. Nolan's secretary, according to later reports, waved Wingate into the inner office, where the lawyer got up from his chair to greet his client. Nolan had gotten his client pardoned for a cocaine distribution conviction, found him a "lucrative job servicing offshore drilling rigs," and, when Wingate had to go out on worker's comp due to a back injury, loaned him what he thought should be enough money to get him through litigation against the oil company. Nolan, fifty-two, reached out to shake the hand of Wingate, twenty-nine. Instead, the younger man reached into his pocket and pulled out a revolver.

Two shots pierced the quiet morning air. As the secretary rose, clutching her chest in terror, a third piercing shot caused her to stumble back. Inside Nolan's office, both men lay dead, client and attorney with bullet holes in their faces.[21] After the murder-suicide story broke, clearing everything else from the headlines for days, reports indicated that Nolan may have neglected, deliberately or unintentionally, to file suit against Wingate's employer before the statute of limitations expired; the insinuation was that Nolan Edwards hadn't wanted to represent this unhinged person, for whom he had already done so much, against a powerful company he would need to keep on his good side for future business dealings or legal proceedings.[22] Regardless, the murder-suicide deprived the Edwards family—and the public—of answers.

Edwin, receiving the news, cried out. When staffers raced to his side, he cradled the phone with a shaky hand and gasped, his voice cracking: "My brother's been shot!" As the story emerged, he flew to see Marion in Crowley; the photo of them embracing, stunned into silence, on the tarmac generated so much sympathy that the entire tone of the campaign changed.[23] The Treen people suspended their operations for several days. They didn't need to say anything. Edwin fell into a kind of a stupor, losing his customary vigor. Gone were the wisecracks and clipped, almost robotic manner of speech. He had pardoned Nolan's killer—sure, it may have partly been because Nolan himself represented the man, but the fact hung unmistakably over him forever after. He would never understand it, Edwards told the press, but "it doesn't matter now." Nolan had left behind a wife and four children and it would be difficult to face them. At the funeral, he spoke little and choked back tears

standing in the receiving line, the sight devastating family and even reporters who had been dogging him for years. "Now I know how I got elected governor," he said, his voice cracking, "by Nolan's friends."[24]

There were two gubernatorial debates scheduled for less than a month
away, and the Edwards campaign wondered if they would make either live
broadcast. The candidate was virtually comatose. West Monroe's *Ouachita
Citizen* noted that while Nolan's death may not affect the outcome of the election, with only eight weeks to go, no one knew how it would play out. Edwards,
attending a fundraiser in Ville Platte, sat "expressionless at the front table
listlessly holding a fork. . . . Edwards' blank expression doesn't change. . . . He
stands and 300 Cajuns stand with him, their expressions as intent as his."[25]

Reporters remained hesitant. At his next press conference, expressionless as usual, Edwards listened to questions about President Reagan, polls,
oil and gas, everything except pardons, scandals, and his family. He was
leading Treen by more than a dozen points, "but what about your own polls
showing that only one-third of your supporters believe everything you say?"

"My wife is one of them."

Tentative, nervous laughter. How about the fact that Bob Hope had
endorsed Dave Treen and was carrying on with a two-thousand-attendee
$1,000-a-plate, tournedos-of-beef-and-veal fundraiser for him at the Lake-
front Airport in New Orleans, despite Edwards' grief?[26]

"Bob Hope is a good friend of mine. I might buy a ticket myself and go."[27]

Murmuring turned into snickering. The tide, it seemed, had turned back.
Within days, Edwards would deliver some of the most memorable one-
liners and speeches of his career, and all of them found him invigorated. He
cracked wise about Treen's contemplative, methodical nature, as before, and
even let the veil slip a bit when he said, "If we don't get Treen out of office
soon, there won't be any money left to steal."[28] Did it bother him when Treen
smeared him? "Treen can say bad things about me, but I won't say anything
bad about him. He hasn't done anything!"[29] If you had been governor for
the past four years, would you be having a tough time getting re-elected? "If
our places in the *polls* were reversed, I would not be a candidate," he said.[30]

At a September forum with the two candidates, the moderator noted that
crime had risen in recent years in Louisiana. Treen pounced—not mentioning Nolan and Wingate, but suggesting Edwards had singled out criminals
he and his own lawyer represented for pardons. Edwards said his administration was "the first to deal with the problem" and thus had a longer list
of worthy inmates to pardon. The discussion finally created some heat in
the race; supporters of each candidate were split on whether Treen should

even be allowed to bring up the "scandal" after Nolan's murder. Then, at the first televised debate, the four reporters posing questions struck hard on "political appointees, raising taxes, job creation, providing aid to private schools, setting spending limits on gubernatorial campaigns, reforming special retirement plans for public officials . . . the environment, prison overcrowding and their response to what the voters view as their negative qualities."[31] Nowhere did they touch on minorities, civil rights, the economy in general, or any of their other fallback planks.

In his opening salvo, the incumbent claimed to have "become alarmed at some of the misrepresentations" of his campaign and of Edwards' storied tenure. He held up a brochure apparently produced by his opponent's campaign, claiming that Edwards had created a whopping ten thousand miles of highway—"absolutely preposterous."[32] When a light flashed in the Louisiana Public Broadcasting studios, he asked whether he had run over his allotment. "Spend some of your time looking for those extra miles," Edwards cracked, pivoting to a more comfortable liberal position—hitting the Republican Party for wrecking public education.

Edwards *did* have a major advantage. He could criticize Treen day after day, tarring him with the labels of incompetence, stiffness, lameness, tax favoritism, bankruptcy, elitism, everything a populist Democrat could hit a right-wing politician with. One questioner did the work for Edwards, claiming that Treen called environmentalists a bunch of "hippies" until it became clear that big business took that as their cue to run roughshod around the state, dumping hazardous waste and ruining local drinking water. The most memorable moment of the otherwise stale debate came during an exchange about honesty.

The panel asked what Treen thought about "Undecided/No Preference" running a close third, voters who didn't believe anything Edwards said, and "people [who] think you are inept." Treen said, "I'd rather be inept than dishonest. Of course, in my defense, the accomplishments of my administration are lengthy. . . . I don't shoot from the hip and . . . I've proven them wrong before and I'll prove them wrong again."

"I'd rather be inept than dishonest, also," said Edwards, barely stifling a smirk, "but since I am neither, I have a hard time commenting on the question."

Laughter.

Edwards finally smiled. He had 'em now. He pontificated on how the *Morning Advocate*, a minor irritant, accused him of "all kinds of skullduggery . . . it doesn't stick but it leaves a mark," he said. "I'll try to be as open as possible . . . in the next four years. I may end up being called inept, but I *am* going to be called honest."[33]

Neither Marion nor Nolan had been mentioned. At the live Jaycees debate in Baton Rouge one week later, the economic effects of 240,000 people out of work finally came to the forefront.[34] The two candidates fired at will over the jobs figures, each blaming the other for not "diversifying the economy" as the oil crisis and Iranian revolution kicked off. With Edwards on the ropes, Treen finally got a joke in; unfortunately, it was mainly at his own expense. "Of course, the crime rate cannot be up as a result of anybody that I've pardoned," he said, "but could very well be the result of someone you've pardoned." He turned serious then, noting that his predecessor had released hundreds of "murderers, rapists, and armed robbers" as well as drug dealers, who "might be considered non-violent but they do a terrible violence to this state."

Then Treen made a final, fatal mistake, setting Edwards up for the spike. "Why do you speak out of both sides of your mouth?"

Edwards drolly replied, "So that people like you with nothing between their ears can understand."[35]

These debates, fought to stalemates, showed that neither man could expect an easy term. The smart play might have been for Edwards to remain on the sidelines for another four years, by which time the Democratic electorate would be sick of Treen and perhaps Republicans entirely. If Edwards would have waited until 1987 to make his triumphant return, he might have coasted to victory, although that would have put him in a reelection matchup with David Duke in 1991 and that might have been too close to call.

In his closing remarks at the Jaycees debate, Treen said he believed the election hinged on whether Louisianans wanted good government at all. Edwards, frankly, thought the voters didn't give a damn. "Let's get back to the good times," he said in his final statement. "Are you ready for the return of your Cajun king?!"[36] Indeed, the people were ready. "The only way I can lose this election is if I'm caught in bed with either a dead girl or a live boy," he boasted.[37]

Invincible, or so he felt, he let loose, haranguing a senate candidate for asking him to campaign for him instead of just riding the proverbial coattails. Edwards joked that he wanted to tell Treen that he spent his earnings from one pardon case on hookers and blow. "Is that what you've been snorting?" someone asked.

"Yeah, whenever I do I get younger and more virile and I attract more Girl Scouts."[38]

He spoke 109 times in seven days, an awe-inspiring effort that reached hundreds of thousands of voters. In 1991, regarding the '83 campaign and John Maginnis's chronicle of it in *The Last Hayride*, Edwards called it "unfair in that it depicts Treen as a total dummy and me as a total crook, which is just partly true." Which part?, the *Los Angeles Times* inquired. "Well, he's dumber than I'm a crook."[39] In later years, he would be more charitable about his opponents, especially with Treen, whom he got close to near the end of the Republican's life. "I had a good record," he said, explaining why, in his view, he won, "and Treen, while a good man, had never connected with average people."[40]

It didn't matter who he offended or which niche groups were up in arms against him. Treen had passed a bill mandating the teaching of creationism in public schools—later ruled unconstitutional; the freewheelin' Edwin Edwards shot from the hip in an interview that would haunt him for a decade.

After confirming his Christianity, Edwards answered questions about the life of Jesus Christ.

"Do you believe Jesus died on the cross, was buried and resurrected?"

"No. I think Jesus died, but I don't believe he came back to life because that's too much against natural law. I'm not going around preaching this, but he may have swooned, passed out or almost died, and when he was taken down, with superhuman strength, after a period of time he may have revived himself and come back to life."[41]

Both the Louisiana Christian Coalition and Christians For Truth would run ads nailing him on this in 1991. Edwards further enraged Christian groups with his refusal to respond to their questionnaire on instituting an abortion ban, implementing school vouchers, and expanding sex education, and he would have a tough time winning over fundamentalists in future battles.

For now, though, most remained unaware of his leanings, including the Edwards campaign. On October 22, they sealed off the fifteenth floor of the Monteleone and installed their candidate in suite 1545, repeating tradition to keep away the jinx. A torrential downpour in rural areas freaked Marion out; Democrats, as Treen's people knew, didn't turn out in inclement weather, historically. The moment the polls closed, however, with no one left to seduce, Edwin took his brother's widow by the hand and lead her to the ballroom floor, making sure reporters jotted down every word: "No one had a better brother than I had in Nolan and no one had a better wife than he had in Eleanor."[42] His powerless years in the wilderness were at an end— he needed only to study the black vote pouring in from nearby precincts; with close to one hundred percent reporting, the Edwards '83 campaign netted 97 percent of the city, more than nine out of every ten black votes, and 62 percent of the total electorate. Treen cleaned up in neighboring Jefferson Parish and his hometown of Metairie, but that's about the extent of his good news. For the first time since Earl Long's heyday, Louisiana had a three-term governor. Edwards never doubted it for a second.

"They tried to indict me," he shouted over the din in the hotel ballroom. "They called me names, they spread rumors about me that were untrue and malicious, but I am glad to have had the jury of the greatest people in the world."[43]

The shrieks and howls of joy that followed from the ballroom masked a few nervous titters. As the crowd whooped and danced into the night, history churned against Edwin Edwards. In Beirut, Islamic terrorists struck the US Marine barracks, killing 310 service members with truck bombs. The campaign was more than four million dollars in debt, with no sensible, efficient, and legal way to repay it for at least another four years. The economy, bad enough already when he originally left office, would get even worse and no penny gas tax increase would save Louisiana now. Worse still, Edwin Edwards would never again face an opponent so ripe for the picking, so obviously the antithesis of the relentlessly charming, good-looking, and politically cunning Cajun Prince. He was about to face his most well-financed, well-liked, and merciless foe. In fact, there were two of them.

CHAPTER 8

The Dragon

Once Edwin Edwards was inaugurated for the third time, prosecutors began building a multi-pronged attack against him. Less than a year later, in February 1985, a grand jury convened by United States attorney John Volz leveled fifty charges against Edwards alone, as well as criminal indictments against Marion, nephew Charles David Isbell, and five business partners.[1] "I never speak ill of dead people or live judges," Edwards reflected, although following two trials in the mid-1980s, he had reason to break either promise.[2] Federal District judge Marcel Livaudais, however, slapped a gag order on the participants, making it difficult for Edwards to defend himself in the press, although God knows he tried.[3]

Before the trial got underway, Edwards admitted to receiving $2,000,000 in exchange for helping a group of consultants land a prized hospital construction contract with the state, but he claimed the payments were for a "legitimate business" deal while a "private citizen." In a poll, only 31 percent of Louisianans believed him, while 39 percent said they would vote for a guilty verdict. Edwards' strategy seemed to be to attack the very idea of a court case, joking as proceedings dragged on that it had become not the Trial of the Century but rather "the 'Century of the Trial.'"[4] In another memorable moment, the governor arrived at the hearings from the Monteleone by mule-drawn carriage. (He claimed to have finally hit upon "some mode of transportation that was indicative of the pace of the trial."[5]) One night, the defendants and their army of lawyers were invited to temporarily take over the bar Molly's at the Market in the Quarter. As dozens gawked from the street or nearby barstools, Edwin couldn't help but once again push the envelope. With co-defendant and nephew Charles David at the keys and Edwin's lead lawyer, James Neal, pouring shots, Edwards, apparently having assumed he could defy the judge's order with a little comedy routine, unleashed a limerick: "When I'm in a happy mood, I eat and sing and drink. When I'm in a sober mood, I worry, work and think." The assembled raised their drinks in unison. Edwards toasted with his water glass. "When my moods are over," he concluded, "and my time has come to pass, I hope they bury me upside down, so Volz can kiss my ass."[6] Hurrah.

Loosened up now, the trio ran through a litany of thematically apropos, boozed-soaked, comical covers, a la a Dean Martin dinner show at the Sands, for the congregation and pesky press people. While one overweight defendant laughed, they ran through the bombastic "My Way," dedicated "Hail to the Chief" to the judge and "Please Release Me" to themselves, and serenaded Edwin with, of course, the Kenny Rogers anthem "The Gambler." Asked why they needed to blow off steam after another sleepy day in an unconcerning trial, one defendant told the Associated Press, "Everybody tries to act like they're in a good mood, but nobody wants to be here."

Indeed, beneath a boisterous public face, the defendants were suitably nervous. While the prosecution sternly presented an unconvincing case like Dave Treen in a gubernatorial debate, and Edwards joshed with spectators and reporters, the defense team privately fretted about the jurors, several of whom seemed unamused by their antics. US attorney John Volz rarely cracked a smile—except at his own earlier bartending gig at Molly's, during which he was referred to as "Defense Exhibit A," due to his apparent mishandling of the case.

Volz grilled the governor on the stand, "You lost two million dollars in Nevada between 1981 and 1984, did you not?"

"It was nothing near that," Edwards shot back quickly. "If I wasn't under oath, I'd tell you what I won."

When the laughter died out and the judge had sufficiently warned the gallery about its outbursts, Volz demanded to know about the million bucks Edwards netted from a single hospital deal. How'd that happen and what'd you do with the money?, he asked.[7]

"You issued subpoenas by the backload, we hauled in documents by the truckload and you have not produced a single witness or a solitary piece of evidence to contradict what I've said."

When Volz countered by pointing out that Edwards hadn't included the deals on his financial disclosure paperwork on file with the state, he shrugged. "I didn't forget," said the governor. "That implies a conscious attempt to remember."[8]

How, spectators wondered, did Volz keep going after such drubbings? Edwards may have hit upon his motivation—Volz once phoned the governor to ask for his help landing a federal judge's post. As the *New Republic* noted, "the man who got the appointment, secure for life and smugly observing" the case? Judge Livaudais himself. The prosecutor continued to let the case slip through his fingers. An assistant GM at a Lake Tahoe casino testified that Edwards had racked up roughly half a million bucks in winnings during his years in exile, neutralizing the prosecution's insinuation that the governor had a debt-driven "motive" for taking payoffs. Then Volz, in a stunning display of anger, accused a black woman of mismanaging the State Department of Health and Human Resources and allowing this "crime" to occur. The move, according to journalists, caused black and/or female jurors to grimace.[9]

Shortly before the jury took up the gauntlet, Livaudais agreed to dismiss charges against three defendants. If there hadn't been one holdout, possibly prejudiced against Edwards, and two others who waffled on a handful of the fifty charges, the jury would've acquitted the remaining defendants. Instead, after thirteen weeks of testimony from fifty-three witnesses and six days of deliberation, the judge declared a mistrial.

"How sweet it is," Edwards shouted for the press's benefit. "I have just won the 16th and most important election of my life and by the greatest majority ever."[10]

It wouldn't stick, and boasting about beating Volz only stirred the beast. Given until the end of February to make a decision, Volz waited until almost the literal last minute before announcing a retrial. This time, only three others would accompany Marion and Edwin, with Michael Fawer representing the governor in "Racketeering Redux." In her wryly hilarious fish-out-of-water tale about her year living in Louisiana to cover the Edwards trials, *Ritz of the Bayou*, reporter Nancy Lemann described Volz's problem thusly: "The Prosecutor was not winning when he moralized about the Governor, who is known for gambling, womanizing, and risqué bon mots, for people hold few things as dear as these." Worse, Volz simply didn't have the temperament. Lemann quoted an observer saying: "You can read the future in a man's face, and John Volz is going to lose this case."[11]

Jurors didn't want to sit through it either. In both trials, they fumbled through a litany of excuses. (One potential juror said during the first voir dire, "I might know him too." Replied the judge, "We all do."[12]) But once they were seated, everyone seemed to have a blast—including, in rare instances, Volz.

Lemann described the courtroom in recess as a collegiate atmosphere, more of a fraternity reunion than a truce in a slugfest. Marion, ever the fundraiser, glad-handed the spectators, meeting everyone and cracking jokes. Stuffed into an elevator with a group of elderly, tittering woman, Edwin seized on the opportunity to do a little politicking for '87. "I know you ladies probably aren't old enough to vote," he quipped, "but if you are, remember me." ("You should've seen him forty years ago," one woman swooned.)[13] Unfortunately, between the two trials and Nolan's murder, Edwards didn't level as many wisecracks or turn on the charm as often. When a reported asked, "What will you do if you are convicted, governor?," Edwards responded, "I'll become a newscaster." He wasn't smirking when he said it.[14]

This time, though, the verdict was never in doubt. Volz lost his main witness, a turncoat named John Landry, due to Landry's volatility. Without an eyewitness to bribery and conspiracy, Edwards might have been able to get the charges tossed entirely. But as with the first trial, he gambled a long prison term against being able to ride an absolute legal vindication to reelection and refused to agree to have the charges dismissed. He had the right instinct. On May 11, 1986, this time after two days of deliberations, the jury gave him that vindication, to cheers and cries of relief from defendants and spectators alike.[15] "Corruption is legal in Louisiana," grumbled one northern reporter.

Another reported inquired: "What do you say to people who think: he's guilty as hell, they just weren't smart enough to catch him?"

"I'd say they were half right."[16]

When someone mentioned that several jurors had been nabbed stealing hotel towels while sequestered, Edwards quipped, "I have been judged by a jury of my peers."[17]

Then, instead of jetting off to Vegas to celebrate, in recognition of the view that the legislature had stalled without him, that hotels had shuttered, that libraries had shut down for lack of funds, he announced he was going back to the office.

"We're going home," Elaine, holding his hand, corrected him.[18]

Even before the tiresome retrial, the public had burnt out on their governor, up for reelection the following year. Silas Lee, a Xavier University pollster, told the *Times-Picayune* he thought Edwards a longshot in 1987. "The trial and its revelations have damaged Edwin. Even more difficult is Louisiana's economy," he said. "I think Edwin's probably finished."[19]

There were numerous problems over those four years, starting with one of his first actions after the 1983 landslide. Marion, saddled with the four-million-dollar problem of the campaign's debts, hatched a plan to sell tickets on a jet to France, where the governor would hold court with his richest donors and maybe shoot a little craps. The trip, dubbed "The Beverly Hillbillies Go to Paris," was unprecedented.[20] Marion and Edwin had decided their crazy idea of having five hundred donors pony up $10,000 apiece to jet to Europe with the administration (plus Bennett Johnston and friendly members of the media) was dead on arrival and almost didn't even announce it, lest they get stuck with a plane half-full, racking up further debts. But after Clyde Vidrine appeared on *60 Minutes* to lambaste Edwin for corruption and sleaziness, national corporations and lobbyists took note: *the Sun King is back and open for suggestions.* The tickets sold out in days; by the January departure date, including comps for staff, elected officials, and journalists, 617 people joined Marion and the "Hillbillies" on a pair of gleaming 747s.[21]

Edwards, still amped from his electoral victory, charmed the pants off Parisians. One, a nun born in Louisiana, kissed him on the cheek ("Don't let me get in the habit," he deadpanned.) He toasted the delegation, including Treen's ex-campaign manager, at an $85,000 dinner at Versailles. "People say I've had brushes with the law," he said, practically boasting. "That's not true. I've had brushes with overzealous prosecutors."[22] But the Paris trip didn't distract the public from the trial, and while it provided numerous short-term benefits to the Edwards image, the spectacle ultimately hurt him. He took office on the coattails (or perhaps contrails) of it, and the public already seemed to regret bringing back the hayride. He inherited Treen's $250,000,000 deficit and had to raise taxes during the lame duck session, with Treen's help, but pissed off big business by slapping on some corporate taxes. The 1984 World's Fair, which cost the state tens of millions and was supposed to have drawn mobs of international tourists in the dead of Louisiana summer, landed with a shrug from Earth's population. After the legislature slashed $43,000,000 from the education budget, teachers, not impressed with the Education Governor, went on strike. All five of the constitutional amendments he backed were defeated by the end of 1984.[23] In a rare public rage, he responded to reports of LSU grads leaving the state for better job options elsewhere by saying not to let the door whack them on the ass.[24] The legislature even rejected his plan to shore up state coffers with a New Orleans casino—the gambler said "hit me" and the dealers told him he had no more credit. His campaign coffers were empty. He missed Elaine, who complained bitterly to the press about being First Lady.[25] He missed Nolan.

When he announced early on in his third administration that he would run for a record-breaking fourth term, the press seemed about as enthused as the public. By mid-1986, he had sunk to a 23 percent approval rating. "I don't think there is any way he can rehabilitate himself politically," predicted state rep. Skip Hand. "No matter what he does, he will not bounce back to his former popularity."[26]

Clyde Vidrine didn't help matters. Edwards' former running buddy and bodyguard had updated his book *Just Takin' Orders* with a new title, padding a 1985 edition with trial transcripts, few additional reminiscences, and an introduction in which he referred to himself in the third-person as a "humble busy honest . . . Cajun farmer."[27] The following year, he escorted a client to court for her divorce proceedings; after the husband didn't show up, forty-eight-year-old Clyde dropped the woman off back at her car and turned back toward his. Shots rang out and Vidrine dropped onto the sidewalk, already dead. The shooter was identified as the woman's soon-to-be-ex-husband, who claimed he had fought with Clyde for the shotgun, but the man's teenage son, standing nearby and who wrestled the weapon away, confirmed that the shooter had been at least fifteen feet away. Vidrine was subsequently subject to post-murder rumors that he had been sleeping with his client, which had enraged his killer.[28]

Luckily for Edwards, the people did not think long and hard about Vidrine or his book, not even in the wake of his headline-grabbing slaying. Voters had turned out for Edwards in record numbers in 1983 and supported his plan to institute a state lottery, as dozens of other states had done. He could run on that. Meanwhile, there were far too many candidates in the offing and not only would Louisianans have a difficult time parsing them, it seemed unlikely one could break out of the pack and rack up a large enough vote to outrun the entrenched Cajun Prince. One presumptive also-ran, congressman Charles "Buddy" Roemer, III, shared the name of his father, Charles II, still behind bars for his corruption conviction related to the first Edwards administration. His jailer? US attorney John Volz.

At one of his first public appearances as a gubernatorial candidate, Buddy Roemer spoke of how 1987 would be a "change" election; the response at the Louisiana Association of Business Industry luncheon included guests picking at the tablecloth or nodding off.[29] Buddy, one of five children born to Charles E. Roemer II in Shreveport, didn't seem like a galvanizing figure at the outset, nor did he have the backstory of a rags-to-riches governor in the post-Long era. Born in the middle of the Second World War, Roemer spent a decade of his childhood at Scopena, the family's Bossier City cotton plantation. In his memoir, Buddy said privileged plantation life along US 71 instilled in him "the value of individuals rather than on the color of someone's skin, and I learned the keys of success that I carried into the world far from there, keys like hard work, team effort, honesty in reporting what you saw. The truth is that the highest hurdle I had to jump in life and the thing that prepared me the most for politics, Louisiana-style, were the demanding standards set by my father years ago —at Scopena."[30]

Back then, Roemer recalled, the biggest "issue was civil rights, how black people were treated on the farm—our farm—and in life. How, in the South, blacks had a poor deal. Eat in separate restaurants, drink in different water fountains. . . . That became the issue [for] our family. Edwards was good—better than all the opponents—on these issues."[31] Charles Roemer saw a chance to hop on the Edwards train and make true systemic changes for African Americans.

His father, however, proved more of a hindrance than a boost when it came to running for office. As campaign manager for the 1971 Edwin Edwards campaign and later as Edwards' head of administration, Charles had the power to sway insider opinions. If Charles wanted to reward the black leaders who had shown up to Scopena to offer their support for the Edwards campaign, the legislature and the cabinet would scramble to find ways to help. If he wanted to eliminate departments, they were gone. And if he thought the Edwards campaign could use a computer system produced by Innovative Data Systems, which Charles happened to own, Charles Roemer would make sure every piece of data, including registered voter contact information, was run through that software, and every call or telegram for a get-out-the-vote effort came as a result of a calculation made by that "Innovative" solution.[32] In 1981, an FBI sting operation dubbed "Brilab" ensnared Charles and mobster Carlos Marcello. The nation may have ignored the story of Charlie and Carlos, for on the day the trial began, President Ronald Reagan was seriously wounded by a crazed gunman. Louisianans, though, could follow two stories at once. They read in hometown newspapers about "the bribery trial of a reputed Mafia leader, Carlos Marcello, and four other men," including Charlie, with US District Court as the arena. The AP wrote, "In the sting, undercover FBI agents posed as crooked insurance executives . . . taking part in a scheme to win a multimillion-dollar state group insurance contract through bribery."[33] Roemer and Marcello were convicted and Roemer would do fifteen months in prison before the Circuit Court of Appeals threw out his conviction on a technicality.[34]

"What did it cost me?" Charlie Roemer asked rhetorically. "Does that count the heart attack and the health problems that were the result of that? Does it count what my children and seventeen grandchildren went through, and my wife? Four million dollars went in expense for the trial and preparation and I lost ten years of my life. What do you think it cost me?"[35]

His son, Charles III, wiped away tears upon hearing the news. Not only did he have his father back but Buddy could reclaim his mantle of being the uncorrupt good government politician. It was his destiny to be incorruptible to the point it clashed with his will to succeed. After graduating from Bossier City High as its sixteen-year-old 1959 valedictorian, Buddy read everything he could get his hands on, especially Robert Frost and works of history and philosophy, blazed through Harvard, and returned to Scopena, savoring a luxurious "gap year" until his father took the helm of the first Edwin Edwards gubernatorial campaign. Thanks to Dad, Buddy received a prime posting in the 1971 slugfest: campaign manager for northern Louisiana. "We developed something else," Buddy reflected. "A telegram that could be sent to the voter. A different telegram, given the voter's interest. We did that by the hundreds of thousands on election day. I'm not saying it won for Edwards, but he won by 4,000 votes out of two million."[36] Just months after Edwards took office, newly minted Commissioner of Administration Charles Roemer arranged for a million-dollar computer systems contract for a Texas business, Software, Inc. The owner of that company soon hired Buddy Roemer at his other startup, paying him $80,000 to consult on data processing. Buddy told a grand jury that he hadn't known about the connection or the deal between pops and Software, Inc. Another company, Honeywell, had meanwhile sold the state $16,000,000 worth of computer gear, and the Roemer family data company collected an even million on that deal. The grand jury declined to proceed with charges against Buddy, Charles, or any of the companies under investigation.[37]

His father's powerful position and Buddy's track record as a campaign staffer soon landed him coveted consultancy gigs, albeit with underdog candidates running against entrenched incumbents. However, in the 1970s, challengers won three consecutive upset victories under his tutelage, including a congressional race. As the closest aide to Superintendent of Education Kelly Nix, whom he had guided to victory, Roemer parked his desk at Nix's door and held out his hand for checks, ostensibly to help Nix retire campaign debt but really building Nix's reelection war chest.[38] Roemer started to think, *Well, if I can make anyone king, why not me?*

In his initial 1978 congressional run, Buddy made it part of his platform to attack retiring rep. Joe Waggonner's proposal to dam Bossier's Red River and make it navigable for commercial traffic. Waggonner, a local favorite and conservative Democrat later to join the Reagan Administration, spread the word: anyone but Roemer. Buddy lost. As with every fight of his career, he seemed to learn nothing from these crushing defeats and continued to stick to his platform. As for what he termed "those peripheral issues, Harvard and my father," admittedly they were hindrances with folks who were unfamiliar with him, "but as I get better known they are less of an issue."[39] Two years later, the same candidates staged a rematch and, after receiving the third-place candidate's endorsement for the runoff, Buddy beat Waggonner's successor handily. After his commanding victory, insiders told one another, "Keep your eye on this guy; Buddy's going places."[40]

He established himself as a conservative Democrat, a hometown-crowd-pleasing independent, a "maverick"—"often wrong but never in doubt," as liberal Massachusetts congressman and House Speaker Tip O'Neill famously said.[41] Indeed, when he vacated his congressional seat, it would be snapped up by his closest Republican friend and legislative director, Jim McCrery. Quin Hillyer said after Roemer's death, "Buddy tried his darndest in public life but didn't always succeed. He was legitimately a reformer and legitimately a good man."[42]

Roemer wouldn't have seen it that way, in retrospect. He spent his life seeking "grace," which he defined as "when I get something I do not deserve." His son, Chas, once went fishing with Buddy for blue marlin in Hawaii; although both men were warned they might not catch anything, even after twelve hours on the water, or even after months of trips, Buddy had a blue marlin on the line almost immediately and subsequently battled it for three hours. The crew kept yelling encouragement, only they thought his name was "Bucky." When Buddy returned to shore with a record-breaking four-hundred-and-fifty pounder, his picture went up on the marina wall under the name "Bucky Roemer." He never corrected it.[43]

It may have been his stubbornness and a dogged determination to achieve true reform without compromise that both elevated and doomed him. Despite several right-wing stances, he never forgot that, like Beth Rickey, he came first and foremost from a civil rights-focused white family, and that informed everything he did in office. "I'm more conservative than they are probably, but in love with that concept [of civil rights]. I still think that blacks have a tough time in America. There's some things we can do, there's some things they can do. But together, we can come out of it."[44]

Together, meaning, with everyone except Edwin Edwards. As a congress-man, Buddy Roemer had moved "further and further away from Edwards," who developed a toxicity even before Charlie went to jail in the stead of—in Buddy's mind—the true culprit. With a lifelong motto of *it doesn't matter what you're fighting for, just so long as you always fight the* good *fight*, Roemer seemed the antithesis of Edwards, who would never have sacrificed certain victory for a cause, and thus each became the other's perfect foil.[45]

Raymond Strother came to see Roemer in his DC legislative office after quitting the Billy Tauzin campaign. "Buddy, I think this is your opportunity to enter the governor's race," he told the congressman. Roemer told him he had already qualified, but, out of curiosity, the congressman wanted to know, why did Strother think Buddy could win? "You have enough political courage to do it—a revolution," said Strother. "Refuse their endorsements, do the opposite of how everything's been done in Louisiana." Roemer, who had already completed his hiring, thought about it for an hour, then called up Strother and said, "I fired my consultant. You want the job?"[46]

Once aboard, Strother recommended including Mark McKinnon, a young campaign strategist for governor Mark White in Texas. White had just been defeated for reelection by a Republican and McKinnon needed a paycheck, fast. Strother told his protege, "If you wanna learn anything about politics, you should go to Louisiana and get your PhD." In the beginning, McKinnon said, no one offered Roemer press, support, or donations. "He was a real longshot, which is partly why I got the job," said McKinnon, who moved to Baton Rouge and found that Strother couldn't have been more accurate: the liberating 1987 gubernatorial primary turned into a four-year degree program rolled up into eight months.[47]

"Roemer was a really gifted campaigner," McKinnon recalled. "If he could get anybody one on one, he could convince them. He could talk the bark off a tree. We went to every newspaper publisher in the state and asked for their endorsements. 'You can't win South Louisiana,' they said. But then we got the *Times-Picayune* endorsement. Just the fact they endorsed was big, but to put it on front page? . . . That got everyone's attention."[48]

"A Revolution for Louisiana," Roemer's TV commercial, became the defin-ing political ad of the era.[49] Strother had come up with the concept while suffering from writer's block and peering out his DC window. As a repeat burglar smashed up car windows on his block, Strother realized the police would do nothing. The ad he sat down and wrote moments later called on Roemer to boast of angering both polluters—by telling them to "clean up or get out"—and bureaucrats in the Department of Education for suggesting their jobs be eliminated to clear budgetary room for teacher pay raises.[50] Roemer himself came up with the definitive line that closed the thirty-second spot: "I love Louisiana, but I hate Louisiana politics."[51] (On the campaign trail, he would laugh and shake his head. "I'll be glad when this is over," he told one fan.[52])

"This election is about three things," a grinning Roemer told an interviewer, "jobs, jobs, and jobs."[53] Actually, the *Times-Picayune* corrected him, "the number one issue was Edwards." That didn't mean everyone with an opinion felt negatively about the Silver Fox. The state's economy had partly rebounded, thanks to doubled oil prices, and multiple no-name candidates were dragging each other down into the single digits. Edwards, with a hardcore base, first thought he might coast to a comfortable win. Roemer, in turn, foresaw that his best path to victory would be eliminating Edwards from the runoff. In his early speeches, Buddy suggested Louisiana needed a governor that "puts our pocketbook ahead of his," a vague, indirect attack but an attack all the same.

In September, a poll showed Roemer in last with nine percent.[54] Three weeks later, he had only crept up a few points and was in fourth, behind even Republican congressman Bob Livingston, as the five candidates met for a live, televised debate September 25 in Baton Rouge.

Livingston fired the first shot, wryly suggesting that Edwards may have been too "occupied" in 1985 to tackle problems like staggering unemployment, illiteracy, and cancer rates, and "not getting indicted *this* week."[55] The audience gave him a booming ovation. Moderator Rob Hinton practically had to search for a gavel to bang.

"The governor's office is not for sale," Roemer said, a statement met with riveted silence. Who was this guy? A Democrat attacking Edwards?

Edwards stuck to his defensive position, comparing himself favorably to a bullfighter, only creeping from his crouch to hit his talking points: removing sales tax exemptions and instituting a lottery. Generally, though, he remained red-faced and on the defensive. Receiving both the right to give the first opening statement as well as having received the first question, Buddy Roemer had the spotlight from the get-go. He got in memorable, Edwards-style quips like, "It was written in the Monroe paper . . . 'The only guy in America duller than Dave Treen was Bob Livingston,'" and as to "whether Bob Livingston is a better leader than Dave Treen. . . ? I don't know, but it's a *great question.*"

"This is not the time for on-the-job training for governors. My bicycle does not have training wheels," said the Silver Fox.

"We need to do things other than take jaunts to Texas ranches and Las Vegas," countered Livingston, shouting over thunderous applause. "Governor Edwards, I think you need to change your act—and I think we need to change governors!"

Edwards struck back, pointing out that he had beat back conservatives in both parties who wanted to close down hospitals and facilities for the elderly and disabled. He was interrupted by interviewer John Maginnis, who reminded him the question hadn't been answered. "A shortcoming?" Maginnis prompted him.

"I didn't beat them bad enough," Edwards replied.

"Whoever's the next governor," Roemer said, showing his toothy grin, "and he's sitting here—I hope it's me—is going to have to make tough decisions."[56]

After all the joshing and horn-tooting, the pivotal moment of the 1987 campaign and of Edwin Edwards' career came out of nowhere, and it was not even during the debate. Had the public missed it, Edwards would have won and thus been term-limited in 1991 and unable to face David Duke. Addressing the Baton Rouge Press Club forum just eleven days before the election, Roemer leveled the line he had been working on for two weeks. At the end of the discussion, the moderator went down the row of four candidates, asking each whether, should they be eliminated, they would endorse Edwards. Three of the governor's opponents hedged, but ultimately suggested they would. Having waited mutely, biting his lip, knowing everything rode on this, the one thing he might ever say that people would pay attention to, Buddy Roemer got to have the last word.

Would you endorse and support Governor Edwin Edwards, were he to win the election outright? the moderator wanted to know.

"There are some things I could not and would not do," he said firmly. "We've got to slay the dragon. I would endorse anyone but Edwards."[57]

In the closing days, he would reiterate this message again—"When I get Edwin Edwards' face up," he would say to voters and a swarm of cameras, "I will slay the dragon." He, Strother, McKinnon, and a growing flood of volunteers then passed out buttons that read "Slay the Dragon," and the iconic phrase soon returned to them on the memo line of checks mailed to the campaign. Edwards was lying down, face up, and, the press piled on.[58]

Most of the state's major newspapers endorsed Buddy Roemer, a major indicator of a political wind shift. Not only did Roemer move into first place in the final poll, there were signs he had not only earned his surging support from the previously undecided electorate but had also pulled huge chunks of votes from the also-rans. But worst of all for Edwards, black voters were abandoning him. He had done everything he could get away with to earn their continued support, but his trials and inability to completely resurrect the economy dampened enthusiasm for a fourth term.

As the campaign wound down, Roemer's optimistic campaign team selected the 7,500-seat Monroe Civic Center for a final, highly publicized rally. Despite creating thousands of "Slay the Dragon" buttons, expecting a surge of new supporters, the arena was one-third full—a terrible turnout on paper, but as many as Edwards could have claimed to have had at any point since his '83 run.[59] "We felt this amazing sense of drama, the thought that something was going to happen," recalled Roemer aide Len Sanderson.[60] Edwards, sensing that the shift that lead to his nail-biter win over Bennett Johnston in 1972 had now begun to shift back, slunk off to the Monteleone—his old rabbit's foot—and waited in suite 1545 for Marion to trudge through the door with the results. Marion Edwards, however, watched the solemn faces of the volunteers coming through the hotel's revolving doors, heading straight to the Carousel Bar for a Sazerac. The governor's brother knew the race would end in a runoff, and knew, too, that Edwin would want nothing to do with it.

The governor's adult children, including Stephen, David, and Victoria, were all there, all livid with the voters for not appreciating how Edwin pulled Louisiana out of a hole. A representative from S.O.U.L., the African American get-out-the-vote organization that had put him over Johnston in 1972, showed up as a symbol of support for a presumptive runoff battle. All tried, one on one and collectively, to kneel down, lock eyes with the candidate, and make a case for him to stick it out. Buddy Roemer had closed the gap in a matter of days; the voters, media, and other candidates hadn't even begun to investigate and weigh in on him. Perhaps they would find out something, perhaps about Budgie Roemer. Why not wait and study the fallout before making a decision on whether to continue in the runoff?

But the voters were decisive. As the returns initially trickled in, the governor fell behind by eight points and never recovered. Technically, he made the runoff, but Edwards trailed Roemer by an insurmountable margin. Once the anti-Edwards also-rans presumably endorsed the frontrunner, Congressman Roemer would collect their voters too. The incumbent couldn't see an avenue to continue, no matter how much it crushed him. Another man would be governor-elect and get to take the credit for the cleanup efforts underway.

Entering the Monteleone ballroom with Elaine and his mother behind him at one a.m. to "On The Road Again" and a booming ovation, Edwards, eyes downcast at his right, motioned for everyone to be silent. This wouldn't be easy for him, but it had to be done. He began, "I want to express my appreciation for the other candidates. I can't truthfully say they were nice to me. I forgive them . . ." He grinned as nervous titters rang out. "There is no person in this state who is more honorable and honest than I am. . . . I have determined, under the circumstances since I did not run first, it would be inappropriate for me to continue this election."

"No, no!" they howled in unison. "Don't drop out!"

"Please hear me out," he said over their shouting. "I have to do what I think is best for this state."[61]

As Edwards noted in interviews, he had needed Republican Bob Livingston to make the runoff, assuming that most Democrats would stick to their nominee; against a fresh-faced Democrat, however, he couldn't compete.[62] John Volz, in a rare appearance without his poker face, quipped to the press, "I guess the big jury has spoken."[63] Volz and his prosecutions, Edwards wrote in 2021, "made the difference" in 1987.[64]

"A lot of people wondered for a long time what this election was about," said Roemer in an uncharacteristically humorless victory speech. "I can say it in a simple, single word: it was about 'change.'"[65]

In retrospect, said Roemer's former campaign worker Mark McKinnon, "Edwards did a strategically brilliant thing by denying [Roemer] the opportunity to win the runoff. No one had time to invest in Buddy Roemer. Livingston and Tauzin's former supporters . . . didn't vote for Buddy Roemer, so there was no emotional investment. You could say it was strategic or inevitable, but [Edwards] was a guy who had never lost an election. Roemer became a governor-in-exile."[66]

In the elevator back up to the fifteenth floor after Edwards conceded, an Opelousas businessman tried to console the outgoing governor: "I can say I had a great governor for four years."

"My man," said Edwards. "I'll be back."[67]

Virtually no one—not Marion, Stephen, or Elaine—agreed. Edwards' defeat shattered the Sun King's legacy, causing far more damage to his image than the corruption trials or Vidrine's book. Nancy Lemann suggested that Edwards might end up being "the last governor of this kind in Louisiana, that a crash or downfall would come, and that a new style would have to emerge from the ashes."[68] While no one had ever previously upset Edwards or Huey Long, Louisianans were tired of the Kingfish's scandals and didn't turn out for him in the 1991 primary. But by the end of Roemer's tenure, one that started in revolution and ended up in the same disappointment and sense of helplessness that has given rise to so many would-be dictators and autocrats, voters wouldn't be motivated to turn out for either insurgent candidate, opening a path for the former Grand Wizard of the Ku Klux Klan to muscle his way through.

As the Shreveport *Journal's* Lanny Keller famously put it: "The only way Edwards can ever be reelected is to run against Adolf Hitler."[69]

CHAPTER 9

"The Race from Hell"

The Reverend James Stovall had been at Duke's 1990 announcement for the Senate, eyefucking him from the back. Duke ignored him then and ignored him again on March 14, 1991, as Stovall told the press, "The image of David Duke is such that he won't get the votes that he once got before."[1]

Pollster Kenneth Johnston disagreed. "The race is going to make history," he said.[2]

The Louisiana Coalition Against Racism and Nazism worried from the get-go about Duke's chances in 1991, whereas the media, political insiders, and anyone with an unsolicited opinion seemed to think Duke had already peaked. (That, Lance Hill and Larry Powell pointed out, was what they had said in the 1989 primary. And the 1990 primary.) Hill was annoyed that the sliver of Louisianans who knew about LCARN saw it as a bunch of hippie-dippy types who thought they could change the world. "The real dreamers," he wrote in a letter to the membership, "are those who believe that the hate movement will disappear if Duke drops a few points in the polls." He pointed out that defeating Duke would be all well and good but if he lost over having had plastic surgery, "we may have struck a blow for vanity but not to racism and anti-Semitism."[3] Hill said that Duke's vote the previous year would have been significantly lower if black voters had turned out in the same numbers as white ones. In such a scenario, however, it would actually be preferable for anti-Duke forces if Duke were to make the runoff so as to perhaps rally the electorate behind another candidate and crush the Republican once and for all. However, considering that was a dangerous gamble, it's no wonder LCARN couldn't agree to risk conserving funds for a not-guaranteed runoff. Regardless, as reporter John Maginnis pointed out in his campaign diary *Cross to Bear*, because no one paid attention to the output of the coalition, they were forced to choose either to expend budget and energy in the primary or stay quiet and regret it.

"The old-liners wanted to take a stand against what [Duke] stood for and the new ones wanted to find him in bed with a dead goat," Beth Rickey told Maginnis. Reverend Stovall added, "We made up our minds early to not try to defeat Duke" on his philandering or any other character flaw.[4] That eliminated the softcore porn book Duke had ghostwritten, *Finderskeepers*.[5] But Rickey pointed out that they had already spent ages gathering opposition research on the man without finding anything that put him away for good. In fact, as Stovall said, here it was two years later and they were still sitting on an avalanche of unused material. The GOP, which might have been open to the information, stuck to the Nungesser plan—don't pay any attention to Duke. The state rep., they figured, would once again lose in the first round of the race, which they expected another Republican to win after ending up in the general against Roemer.

Before Duke had any other opponents in the race, however, Stovall made overtures with centrists to make sure they stuck with Roemer—or at least didn't wander away to Duke Country. Stovall's presence in the group was supposed to shore up the religious Left *and* Right. The anti-Duke movement had tried to enlist fundamentalist Christians in 1989 without success, however. The archbishop of New Orleans wrote a letter to religious leaders in Metairie, imploring them not "to resent 'outside' involvement" in the race.[6] It, like most letters he sent regarding Duke, was met with silence.

The vibe on the street was that Roemer would stomp Duke in the primary, that he would go head-to-head and "cut him like he did Edwin," as Maginnis put it.[7] But as one commentator noted, "If you've gone to Satan once, you know, it's not hard to do it again."[8] LSU political science professor Wayne Parent agreed, noting that at the time, insiders believed Duke would retain his base of 44 percent of the vote and then add to it, now that people believed he had a real shot at a prize, especially in the wake of Roemer's failure to reform state government.[9] "It became clear that Duke was not a one-off event and that he had legs," said Larry Powell. "One time, we were talking about Roemer in the office and the difficulty of reform, and the next thing you know, local lawmakers in Jefferson Parish were talking about race."[10] That wakeup call—that now everyone was piggybacking on

Duke's platform—helped coalesce the anti-Duke forces, but it also proved to lackadaisical parties that his message had momentum.

Duke and Huey Long conquered roughly the same parishes in their respective Senate races, only, as Duke pointed out, he may have been "a populist like Huey Long . . . but we need a Huey in reverse. We need a populist for *less* government and *more* power to the people."[11] Long had been a radical liberal whose entire plank was to give himself power to enact social change to benefit everyone, not just the elites. The anti-government conservatives and Reagan Democrats that had elevated Duke to power were the ones most disappointed by social progress and liberal reforms, however, and in particular Roemer's stabs at them.

Governor Buddy Roemer had been in trouble from the moment Edwards blindsided him by dropping out on primary night 1987. He instantly became governor-elect, before he could manage a runoff campaign that would give him a chance to receive endorsements, make his case before a larger, more attuned public, and build a coalition. He instead became an unusual kind of lame duck, forced to twiddle his thumbs as he waited several months for March 1988 and Edwards's departure from office. In the meantime, he became less cheery and more reserved and kept to himself. Soon after he took office, his wife, Patti, more than a decade younger and relegated to entertaining honored guests at the Mansion while Roemer watched sports, left him and took ten-year-old Dakota to Grand Junction, Colorado. Patti was later discovered hiding out from the press at a Howard Johnson's hotel. Roemer fell into a funk that rivaled governor Earl Long's famous crackup of decades earlier, highlighted when Long snuck around with striptease legend Blaze Starr, railed about segregation, flew by helicopter to bet on ponies in Arkansas, and had to be committed to a mental institution.[12] Roemer, who took to wearing a rubber wristband and snapping it against his skin when he had "impure" thoughts, alarmed his staff nearly as often. Staffers were particularly put off by his staging an almost cult-like weekend retreat by a company called "Adventures in Attitudes"—its title a major clue to its focus— which Patti Roemer grudgingly joined for all of one day before fleeing.[13]

"I asked him about that race quite a bit," said Carlos Sierra, a campaign staffer on Roemer's 2012 presidential campaign. "It wasn't politics, it wasn't policy. He wasn't used to failing at things. His honest answer is the divorce kicked his ass."[14] Roemer lacked the fire of the first gubernatorial race, when he was all-in on the poker table, traveled relentlessly to reach voters and get his name out, and came from the basement to hand Edwards his first defeat, all in a period of two weeks. When Raymond Strother dropped in on the Mansion, a receptionist told him that his former boss was too busy to see him, but when Roemer heard who was in the lobby, he "screamed" out Strother's name. Beckoned into the inner sanctum, Strother found the governor behind a barren desk—only a pen and a single sheet of paper lay before the state's most powerful politician.

"Patti left me," he said. "She left me and I wanna write her a letter."

"A letter?" said Strother, already shifting in his leather chair. "Hell, I don't know, Buddy, I'm not the best person to ask. My wife left me two weeks ago."[15]

Roemer's failure to woo back his estranged wife seemed to transfer to the legislature. Roemer not only became the first governor to split from his spouse while in office, damaging him with evangelicals and conservatives, he also became the first in state history to have his veto overridden by the legislature. Worse still, it was the government's third attempt at an anti-choice abortion bill, and one that that had been somewhat watered down after his critique and *still* vetoed.[16] That opened up a lane for anti-choice Republican Clyde Holloway, who announced he would challenge Roemer for evangelicals.[17] Roemer suddenly found himself without a lane—Edwards had the hardcore Democrats, Duke, a ragtag coalition of the disaffected on either side; Holloway religious folks who couldn't stomach a "racist"; and Roemer had whatever remained of the "Roemeristas," his diehards from 1987. "He had difficulty balancing his idealism with the pragmatism that's required to make things change, but he did accomplish quite a bit," lamented reporter Clancy Dubois. "He strengthened our campaign finance laws . . . pushed through many of the elements of that fiscal reform plan. . . . By the time he finished his first term as governor, he had made significant reforms working with lawmakers."[18] As Earl Long said in the fifties, "One of these days Louisianans are going to get good government, and they ain't going to like it!"

Then Buddy Roemer—or perhaps more specifically, the president of the United States—had a stroke of genius. George Bush wooed his old squash partner from Buddy's days in DC: *Join the Republican Party*, he said, *we don't bite. Much.* Roemer mulled his commander-in-chief's advice. Doing so, he knew, would earn him RNC financing and a head start in the run for the 1996 GOP presidential nomination. Chas, his son, would later say, "He never really fit in any party completely. It probably added to his downfall politically. But that's who he was."[19]

No sitting governor had ever switched parties, but Roemer suspected that the conservative movement could use someone like him in the South—a sane, balanced centrist who kept the state out of bankruptcy and cut the budget and was against abortion but knew that *Roe v. Wade* meant any-thing extreme would be ruled unconstitutional and cost the state millions in legal fees. (Or, at least, that's what Governor Roemer *believed* Republi-cans would think.) But success in politics is only visible in the tangible—potentialities that don't or *didn't* happen don't count with voters. They are only interested in the facts of a situation.

After telling his family he was thinking of leaving the Democratic Party and that he might try to succeed his friend President Bush in 1996, they almost unanimously tried to talk him out of it. The one person he should have listened to didn't get to weigh in until after Roemer's press confer-ence announcing his stubborn decision: Billy Nungesser, the head of the Louisiana Republican Party. Roemer's newfound surliness, developed during his five-month wait to take office, translated everywhere: his mar-riage, dining out in Baton Rouge, talking to the legislature, and when invit-ing Nungesser to the mansion to explain his decision and, ostensibly, to ask the GOP Chairman for his support in the fall.[20]

In Tyler Bridges' telling, it started out cold but cordial. Roemer's mother, who had moved into the Mansion after Patti departed, sat mutely in a cor-ner, probably in attendance to calm down the wrist-snapping, bad-thoughts-plagued governor. When Nungesser tried rather delicately to suggest that he was disinclined to support a liberal who had just made the switch in name but perhaps not ideology, Buddy exploded. "If you don't get into line and cut this shit out," he shouted, "I'm going to kick your fucking ass out of the Mansion."[21]

Billy Nungesser almost didn't speak to Roemer again. He immediately set to work one-terming Buddy Roemer. When Roemer surrogates John and Dave Treen worked behind the scenes to get the Republican convention scrapped, likely enabling Roemer to become the GOP nominee for governor, Nungesser pressured his bloc to vote down the proposal, which kicked off the convention at the Cajundome in Lafayette.[22] Thousands of Republicans cheered for the party itself, deeply divided over the three solid candidates in the hunt—the incumbent Roemer, congressman Clyde Holloway—the now odds-on favorite—and state representative David Duke.

But Nungesser rigged the vote without making major changes. As part of a quirk of the party's nominating process, every candidate for the GOP nomination had to swear an affidavit that they would drop out of the race if they were defeated in the nominating process. Duke and Roemer weren't stupid enough to fall for that, and Roemer, well aware of how humiliated he would be if he turned this into a battle and came up even one vote short, sat out the convention entirely. All those cheering, shrieking Republicans in the Cajundome, though? Duke had packed them in.

Duke, having refused to sign Nungesser's whiny little pledge, stage-invaded the convention to wild cheers. They chanted "Duke, Duke, Duke" for several minutes until a spokesperson for the party had to come out and tell the crowd Duke would be allowed to speak before the roll call vote.[23] At first, none of it seemed to make any difference in the makeup of the race. Clyde Holloway won the nomination, capturing 50 percent more electors than Duke.[24] Holloway would have a substantial baseline: 10 percent of the state's voters were also evangelical Christians. The GOP, it seemed, had turned into the anti-abortion party. "Goddamn it, sonofabitch," Roemer barked at Nungesser in a closed-door meeting. "I don't need you or Dave Treen or the Republicans or the Democrats. I won without any of you last time."[25]

Another person who stopped speaking to Roemer—his close confidante, Ray Strother. The consultant returned to the Mansion, where he was living during the campaign, to grab a change of clothes before a flight, and one of Roemer's attachés blocked his path. "I looked in the doorway," Strother recalled, "and there's a foyer and beyond it the state seal and a twenty-four seat dining room. I saw Mary Matalin in there." When Roemer emerged, he convinced Strother that he wouldn't switch, that he was just making nice with the Bush Administration to keep Federal funds flowing to Louisiana. The next day, Strother, a diehard Democrat, woke up at the Driskill Hotel in Austin, walked out of his room for breakfast at seven a.m., opened the newspaper, and saw a headline that caused him to drop his coffee mug.[26]

Beth Rickey tried to alert Roemer to this tactical mistake, writing to fellow Republicans that Matalin and Bush's involvement "is a double-edged sword. What Roemer does not realize is the depth of resentment Louisiana Republicans have toward Washington political operatives."[27] She believed Republican favorite Henson Moore lost his 1986 US Senate race because outside consultants suggested disenfranchising people from predominantly black districts, which backfired on Moore and lead to higher-than-expected turnout from African Americans. She worried most of all about a three-way split, which "promises to be a divisive, costly battle" and pointed, as evidence, to the mayhem with the endorsement of Bagert in 1990.

"Gov. Buddy Roemer's decision to defect from the Democratic Party and run for re-election as a Republican is another clear signal of the resurgence of the race factor in American politics today," said the *New York Daily News*. "If Roemer had run as a moderately conservative Democrat, which is what he has been, he would have faced the prospect that most of the white vote in

Louisiana—roughly three-fourths of the total—could have been split among himself, David Duke and a Republican candidate of some prominence such as former Gov. David Treen." The *Daily News* also noted that "the race factor is touchy enough to give [Duke] an imposing base," but it wouldn't be enough to get him into the runoff with a Republican incumbent.[28] Instead, the African American bloc would go to Edwards and Roemer would likely collect enough of the rest to edge him into second—and everyone else into the elimination column—in the primary.

As usual, though, David Duke saw several moves ahead, as did Edwin Edwards. Roemer, the famed strategist, couldn't seem to effectively manage his own reelection campaign. Turning his focus on the incumbent, Duke reminded voters of how he had achieved power in the first place, through his support of the homestead exemption, which Roemer tried to shred. Duke returned to the legislature and set about building up his record to compete with his two opponents. (Holloway faded deeper into the single digits.) Duke pushed bill after bill; it didn't matter that they were later watered-down to the point of worthlessness, he was proving to his constituents that he wouldn't get into the Governor's Mansion and just watch TV and brood, or dream up one-liners instead of signing bills. One might hear Duke got his welfare reform bill through, and it came off as a triumph, so long as one avoided the fine print—his initial plan to offer dole recipients five hundred dollars to receive the Norplant birth control treatment turned into a laughable provision to give women literature about preventing unwanted pregnancies.[29]

Edwin Edwards had few successes to point to over the past four years. While Patti Roemer was packing her bags, across town, Elaine Edwards was doing the same. After forty years of marriage, she'd had enough of the rumors, the confirmed infidelities, the literal trials and tribulations. She decamped for New York City with her daughter and tried to break into acting. Marion Edwards' cancer had returned and he wouldn't be back for the 1991 race. Edwards, working the phones himself, now realized how much of his success was due to his brother's persuasiveness. Cold called by the Cajun Prince, even those who had stuck with him through the trial and the '87 campaign turned him down.[30] No funds, no wife, no Marion, and no Nolan.

The magic touch, thought to have vacated him circa the previous cycle's debate, was not in evidence at his 1991 kickoff event at the Monteleone. Only about one hundred showed for the launch, one-fifth the turnout for his 1983 party.[31] The campaign asked staffers and Edwards' family, including daughters Anna, the beleaguered campaign office manager, and Victoria, who produced his 1983 campaign ads, to pad out the room and take food home so it wouldn't look pathetic when entire garbage bags' worth of catering had to be tossed. Little noticed by most of the attendees was perhaps, to Edwards, the most important guest, a nervous but charming, blond twenty-six-year-old LSU nursing student named Candy Picou. But the sixty-four-year-old Edwards didn't introduce everyone to his new girlfriend just yet.[32]

After explaining to the crowd his thinking on the campaign—going for Roemer's vulnerabilities, including his competence, betrayal of the Democratic Party, etc.—he dismissed the other candidates one by one, including Democrat Kathleen Blanco, a member of the state's Public Service Commission.[33] "She thinks if she hangs in long enough, people will come to her like they did to Roemer. But she lacks three things: one, the conspiracy of the press; two, she's not as smart, articulate or conniving as Roemer; and three, she's truthful."[34] Then Edwin turned the microphone over to the assemblage, which had so far remained lethargic, for questions. *Yeah*, someone grumbles. *What are you gonna do about David Duke?*

The informal pollsters (random Edwards fans who took the measure of their communities) stood, one at a time, including one man who claimed Duke was running strong and could even win in Jefferson Parish, Bossier City, West Monroe, and Livingston, as well as the northern parishes La Salle and Franklin. Another impromptu speech included the prediction that Edwards would lead after the primary, but that he should be careful about going hard on Roemer.[35] Edwards nodded, as if indicating he already knew—not impolitely, though. He seemed wary of losing focus on his strategy of attempting to go one-on-one with Roemer.

"No, no," came another voice from the darkness. "He won't make the runoff."

Edwards, trying out a one-liner, joked, "I'm trying to help him all I can. Unless there is a dramatic change, I will be in the runoff with Roemer." A moment later: "Wait, you don't seriously think Roemer will not make the runoff?"

Edwin Edwards, for the first time, may have been the least attuned person in local politics. After just a few speeches, it became apparent that most of Edwards' key supporters expected a Duke surge. The only people who didn't see it coming were, it seemed, Duke's competitors. As the music petered out, the loudest sound was the air conditioner humming low through the ducts. Seemingly baffled, Edwards asked everyone to raise their hands if they thought he would go head-to-head with someone other than the incumbent in the general. A slim majority believed it. Sheriff Harry Lee, at the back of the dais, sidled up to the podium and said he didn't believe for a second Duke could win in his parish (Jefferson), since the latest poll had Duke in third and Edwards in first. But the poll, unbeknownst to many, was set up by Lee himself and may have been a push poll, designed to encourage positive responses for a candidate. Overall, in any case, the word on the street was that Duke had rows of yard signs, people wearing his buttons and t-shirts, and informal surveys on his side in white districts. It was 1990 all over again, itself a repeat of 1989. Would anyone in a position of power do something about it?

Just weeks before the 1991 primary, Powell recalled, there was a general sense among Lance Hill, Beth Rickey, and LCARN that Duke would win. "There was a kind of wake-up call, a sense of existential dread that all of us felt. Lance and I [felt that, normally] if you give Louisianans a choice between a Nazi and a rogue like Edwin Edwards, the rogue's gonna win every time." But it was a major risk to sit it out and imagine Edwin Edwards would do the work for them. Powell, a history professor, marched over to a meeting of the Tulane Board of Administrators and told them, adamantly, to start planning for a Governor Duke. In a surprising twist, Tulane's board proved to be one of the few groups sufficiently mortified by that probability. Another Tulane professor arrived promptly at Powell's office door with a check for $5,000, which Powell immediately handed over to the New Orleans NAACP field office for their get-out-the-vote campaign. "It was just rolling in," Powell said. "This was kind of a showdown, and we had done a good enough job of shaping and defining the perception of who Duke was, the meaning and significance of the election. It wasn't an electoral contest; it was a moral crisis."[36]

Tim Wise, another anti-Duker, had graduated from Tulane and begun working under Larry Powell at LCARN headquarters. "[Powell] asked if I would be interested in doing the coordinating for the student anti-Duke network on all the campuses" for the 1990 race. Surely, Wise thought, Duke wouldn't get anywhere—hell, he'd only won his House seat by 227 votes. No way could he "mount a credible Senate campaign." But after turning Powell down and heading back to the east coast to become the editor of an underground newspaper, Wise caught Duke's live press conference announcing his 1990 run at Johnston and watched in horror as the Republican's poll numbers exploded. "And we all knew he polled well below the radar," he recalled.[37] Wise got back down to Louisiana immediately, and went straight to LACRN HQ, racking up seventy-hour weeks until the stunning moment on Primary Night 1991 when Duke took the podium.

Meanwhile, Beth Rickey's contributions, especially her continued dogging of Duke's past, mainly off the record and behind the scenes since their disastrous Chinese lunch, clearly got under Duke's skin. In a 1992 interview with the *Texas Observer*, Duke had plenty to say about her:

> INTERVIEWER: Now in 1989, according to Rickey—and of course she's a Republican here—
>
> DUKE: Yeah, she's a liberal Republican. She's in favor of affirmative action. . . . Very Leftist on all subjects. She's a very biased individual.
>
> INTERVIEWER: Did she misquote you when she said that you were saying basically that white Aryans are superior, Jews are evil . . . ?
>
> DUKE: That's just malarkey. And she taped me for many different things, and it's amazing she's never come up with any tapes on these things. She's got plenty of tapes of conversations she's had with me.

When pressed on several of Rickey's major claims about Duke's statements, he denied ever saying that Jews were Satan's spawn or that he supported Nazism and Hitler.

"That's just total garbage," Duke said. "In the recordings that she's presented and the Coalition has presented, you look at all of them, you go through all of it, there's many places where I condemn . . . Hitler, as I do today. He was a disaster for the European people and for the Western Christian civilization that I love and represent. In their own stuff that they distribute they have me quoted as saying those things. That's just one person's word."[38]

But the evidence remained strong—and now he'd pissed Rickey off. When asked what she might say if ever face-to-face with him again, she deadpanned, "Sweetie, I've been too nice to you."[39] The gloves came off. "David Duke has carefully repackaged himself," she wrote in a 1991 newspaper op-ed. "He is a Nazi, posing as a Klansman, posing as a conservative Republican. His plastic surgery is a metaphor for the makeover he has given his racial beliefs. While he looks different, David Duke has not changed. He merely appears more polished. He still believes in the tenets of Aryan superiority, African inferiority, and Zionist conspiracy. He has put a pretty face on his hate, mainstreaming his rhetoric and using carefully chosen code words. . . . However . . . he openly espoused anti-Semitism well into 1990."[40] Hill was able to parse Duke quotes from Rickey's notes, Duke speeches, NAAWP newsletters, and archival newspaper clippings for mailers LCARN spread in 1990 and 1991. He and Rickey agreed that, regardless of what pollsters, donors, and even other LACRN board members wanted, suggested, or outright demanded, the mission wasn't to *elect* a Duke opponent but to keep Duke out of the running. It may have hurt their fundraising, as potential donors often asked—pen hovering over the "amount" line on a personal check—who the Coalition would support in the 1991 primary. By July 19, 1991, the group had $40,000 to spend but had already accumulated bills totaling $22,000.[41] They decided to stick to direct mailers and avoid television ads to conserve funds, leaving Roemer alone to replicate his powerhouse 1987 strategy. Duke, meanwhile, collected cash by the bucketful. Calls and letters came in at nearly a rate of one per minute after his State House victory, an interview on *The Morton Downey Jr. Show*, and a May 1989 appearance on *The Phil Donahue Show*, America's longest-running television talk program.[42] "Want to congratulate you on how you did on Donahue," one phone receptionist wrote in a memo book, quoting a caller. (One complained that their local affiliate had "dubbed in words for 1/3 of show, then showed Cosby show instead of the rest of Donahue.") Another, having seen his TV appearance, offered some unsolicited advice: "When asked if you think there is a difference in the intelligence level between Blacks + whites, you should pull out a list of philosophers" who agreed with Duke on genetics. Others wanted to thank him for "doing a great job for your people," invited him to swank soirees in uptown New Orleans, or wanted to share intel on Democrats abusing children.[43] His 1991 appearance on *Donahue* triggered a similar reaction and a mountain of cash donations.[44] Duke started to rack up donations all day, every day. In 1991, Duke Country came through with $2.1 million in donations via twenty-six thousand contributors, which one reporter suggested was mainly through paper currency. These contributions were supposed to be banned under a campaign finance deal signed by Governor Roemer, which included a cap of $100 cash or $5,000 in checks per person. Anonymous cash was a big no-no, too, but that didn't stop Duke from raking in oyster buckets full of tens and twenties at his 1991 rallies, and since these sometimes anonymous letters often arrived accompanied by cash but didn't include the contributor's full name, mailing address, and Social Security number, a legal issue developed. The Louisiana Ethics Board took him to court over these monies, and campaign worker Robert Hawkes testified in a 1993 deposition that he would see cash in about half of the two thousand pieces of mail Duke received at his peak. Another eyewitness, Paul Allen, backed Hawkes up. Allen claimed he hadn't known cash contributors were supposed to receive a receipt. The state thought it had this one locked up, as ignorance of the law is no excuse, but a judge tossed the suit, saying, "The person who gives $1, $2 or $5 certainly is not looking for something in return. And if they are, they're insane."[45]

Not all of Duke's appearances triggered a tidal wave of support. At a March 28 appearance in Boston, he was delayed for several minutes while Steve Curwood, the black host and vice president of the Ford Hall Forum, where the event was being held, tried to silence the crowd. "We're opposed to fascism in any form," Curwood said, getting everyone to applaud at last. He reminded them that "Margaret Sanger spoke here on birth control when a condom was still a crime. Malcolm X spoke here when other people did not want him to speak. We had neo-Nazi George Lincoln Rockwell—he preached white supremacy from our podium. Many people have hated what these people said, but that is no reason not to let them speak. If you want fascism in this country, where people who don't agree with you aren't allowed to speak, why don't you move to a place like Russia or Iraq?"

The chanting resumed and Duke sat mutely, pretending to reread his notes, even as Curwood pointed out that his own ancestors had been brutalized under slavery and by the KKK. He also noted that unless outlets were given to angry people, violence would inevitably break out. "When any point of view is censored, *that* is the beginning of tyranny." Duke nodded vigorously.

"Sellout," they chanted. "Oreo!"

"Oreo's a good cookie," cracked Curwood.

"It's a little bit ironic, isn't it?" said Duke. "If David Duke had prevented you from hearing our gracious black host here, he would've been called a white racist. What should we be called here? Obviously, the irony is that freedom of speech must live in this country for all points of view."

He tried to bring up failures of liberalism; to discuss freedom of speech and the American Revolution, which had kicked off in that very venue; to address the term "politically incorrect speech" and argue that it didn't matter if something was incorrect or otherwise; but the chants went on unbroken. He was interrupted by applause only after police officers removed unruly protestors. While the cops had their backs turned, escorting one person out, an audience member lunged at a protestor, leading to an arrest for assault and battery. Five more anti-Dukers were ejected. One, a middle-aged black man, hugged a pillar until cops were able to yank him away, upon which he swung wildly and took a blow to the face. The crowd roared.

Duke pressed on. He told them that he had taken no fee for the engagement and would press on all night, if need be, to wait out the chanting.

"Violence is not going to be tolerated here," Curwood interjected sternly. "Anyone who throws any more material will be arrested, the police have promised."

"KKK terrorist!"

"Racist," went the chant as he tried to speak again, the chant and accompanying claps picking up speed in tandem.

"These people are guilty of everything they accuse me of," he said. "Listen to this!"[46]

Duke, clearly shaken, adjusted his tie, and suggested everyone meet him on the ground floor after his speech for a debate. Over the past two dozen years as a provocateur and right-wing movement leader, he had faced dozens of hostile crowds. The Boston protestors, however, seemed to have prepared these chants, secured their spots in the gallery, and committed to drowning him out for the entirety of the event. Eventually, he powered through his speech as if the crowd were studying him in rapt silence, making the case that he was the true crusader for equality, eliminating biases in favor of one race or another through his anti-affirmative action bill, and how social justice crusaders were hypocrites, discriminating against white people instead of supporting equal rights for all US citizens. This, though, was a far cry from Free Speech Alley, where Duke had been able to go toe-to-toe, giving as good as he took against a handful of casual, relatively bemused hecklers. The vociferousness of the crowd blindsided Duke. Such reactions, however, were about to become the norm everywhere.

CHAPTER 10

The Gamblers

David Duke didn't trouble himself over tired and tiresome ol' Edwin Edwards. In fact, as Duke may have known, Edwards's presence in the 1991 primary helped him immensely. Since the Silver Fox drew at least three-quarters of the black vote, of which there were tens of thousands in New Orleans alone, he deprived Roemer of a crucial base to grow from. Edwards later claimed that he saw Duke's ascendancy months in advance, but all evidence points to him targeting Roemer throughout the fall. After all, the two competitors were facing off practically every week at the Governor's Mansion, for, of all things, poker.

It was a strange sight, the governor and the ex-governor he'd vanquished, now challenging him to a rematch, playing through the night with thousands of dollars piled up between them. Roemer, despite sometimes winning $20,000 per night playing poker at Bob Woodward's DC townhouse, abhorred casinos, Vegas and Atlantic City alike, and ran as the anti-gambling candidate in 1987 to contrast with Edwards.[1] Now, pushing the state lottery through to passage, which Edwards had lobbied for relentlessly during his third term, seemed a rich irony, yet no one commented on it during these games. The two were among half a dozen regular players, all of whom talked smack but never made it truly personal—or political. Edwards, though, quietly stewed. Roemer had been his campaign staffer and had soured on Fast Eddie. He had "slain the dragon," a personal insult to his old boss. And while Edwards told supporters he believed he'd "evolved mentally and emotionally," he couldn't resist some relatively childish digs at the incumbent, usually once Roemer had retired for the evening, but sometimes in public or to his face. "I'm the solution to the Revolution," a banner behind him might read. "[Roemer] said read my lips. He meant kiss my hips," said Edwards. "Oh yes, Louisiana, there is a Santa Claus."[2]

But although Edwards tried to make it a two-man race with the incumbent, all anyone wanted to talk about that year was David Duke. "He's not a respectable Republican. I cannot believe that anybody who wears a Nazi uniform or wore a Klan sheet is respectable. I hope he has changed, but it is not for me to decide." Edwards was still trying to stay on Duke's supporters' good sides to be able to lobby for them in a runoff. He wasn't campaigning to stop a Nazi or get revenge on Roemer, or so he claimed. "[Being governor is] what I want to do when I get up in the morning. It's what turns me on."[3]

Unable to prove the necessity of his candidacy, Edwards suffered an unsurprising uphill slog for money. He told a local car dealer to stop wasting money on obnoxious commercials and donate the savings to the Edwards campaign. The candidate was half joking. He attempted to get each candidate to agree to run only on name recognition, free media coverage, debates, in-person campaigning, and on their records, without political ad buys. The others laughed. Of course, the Edwards brand was better known, giving him a head start. After the March Federal Election Commissions report showed his fundraising somewhere between "embarrassing" and "nonexistent," he returned to the familiar way of doing things.

Roemer continued to believe his true competition came from the Silver Fox, as did Caroline Roemer, initially. But then the governor's daughter, twenty-four, rode in the New Iberia Sugar Cane festival as a campaign surrogate, waving to the crowd, expecting it to be like all the other campaign events she'd attended since birth. Instead, as people read the "Roemer" sign on the car, they broke into relentless heckling. Worse still, the response to David Duke, who rode in the convertible ahead of her, was thunderous and chilling. Chanting broke out whenever he appeared up the block, and blue "Duke" signs flashed above the crowd every few feet. Duke seemed to have operations at full throttle everywhere, while Buddy Roemer, who hadn't started formally campaigning and claimed to be concentrating on working his bills through the legislature, had none. He didn't appear in front of the tens of thousands at the festival to, say, promote the lottery system, education programs, or his civil rights vision for the nineties. Even after Duke had to duck to avoid empty glass bottles while passing through certain sections of the parade route, Caroline Roemer, a resident of the Mansion since her stepmother's departure, came away convinced that she had to confront her father about kicking his reelection into high gear, pronto.[4]

Raymond Strother agreed with Caroline Roemer. (Roemer convinced Strother to stay on after the party switch by pointing out that not helping him would be helping the "corrupt" Edwards instead, a "philosophical inconsistency" of choosing party over morals.) Strother planned a media campaign, including television ads, but when he came to Louisiana, he immediately ran into a succession of stone walls. Roemer didn't want to campaign (at least, he said, not while the legislature remained in session); the Republican National Committee and Republican Governor's Association were suspicious of Strother, a holdover from the governor's time as a Democrat and perhaps of new turncoat Roemer himself; and while Strother wanted to refocus the primary campaign on David Duke, Roemer was unmovable.[5] Focusing on Edwards only played into the dragon's hands, as it allowed Edwards to respond with pithy one-liners that served as the focus of, say, a newspaper. Ignore him and Edwards wouldn't be able to generate any publicity on his own. Duke, however, had sailed through a Senate race with only weak-kneed or minimal attacks from the Left. Would his approval rating nose-dive with a few commercials throwing his words back in his face? The Republican Party thought better of it, instead echoing Billy Nungesser's strategy: leave Duke alone and he can't boost his profile. Roemer, unconvinced by his daughter's experiences touring the state or his media consultant's pleading about a hidden Duke bloc, kept pointing out that he and Edwards were neck and neck for the lead and the ex-Grand Wizard had less than half their support, which would mean his elimination from the runoff. Strother managed to convince the governor to at least let him conduct a secret focus group in order to determine what the state's voters truly thought, polls be damned, and settle the bet.

In a sealed-off room in a nondescript building on the Westbank of New Orleans, part of Jefferson Parish, a dozen undecided voters sat with their arms folded, waiting to be told what this was all about. Right away, when Roemer's image flashed on screen, most recoiled. It kicked off Strother's thirty-minute ad buy and, behind nearby one-way glass, the consultant, hand on chin, started to sweat. When the moderator flicked on the lights and asked about the uplifting spot and its claims that "victories grew" and that "slowly, hope is taking root" under the Roemer administration, participants simply shook their heads. They mumbled verdicts of their reformist governor like "manipulative" and "a disappointment." Once the persuasive debater who got things done, Governor Roemer had lost the legislature, his campaign team, and his early supporters.

The moderator tried another tactic. *Let's talk about an imaginary candidate*, he began. *This person is a draft dodger, a prima donna, has had cosmetic surgery, has been involved in a hate group, and never worked a day in his life. What would you say about his candidacy?*

The focus group shifted uncomfortably in their seats. Regarding the plastic surgery claim, one man said, "I'd wonder about his sexuality," to nervous muttering. A draft dodger? None could stomach the guy who refused to serve. Personally, they said, we're not racist and don't want to go back down *that* road. And what the hell qualifications would a lifelong mooching loafer have to run for office?

Strother's tactic seemed to be working, but in the second group, the moderator grew bolder. At first, the focus group seemed open, using positive language to describe the incumbent, calling him "intelligent" but a bit "glib." Then came the reveal— David Duke was the "imaginary" second candidate.

"What's wrong with a politician having plastic surgery? Movie stars do it."

"Only dumb people pay taxes. Politicians and millionaires don't because they're smart. Duke must be smart."

"He's a politician. Politicians don't work."

"It [the Klan] was when he was a lad. Kids do crazy things."

This time, Strother made sure the participants were asked who their neighbors were voting for. The moderator blanched and started out of the meeting room. They're all voting Duke, he said.[6]

Strother's team did find one weak point. When pointing out that many out-of-state groups, including major conventions, would boycott Louisiana were Duke elected, creating a four-year economic hit, Duke's rating dipped. It would be incredibly difficult to produce an effective anti-Duke spot from a position of power, but Democrat Raymond Strother felt that he could pull off a tightrope act of an attack ad that hit Duke—not too hard—on the economic concern, and Roemer might just win it.[7]

Buddy Roemer said no. Another staffer told Strother the campaign wouldn't win by being negative, which, in a normal election, would be a wise position for the incumbent to take. But David Duke had become a serious political figure practically unchecked, and without drastic measures, his support would rise incrementally every day. Strother showed a half dozen test ads to Roemer, with well-dressed actors signaling "business leaders" and fretting over the possibility of shuttered companies and job losses. Roemer called them "a bunch of yuppies" and stormed out without explanation. Strother, despondent, couldn't speak.

The focus group and Strother's anti-Duke spots could have become a major turning point. Instead, the campaign's failure to air them proved catastrophic. "[Roemer] never took Duke seriously," Strother said later. "He did not want to alienate conservative voters in North Louisiana . . . for the runoff. He would not allow any attack on Duke, ever."

Regardless, Roemer's former supporters were busy attacking *him*. Jack Kent, owner of a hazardous waste company, had been on board the Roemer Revolution in 1987. But when Buddy assumed office, he asked the Department of Environmental Quality to look into Kent's operation, Marine Shale Processors. The DEQ subsequently slapped Kent's business with millions in fines for violating cleanup and safety standards for hazardous waste. Overnight, he turned Kent into a hardcore enemy.[8] The tycoon rationalized what he did next thus: "He's tried to put me out of business. I can do the same to him."[9] Kent flew to Washington, hired a consultant to produce a series of flashy anti-Roemer ads hitting the governor on his setbacks, indecisiveness, and flip-flopping. In focus groups like the ones Strother had led, Kent's team discovered that people muted the sound when Buddy Roemer spoke, such was their fear that he would manipulate them into voting for him again. Armed with this intel, Kent threatened to air his anti-Roemer spots unless the governor backed down on his pledge to shutter Marine Shale.[10]

"I didn't become governor to make deals like this with people like Jack Kent," Roemer snapped. Within days, Kent had the ads running on TV in primetime, spending a reported four hundred thousand to a half million dollars to have them air relentlessly in the two weeks before the primary.[11]

A few days after his official but late-in-the-campaign launch, Roemer was at the Pickin' and Ginnin' Festival in Rayville, shaking hands, when he heard a voice beside him, one that had grown increasingly familiar lately: "Welcome to Duke Country, Governor."

"Well, thanks, Dave," said Roemer, shaking Duke's hand amiably, "I thought this was Louisiana."

Duke, not missing a beat, shot back: "Louisiana *is* Duke Country, Governor."[12]

The governor may not have believed it, even after seeing Duke stickers on a third of festival attendees, compared to almost no visible support for him. The fault was entirely his own, which became clear when he told a radio interviewer that his campaign had become "very aggressive, encompassing and positive." The interviewer bluntly asked the governor when he might "start."

"Why, I think I have," said a startled Roemer. "I mean, I'm out here on a Saturday, it's hot as a dog and it's going well."[13]

But he didn't campaign that aggressively at the Pickin' and Ginnin' Festival. He stayed in the middle of the street, shaking hands only when someone approached—unless they were also wearing a Duke sticker. He fell into a conversation with a supporter from 1987 who worked in healthcare and wanted to talk about the state's growing child abuse caseload, but Roemer demurred. "Linda," he said, "I know you can talk. Now let's see if you can write."[14] State rep. Ralph Miller may have put it best. When asked about the plan to exhume Huey Long's body to determine which gun, the assassin's or his bodyguard's, truly felled him, Miller quipped, "They're trying to dig up Buddy Roemer, but they can't find where he's buried."[15] At the time, Roemer *led* by six points.

"No poll ever showed him losing," Strother noted, and Buddy Roemer, seven for eight in his political career, including wins as a campaign manager and three consecutive congressional elections, bought his own hype.[16] In the last days of the campaign, he made cursory attempts to tamp down Duke's support and remain in first place. He scored an image-boosting coup by co-headlining a fundraiser with George H. W. Bush. Journalist John Maginnis gushed that it was a "big historic moment, the first time a sitting President of the United States has campaigned on behalf of a sitting governor."[17] Communications director Gordon Hensley seemed even giddier, watching one hundred couples line up for $5,000-a-pop photos with POTUS, and between those and 750 $1,000 banquet dinner tickets, the Buddy Roemer campaign walked away with a million bucks for one night's "work."[18]

Bush pushed hard for Roemer's reelection: "I think we've got a lot in common," he said. "We both can be a bit stubborn. We don't always get along with the legislature."[19] As the laughter simmered, the president rattled off his own administration's accomplishments, which were similar to what he saw as Roemer's: commitments to combatting toxic chemicals and pollution, an increase in childcare assistance, and a pro-capitalist mentality.

"Let's look at civil rights," Bush said. "Some in Congress want a bill that divides our people. I want one that brings us together. . . . I don't like these allegations made that we're not interested in the rights of all Americans. We are. Education, the environment, a strong economy, and true civil rights: Buddy changed parties to crusade for these causes. And Churchill said, 'Some men change their principles for their party. Others change their party for their principles.' Some would rather fight than switch. Some would rather switch than fight. Buddy decided to switch and fight. And tonight, I ask you and all the people across this State of Louisiana to fight for him, to keep him as Governor of this State."[20]

As cheers rang throughout the ballroom and patrons stood to applaud, Buddy Roemer took the stage, grinning. But when his speech got down to brass tacks, the audience shifted silently in their seats. "If you don't have a bumpersticker on your car, you're not committed," he said, "If you don't have a sign in your yard, you're not committed."[21] Not familiar with being chastised for activities normally reserved for commoners, the wealthy Republican attendees scowled. They would not be putting bumperstickers on their Cadillacs.

"The governor came in wanting to make major changes in a blitzkrieg fashion," a local economist noted. "But now he is taking a much more gradual approach, seeking smaller changes and assuming a lower profile himself." That diminished presence cost him his frontrunner status. "For my first 30 months in office I tended to be angry. I had good reason to be angry. I fed on my anger. It was a source of energy, but I paid a high price for it."[22]

Now, he fought like a wounded animal. He gave TV interviews, visited the northern part of the state for the first time all year (Duke visited six times), and rushed to schedule events, often without proper planning. A major rally in one town was attended by dozens instead of thousands, as the state fair was underway a mere two blocks down. As Edwards put it when seeing the numbers, if "the Roemer campaign says they had 300 at their Bossier rally," it's double what they really had. (Regarding that Bossier City event, Edwards also noted 300 attendees would only cover ten percent of Buddy's turnout at the same venue in 1987.)[23] Already miffed about the poor turnout, Roemer again went against his better instincts and informed his supporters that they'd better start slapping his bumpersticker on their cars. This speech went over no better than the one at the Bush fundraiser.[24] At least, though, Buddy finally did something about Jack Kent's relentless, disparaging ads—he embraced them.

At the LSU football game one week before the primary, Roemer was quizzed about the Kent ads, which by then were running almost constantly, during most commercial breaks, on every network. "When I saw that ad, I said 'Victory!'" he claimed. "These guys have just given me something I've needed— an enemy."[25] Indeed, he seemed sunnier, even invigorated. But when pressed about how his campaign would respond, Roemer said they were carefully considering their counterattack, "but we find that the media is a more effective way to answer that. I've found that people are skeptical of my spots. And that increases with each election I've run. So I try not to react." As for whether Kent was secretly, specifically helping Edwards, Roemer hinted he knew journalists were working on "something" that'd turn Kent's ads against Fast Eddie. Now, if they didn't mind, he had a game to catch.[26]

With only days to go until Election Day, Roemer's opponents had already spent months crisscrossing the state, holding galvanizing rallies, running carefully calculated attack ads on each other, and getting their pictures in the local papers—all essential practices that Roemer had neglected until he noticed that few supporters had posted "Buddy" yard signs up along the routes he traveled. Meanwhile, holocaust survivor Anne Levy made a wrong turn in Metairie one afternoon and found herself on a suburban street bursting with blue-on-white Duke signs. She had never seen such unanimous support for a candidate anywhere.[27]

David Duke had never smiled so much. Not far from that LSU game where Roemer had made a triumphant but little-noticed appearance, Duke held a rally at the Hilton, site of his gubernatorial announcement months earlier. Then, only about one hundred had turned out; now, he returned to more than six hundred screaming fans.[28] Journalist John Maginnis, having followed all three major candidates across the state that year, marveled at the demographics—Duke's supporters were mostly thirty years old or younger or fifty-plus, not a yuppie in sight.[29] (The anti-Duke ads Strother wanted to run for the governor might have worked on the upper middle class, or they might have been reaching people who wouldn't bother to vote at all.) Duke's lawyer, Jim McPherson, now running for attorney general, came up with a devastating line: "Four years ago I voted for Buddy Roemer," he said. "I wanted a revolution, and now I'm going to get it if we put David Duke in office!"[30]

Duke took the stage in what the *New York Times* called a "big-shouldered" suit and blond, perfectly coifed "blow-dried" hair. "On his lapel he wears a pin shaped like a fish, an ancient symbol for Christ. He speaks with fervor and sincerity, and there is none of the anger common to the segregationist politicians who were the heroes of his youth."[31]

"Are you ready for a new governor?"

"Yeah!" the throngs roar back.

"The pollsters say my voters fly beneath radar. Well, we're up on their radar screens tonight."

"Yeah!"

He hit Roemer on nickel-and-diming the state to death: "A lady came up to me in church the other day. A feisty lady. She told me the next thing they're going to license is having sex—and if Roemer is governor, they'll raise the fee every year."

On his other, almost neglected opponent: "Going back to Edwards is like moving from New Orleans to Detroit to escape crime."[32]

On an apocryphal story of a robbery in Metairie: "The officers grabbed the [suspects] and threw them against the wall and said, 'Are you guys crazy? Don't you know this is David Duke's district?'"

"Duke, Duke, Duke!" they chanted.[33]

But when he railed against the "far-left" NAACP, he temporarily lost them—until he suggested that "the NAACP stands for gun control. I believe in the right of law-abiding citizens to bear arms. I believe in the rights to be judged on your merits and not your race."

"Shame, shame," someone called out.

"When I saw Clarence Thomas during some of those hearings, my heart went out to him. The forces that tried to destroy his character are the same forces that tried to destroy mine."[34]

Duke supporters, hesitant to speak to the media—"the press is out to get him because they can't control him," one man suggested—occasionally let something loose to a reporter. "I was saved," another man said. "I'm a Christian. I wouldn't want someone to come back at me about my past and say I haven't changed."

In his closing argument, Duke outlined his plan: tough on crime, increased employment, more cops. How he might inspire job creation or keep businesses from fleeing the state, as they threatened to, he didn't elaborate. Instead, perhaps worried about the FEC and state government investigations into his donations, he implored followers to accept a Mardi Gras doubloon to turn the donation into a cash sale—"that's Buddy Roemer's law," he grumbled. "If you want to give more than twenty-five dollars," he added, "you can write a check."[35]

It worked. "Former Ku Klux Klan leader David Duke is pulling 10 times the number of campaign contributions as Edwin Edwards in the Louisiana governor's race, and opening checkbooks nationwide," the AP noted in November.[36]

Confronted about allegations that he, like Edwards, had bet five figures per game of craps, allegedly with funds that were supposed to go to an organization or campaign, Duke demurred. "I've played dice before, but I've never ever made a bet of anywhere near that size." But, he admitted, "A couple of times in my life I've been at a table where it's run up real high during the course of an evening."[37]

Edwards, meanwhile, appeared on the verge of going broke. In the final week of the 1983 election, he blew through $500,000 in cash reserves; this time, he had only $60,000 set aside, including for all his GOTV efforts. If he couldn't afford to pay black organizations to bus supporters to the polls in New Orleans and Shreveport, he could end up in third. Luckily, the Democratic National Committee paid for ads using "soft money," meaning that it didn't have to be counted as campaign contributions, as the RNC had done for Roemer.[38] It didn't amount to much, but it might be enough.

Had he raised more cash, however, Edwards might have clobbered David Duke on TV. As it was, he was still able to inspire eleven hundred supporters to turn up for the final rally of the primary, and perhaps of the Cajun Prince's career, at the Shreveport Holidome. Fully half of them were black, and hundreds more were turned away. He had stunned reporters when he packed an all-time high (for him) eight thousand supporters into the Cajundome, seizing headlines in the last days of the campaign.[39] Tom Stokes, a young staffer concentrating on turnout in Lafayette, organized the definitive rally of the 1991 election, sealing Edwards' comeback.

Stokes had met Edwards during the tail end of the governor's third administration. He and his blond girlfriend, both eighteen, broke down in Stokes' new (used) vehicle on the side of the road outside Baton Rouge. A passing limousine with tinted windows circled the block, crawled close, and a window came down, revealing a decked-out black limo driver, Jaubert Ambeaux, at the wheel, offering them a ride to the Governor's Mansion. "I was very young and pretty easily wowed," Stokes said. He lunched with the governor the following week and immediately signed up for the 1987 campaign.[40] In 1991, Stokes got sober and ran into another former staffer at an Alcoholics Anonymous meeting in Lafayette. His older cohort told him that he had rejoined Edwards for the race against Duke and Roemer, and Stokes asked to be hired on somehow, somewhere.

He ended up saddled with the command of the Lafayette to Lake Charles region, a swath of seventy-five miles with more than a quarter million people. He was twenty-two, full of himself, eager to introduce his famous friends at events. "I didn't know my dad and grew up in a boy's home in New Orleans," he reflected thirty years later, so Edwards and his campaign surrogates stepped in, turning Stokes into a fundraising and door-knocking force.

The campaign, he said, ceded northern Louisiana to Roemer. It was a near suicidal strategy, but, Stokes said, they had no choice but to concentrate on turning out their base and not trying to change minds about the crook, Edwin Edwards. "The campaign was very grassroots," he said. "It was parish by parish. Edwards was a people person, people loved him. I was with [Edwards] in Crowley on the campaign trail, just amazed. I was just sitting there at a barbecue, there were a couple hundred people there, and there is Edwards, speaking in three fucking languages."[41] With such charisma, ease with women, and ability to raise checks with a series of zeroes in a blip, the candidate became Stokes' idol. He soon developed the boss's cocksure approach to negotiating, getting in the personal space of business owners and collecting checks. He was given three cellphones, a mind-boggling luxury, including one to receive direct dials from "the Bat Phone," Edwards' personal cell, and the others to call either for the campaign or to receive personal calls. (Outgoing calls were prohibitively expensive.) If Duke had won the ground game in the primary, Edwards was determined to battle him for it in the general, albeit without competing in angry, conservative parishes, but certainly in terms of headline-grabbing, high-turnout rallies.

The rally at the Cajundome had been dumped on the campaign's under-lings, but with Stokes in charge of Lafayette, the make-or-break event fell to him to make or break. "We pulled that whole thing together in thirty days," he said, still amazed. Stokes said the team effort included contributions from Lehman Brothers executives, wealthy matron Johnnie Reese, former mayor of Lafayette Kenny Bowen, and "the guy who did all the construc-tion of I-49 for Edwards."

"When Edwards came out, you would've thought that guy was Elvis," said Stokes. "It really fucked me up for the rest of my life. Everything's been a letdown."[42]

Edwards took the stage in his trademark blue suit, red tie, and yellow-on-black "Edwards for Governor" pin and whipped them into a frenzy talking about the old times and the good times, one and the same in Edwards coun-try. "I'm sixty-four," he confessed during these last rallies. "I've made my mistakes but I've tried to be available. Anytime I can be of service, let me know. I'm not a perfect human being. But when I'm ready to go from this earth to my reward, I know I will be judged by that infallible judge." Echo-ing a line unknowingly cribbed from Buddy Roemer, he said he stood by his record because he always "fought the good fight."[43]

His ragtag campaign team, composed of mostly unfamiliar faces (at least to the candidate), had pulled it—and a stunning comeback—off. Edwin Edwards had fought for eight months and battled back from disappoint-ing fundraising totals and poll numbers to take the narrowest of numerical leads. The final poll had Edwards at thirty-one percent, Roemer with thirty, Duke at twenty, and Holloway, the forgotten Republican nominee drawing support away from Roemer, at six. Twelve percent were undecided. In the *New*

Orleans Times-Picayune, every pundit surveyed picked Roemer and Edwards to make the runoff (in that order), although one said Edwards would place first. Another little-seen poll had a much more interesting result—all three were tied at roughly 29 points, but as in 1990, pollsters, journalists, and campaign staff themselves considered it an outlier, and therefore highly suspect.[44] They were soon to be embarrassed for the second year in a row.

The Louisiana Coalition Against Racism and Nazism had been waiting for this final week to make their move. Lance Hill and Beth Rickey decided that the smoking gun, the most damaging piece of information, came from a tape they had acquired through backchannels that Evelyn Rich, then a doctoral student, had made in 1986, of Duke dropping in on her chat with Joe Fields, a proud, public neo-Nazi.[45]

Duke, in an apparent attempt to show Fields how he would run for president in 1988, told him that he would tamp down his rhetoric, which he told Fields was much more closely aligned to Field's ideology than it might sound.

"What did Hitler do with the Jews?" Duke asked Fields, seemingly genuinely curious.

"I think he wanted to break their influence," said Fields.

Duke suggested, "I think he wanted to resettle them."

Regarding extermination, Fields started to say that the Jews didn't deserve to be exterminated, but Duke interrupted him with his laughter. "No seriously, they actually do deserve everything they get. And if it was extermination, they would have deserved it."

"They're a pest," Fields went on. "You know, when your house is rotting, you have termites, you get rid of the pests."

Duke seemed partly taken aback by this: "Well . . ." he began, "People generally deserve what they push on other people. I think they're trying to exterminate our race. I think probably in a moral sense, the Jewish people have been a blight. I mean as a whole, not every Jew, and they probably deserve to go into the ashbin of history, but saying that and actually shooting or killing people in masses are two different things. I'm not advocating some sort of extermination. I think the best thing is to resettle them some place where they can't exploit others."

"A parasite can't live unless it's attached to a host," said Fields.

When Rich got them talking about being called Nazis and whether that branding stung them, emotionally or at the ballot box, Duke affirmed that it hurt his standing on the political scene.

"Why not say . . . 'What are you going to do about [my Nazism], Jew?'" asked Fields.

"I'm trying to bring new people in, like a drummer," Duke can then be heard saying. "The difference is, they can call you a Nazi and make it stick—tough, really hard—it's going to hurt your ability to communicate with them. It's unfortunate."[46]

These comments were incendiary enough, but buried further down the transcript was a potentially more damaging exchange, in which Duke agreed that an economic collapse would help the Far Right. He looked "forward to" another depression, he said. On top of that, there was an exchange about Duke's true, current beliefs and plans for the future after achieving power, which contradicted his statements since 1988.

"It doesn't take that many people though to start something rolling," Fields said encouragingly. "Hitler started with seven men."

"Right!" Duke exclaimed. "And don't you think it can happen right now, if we put the right package together? Don't you think that there are millions of Americans that are alienated and are looking for something, and the truth is the truth, and give 'em something to believe in?"

"And Guru Duke will come along!" Evelyn Rich said, half-jokingly.

Duke demurred. "I might have to do it because nobody else might come along."[47]

The Evelyn Rich tape, aired almost in its entirety on a local New Orleans television station and published in part in the free New Orleans paper *Gambit Weekly*, would have stopped Duke if it had been published early enough and in a normal election. But this was a Louisiana gubernatorial jungle primary, with all the candidates thrown together in a one-vote free for all, and most undecided voters didn't hear of it before Saturday, October 19, 1991. Those who did were incensed, for the most part, but more than eight in ten voters had already made up their minds.

Some voters were furious about the tape, however, and Beth Rickey's "betrayal" of Duke. A truck had tailgated her on the highway and seemed to be following her as she exited and made maneuvers to shake it.[48] "She had 'countless' harassment calls," the *Texas Observer* claimed. "A lot of hang-up calls at night during the 1990 Senate race, and then, during the governor's race, 'it was like all day long—it was crazy.' People followed her from her home; one night, she said, a car tried to run her off the road."[49] After that, for a week, Kenneth Stern had the American Jewish Committee pay a former policeman to provide security for her, and "things stopped."[50] On election night, she stayed home on Coliseum Street and tried to focus on the returns coming in, but she kept feeling as though someone was watching her apartment from the park across the street.

Buddy Roemer had retreated to the Governor's Mansion the previous Sunday to watch NFL games, exercise, read philosophy, and generally try not to get worked up. His complete lack of campaigning in the final week terrified his staff and core supporters, but the explanation was simple: after attacks on his marriage by Edwards and on his record by every candidate who had even *thought* of running, as well as disappointing poll numbers, Charles "Buddy" Roemer III had had about all the politicking he could take. "Last time I had the anger [on my side]," he told reporters. "Since then, I've been through eleven sessions of the Legislature. No one should have to go through what I've gone through. It changes you."[51] But voters, he knew, don't turn out for lowly, battered candidates; they didn't vote for Edwards in '87 or Michael Dukakis against George Bush in '88 after Willie Horton and other debacles. They wanted to see the electrifying ex-Nazi speak, he believed, "because he's new, he's a novelty."[52]

He knew there was a very real possibility of a humiliating or heartbreakingly close defeat. But he swore to reporters that he would stay in the fight. "Let me tell you, if Duke wins, there will be a real problem," he said. "Can you see him and the Legislature?"[53]

Roemer did, however, muster the energy for one more push in New Orleans on Friday. (It and Baton Rouge are less than ninety miles apart.) There, and in a stop back in the capitol, the politician who had won four years earlier on a message of support for chemical workers worried about jobs *and* on a promise to clean up the environment now had a bigger worry. "My greatest nightmare . . . would be having to choose between Edwin Edwards and David Duke." The *Times-Picayune* assured voters they wouldn't have to: Roemer remained the odds-on favorite, James Gill wrote, so the state didn't "have to decide whether to turn the clock back four years with Edwards, or 100 years with the other guy."[54] With a two-point edge on Edwards and ten over Duke, who should the incumbent have believed, anonymous registrants or his own lying eyes?

One thousand turned out for the David Duke Election Eve rally at the Pontchartrain Center one town over from his district, a turnout that he would match exactly twenty-four hours later, for the real party. "Roemer and Edwards are the same side of the pancake," he argued. "One side is burnt, the other is light and fluffy. It's time to throw out the pancake and get some real meat and potatoes!" Without evidence, he suggested that, with his victory the following day, Louisiana "will have so many businesspeople come to the state because business wants a policy to hire the best-qualified person . . . not by race."[55]

Edwards returned to the Hotel Monteleone and took over his customary suite, 1545, despite the fact that everyone else on the campaign had asked if they could have their victory party at another hotel this time. Perhaps something "modern." But Edwards never risked a jinx, even though the Monteleone had let him down in 1987. Unbeknownst to most, with his marriage in ashes and a new, young, New Orleans-based girlfriend, Edwards had been in his suite since August. If asked, he might hint it was all part of a winner's mentality. With no scheduled events the last week of the election—he told John Maginnis he wanted to focus on fostering relationships with black political organizations in New Orleans to boost turnout—and the campaign airplane idling at the Lakefront Airport, Edwards set up four phones on a glass coffee table, sent his ladyfriend, Candy, out shopping, and started making calls. By Election Day, he had S.O.U.L. lined up again, to counter B.O.L.D., the African American-led GOTV effort aligned with Buddy.[56]

The idea, according to *Cross to Bear*, was to not repeat Johnston's mistake of taking the black vote for granted in a race against David Duke. Not that Duke had even one percent of the black vote; rather, in this instance, they might vote for Roemer or assume Duke would finish third and instead let the two disappointing white Democrats slug it out, which wouldn't require their vote in the primary or a runoff. But at the start of Election Day, October 19, 1991, Edwards' four phones started ringing in the Monteleone: it was Ben Jeffers, at the official New Orleans headquarters on South Galvez. Jeffers, the 1979 Democratic candidate for Secretary of State, who had earned the most votes of any black person in a statewide race in Louisiana history, had a report from Treme, the historically black, traditionally Democratic, *always* Edwin Edwards neighborhood. Turnout, he said, was at seventeen percent. Worse, Jeffers and the team at S.O.U.L. had collectively driven past several precincts and could find no lines of voters anywhere.[57] To win, Edwards knew, he needed high turnout in Treme and other New Orleans neighborhoods, but the poorer the district, the worse the turnout, historically. The downtrodden, rarely receiving the help they pleaded for, had been coming through for Democrats only intermittently since Huey Long.

Edwards turned on the charm and picked up the phone. "I don't think your man Duke is going to make it," he joked to a wavering black Edwards supporter. "You'll have to be with me in the runoff."[58]

Roemer experienced similar stumbling blocks in the city's upper crust uptown neighborhood, and without it and other GOP strongholds in the state, Duke and Edwards could squeak past him. Meanwhile, reports that

Edwards, not Duke, might have the lead in Jefferson Parish, which encompassed Metairie and thus much of Duke Country, brought audible sighs of relief in Suite 1545 after a morning of setbacks.

Once the polls closed, the campaign hung up the phones and waited for poll watchers to call with results. In the long interim, they watched replays of Anita Hill's testimony in the Clarence Thomas Supreme Court nomination hearings, wondering if the hard-right Republican judge would squeak through.[59] C-SPAN had Texas Democratic congressman Chet Edwards (no relation) on to discuss the previous day's mass shooting in Killeen, Texas, in which nearly two dozen were slaughtered. As Edwin watched, Chet said that his constituents were more concerned with the victims' families than the legislation he helped pass hours later, which banned the sale of assault rifles. Congressman Edwards affirmed his support for the ban, a change in his view which he said was a direct result of the horrifying events in his home state.[60]

Duke turned out another one thousand supporters at his election watch party in Pontchartrain Center. He brought his two daughters in from Florida for the shindig, both girls sporting fall sweaters and leaning on their father as cameras blinded them. He escorted Erika and Kristin off stage to thunderous applause and ducked behind a black curtain to watch returns. Hundreds crammed around and craned their necks to see two Sharp TVs displaying WWL-TV's election results coverage, and other folks felt emboldened enough by the spirit of the proceedings to address out-of-town media.[61]

"[David Duke] is good for Louisiana," one man proclaimed. "He's trying to get the parasites off welfare."

"Duke says what I really feel," said another woman.

"All them n***s on the west side of Louisiana are gonna go to Texas" when Duke becomes governor, said another man. "This is the beginning of the end. White Protestant Anglo-Saxons are gonna rule, because we're god's people."[62]

What about his Klan affiliations and so on (and on)?

"His past is all out of the closet," one woman in a miniskirt and sequined blouse said. "You can't get any more out than he is." A moment later, she added: "Look, you'd find some stuff if you dug into Roemer's closet, and, of course, Edwards."[63]

As the returns came in, the Monteleone ballroom swelled. There was a sense that this wouldn't be a repeat of '87 for Edwards, that the old dog still had it in him. They murmured as the early numbers seemed to indicate their optimism had been misplaced. Incumbent Buddy Roemer burst out of the gate with a commanding lead, which he held onto even as precincts piled up. With 3 percent of the votes in, he led, with Edwards in fifth. His campaign shrugged off the early numbers, although they couldn't stand the suspense of waiting for New Orleans black voters to show up on the board. At 10 percent, however, Roemer maintained his lead, and at 15, Duke seemed in danger of elimination. The polls, it appeared, had been right all along—Roemer, followed by Edwards, with Duke mathematically eliminated and Holloway a non-factor. Then another set of numbers flashed over the state's televisions.[64]

Duke Country erupted; for the first time in his political career, Duke lead in a statewide or national race. With one-quarter in, Edwards vaulted into first with him. Edwards silently pumped his fist. Soon he would stretch into a comfortable lead and never really lose it. Bennett Johnston, at senator John Breaux's private watch party in DC, cracked, "Here he comes, our guy Duke."[65] Johnston and Edwards, it seemed, took an almost masochistic, gratifying pleasure in seeing the insurgent oust an entrenched enemy. They relished Duke's totals more, it seemed, than their party's or even their own victories.

"The Chinese have a saying that if you wait on the riverbank long enough, the bodies of your enemies will float by," Edwards told supporters, clearly referring to Roemer.[66]

Eighty miles from the Monteleone, at the Sheraton in Baton Rouge, the Roemer campaign settled into a collective murmur, and then, as Duke held firm in second, silence. Was Louisiana really suggesting a preference for an ex-KKK Grand Wizard? The thought broke Caroline. Her bawling across the hall, loud enough to alert Governor Roemer, who was busy watching baseball, told him he needn't reach for the remote. Governor Roemer believed in polls, convinced Caroline to trust them, had enough faith to watch baseball instead of the returns, and had been proved wrong, a brutal lesson in political reality. Edwin Edwards believed in them, too, but only up to a point; the vibe on the campaign trail mattered more, he had long since realized. And David Duke, of course, had been underestimated once again by everyone except David Duke. As Stanley Cohen had written exactly ten years earlier, "The box score is the catechism of baseball, ready to surrender its truth to the knowing eye."[67] The last box score on October 19: Edwards 34 percent, David Duke 32 percent, Buddy Roemer five points out of the running. Political analyst Warren Smith noted that there were multiple paradoxes in the election, including the fact that the candidate who beat all the other candidates in head-to-head matchups had lost.[68]

Four years earlier, Roemer's campaign slogan had been "This Time Louisiana Wins." In 1991, it could have been "This Time It Might Lose."

CHAPTER 11

The Wizards

"Could it really happen?" asked the *Christian Science Monitor*. "Could David Duke, a former imperial wizard of the Ku Klux Klan, be on the verge of winning the governorship of Louisiana? Political analysts, speaking anonymously, say they now expect Duke to win the Nov. 16 contest, although narrowly."[1]

The *New York Times* agreed, saying few pundits had the guts "to underestimate Mr. Duke, who has made a career of defying predictions."[2] Democratic pollster Geoffrey Garin called the race "very close" and echoed the toss-up prediction of other insiders. "People who don't take the possibility of a Duke victory seriously ought to think again," he said.[3] The *Monitor* suggested a Duke victory would be damaging for American race relations and taint the Republican Party nationally one year from a tough reelection campaign for its leader.[4] A Duke victory seemed impossible to believe, but people were finally waking up to it. And while more than half of Louisianans said they would never support Duke, pollsters had already admitted their models could not predict the "secret Duke vote," which could include adults who pretended to hate the Republican to maintain social graces.

Wayne Parent, LSU political science professor, visited New Orleans the day after the primary for a Saints game. Meeting up with a friend with the tickets, Parent noticed a strange hush over the city. Parent struggled to explain to his friend, who had just moved to Louisiana, why Edwards was going to be in the runoff but not Roemer. "I was thinking there was no way, it just seemed so unimaginable" that it wouldn't be those two candidates. But in the week after the primary, having taken the measure of the state's political winds, Parent said, "there was a sense that Duke could win. The tides were [turning]. It was such a strong perception that I just assumed everyone thought this."[5]

"So disliked is Edwards today," the *Monitor* noted, "that Duke leads him among white voters by a 58 to 25 percent margin, according to Mason-Dixon. His unfavorable rating among whites is 62 percent. That puts the heat back on [President] Bush. Perhaps the only way the prevent Duke's election would be for Bush to throw his arms around Edwards, a gesture no Republican would relish."[6]

The president said, "I could not possibly support David Duke because of the racism and because of the very recent statements that are very troubling in terms of bigotry." When asked if he would endorse Edwards, however, Bush nearly fled the White House briefing room. "I'm not going to inject myself in here," he stammered, "except to say that we can never in any way support David Duke. . . . please don't try to draw me into a runoff in that state."[7]

Mary Matalin, heading up the Republican National Committee staff, though, spoke frankly with the *Times* that Sunday. There was no way in hell, she suggested, Duke would get financial or structural support from the GOP. "We never considered him a Republican," she said. "There will be no involvement in his campaign whatsoever."[8]

Most Roemer campaign workers were livid, though, but not with the Republican from the KKK. They relished the chance to crush Edwards for running for a record fourth term despite his past, unpunished crimes. Now, for the same reason Edwards had run, Roemer's people would run against *him*: vengeance. One staffer, Michelle Schauer, had been a fundraiser for Buddy Roemer in the primary, and when forced to choose between the Dragon and the Wizard, she realized the Dragon and his liberal values repelled her significantly more.[9]

Howie Farrell, Duke's campaign manager, lured her in, promising focused work alongside him and the candidate. "I spent fourteen years in the Republican Party," Farrell assured her. "I know what you're going through. We need people from the establishment who know how to do things like run phone banks."[10]

Phone banking she could do and better than anyone. After toughing it out when Republicans and Democrats alike hung up on her calls from the Roemer campaign office in New Orleans, Schauer thought she had prepared herself for working under Duke. But an in-person conversation with a member of the Republican candidate's base gave her serious pause. He told her he wanted to set in motion plans to make better use of the Louisiana Superdome. "He goes, well, we're going to figure out how to get all the black people—and of course, he didn't use the word 'black people'—into the Superdome. And then we're gonna blow it up. And I just looked at him like, 'are you crazy?' And he was not crazy. He was serious. And talking about it like this was something that he could accomplish. And I just remember sort of turning around and going, wow." She was in it now.[11]

Elsewhere, the far-right tide had begun to sweep Republicans into office in places they hadn't been viable in decades—or centuries. Mississippi had just elected its first Republican governor since Reconstruction on a platform attacking racial quotas and welfare queens.[12] And as the country gradually realized a former Klansman might become governor of a US state, the media, voters, and political insiders turned their guns not on him but on Edwin Washington Edwards. What in the hell, they wanted to know, had Fast Eddie been thinking pushing Louisiana this close to the precipice? In one interview, Edwards claimed he did not try to put Duke in the runoff with him, specifically. "I didn't do that because I didn't think it was necessary and I would've maybe got caught," he said. "I just let him run his race. I ran mine."[13] However, he admitted it "sure was" disappointing not to be able to go head to head with Roemer the dragonslayer, if for nothing else, "to show how he had misrepresented his real philosophy." Quin Hillyer said that Edwards helping Holloway drag Roemer down was "completely without regard to the morality of trying to help David get into the runoff and whether or not that would be good or bad for the state of Louisiana. It certainly was playing every political angle, and it was Edwin Edwards and his people" who tacitly arranged it.[14]

"Just one screw-up, one sleazy friend to get indicted, one more grand jury investigation that sticks, would really turn people against him," said Maginnis.[15]

Duke, in a front-page *New York Times* piece, ignored these self-defeatist arguments and made his case for Roemer diehards—convincingly, at that. "The rank-and-file Republicans of this state voted for me, and the rank-and-file Republicans in this country believe the way I believe," he said. "I think I offer a tremendous opportunity for the Republican Party. I am the first Republican candidate that actually bridges the gap between fiscal conservatives and labor."[16] He needed to make nice with *all* Republicans, however. Sixty-three percent of Louisianans had voted GOP in the primary, a staggering number for the state, but with the incumbent Republican gove rnor and official Republican nominee both eliminated, they were up for grabs.

He slammed Bush and Roemer throughout the primary and, after the Bush fundraiser, wisely foresaw that Bush's support could actually backfire on Roemer with working class people, especially union Democrats. Duke called it the "turning point" in the race, when Roemer "got a lot of money but he lost a lot of votes." The governor, in his estimation, "realized too late I would win. He made the classic mistake of preparing for the old foe instead of the young foe."[17]

Wealthy or otherwise politically engaged Jewish people may, like African Americans, have underestimated the young Republican's chances of making the runoff, as well, but they were among the first to head straight for Edwin Edwards and pledge unlimited support. Hippo Katz, who had plenty of fundraising experience under his belt, had already been aboard the Edwards train, but watching the returns come in at the Monteleone, he immediately gathered campaign staff, fellow Jews, horrified LCARN volunteers, and everyone within earshot. "We need to do a commercial with taxi drivers and working people. The message is economics," he said. "You may like [Duke] but can you afford him?" Riled up, Katz rubbed his hands together furiously. "David Duke thinks he hate Jews now," he told John Maginnis. "Wait till we're through with him."[18]

Louisianans were fired up about the runoff, so much so that when the registrar of voters opened Monday morning, most parishes had a line around the block. "We've never seen anything like it," said the Commissioner of Elections. "Everyone wants to be able to vote in this election."[19] The Edwards campaign rejoiced, although their celebration turned out to be presumptuous. When local news stations ran footage of predominantly black Southern University students lined up to register, whites hightailed it to the Board of Elections in their towns. Ultimately, less than half of the sixty-seven thousand new registrants (in the first forty-eight hours) were black.[20] The race, it seemed, would stay hotly competitive.

The Louisiana Coalition battled over what to do about Duke in the runoff. If they were going to try something, though, it was now (at what seemed to be his peak) or never (if he got elected, it would make him almost invincible). No one at LCARN thought to ask Roemer's campaign strategist Ray Strother how to stop Duke. "The economic issue," he told an Edwards staffer, "is the only thing that works."[21] The plan LCARN decided on was to run two types of ads: one a series of print ads on Duke's "racist" past, another a hard-hitting television spot on the Nazi connections. "The full cost of the campaign is $550,000," Powell and Hill determined, "$150,000 is needed immediately in order to run the television spot statewide for the two weeks preceeding the election."[22] With wealthy interests financing the ads, hundreds of thousands of people saw a thirty-second spot that concluded "Vote for Duke, Create a Fuhrer." It also alerted "undesirables" to the existence of the Louisiana Coalition Against Racism and Nazism.[23]

Savannah, Georgia, respondent A. C. "Sparkplug" Jones wrote a letter addressed "To Race mixers" and said he had been forwarded LCARN's "appeal for money to promote race mixing and to oppose Biblical teaching of racial separation." After saying he had enclosed forty dollars, he wondered "how many darkies you can get to take a bath on Saturday night with this $40.00. Failing that, please let me know how much socialism you can promote with this money." He then explained that it was all a lie and that he really sent a check in that amount to the Duke campaign.[24]

The Coalition's pleas for money often came back defaced with racist edits. The line "I want to eliminate racism and Nazism from Louisiana" sometimes returned with an added, handwritten "don't" between "I" and "want." "Thank you for your letter white boy," one said.[25] Others were more impolite.

"There is one thing I hate even more than Blacks and Jews . . ." and on the other side of the page: ". . . it's shit like the Louisiana Coalition. David Duke has 10 more votes since I received your crap in the mail. Go Duke!!"[26]

"You fucking n*** assholes!" a handwritten, all-caps, anonymous letter to LACRN's New Orleans headquarters read. "If someone kills David Duke I will personally kill every n*** in this shit state!!! Duke has changed!!! I have changed —a girlfriend I had used to piss on me. Now we are not together and I piss on girls now. I've changed. Jesse Jackson used to spit in white people's food and was a member of the Black Panthers. He's changed. You all just can't leave it alone!!!"

"Apparently you and every other freeloading black is scared that your FREE govt. and society handouts may come to an end when Mr. Duke is elected Governor—I'll certainly vote for him to help end the real racism and discrimination in this state and nation. The Honorable Judge Clarence Thomas is also against the so-called 'minorities' (freeloaders is a better word) who want govt. and society to give everything FREE."

"Tell your racist blacks who hate whites to stand up for themselves intelligently and not by riots, boycotts and crying to already weakened govt. system for more handouts and welfare!"

"The Jews crucified Jesus, and he forgave them . . . the Jews are crucifying David Duke."

"Your organization is despicable," someone wrote across the back of a reply envelope. "Because it hides behind a name to attack one human being!

Shame on you Rev. Stovall for spreading unforgiveness [*sic*] and hatred of another human being. Who made you the judge and jury against others?"

"What did your minister do about fornication adultery too [*sic*] many fatherless children . . . what about dope in welfare residences."

"May it be God's Will for people of Louisiana to wake up and VOTE RIGTH [*sic*]. You know, you go around + ask as i did and you too will be shocked to see how many blacks are tired too of the WELFARE ABUSERS. As for Duke, he was doing something silly in his younger days, something he believed in as you believe in your cause which could mean you are a racist."

"I'm for racism and anti-Semitism. That's my right. What are you going to do about that?"[27]

Letters like these put pressure on the group to hit Duke on racist inclinations and past statements rather than rehash the economic implications of a Duke governorship. Tim Wise recalled years later, "One particular faction felt one way, one another. One, the old-line liberals and Lefties: Lance, progressives like Larry, Reverend Stovall, who was a liberal minister, wanted to make Nazism and racism the issue, make his extremism the issue. Another group, mostly Republicans, New Orleans business owners, were very nervous about making racism the main issue, as they didn't disagree with much of his platform."[28]

"We're strongly committed to removing Duke from office," LCARN announced. "However, we refuse to accomplish this through attacks on Duke's personal life. We leave this to the sleaze-wizards of the major parties."[29]

As the campus coordinator for LCARN, Wise had to serve hors d'oeuvres in uptown New Orleans for the group's fundraisers. The neighborhood, originally part of Jefferson Parish, had been the home base for many free black people prior to the Civil War and had a deep connection to anti-slavery and progressive causes. Wise, however, soon discovered his hosts weren't the liberals he'd imagined. "I was at a New Orleans 'money people' house party, walking around with plate of lemon squares" and saw the walls lined with images of the hosts posing with a beaming vice president Dan Quayle and far-right senator Jesse Helms at the 1988 Republican National Convention. "I was thinking: 'Oh my God, where am I?'"[30] It dawned on Wise that David Duke was destroying the GOP brand, and these people were making an investment in the future of the party by stopping a virus from spreading within it. Wise recognized that, although Rickey was on that same plank, her main goal was always to defeat Duke; saving the Republican Party was a secondary consideration.

Also tied for distant second in Rickey's and LCARN's hive mind: Edwin Edwards. Her goal was, as always, not to *elect* anyone but to defeat Duke. "We all preferred Edwards except Beth, who preferred Roemer, but we referred to ourselves as a campaign without a candidate," Wise said. Rickey had had time to plan for a Duke-Edwards showdown, having agreed that the political winds were slapping Roemer in the face over his party switch and pro-abortion stance. Even with Buddy out, Wise concluded, "you had the Duke Republicans in the northern part of the state, in St. Bernard and the other parishes adjoining New Orleans."[31] Duke was in a great position to win, which meant that to defeat him, Rickey needed to swallow her partisan pride, put the geriatric Democrat in a wheelbarrow, and shove him over the finish line. But she refused.

Rickey subsequently stayed out of the spotlight for much of 1991, signing her diary, "I remain, yours from the Twilight Zone."[32] She fed material to LCARN members and fielded calls from reporters or groups asking her to speak about discrimination but generally let Stovall take the lead. Other LCARN members, including Mitch Landrieu, took her research and incorporated it into their own stump speeches.[33]

But even on the sidelines, Rickey proved instrumental in the campaign. The summer 1991 strategy guide Hill produced included Rickey's ideas to call WWL NewsTalk Radio and comment on-air and to write letters to newspaper editors disseminating Duke's damaging interviews on Nazism, which Rickey had uncovered, and, if they felt they *had* to, absolutely *must* do so, they might mention Edwards was the lesser of two evils. "Keep Edwin Edwards informed of what we do," Hill and Rickey told their membership. "Encourage him to seriously address the concerns of individuals who are worried about his past."[34]

Buddy Roemer had serious reservations, as well. While Edwards drove at high speed between campaign events to woo 145,000 ex-Roemer supporters before Duke could snatch them up, the sitting governor remained silent on the race. It could've been that he was licking his proverbial wounds, but Edwards didn't buy it. He later complained to reporters that he had spoken with Roemer several times: once, the sitting governor called to set up a meeting, Edwards agreed to a date and time, and then Roemer called back to postpone because he was still thinking about what he was going to do about endorsing or staying out of the race. "Finally, I go to meet with him," Edwards said. "He has a legal pad of notes. . . . He's going through all these machinations and details, like he's writing the fucking UN charter. He says he's not ready. I say, 'Okay, that's fine, do what you want to do.'"

Of course, truthfully, Edwards might have said more than that—and certainly must have been steaming after the pointless meeting. When Roemer called back that evening, claiming to have had a speech prepared, Edwards tried to get off the phone without hearing anything further.

"Buddy, I don't give a shit."

"No, I want to get it right."[35]

Roemer read Edwards the entire speech, Edwards agreed it seemed fine, perhaps even excellent, and Roemer backpedaled. He wanted to adjust and edit further before the Halloween morning press conference announcing the endorsement. When Roemer called the Hotel Monteleone once more, Edwards barely restrained himself from exploding.[36] This was a race against *Republican frontrunner* David Duke—how could Buddy Roemer *not* endorse the ex-Klansman's opponent? And how could he think anything but an unqualified endorsement would help? Finally, the governor alerted the media.

"I have sat at my desk and cried at the anger, and shock and shame," said Governor Roemer, the press riveted to every word. "I cannot, will not, must not vote for David Duke. It would be suicide for Louisiana. And, since my choices are only two, Edwards gets my vote. He does not get my endorsement. His actions over the past eight years prevent that. [He] is at least saying the right things about integrity in his appointments and in his commitments to maintain environmental sensitivity, educational excellence and economic rebuilding.

"I could never vote for Duke—too much hate, too much hurt, too little truth, too bad for Louisiana. So I will vote for Edwards with all my fears and hopes and tears and doubts and prayers going to the polls with me. Duke has no chance to help our state. Edwards has one chance. I pray to God that he takes it."[37]

While he claimed the non-endorsement endorsement "did not matter to me by then," instead of cakewalking to victory, Edwards had to continue fighting for Roemer's voters.[38] He first concentrated on Roemer's high dollar, most visible, and wavering supporters, humbling himself before the Baton Rouge City Club, a big business organization.[39] Marion joined him for a last hurrah of polite, legal shakedowns for checks.[40] With ex-state senator Tommy Hudson as a go-between, Edwards made the rounds of dozens of sullen, mostly middle-aged white men from Buddy Roemer's 1987 booster club. Edwards set the jokes aside and listened to these people for the first time; learning of one man's mother's recent passing, Edwards let him go on for several minutes about it without moving on, and then told the young man he knew of his mother's family, expressed affection for them, and offered everyone, especially the grieving man, some kind words of condolence. The man later admitted, "Buddy Roemer would never do that."[41]

Duke was after these people, too, but he didn't quite know how to go about it. He thought rallies, which often drew in undecided or wavering voters, were the answer. He tried to keep in the spotlight day and night, even when out-of-state cameras were the only ones trailing him. It was the scattershot screams from young women that kept him jogging toward the next event. The girls, students or recent graduates in many cases, shrieked as he passed them in parades or bumped into them in crowded college bars, where he went on weekend nights to see and be seen by mobs of white people. Single women seemed to make up the bulk of his new supporters, despite or because of his plastic surgery, while the geriatric Edwards, once "the Silver Zipper," shook hands with stern-faced lawyers and young married oilfield workers.

With the race still stubbornly within the margin of error, twelve percent of voters undecided, and only a fortnight until the runoff, the election started to receive "global attention," as *New York* put it.[42] No one had been paying attention just three months earlier, when the two foes had met at the Louisiana Municipal Association Forum, and now, with two televised debates looming, the candidates, press, and public all focused on a little-noticed exchange in July.[43]

At that earlier debate, Duke had attacked the press for insinuating that his gubernatorial term would be fatal to the state's economy, but, he said, he didn't think the state's economy could do worse than it had under Buddy Roemer, with his obsession with snapping rubber bands against his wrist, or Edwin Edwards, with his womanizing, "though," Duke added, trying for a gag, "I happen to like his taste in women."[44] Instead of getting a laugh from Edwards that might have put the competitors on even footing, Edwards seized the moment to make a final stab at what would become the year's— and his— definitive soundbite.

"David Duke and I both have this much in common," he'd quipped previously, "We're both wizards under the sheets."[45] Now he repeated the catchphrase, adding: "But at sixty-four, I don't qualify for that anymore. But I'm a pretty good governor."[46]

The two met again at LSU on September 28 with the four other candidates.[47] Roemer, then a competitor, named freedom-lovin', party-switchin' Boris Yeltsin as his hero, which Duke pounced on by saying that, first and foremost, Yeltsin was a hero because he "stood up against the *establishment*."[48] Duke then named "black leader" James Meredith as his idol, for standing "up for his civil rights and the civil rights of all human beings."[49] He then pivoted to an attack on forced busing, teachers who strike and misspell words on their signs, waste and extraneous positions in state government, new taxes, toxic waste dumping, carcinogens in the water, and the welfare state under liberal governments. He was his own hero and the state needed his courage. "And I honor the man who is willing to sink half his present repute for the freedom to think. . . . Will risk t' other half for the freedom to speak."[50] The audience spontaneously applauded. Edwards named Billy Graham ("The man I nominate is like a tree planted by the rivers of water," he said, quoting from Psalm 1:3[51]) and countered Duke with wry humor about getting rid of the out-of-state residents Roemer had paid "high salaries" to balance the budget.

"Anybody could balance the budget," Duke joked, just by "getting out your credit cards. That's what Louisiana did."[52]

Then the journalists on the panel hit Duke. Karen Nachman wanted to know what Duke would do about a speculatively raped and impregnated daughter. Duke was ready for this, saying that he was pro-life and a Christian, and that he thought the state's poor needed more contraceptives to prevent unintended pregnancies. Edwards got loud but limited applause by saying he would take the daughter to another state, although it did not earn him points with evangelicals, increasingly leaning toward Duke.[53]

A reporter pointed out that Roemer had won the 1987 election and helped push "the lottery, riverboat gambling, video poker, horse racing" through—all of which were Edwards proposals rejected by legislature during his third term. If those were already on the books, what new ideas did Edwards have for closing the budget gap?

Edwards quipped, "Met a fellow the other day, told me, 'You know, *cher*, they told me four years ago if I voted for you, we'd have gambling. I voted for you and we got gambling.'"

"The only gamble I know," Duke said, "would be voting for Governor Edwards or Roemer again in Louisiana."[54]

The others, especially Duke, struggled to get zingers in and grab headlines. Mentioning that five people had been executed by the current administration, Duke mused, "The trouble is, we've had two thousand murders in that time. Until we begin to execute more than six, more innocent people are going to suffer in our state."[55] The audience exploded in cheering, and Duke basked in the glow of an audience warming to his message. He solidified his frontrunner status when the debate aired and re-aired over the next two days.[56]

Expectations were high for more wit and some fireworks in the runoff debates to at least help a few undecideds break to one candidate or another. Their first taste was an informal appearance between the two remaining candidates in front of the American Association of Retired Persons Louisiana chapter. Edwards, mistakenly assuming seniors collecting social security would be partial to the welfare state, attacked Duke for trying to take away benefits, including those for sixty-nine thousand older persons. He swore he'd "never get so big, so mighty that I won't take time to help the unfortunate.

"Can you really in good conscience think that this woman [receiving less than two hundred dollars per month in welfare] is going to sit around the table and wonder how she can get pregnant again to collect another eleven dollars a week?"

"Yes!" the AARP members roared back.

What about the fact that "only three percent of the state budget goes to all forms of public assistance?"

"That's three percent too much!" someone called out.[57]

Edwards had committed a newbie's mistake—twice—asking a crowd mixed with supporters and detractors a question he couldn't control the answer to. Duke pounced, claiming that the rate of single parenthood and a welfare system in which even "convicted criminals have central A/C and color TV" was instead to blame.

Edwards, almost stammering, tried to appeal to anti-abortionists with a line about how it wasn't "the child's fault it is born illegitimate," but when Duke snapped back—"neither is it the fault of those who must pay for it"—the audience roared. Edwards, stunned, scrambled.

"He's appealing to your base emotions," he shouted. "Who is going to be next? The disabled? The old? You better think about it."

The old folks worked themselves into a good Bronx cheer.

"The elderly who have contributed all their lives have been forgotten by a welfare system that encourages laziness, and there is no more important freedom than the freedom to live without fear," said Duke, rolling. "You have worked, sacrificed and produced all your lives while the welfare system expands because people won't work."

Edwards tried to settle down, to give off the air of the Silver Fox, totally at ease, in control, and the master of standup comedy. "I don't know why you complain about taxes so much," he said. "Until they caught you, you didn't pay yours."

With this pivot and zinger, Edwards turned the audience against Duke. The representative only made it worse by claiming he hadn't made enough money in the previous couple of years to pay income taxes.

"Let me tell you a couple of things about this fella—" Edwards started to say, but he was interrupted by a woman, loudly applauded, who demanded he not personally attack Duke.

"Man, we've got Edwards," said Jim McPherson, a Duke deputy campaign manager. "We're going to win."

Edwards tried damage control, telling an aide in earshot of the press, "In my entire career, I've helped people like these seniors by making sure their needs are met. They have no earthly idea what Duke's ulterior motives are."[58]

Of course, some of the more conservative seniors (and many other Louisianans) were licking their lips in anticipation of those ulterior motives, figuring he would throw black people off welfare, tear down the state's entire political structure, and pass an even more restrictive abortion bill, all of which they were chomping at the bit for. They packed into the first televised debate later that week, firing Duke up with their chants and applause for his every line.

Duke needed a "win" in the debate to prove his palatability, and Edwards had to come across as having momentum, which could have solidified his support from Roemer voters. But choosing any position could alienate undecideds on the Left or Right, so both men entered into the debates hoping for unforced errors from their opponent.

"Vote for Edwin Edwards," Duke said right out of the gate, "[and] you'll get more of the same: more environmental destruction, you'll get lower salaries for teachers, more crime in our streets, our schools will continue to decline. We need change."[59]

Edwards tried to seize on the teacher salary reference to hit Duke for saying he had voted for pay raises. "You're going to lose your newfound religion if you don't quit lying," Edwards deadpanned.[60]

Duke wisely avoided getting into the weeds on that topic, shifting to Edwards' pardons: "Armed robbery. Contributing to the delinquency of juveniles. Murder. Murder. Murder," Duke said. "Hundreds and hundreds of them. Some people say he sold these pardons. Maybe giving them away is worse."

"I wouldn't think he'd get so upset over some pardons," Edwards said later, unfortunately saving most of his greatest hits for the encore, when everyone had left. "After all, he got a suspended sentence when he was convicted for inciting to riot."[61]

Duke clapped back, "Edwards freed more violent criminals in this state over the past twenty years than all the other governors in this century combined in Louisiana."

Tyler Bridges called the remark "an exaggeration" but pointed out that since Duke, who spoke last, included it in his closing remarks, the statement went unchecked.[62]

Duke positioned himself to the left of Edwards on the environment and, from there, hit the Silver Fox on his "politics of neglect and ruin." Edwards, normally sharper and usually on the attack, was stuck on defense all night. Bridges also criticized the former governor for being too "tentative" in the debate, sentiments echoed by pollsters at the University of New Orleans, who claimed Duke had won the first round.[63]

After Duke won two debates in a row, a *Christian Science Monitor* poll showed that only two percent of the black vote and one in ten white voters were undecided, but Duke lead 58 to 28 percent with white voters, and a majority thought him more honest, while only 5 percent said the same of Edwards.[64] Duke grabbed headlines one more time by releasing a recording of Edwards either correcting an allegation ("It was forty-five thousand dollars," not thirty-five thousand, he accepted as a bribe, he said in the tape) or admitting to a scheme with Clyde Vidrine.[65] But it was too late in October for an October surprise and most were unpersuaded.

Edwards had just four days to prep for the final debate and rescue Louisiana from David Duke. The "master politician" read over newspaper clippings on the ex-Klansman, watched a videocassette of the previous debacle, and generally stayed off the campaign trail and the media's radar, which lead to a belief among reporters that Duke really had sapped the life out of him. Certainly most of the undecideds who had tuned into the public tête-à-tête were convinced and wouldn't need a second hourlong slugfest to make up their minds.

Duke campaigned relentlessly over those ninety-six hours. The day of the concluding debate in Baton Rouge, he started at an American Legion Hall, site of his campaign victory parties, for good luck. Unfortunately, this wasn't the Metairie location but the uptown New Orleans one, where white voters were split between the two remaining candidates. Protestors nearly blocked his way in, screaming "shithead," "Klan bastard," and "Nazi" in his face. If this did not unnerve him, traffic on the way to Baton Rouge, only an hour and half distant on most days, panicked his team.

Meanwhile, at WLPB, Beth Courtney, the head of Louisiana Public Broadcasting, awaited Duke's arrival in the parking lot. "I wonder if he'll make it,"

Courtney murmured.[66] There were under five minutes remaining until the debate went live, worldwide, with or without him. It was Duke's ultimate moment in the spotlight, his best chance to put Edwards away for good, and he was blowing it before the cameras rolled. Edwards, meanwhile, sat till the last moment in the makeup chair, silently going over his prepared statements for the opening and closing, and let his handlers make sure the aging candidate's hair and makeup were perfect before easing into his seat around the semi-circular anchor's desk.

Outside, with less than one minute to go, a black car came careening into the parking lot, screeching haphazardly across a pair of lined spaces. Paparazzi sprinted as if catching Jacqueline Onassis using the service entrance. Duke bolted from the vehicle, trailed by two slower bodyguards and the camera crews, who had to do a one-eighty to keep up with him as he bolted for the door.

Inside, the camera crew counted down to three, held silent for "two" and "one," and signaled to moderator Robert Collins: *you're live*. Duke, having seated himself five seconds before the countdown commenced, tried to brush the hair out of his face and touch up his appearance with makeup before abandoning the effort without a moment to spare. He had survived the test no one asked of him.

Without the live audience of previous debates, Duke would accordingly be without a stacked deck in his favor; no one would resoundingly applaud his canned attack lines. Then again, Edwards' unscripted wisecracks wouldn't cause Duke supporters to cackle against their will. With only four journalists blinking back, their antics would be met with stony silence.

"It's really good to be here," said Duke, without his trademark peppiness. "It's an opportunity I really need because I don't have the special interest money Edwin Edwards has. . . . I need to reach you personally, and that's what I hope to do here tonight."[67] His opening statement attacked his predecessors on letting Louisiana become "the biggest toxic waste dump" in the entire country, for letting the state slip to the bottom in national rankings on education, for rampant crime, and, of course, welfare.

Right off the bat, Edwards exhibited zip. While Duke the jetsetter traveled the nation to raise his national profile for a rumored presidential run, Edwin Edwards wanted only one thing: "to be your governor."[68]

"When he was parading around in a Nazi uniform to intimidate our citizens," Edwards claimed, "I was in a National Guard uniform bringing relief to flood and hurricane victims. When he was selling Nazi hate literature as late as 1989 in his legislative office, I was providing free textbooks for the children of this state. When he was writing porno books, I was signing anti-pornographic legislation."[69]

"Unless we reform the welfare system in our state," Duke countered, "we have no future because fewer and fewer people are pulling the economic wagon and more and more are riding in it. The people who really need help, the elderly, the veterans, are not getting the help they need. At the same time the system encourages people to have illegitimate children irresponsibly, our medical system is overloaded by all of this. Our handicapped are not getting the help they need. We've got to make some changes. We've got to have honesty in government, and we can't ever make a better government in this state, or this nation, until we begin to have clean government."[70]

Duke, accustomed to playing defense in interviews, struggled to adequately answer preliminary questions from press persons. When asked about his administration and who he would appoint to key roles in government, Duke seemed distracted and kept looking off-camera at his campaign team, whom he rattled off by name and suggested would help reduce crime.

Then questioner Norman Robinson set the state aflame.

There had been warning signs. After Robinson, a black news anchor, asked Edwards for three specific bills he would submit to the legislature in 1992, Duke had ninety seconds to muster his own answer, but instead of suggesting three bills, he attacked the ones Edwards had proposed, including "tax reform," which Duke saw as a sneaky liberal attempt to get new tax increases through. Halfway through his response time, Robinson interrupted to complain that candidate Duke was ducking the question. Duke countered by suggesting Robinson wouldn't let him get to the damn answer with his interruptions. "I'm attempting to address the issue, if you give me the chance," said Duke. "What you oppose as governor is just as important as what you propose." When Robinson started to interrupt yet again, Duke said, "He's breaking the rules, he's breaking the rules" and, feeling the debate slipping into the chaos of forums past, Collins signaled for Duke to answer without restrictions on the content of his answer. Duke went on a rant about welfare recipients hurting the middle class.

"Mr. Robinson, do you have a follow-up?" Collins wanted to know.

"That was my follow-up," Robinson said tersely.[71]

All his life, David Duke had been working to this moment, defending himself, guilting detractors into second-guessing their preconceived hunches about him. Now, with a chance to reflect or turn the discussion and campaign around, he instead owned his flaws, albeit not in the way that he had done to inspire voters in 1989. After threatening to identify specific people who received a quid pro quo arrangement from an Edwards administration, Edwards, shrugging, challenged him.

"Name them," he said. "Name 'em."

Duke, stammering, had to ask Jim McPherson to bring him the list on-camera.

Challenged on what he'd done with his life for work, Duke got defensive again and had to be pressed to name the "nonprofit organization" he'd run, which, of course, was the National Association for the Advancement of White People. He quickly moved on to discussing the campaign and comparing how well it had run against "entrenched power."

"Where did that million dollars come from?" Duke asked Edwards rhetorically, referring to Edwards' supposed admission that he had lost seven figures in Vegas. "I'll tell you where it came from," Duke went on without drawing a breath. "The people that produced and worked in Louisiana and the political connections you've had."[72]

"Fella never had a job!" Edwards exclaimed. "He has been in seven elections in eight years and won one. Heaven help us if that's the kind of efficiency he's gonna bring to state government . . . professional politicians who make a living by running for public office . . . aren't qualified to be governor!"[73]

"Mr. Duke, I have to tell you I am a very concerned citizen," interviewer Norman Robinson began, his eyes drifting down and away from the papers before him. "I am a journalist . . . and as a minority who has heard you say some very excoriating and diabolic things about minorities, about blacks, about Jews, about Hispanics, I am scared, sir. I've heard you say that Jews deserve to be in the ashbin of history. I've heard you say that horses contributed more to the building of America than blacks did." Norman Robinson appeared to struggle to form the words.

"Given that kind of past, sir," Robinson went on, undeterred, "and given that kind of diabolical, evil, vile mentality—"

"Mr. Robinson," Collins began scoldingly, his voice soft but tinged in deep concern. Later, he would say that his life flashed before his eyes.[74]

"Convince me, sir," Robinson went on, "and other minorities like me, why they should entrust their lives and the lives of their children to you?"[75]

Duke needed a moment to recover, but he had been hit with such charges before, and he thought he could handle this one, no harsher than most of the others, deftly. First, he decided to mention how Edwards had said he would use "*green* power to buy black power" in the runoff.

"I don't think there is a human being on this Earth or in this state, who hasn't been at some time intolerant in their life," Duke claimed. "And I think that's true of white people, I think that's true of black people, I think that's true of everybody at one time or another. Now, I regret some of the things I've said in my life. I have been too intolerant at times, no question about that. But that's not how I live today."[76]

Robinson's follow-up was no less incendiary. He accused Duke of "dastardly" insulting the state's minorities and demanded an apology.

"Mr. Duke, you have thirty seconds," said Collins.

"Thirty seconds?" Duke asked, snorting. "Of course I apologize for things I've said . . . I repudiate the Klan . . . and any other racist organization . . . but you don't make up for past discrimination by putting new discrimination on people with these new affirmative action plans and policies.

"Mr. Robinson," Duke said a minute later, having been repeatedly interrupted by his interlocutor. "I don't think you're really being fair with me."

"Well, I don't think you're really being honest . . . sir."

"You're not even doing the debate here, are you?" Duke shot back. "You're here to ask me questions, you're here to put me down! That's your prerogative."[77]

Edwards, content to let Duke dig his own political grave, had remained mum for several minutes, then broke his meditative silence by pointing out that members of the Klan in Iowa and other states were supposedly en route to Louisiana to stir up trouble, a.k.a., to "help their friend Mr. Duke. If they come . . . and any of them get in the way or interfere with the election process, they're going to be dealt with harshly.

"Mr. Duke has given us twenty years of hate and hurt," he said evenly. "If he's really reformed, let him go back into the community and give us twenty years of healing and help, *then* come back and ask to be governor."

After Robinson asked about the street-fighting manual for black people Duke had written under a pseudonym and Duke's record of nonpayment of taxes, Duke retorted that he didn't have enough time to answer all of those allegations properly. "That's a cheap shot on your part," he said, shaking a pen at the interviewer.

"It's your record, sir."

"I'm going to use the next couple minutes to show you the unfairness of this."[78] He spoke in his closing argument about the meeting at the Uptown New Orleans American Legion, in which he had been "spit on," and praised the supporters who would "not be intimidated" by the protestors. Reporters seemed to think this statement and the argument he had with Robinson had actually made Duke look like a victim of unfair attacks, which was part of his strategy.

As a stunned Charlie Zewe of CNN put it, "I thought Norman Robinson just elected David Duke."[79]

CHAPTER 12

"The Last Race"

"Will you promise that if elected governor, no more gambling, no more womanizing, no more cronyism?"

Meet the Press host Tim Russert was shouting at Edwin Edwards, and David Duke was smirking. But Edwin Edwards and his past were old news and he just laughed off Russert's terse attack. "I'm not a gambler," he said, cackling.[1]

Russert soon tired of Edwards and turned his focus to Duke. On the Sunday before the election, the national tide was about to turn back against the ex-Klansman.

"What was it about this country, this society, that you chose to become a Nazi? What did you find so offensive and so objectionable about the United States of America that you found Nazi Germany to be preferable?"

"All right, first off, I was never a member of a Nazi party or anything like that. My—what happened to me is, I was— . . . I'll tell you what happened to me in my life. I became frustrated. As a young man, I saw . . . our schools declining with forced integration and forced busing, which hurt them. I reject Nazism, I reject communism, I believe in less government."

"Do you still think that Adolf Hitler is the greatest genius—"

"Listen now . . ."

"Excuse me," said Russert tersely. "Do you think he's the greatest genius in the world?"

"I never said that."

"Well, you did—"

"I don't believe that. Listen, I don't believe that. I think Hitler was a disaster for the Western world."[2]

When asked the names of the three biggest manufacturers in Louisiana, Duke tried to deflect, giving a stock answer. While Duke licked his lips and looked blankly back at his pursuer, Russert pressed.

"I couldn't give you their names right off the [bat]," said Duke. "I don't have the statistics right in front of me," He turned, silently appealing to viewers who might have thought the question unfair. But Edwards later gave the correct answer: Avondale, AT&T, and General Motors.[3]

In the final days of the campaign, with the help of the press, which unanimously endorsed him in repeated local and national newspaper columns and TV editorials, Edwin Edwards closed the gap. He had the momentum, with his second debate performance, Duke's embarrassing *Meet the Press* appearance, and a pair of popular bumperstickers that turned up everywhere: "Vote for the Crook—It's Important" and "Vote for the Lizard, Not the Wizard." And he finally had George Bush, sort of. After the *New York Times* criticized the president, running for reelection, for "remaining disturbingly equivocal" on Louisiana's Republican hero, Bush called a press conference.

"When someone asserts the Holocaust never took place, then I don't believe that person ever deserves one iota of public trust," Bush told the press on November 7, with nine days remaining before the election. "When someone has so recently endorsed Nazism, it is inconceivable that someone can reasonably aspire to a leadership role in a free society."[4]

Duke scrambled to launch a new ad, in which he said, "After twelve years in office, Edwin Edwards left our state in shambles. Teachers in Louisiana had the lowest salaries in the nation. Violent criminals were pardoned by the hundreds. Welfare abuse was rampant while veterans and the elderly were neglected. I can do better, please give me a chance." He told *Good Morning America* that he believed "millions" of Republicans supported his positions. On November 16, he would find out whether enough of them lived in Louisiana to put him over "the Crook."[5]

"You are dealing with two very controversial people in this election," Edwards said in a front-page *Times* article that ran in the concluding week, referring to a poll that showed a paralyzed electorate and fourteen percent undecided. "There is a great deal of emotion and concern on both sides. So you are going to have a difficult time in advance predicting the outcome of this election."[6] Wayne Parent, a political science professor at LSU, paid close attention to the race and believed it all hinged on the business leaders of the state, as Ray Strother, Roemer's media consultant, had warned friends in the Edwards camp.

"My perception was that when businesses said they would boycott the state, everyone thought, 'This [Duke's campaign] was fun while it lasted, folks, but . . .'" Parent recalled. "The tide turned real hard. . . . Business people and Roemer voters were not crazy about Edwards. Roemer ran against populism and good ol' boy politics, but they were told, 'you're going to screw your business if Duke is the winner. You're gonna lose a lot of money.' My perception was that it was logical" for conservative Roemer voters and business leaders to slowly ebb toward Edwards.[7]

Edwards also had the Louisiana Coalition Against Racism and Nazism on his side. During an interview with WDSU, he made a damning case for Duke's unfitness using a resource packet produced by LCARN's Loyola Avenue headquarters that fall, in which the Coalition quoted Duke calling Jews "the most racist people on Earth." Even more damnably, Duke had included an insert in the same newsletter, in which he wrote, "It is painfully obvious to me that the major organized Christian churches have been converted into a deadly enemy against the white race."[8] LCARN's Lance Hill cut Duke deeply in a newspaper interview, saying, "When Duke says welfare, everyone knows he means blacks. When he says New York, everyone knows he means Jews. When he says Western values, everyone knows he means whites."[9]

Taking another page from the Coalition's behind-the-scenes mailers and the group's wealthy, often conservative board members, Edwards attacked Duke on the damage his election would cause the state's convention business, a huge tax base. After his "Unity" ad, in which he noted that a newspaper endorsement stated he had the "skills to pull various factions together" and never mentioned his opponent, he pivoted to noting that affirmative action, if outlawed in Louisiana, would cause the feds to withhold an expected $300,000,000 in grants that kept Louisiana's highways functional.

Meanwhile, it seemed only racists were willing to admit to supporting Duke. We "think like he [Duke] does," a boat captain told a reporter. "I like it down here, man. . . . No n***s, baby," he said. "No n***s down here."[10]

"No person in Louisiana thought four years ago, or two years ago, or even six months ago, I would ever have the opportunity again given me to leave a legacy and leave a good record," Edwards told attendees of a fundraiser in Lake Charles. "I can't tell you how important this is to Edwin Edwards. I'm not going to miss this opportunity."[11]

When the *New York Times* asked him what he wanted people to remember about him, Edwards responded, simply, "He had his last best chance and he used it."[12] Edwin Edwards had been saving his "best chance," a coup de grace, and he employed it at the right moment.

The Silver Fox's famous line, repeated in almost every newspaper article or television story in the days that followed (and for the rest of Edwards' career) and picked up on by undecided voters, served as the true "closing statement" of his career and, in a way, for that of David Duke's. He'd been testing it out since the debates before the primary, and he had now fine-tuned it to the punchline that would serve as his calling card.

"The only place," he said, "where David Duke and I are alike is we are both wizards under the sheets."[13]

If that weren't enough to appear confident in victory—often itself a way to eke out a win—when asked what else he still needed to do to triumph, the sixty-four-year-old said simply, "Stay alive."[14]

After three dozen years in politics, it all came down to this. Losing now would cement his disastrous, tainted legacy; for Duke, defeat would mean something worse than the fate of Buddy Roemer. A failure, to be sure, but one that would mean he never truly "made it" in the first place. The week of the election, campaigning in Shreveport, Duke opened a fortune cookie from a Chinese restaurant, and the slip of paper said, "Your past success will be overshadowed by your future success."[15] If ever David Duke wanted to believe in an omen from "the Orient," he believed in that one. Edwards, meanwhile, sarcastically wondered if Duke had enough lung capacity to go the distance in the closing week "because he's around so many burning crosses."[16]

Edwards himself sat in his van throughout the Crowley Rice Festival Parade, one of the campaign's final events, no longer the go-getter of twenty years before, while Duke pointed out the dour faces of Edwards staffers to reporters. "The most famous statewide candidate in the world," sold "More Duke" stickers and sent his hype man ahead to whip up white people along the parade route before his red convertible reached them. (Maginnis reported seeing the hype man bypassing a mostly black high school cheerleading squad without trying to get them excited about Duke.)[17] As in Edwards's first campaign for governor, snipers were perched on two-story buildings, looking for gun-toting racists. As in 1971, the polls were tight and both candidates had about the same level of name recognition statewide, drawing about three thousand supporters at each of their election week rallies. "On Saturday," Duke claimed, "the 'silent majority' is not going to be silent any longer."[18]

"I can't think of a state-level race that's had this level of discussion," UCLA professor Joel Aberbach said.[19] He and most others still expected an Edwards win, albeit a narrow one, factoring in major underselling for the Republican. "A lot of people represent Duke as being supported by tooth-less bigots," a New Orleans pharmacist told the *New York Times*. "They don't want to accept the fact that there are many intellectuals out there—doctors and lawyers—who are supporting him." A Metairie businessman suggested a secret bloc vote surging toward Duke: "David Duke is expressing a lot of hidden views of people around the state—their fears of being displaced and of losing jobs. Why would you be concerned about his views toward Jews and blacks? He's not going to do anything about Jews and blacks."[20]

Edwards would say of Duke that "people did not share his policy about race" and that it ultimately badly damaged the Republican.[21] LCARN board members, including Larry Powell and Quin Hillyer, thought the ads, state-ments, and editorials referencing or starring the state's business gurus kept Duke from pulling ahead.[22] Others still pointed to several small but highly publicized blows the week of the election. Bryan Adams, whose recent num-ber one single served as Duke's rally anthem, requested that stations stop playing "(Everything I Do) I Do It for You" until Duke's defeat.[23] Then Duke made a truly crucial mistake.

He'd been asked about his religious leanings before. When pressed in the first one-on-one debate with Edwards, he had flippantly named the Evangel-ical Baptist Church as his spiritual home, and interest in this line of ques-tioning petered out. But then the *New York Times* looked into his statements.

"New doubts were cast today on the assertion by State Representative David Duke that he shed his racist and anti-Semitic beliefs as a result of a Christian conversion," wrote the *Times* in a section A story five days before the election. "Mr. Duke said he attended the 'Evangelical Baptist Church,' but there is no such church in the New Orleans area. Last week he admit-ted that he did not belong to a specific church but said he participated in an informal Bible study group that meets in its members' homes."[24]

With business leaders lining up to appear in Edwards ads on one side and the religious Right bailing on the Republican or even running anti-Duke spots of their own on the other, Fast Eddie suddenly found himself the most popular Democrat in America. "Edwin Edwards vs. David Duke is the choice of our lives," the *Times-Picayune* intoned in its Election Day edi-tion. "For those who are tempted to sit this one out in disgust or compla-cency, we repeat: Edwin Edwards, our flawed former governor, is the only alternative to David Duke."[25]

They weren't—sitting it out, that is. The Edwards campaign, based out of New Orleans, spit out dozens of paid Election Day workers and volunteers, fanning them out across New Orleans and other strongholds, and sent buses to all sixty-four parishes with paid drivers and team members to get voters to polling sites. With $337,000 in get-out-the-vote expenses and salaries for the final month alone, Edwards for Governor far surpassed the Duke operation, based in the candidate's Metairie basement, which oversaw seven statewide offices but little in the way of unified GOTV operations.[26] Edwards went for the black vote and persuadable upper or middle-class white voters worried about the economy; Duke went after the substantial white majority, especially working white people who were already *dealing* with the economy.

Rarely in US history had so many people come together from so many disparate groups and demographics to *stop* a candidate, but on November 16, 1991, they rallied not *for* Edwin Edwards but to stonewall Duke's progression to power. They had seem him on *Nightline*, *Donahue*, *Good Morning America*, *Morton Downey*, and *Meet the Press*, and while Duke raised a sustaining amount of money through thousands of small contributions through the mail, Edwards benefitted decisively from negative reaction to these Duke appearances, to the tune of thousand-dollar checks instead of ten-dollar bills. Dustin Hoffman and other Hollywood A-listers wrote sizable checks to the Edwards campaign. The CEO of Time Warner, one of the country's most powerful corporations, asked Edwards what he needed to stem the tide. LCARN itself raised "millions" in the final two weeks of the campaign.[27]

On election night, Beth Rickey brought Quin Hillyer, Lance Hill, Larry Powell, and other LCARN mainstays to her apartment on Coliseum Street to watch the returns.[28] Everyone cracked open beers or poured red wine and chatted about what they had seen when they had stepped away from the office to vote earlier in the day. They sank into Rickey's handful of stiff chairs, guzzled their wine, and tried to think of other things to talk about while they waited for the polls to close.

A few miles away, Edwin Edwards moseyed into the Hotel Monteleone for the last hurrah. The ballroom was jammed, a far cry from 1987 or even this year's primary. Police officers eyed the mobs warily, concerned about reports that TV stations that had endorsed Edwards were inundated with death threats; worried cops noted that a single bullet would automatically make Duke governor-elect, kicking off unimaginable rioting. A few miles still further, on Cypress Street, Duke staffers weighed whether to clear out the team over for a bomb threat, while outside his Baton Rouge rally, a giddy Duke heard reports of a heavy, possibly record-tying turnout, and felt that the numbers would likely "help my race," he said, adding prophetically, "Unless they show me twenty-five points behind, we're gonna win."[29]

There were lines down the block of each New Orleans precinct before polls opened after sunrise. Eight out of every ten black Louisianans voted that day. The Louisiana Voter Registration/Education Crusade, which had signed up staggering numbers of new voters, particularly black New Orleanians, had done its job, and so had the bus drivers and Edwards staffers in the Hotel Monteleone and Galvez Street storefront campaign office.[30] Edwards, seeing the numbers, felt even more confident in the bet he'd made earlier: a 60/40 vote split in his favor.

A close reading of exit poll numbers showed an even worse situation for Duke. Ninety-four percent of those surveyed had claimed business and job losses were a major factor in their decision, although there was a smidgen of hope for Duke: 60 percent said they hated Edwin Edwards, including many who voted for him.[31] Duke, meanwhile, was pulling a majority of the white vote. "I think it's beautiful that the white people stuck together on this one like the n***s did," said a Metairie bar owner. "I can't wait for Duke to win. I just can't wait." It seemed the final outcome would come down to turnout in northern Louisiana.[32]

When the polls closed at eight p.m., the national networks cut to coverage of the gubernatorial runoff that the *Times* had called the most closely watched local race in history. Bob Schieffer of *CBS Evening News* was still on the air at nine o'clock eastern time with a special report on the "election day showdown."[33] At the same moment, CSPAN started its election night coverage from Louisiana with a feed from WDSU featuring local anchors Lynn Ganser and Norman Robinson. "We'll know in a few hours," an announcer said in a prerecorded message.[34] Seconds later, however, the result from a seventy-one-precinct, forty-one-thousand-voter exit poll flashed across the screen.[35]

"NBC News Exit Poll Projects: Edwin Edwards."[36]

The Hotel Monteleone erupted—a deafening roar shook the ballroom. Bars in Metairie went dead silent. A cry of horror collectively rang out at Pontchartrain Center, where another thousand had turned out to replicate David Duke's stunning primary night party. Jim Cummins of NBC News made a projection: "Lynn and Norman, based on exit polls at NBC News and the other three networks have been taking all day," said Cummins, breaking into the broadcast, "we project that Edwin Edwards is going to be the winner of this election . . . one of the most hotly contested gubernatorial races I've ever seen."[37]

David Duke, politicking in Baton Rouge until the moments the polls closed, disputed the report. "Well . . . they haven't really been able to poll me . . . I think we're going to do really well tonight."[38] Edwards, however, told the press, "You can definitely call me governor."[39] With only 1 percent of the vote in, Edwards led by six points and would never fall behind. His prediction—and bet with campaign manager Bob D'Hemecourt—proved accurate. Edwards won about 61 percent of the vote to Duke's 39.

Dave Dixon, the "man who built the Louisiana Superdome," couldn't stop grinning. "I think it's one of the great events in the history of this state and a marvelous thing for the United States of America," he said. "It shows that hatred and bias will not be tolerated." He added that he helped Edwards for three reasons: the possibility of economic devastation should Duke have won, possible boycotts of and recruiting problems in LSU sports programs, and Duke's "fifty-years-out-of-date" hatred.[40] SOUL founder and state rep. Sherman Copelin also addressed cameras at the Monteleone: "I am very enthused about the turnout, especially in the black community," he said, and called out a high rise building with an estimated 98 percent turnout. "We have blacks and whites, rich and poor, and everybody coming together in New Orleans and throughout Louisiana. I just hope we can keep this coalition together, because it's simply good for Louisiana."[41]

The data backed up his assertions about a broad coalition. Edwards not only won almost all of the New Orleans black vote, he had triumphed among Duke's Jefferson Parish neighbors *and* Republicans, winning half of each. He had also captured more than three-quarters of Roemer's primary voters, perhaps the key metric.

At Rickey's place, "there was this little band of people who had been in this fight against Duke," Hillyer reflected. "It was a very little apartment, everyone sat around in a semi-circle, and it became apparent very early that Edwards had won. I can remember we all looked at each other with smiles on our faces. It was this sense of satisfied relief rather than elation: 'thank God it's over.' There was something poignant about it, as the only connection we had was Beth. There were very different political viewpoints in the room and, although a lot of other people did work in making sure he lost, the small original cadre was here." The coalition's collective "sense that somehow, decency would prevail" through almost three years of crushing disappointments and near-misses finally paid off.

"I can remember Beth had a sort of wry smile on her face," Hillyer said, "as if she was saying, 'Okay, we think we've won, but is there another shoe about to drop?'"[42]

"Duke lost because, as in the [2020] election, black voters saved us from catastrophe," recalled Kenneth Stern. "One of the things that still perplexes me is that he lost statewide because of the black vote, but he could've become a member of Congress" but decided not to run.[43] Certainly, Duke could have run for the House of Representatives in 1992 from a heavily white district and been the frontrunner, but he strangely demurred.

In the early nineties, political analyst James Brady noted, "Republicans are beginning to say . . . 'We're gonna start getting creamed with all the candidates coming in from the far right.'"[44] In 1992, the *Texas Observer* interviewed Rickey about Duke and the national Republican Party. "I think we need to do some serious soul-searching," she told the interviewer. The paper said that "although she believes there is hope that the GOP's national leadership can regain control over the monster," it quickly became apparent they would not, when Duke almost immediately announced a run for president in 1992.[45] "Perhaps the messenger was rejected" in the governor's race, Duke had said, but "the people believe in what I believe. The polls all show that."[46]

Before that information settled in, far-right Republican Pat Buchanan announced he, too, would compete in the Republican primaries.[47]

In his official announcement, Buchanan attacked his party's incumbent, George H. W. Bush, on foreign aid, globalism, elitism, and tax hikes. He claimed that his movement starkly contrasted with the mainstream GOP. Bush, Buchanan said, "is a globalist, and we are nationalists. He believes in some *pax universalis*; we believe in the old republic. He would put America's wealth and power at the service of some vague new world order; we will put America first."[48]

"America First" was also the theme of David Duke's presidential campaign, which included attacks on Free Trade programs, foreign aid, and taxes. Having already warned everyone that "my star is still rising," Duke added, "My politics are coming in America."[49] They were, although not in the personage of David Duke. "The similarities between the two men's views have not gone unnoticed on the Far Right. In obscure racist and anti-Semitic journals and in interviews, many of those usually thought to be outside the standard electoral system voice support for Mr. Buchanan."[50] Pat Buchanan lifted nearly every plank from Duke's gubernatorial run and used it to hammer Bush throughout the fall and winter, leading to an endorsement from

Billy Nungesser and Buchanan earning a stunning 38 percent in the first-in-the-nation primary in New Hampshire.

"When you look at political movements," said Kenneth Stern, "people on the extremes, in this case, the Right, make it so that the centrists feel obliged to adopt some of that hateful rhetoric to keep their political chances alive. That was partly Duke's contribution—mainstreaming that white nationalist view of the world for more capable politicians to articulate."[51]

While Buchanan ultimately earned merely 23 percent of the primary vote, each percentage served as another repudiation of the "liberal" Republican president who led America triumphantly into the Persian Gulf War. David Duke, however, ended the race with the most embarrassing total of all three, garnering less than one percent of the total Republican primary vote. "Critics and organizations who follow far-right groups say Mr. Buchanan, who has stolen the conservative thunder from the former Klansman David Duke, has done nothing to repudiate his most extreme admirers or to distance himself from Mr. Duke,"[52] said the *New York Times*. "What Buchanan has catalyzed is a racist movement, whether or not he is personally anti-Semitic," said Leonard Zeskind of the Center for Democratic Renewal. "I expect it to produce . . . an extremist, conservative movement, in which race, ethnicity, nativism, nationalism, play a greater role than the anti-communism of the past."[53] David Duke became the ultimo candidate, last month's news, non-viable locally, a pariah nationally.

After a decade of victories, including Duke's 1989 local run, but also a string of setbacks, murder, and mayhem, observers believed the KKK itself would soon achieve legitimate national power. Instead, in 1992, the Klan declared "war on the government."[54] During a Klan march that year in Janesville, Wisconsin, Klansmen and neo-Nazis "carried clubs, ball bats, pipes and metal poles wrapped with wire and chains, sticks, boards, tire irons and spike shields . . . wore Klan sheets and hoods, swastikas, combat fatigues and boots, gray shirts with military insignia, berets, ball caps with racist logos, and black bandit masks, fishnet stockings and ski masks over their faces."[55] After a neo-Nazi allegedly shoved Jewish TV host Geraldo Rivera, Rivera returned punches and both men were arrested. T-shirts featuring Confederate and Klan founder Nathan Bedford Forrest outsold ones starring Robert E. Lee.[56]

Thirteen alleged white separatists were charged with seditious conspiracy in federal courts after dozens of gallons of cyanide were found before they could be dumped into a water source; the same white supremacists arrested in the case were tied or rumored to have been connected to the

Alan Berg slaying. "Witnesses described how separatist compounds man-ufactured their own Claymore-style land mines and trained in urban war-fare," the *Times* wrote, but after some questionable remarks from the jury, including from a juror who said the Bible prohibited race mixing, the accused were acquitted.[57]

After the Feds' disastrous attempt to storm a reported cult compound in Waco, Texas, in 1993, white power advocates plotted revenge, eventu-ally carrying out the Oklahoma City bombing that killed 168 people at the Alfred P. Murrah Federal Building two years later. The primary culprit had been inspired to join the white power movement, shave his head, and attack Jews and the Federal government after reading William Pierce's *The Turner Diaries*, the book Beth Rickey purchased in David Duke's basement. Shortly before the perpetrator's execution, Pierce publicly praised his prin-ciples; in the thirteen years following those comments, Pierce's neo-Nazi group, the National Alliance, doubled its membership to two thousand.[58]

The year of Bill Clinton's reelection, 1996, was particularly brutal. At the Atlanta Olympics, an anti-abortion, anti-gay terrorist aligned with the white supremacy movement set off a bomb that caused two deaths and injured more than one hundred.[59] A fire nearly destroyed a church in Knoxville, Tennessee; later, explosives were discovered in the sanctuary, where racist messages had defaced furniture. Four black Baptist churches were burned down within a six-mile radius near Baton Rouge.[60] In 1999, white separat-ists were responsible for a series of arsons that targeted Jewish temples in California and for the Los Angeles Jewish Community Center shooting that left five people wounded.[61] A twenty-one-year-old Illinois man, possi-bly inspired by the Racial Holy War movement discussed on white suprem-acist websites, murdered Ricky Byrdsong, who had been Northwestern University's first black basketball coach, and a Korean grad student, both apparently at random. The killer had previously told a documentary crew that, if the authorities kept trying to prevent him from passing out right-wing literature, he would "have no choice but to resort to acts of violence and really to plunge this country into a terrorist war they've never seen before."[62] The culprit committed suicide on Independence Day as police rushed his getaway car.[63]

On April 28, 2000, barely a year after the Columbine Massacre, an anti-Semitic serial killer targeted his Jewish neighbors, local synagogues, Indian grocery stores, and African Americans in a one-day rampage, murdering five.[64] Later, investigators discovered that his website advocated for "an end to non-white immigration."[65] Such racially motivated attacks spiked after

Middle Eastern terrorists—dubbed "very brave people" by the American Nazi Party chairman—attacked New York and Washington, DC, on September 11, 2001.[66] As the organization South Asian Americans Leading Together noted: "Since September 11th, South Asian, Sikh, Muslim, and Arab Americans have been the targets of numerous hate crimes, as well as employment discrimination, bullying, harassment, and profiling. In addition, places of worship have been vandalized and attacked, including the tragic shooting of the Sikh gurdwara in Oak Creek, Wisconsin, and the numerous alleged hate crimes in the Muslim community that followed."[67]

But nothing seemed to inspire the Klan and its fellow travelers like the election of the country's first black president. From 2008 to 2016, the years encompassing Barack Obama's two terms, the amount of racial violence surged yet again.[68] On May 8, 2009, just three months after Obama assumed office, a member of Alabama's International Keystone Knights of the Ku Klux Klan was arrested after burning a cross outside a black housing development. The KKK, the Equal Justice Initiative suggested, "targeted the neighborhood because of the race of its residents."[69] No one has been able to solve the supposed "accidental drowning" of Jason Smith, a black teenager who died in Eros, Louisiana, on a school day in 2014; the story never made any major news outlets and was subject to internet rumor in which family members and friends of the deceased speculated he had been lynched by the KKK for unknown reasons.[70] That year, Robert Jones, Imperial Wizard of the Loyal White Knights of the Ku Klux Klan, appeared in his Klan robe on Middle Eastern TV network Al-Jazeera and called Obama a sellout on immigration, suggesting that the way to stop illegal immigrants would be to "leave their corpses" at the border. "An estimated two million plus illegal aliens entered the United States this year," he wrote in the 1980s. "With these Hispanic aliens' high birthrate—three times as high as whites—they are adding to the already bad problem of the nonwhite population explosion in America. Create a narrow no-man's land on our southern border. Shoot interlopers if necessary and establish army bases all along the border and use soldiers to help patrol the border if the above measures don't meet with enough success."[71]

The following year, another twenty-one-year-old white neo-Nazi gunned down nine black people, including the pastor, a state senator, in the aisle and pews of South Carolina's Emanuel African Methodist Episcopal Church. After his arrest, investigators unearthed a manifesto with photos of the shooter posing with the Confederate flag. He claimed to have been inspired by the Trayvon Martin killing and right-wing propaganda outlets like the

Council of Conservatives, which pushed the narrative of a media coverup of "black-on-white" murders.[72] An even larger massacre in 2019 ended the lives of twenty-six churchgoers in El Paso; the murderer admitted he had been convinced that white people were becoming the minority.[73] Members of the Klan had burned down a South Carolina church in 1995, the same year its State House became majority-Republican, and almost exactly two decades later, someone set the African Methodist church ablaze again as part of a spree of possible copycat crimes related to the state's recent mass shooting.[74] That same year, the number of Klan chapters more than doubled nationally.[75]

ABC News's *Nightline* program, on which David Duke had regularly appeared, started covering the Klan in earnest in 2012 and broadcast a report in October, just days before Obama's reelection. In one revealing story, the show detailed a secret meeting outside Washington, DC, at which one man called out, "Klansmen, the fiery cross!" and dozens of women and men in Klan robes roared back in unison, "For God . . . for country . . . for race! And Klan!"[76] It wasn't the only Klan rally that week—in Mississippi, near the birthplace of Elvis Presley, Klansmen chanted "white power," and anti-racist observers called Obama's ascendancy a boon to Klan recruiting.[77] The SPLC said, "Immediately after Obama was elected, we saw two of the largest hate websites in the country crash."[78]

One of those was Stormfront. In 1990, Don Black, husband to David Duke's ex-wife, created what critics called the original right-wing "hate site" on the internet.[79] Initially an online bulletin board system geared mainly toward promoting Duke's candidacies, by the mid-1990s, Stormfront had become a mainstay on the emerging World Wide Web. Over the following years, it warned white people of a coming race war, criticized Dr. Martin Luther King, bad-mouthed Jewish people, and pushed for Ron Paul over Obama in the 2012 election.[80] Paul, an insurgent candidate within the Republican Party, was backed by Duke and Black and raised millions for the primary, much of it from grassroots donors, but he came up short after researchers discovered newsletter articles he'd signed warning of a race war, the "disappearing white majority and . . . the federal-homosexual cover-up on AIDS."[81]

"The far right felt that the deep story was their *real* story and that there was a false PC cover-up *of* that story," Arlie Russell Hochschild wrote of the surging right-wing. "They felt scorned. 'People think we're not good people if we don't feel sorry for blacks and immigrants and Syrian refugees,' one man told me. 'But I am a good person and I *don't* feel sorry for them.'"

Another said, "I know liberals want us to feel sorry for blacks. I know they think they are so idealistic and we aren't."[82]

"I think [Duke's message] became the Trump message later without the overt racism," said Roemer strategist Raymond Strother. "I don't know if they did it consciously. It is a current that was running under the surface all this time."[83] The current swept up a silent majority of "white nationalism and racial resentment," observed one pollster, Americans "whose overwhelming motivation is a deep worry that Black people and immigrants will control the country."[84]

Mitch Landrieu, then mayor of New Orleans, noted, "[In 1991], Louisiana politics demonstrated the raw susceptibility of voters—particularly Evangelical Christians—who rallied behind David Duke, trailed by TV spots exposing his Nazi beliefs as a would-be defender of human life. It is the same phenomenon that allowed Christians in 2016 to support Donald Trump, despite the women who accused him of sexually assaulting them."[85] Evangelicals, however, mostly saw through Duke's "Christian conversion" by the gubernatorial runoff, while the same bloc overlooked Trump's hypocrisy and failure to attend church thirty-five years later. "Nazism has nothing to do with race and nationality," one critic observed of the rise in American Nazism. "It appeals to a certain type of mind."[86]

At a 2016 Trump rally at Lakefront Airport in New Orleans, signs mentioned the Silent Majority and suggested Trump "Make American Great Again," references to Nixon and Reagan, respectively. Buchanan and Duke planks had been included in Trump's speeches, including attacks on illegal aliens and government spending. An elderly person in a suit held up a sign reading: "KKK for Trump." On the flip side, the sign read, "Trump, Duke for 2016." Unable to tell whether the man was a troll or a hardcore supporter, organizers ejected him. (They also kicked out a protestor who brandished a sign reading, "No Trump, No KKK, No Fascist USA.")[87]

Duke had been quiet for much of this period, declining to run for elected office again after devastating losses in the nineties. But he had continued to wield influence, especially in Louisiana. In 1995, when Governor Edwards declined to run for a fifth term, several notable political figures including Buddy Roemer leapt into the mix to replace him. Among them was Democrat-turned-Republican state senator Mike Foster, even older than Edwin Edwards had been in 1991 but a fresh face in the sense that few had heard of him.[88] Suddenly, almost overnight, Foster leapt from last place in polls to rungs ahead of Roemer and Mary Landrieu, considered the Democrats' best shot at retaining the Governor's Mansion. Was it the successful businessman's pro-gun stance, or his brilliant decision to switch parties and run to the right of Roemer, leaving the ex-governor fighting for the increasingly nonexistent middle? The Feds believed something different.

Foster had secretly purchased Duke's mailing list of financial contributors and diehards. "What was even more remarkable" to the *New York Times* was the payout: $150,000 for a mere eighty thousand names, "most of which were available for just a few hundred dollars at the state Ethics Board." The implication was that Foster had bought Duke off—off of the ballot in 1995. He also received Duke's endorsement.[89]

While an investigation turned up campaign finance violations (Foster had listed the mailing list purchase under "computer software" in one filing[90]), Foster survived the ordeal and avoided both an indictment and defeat in 1995 and his 1999 reelection contest.[91] Duke, however, invoked the Fifth Amendment in front of the grand jury and thus opened himself up to scrutiny by the IRS, eventually leading to major felony charges.

While Louisiana's far-right Republicans were under attack from liberal forces or government agencies, the party was eating itself from within. Tim Wise, previously of the Louisiana Coalition Against Racism and Nazism, accompanied his girlfriend to the 1992 Republican National Convention, where he witnessed a prophetic scene. Supposedly there to re-nominate President Bush, the party, unable to crush Buchanan's movement and message, seemed to double down on his planks.

LCARN, with Lance Hill as director and Wise as research director, had tried to transition to a freestanding anti-extremist PAC, but when the group's fundraising letter went out, it generated few responses and even fewer contributions. Everyone thought Duke and his movement had been "conquered," Wise said bitterly, and "there was just no interest in terms of funding." Wise never saw Beth Rickey again. He briefly moved to Houston, where he received an invitation to the RNC as his interior-designer girlfriend's plus-one. Ostensibly there to check on the work his significant other had done to spruce up the VIP rooms at the Houston Astrodome, Wise instead set out to explore and marvel at the convention as a liberal interloper. "We were actually there the night Buchanan gave his 'Culture War' speech," Wise recalled.[92]

The Republicans had given the insurgent right-winger a nationally televised, primetime speaking role at the convention and, in an about-face in decorum, Buchanan used it not to heal divides and push for unity behind, in this case, a centrist, but to further his and Duke's far-right message. He didn't waste a second getting to his attacks on the Democrats and their ilk:

My friends, like many of you, last month I watched that giant masquerade ball up at Madison Square Garden, where 20,000 liberals and radicals came dressed up as moderates and centrists in the greatest single exhibition of cross-dressing in American political history.

The presidency, my friends, is . . . "preeminently a place of moral leadership." George Bush is a defender of right-to-life, and a champion of the Judeo-Christian values and beliefs upon which America was founded.

. . . The agenda that [Bill] Clinton & [Hillary] Clinton would impose on America: abortion on demand, a litmus test for the Supreme Court, homosexual rights, discrimination against religious schools, women in combat units. That's change, all right. But that's not the kind of change America needs. It's not the kind of change America wants. And it's not the kind of change we can abide in a nation we still call "God's country."

. . . Yes, we disagreed with President Bush, but we stand with him for the freedom to choose religious schools, and we stand with him against the amoral idea that gay and lesbian couples should have the same standing in law as married men and women. We stand with President Bush for right-to-life and for voluntary prayer in the public schools.

. . . There is a religious war going on in this country. It is a cultural war, as critical to the kind of nation we shall be as the Cold War itself. For this war is for the soul of America.

Friends, in these wonderful 25 weeks of our campaign, the saddest days were the days of that riot in L.A., the worst riot in American history. But out of that awful tragedy can come a message of hope . . . the mob was headed in, to ransack and loot the apartments of the terrified old men and women inside. The troopers came up the street, M-16s at the ready. And the mob threatened and cursed, but the mob retreated because it had met the one thing that could stop it: force, rooted in justice, and backed by moral courage.

And as those boys took back the streets of Los Angeles, block by block, my friends, we must take back our cities, and take back our culture, and take back our country.[93]

Wise realized Dukeism had won when he walked into the Astrodome at ten o'clock that morning, carrying high top tables and leather chairs to complete the VIP room. "I look up," he recalls, "and on the Jumbotron is a freeze frame of a snarling image of Ice-T, the rapper."[94] Ice-T released the single "Cop Killer" with rap-metal band Body Count in 1992. The first-person story of a fed-up inner-city dweller raging over police brutality and promising to "dust" police officers with a sawed-off shotgun provoked President

Bush and future Second Lady Tipper Gore to call for a near boycott of all Time Warner properties until it was pulled from the album.[95]

Wise realized the thirty-foot freeze-frame of a sneering hip-hop artist, reminiscent of a still from President Bush's persuasive, racially charged 1988 Willie Horton ad, would serve as the first impression of the convention for Republican National Convention attendees.

This, Wise thought, *is the party's way of signaling "Here is where we're going."*[96]

PART IV

THE RIGHT

CHAPTER 13

The 5,784 Days

Louisiana politics is of an intensity and complexity that are matched, in my experience, only in the Republic of Lebanon.

A. J. LIEBLING

"Did the David Duke thing bother you?" the host asked. "Fifty-five percent of the white vote . . ."

"I hate seeing what it represents, but I guess it just shows there's a lot of hostility in this country, there's a tremendous amount of hostility in the United States."[1]

On November 19, 1991, three days after the Louisiana gubernatorial run-off, Donald J. Trump, then a supposedly liberal Democrat, appeared on *Larry King Live*.

"Anger," Larry King said, meaning for it to serve as a prompt, and Trump ran with it.

"Anger, I mean that's an anger vote," Trump said. "People are angry about the jobs. If you look at Louisiana, they're really in deep trouble."

As for Bush, Trump said: "I think if he had it to do again, he might not have gotten involved in that campaign. . . ."

"But Bush morally had to come out against him," King suggested.

"I think Bush had to come out against him," because, Trump said, Duke (or perhaps Buchanan) would take away votes from the incumbent Republican president.[2]

George H. W. Bush, hit from the right by Buchanan and eventual third-party challenger Ross Perot, lost the 1992 election to Bill Clinton. Clinton tap-danced alongside Buchanan's cultural wars, attacking singer Sister Souljah and other rap artists, neutralizing Bush on those issues. The Far Right finally achieved true power in the US during the Republican Revolution of

1994, which swept right-wing activists into Congress and turned the legislative system into a near-stalemate that has persisted, with brief interruptions, to this day.

John Boehner, an Ohio Republican who became Speaker of the House after the racially charged Tea Party wave of 2010, fostered the rise of the Far Right. In his fourth year in Congress, he and Newt Gingrich wrote *Contract with America*, which promised that, should the GOP gain control of the legislative branch, they would slash taxes and welfare benefits. (In 1994, after the Gingrich revolution, Democrat Senator Pat Moynihan said, regarding welfare, which he had previously refused to reform, "The Republicans are saying we have a hell of a problem, and we do."[3]) Though the *Contract with America* propelled Republicans into control of the House for the first time in forty years and Boehner into a role as the House Republican Conference chair, Boehner only lasted in his post for three years before hard-rightists ousted him. In those days, wrote the *New York Times* in a review of Boehner's memoir, the "party . . . was extremely different from its current incarnation, at least until Sarah Palin became the party's vice-presidential nominee in 2008."[4] Boehner claimed he avoided the Fox News "Looneyville" in his career, but from day one, the Republican encouraged his party to ignore "civility" and support Gingrich, suggested "the Tea Party movement has done this nation a great service," and encouraged right-wing talk radio to propagandize for the *Contract with America* and legislative goals. "Partisanship, rather than reform, drove his actions."[5]

Following years of voting to bury liberal illicit drug reform measures, Boehner quit to become a marijuana lobbyist. "Until senior Republicans acknowledge how they helped radicalize the party," wrote the *Times*' reviewer, "there is little hope that it will transform itself."[6]

In 2000, right-wing operative Karl Rove managed President Bush's son, George W., in a victorious presidential campaign built on tax reform, family values, diversity, strengthening social security, and a de-emphasis on nation-building. Over Bush's two terms, the right-wing did an about-face on most of those issues; instead, it pushed ultra-conservative platforms—ban gay marriage, overturn *Roe v. Wade*, support preemptive military invasions—as part of a new hyperpartisanship.[7]

After George W. Bush's presidency became bogged down in wars in Afghanistan and Iraq, as well as failed attempts to install cronies on the Supreme Court, the Hurricane Katrina disaster, and the administration's inept response, Americans elected and re-elected black Illinois senator Barack Obama. However, Obama, entering into the hyperpartisanship of the post-Republican Revolution and the Tea Party wave that overshadowed it, never had a chance. Senate Majority Leader Mitch McConnell, who pushed for a ban on affirmative action in government contracts, pivoted to supporting restrictive national voter ID laws that experts believed would prevent minorities, students, and other adults more likely to be Democrats from voting. He also proclaimed that he didn't believe black people were still victims of voter discrimination.[8] After Tea Party candidate David Brat defeated House Majority Leader Eric Cantor in his 2014 Republican primary, and Joe Arpaio won a race for sheriff in Maricopa County, Arizona, by suggesting illegal immigrants be kept in "concentration camps,"[9] the *Times* wrote in a headline, "Much of David Duke's '91 Campaign Is Now in Louisiana Mainstream."[10]

Amid the chaos, Donald Trump, a New York real estate kingpin, developed a Twitter following by slamming Obama for being born "in Kenya."[11]

"Why doesn't he show his birth certificate?" he asked on *The View*. When pressed on these racially charged and unsupported allegations, Trump pointed out that Hillary Clinton supporters supposedly crafted the Kenya conspiracy theory during Clinton's 2008 primary run. For four years, Trump made insinuations that Obama was a Muslim and had not been born in the United States, making him ineligible to be president.[12] When Trump announced he would run for the presidency in 2016 as a Republican and attempt to thwart Clinton, the media pressed him repeatedly on his comments about Obama, immigrants, and affirmative action.[13] He didn't back down on his behavior during the 1989 Central Park Jogger Case, which included running an $85,000, full-page advertisement, in which he called for the reinstatement of the death penalty to punish the five accused young black men, and which touched off a wave of support for the prosecution.[14] (All five defendants were exonerated through DNA evidence and brought a successful lawsuit against New York City. During his 2016 campaign, Trump insisted "the fact that that case was settled with so much evidence against them is outrageous."[15])

In 2016, Trump also claimed he didn't even know who David Duke was, and when asked whether he would reject the support of the white nationalist movement and the KKK, he said, "I have to look at the group. You wouldn't want me to condemn a group that I know nothing about . . . you may have groups in there that are totally fine, and it would be very unfair. Honestly, I don't know David Duke." The next day, he walked back his statements, claiming he couldn't hear well with the earpiece he had in.[16]

Trump and Duke had a lot in common, which the media picked on and tried to stress both before and after the election. "Both were Republican interlopers," the *Chicago Tribune* noted. "Both repudiated by the party's mainstream, a rejection that turned into an advantage. Both exhibit a grandiosity they seem to confuse with greatness. Both have built their power by exploiting racial fears and economic insecurity. . . . Duke, who long ago traded his white KKK robe for a stylish dark suit, was a pioneer in the modern art of whitewashing white nationalism. Trump benefits from the generation he helped cultivate."[17]

But Trump had fleeting KKK connections and a checkered past as a possible racist. His father, Fred, was arrested at a 1927 Ku Klux Klan rally, but apparently released without charge. In the 1970s, while both men were landlords in New York, they were sued twice by the US government for allegedly discriminating against black people by refusing to rent them spaces in Trump properties; ten years after the first case, the buildings were 95 percent white, according to the Division of Housing and Community Renewal.[18]

In 1991, Jewish and other anti-racist forces marshaled, scaring off middle class workers and wealthy business owners from Duke, claiming that his election would cause a boycott of the state and kill the economy. But if the "canceled" politician becomes the country's Commander-in-Chief, how do you boycott him then?

In light of much of this and Trump's platform, Duke unsurprisingly came out early and in strong support for the Republican candidate. In 2015, he praised Trump for pushing the immigration issue, for hitting the Obama administration for accepting waves of new immigrants, and for saying what his opponents in the GOP primary wouldn't say on visas and deportation. "Donald Trump is not a racist," Duke told NPR. "And the truth is in this country if you simply defend the heritage of European American people then you're automatically a racist."[19] Five days before the 2016 election, Duke appeared at Dillard University in New Orleans, a historically black college, for a US Senate debate as part of his latest campaign.[20] (LCARN reformed with Lawrence Powell and Karen Carvin Shachat at the helm to blunt his chances.[21]) Over chants of "No Duke, no KKK, no fascist USA" from anti-racist activists kept out of the event, the ex-Klansman dubbed Black Lives Matter a radical terrorist organization, boasted "I'm against Jews or anybody else that puts the interests of some other place over our own country," called the moderators media hacks, and had to be helped off campus by a police escort for fear of assault from protestors.[22]

Near the end of Obama's presidency, a survey found that fewer than a third of white people without a college education viewed Black Lives Matter favorably and only half of those with degrees felt positively about it.[23] The backlash inevitably lead to the Far Right's ascendancy and, with left-wing activists attacking the Democratic nominee for calling African Americans "superpredators" in the nineties, and criticism on the right of Obama's supposedly preferential treatment of black people, Trump rode a surge of far-right energy to the Republican nomination. Clinton slammed Trump for his past statements, including racially insensitive or degrading remarks about women and for not paying his taxes, and Trump's approval rating slid.[24] (As in 1991, the two leading candidates had net negative approval ratings—at one point in 2016, Clinton and Trump both were at roughly a -21 percent rating. Clinton had a majority unfavorable rating for the entire campaign.[25]) Down ten points one week before the general election, Trump warned supporters the campaign wouldn't prevail. Clinton, like John Treen before her, ran a campaign "mired in complacency. Believing all the expert analyses that showed him winning easily, Treen quite simply failed to expend much energy on the contest."[26] Then the head of the FBI threw everything into turmoil.

James Comey faced a revolt from within his own bureau, seemingly for refusing to do something, *anything* to stop "crooked Hillary" from achieving high office, a reverse Edwards-Duke situation. Immediately after Comey quietly informed Congress that Clinton was under investigation, right-wingers gleefully leaked the revelations to the media. With a series of breaking news alerts regarding the supposed investigation on the *New York Times* app keeping the story fresh in voters minds until November 8, Trump pulled within three points of Clinton. The race became a toss-up.[27]

Kenneth Stern thinks Trump's ascendancy during the Obama years paralleled Duke's in the Edwards era for the same reason—because of white America's fear of living in a "a majority non-white society," he said. Buchanan and Trump both tapped into that fear, but Buchanan was thoughtful, while "Trump came across as the anti-intellectual and was able to resonate with that message much more."[28]

"My sense is Trump in 2016 in a lot of ways ran the same campaign that Duke ran," said Duke biographer Tyler Bridges, "against the elites, trying to give voice to the dispossessed. Trump did not have the baggage of the Klan . . . his campaign was not as race-based, but both were about 'sending them a message.' There were a couple of issues where there was a direct overlap between the two, mostly immigration and trade, but the same wave that swept David Duke into office in 1989 and got him half the white vote [in 1990 and 1991] was what washed Trump into office in 2016."[29]

That Tuesday, after Trump crossed the electoral college threshold with wins in battleground states, including Wisconsin and Pennsylvania, Duke rejoiced. He called the upset victory one of the most wonderful moments of his life and insisted Trump eked out the win thanks to "our people." Duke was further impressed with the work Trump did in his administration, especially blocking the Equal Employment Opportunity Commission from asking corporations about pay discrepancies between black and white workers; banning travelers from heavily Muslim countries (excluding, notably, Saudi Arabia, provenance of most of the September 11 hijackers) and Haiti (because, he claimed, all Haitians "have AIDS"); revoking or trying to revoke protections for Salvadorans, immigrants brought to the US as children, and immigrants who were parents of US citizens or legal residents; railing against supposed "open borders" and "chain migration"; resuming federal executions; and undoing Obama-era Affirmatively Furthering Fair Housing anti-discrimination rules.[30] (Beth Rickey had marveled in 1989, "I cannot believe the lengths these people are willing to go to protect their Duke base."[31]) But nothing solidified Trump's far-right base or anchored right-wingers' love of the president more than Charlottesville.

As Black Lives Matter and other groups attempted to take down a statue of Robert E. Lee and other symbols of the racist Confederacy in 2017, neo-Nazis and members of the National Socialist Movement operating under the umbrella term "the Alt-Right" organized an August rally in Charlottesville, Virginia, under the banner "Unite the Right." There, confirmed neo-Nazis chanted "Jews will not replace us!" and paraded across the University of Virginia campus armed with shields and lit tiki torches. The next morning, protestors wielding flags emblazoned with swastikas or the Confederate symbol, massed in the former Lee Park, now Emancipation Park, where the Confederate general's statue remained. There, the counterprotestors waited, taunting neo-Nazis. Conflicting reports indicated that either neo-Nazis lunged at the left-wingers or provocateurs on the Left threw projectiles at the right-wingers. Regardless, the two sides exchanged blows, leading to three arrests. Virginia's governor called for the park to be cleared. David Duke, one of seven keynote speakers from the white nationalist movement scheduled to address another rally the following day, was one of the last to leave, raising his arms in triumph and flashing a thumbs up. Two hours later and mere blocks away, an Alt-Right supporter rammed into a crowd of counterprotestors with his Dodge Charger, causing one death and numerous injuries and plunging the city into pandemonium and terror. One counterprotestor, hit by the Dodge, sued David Duke for inciting violence that lead to his potentially permanent unspecified injuries. Duke was slapped with a $5,000 judgment to pay for the plaintiff's medical bills; Richard Preston, the Imperial Wizard of the Maryland Klan, was sentenced to several years in prison for firing a gun at a counterprotestor.[32] The mayor of Charlottesville implored the Federal government to prosecute the vehicular homicide as terrorism and, for once, the general public seemed to agree that right-wing violence had been just that: terrorism. Still, Duke saw Unite the Right as a triumph.[33]

"This represents a turning point for the people of this country," he tweeted. "We are determined to take our country back. We are going to fulfill the promises of Donald Trump. That's what we believed in. That's why we voted for Donald Trump, because he said he's going to take our country back."[34]

But Trump, at first, did not seem to appreciate the idea of the right-wing in all its many permutations uniting behind his presidency. "We ALL must be united & condemn all that hate stands for," he tweeted. "There is no place for this kind of violence in America. Lets [sic] come together as one!"

"I would recommend you take a good look in the mirror & remember it was White Americans who put you in the presidency, not radical leftists," Duke fired back. "So, after decades of White Americans being targeted for discriminated [sic] & anti-White hatred, we come together as a people, and you attack us?"[35]

Trump backpedaled. He claimed there were fine Americans on "many sides," which outraged the Left, the media, and moderate Republican officials, but fired up the Far Right. (There were seventy-three murders tied to white supremacists in the US in just the two years following Unite the Right, according to the ADL.[36]) They turned out in Arlington later that month, gathering at the site of George Lincoln Rockwell's murder to commemorate the fiftieth anniversary of the Nazi's death.[37] They stuck with Trump's congressional acolytes in the 2018 midterms, in which Republicans lost control of the House of Representatives after seven years, in no small part because of Charlottesville and Trump's having covered for white supremacists. They were still with him in 2020, when he lost the presidency by seven million votes to Joe Biden, and they stayed with him right up through the Stop the Steal Rally and its aftermath.[38]

Even before the DC rally, the warning signs were there of a violent far-right insurgency. For starters, attacks on Jews represented half of all hate crime reports in 2020, despite being 2 percent of the population.[39] Then, during that year's presidential campaign, far-right activists tried to run a Biden-Harris bus off the road in Texas, stormed the Michigan legislature with high-powered weapons to kidnap the female Democratic governor, and charged police officers outside the Salem state capitol in Oregon and had to be pepper-sprayed. A shooting at a Washington, DC, pizza restaurant turned out to have been inspired by a right-wing internet rumor started the week prior to the 2016 presidential election that suggested Hillary Clinton was running a sex slavery operation in the restaurant's nonexistent basement.[40] Marjorie Taylor Green, elected to the US House of Representatives in 2020, ran on a platform of cobbled-together conspiracy theories, including Pizzagate, and a suspicion that Jews used a laser beamed from space to spark a California wildfire.[41] Many of these theories rose from the cult of QAnon, an anonymous, likely imaginary employee of the federal government leaking unproven or debunked information on the "Deep State."

At the Stop the Steal Rally (the "steal" being the certification of the election for Joe Biden) on January 6, 2021, Congresswoman Mary Miller told the crowd that "Hitler was right."[42] Trump spoke, concluding his remarks by telling his fans, "We fight. We fight like hell and if you don't fight like hell, you're not going to have a country anymore."

A crowd of Trump supporters quickly gathered outside metal barricades, which were then mysteriously moved aside by police officers, allowing the enraged mob to reach the locked entrance to the Capitol. Senator Josh Hawley allegedly beckoned the protestors to follow him to the doors.[43] As cops barricaded the entrance, protestors smashed the glass and tried to ram their way in; after a breach, the House of Representatives had to be cleared out of all personnel, including vice president Mike Pence, who had been presiding over the vote certification. Trespassers, who called for Pence's hanging, were within one hundred feet of him when the Secret Service hurried the VP out. The rioters soon invaded Democratic House Speaker Nancy Pelosi's office, rifled through paperwork, and were photographed beaming triumphantly with their feet up on her desk. A black Capitol police officer backed through a series of corridors, effectively misdirecting insurrectionists away from their liberal targets.[44]

The videos immediately started rolling in on Facebook and Parler, a new right-wing social media network. A woman identifying herself as Elizabeth from Knoxville, Tennessee, was seen on video wiping her eyes of pepper spray. When asked if she had been trying to get inside the US Capitol, she said, "I made it like a foot inside and they pushed me out and they maced me." When the interviewer questioned her motives, she shouted, "We're storming the Capitol! It's a revolution!"[45] Another woman, seen attempting to break into the barricaded Capitol, was shot and killed by police; the Far Right attempted to lay the blame on left-wing operatives. A press release purportedly from the nonexistent organization "Antifa," claimed antifascist forces had infiltrated the DC march and had pushed for violence. Some Trump supporters claimed on Facebook that "antifa dressed in trumpwear started rioting and going into the capital [*sic*]." In one post, a woman claimed that people with MAGA hats turned backward had perpetuated the violence, but another said: "I know someone who was there today . . . and I can assure you it was no one pretending to be a Trump supporter."[46]

"There is a straight line from the Ku Klux Klan to January 6, 2021, and it's not pretty," wrote a reviewer of *Blood in the Face*, a 1991 documentary on neo-Nazis and the KKK. Another Letterbox.com reviewer wrote simply, "26 years later. . . . They all won."[47]

In the wake of what became known as the Capitol Riots, Donald Trump and David Duke were permanently banned from Twitter and both Congress and the authorities launched investigations, making arrests of small-town right-wing lawmakers, QAnon cultists, and Alt-Right leaders.[48] The tide seemed to turn against the Far Right overnight. The following day, Democrats won both US Senate seats in Georgia. The NAACP invoked the so-called Ku Klux Klan Act of 1871 to sue the far-right groups the Proud Boys and the Oath Keepers, as well as Trump, for allegedly inciting the Capitol Riots and subverting democracy in the 2020 electoral vote count.[49] In January 2021, GOP registrants made up about one-third of the electorate; four months later, they represented roughly one quarter. The Republican Party lost thousands of moderates and firmed up its white supremacist base.[50]

The continued strength of the Far Right is readily apparent though in the passage of voter suppression laws in Texas, Georgia, and several other states with Republican-controlled legislatures; in QAnon repeatedly postponing the date in which Trump would supposedly resume power again; the number of defense contractors or members of the military involved with the neo-Confederacy; the defeats of forces marshaled to impeach the ex-president after he left office; and the removal of Republican Liz Cheney from her House leadership role for her vote to convict Trump.[51] Strongmen such as Fascist Italian leader Benito Mussolini, to whom Trump is often compared, and Juan Peron have returned to power on a wave of "how bad could it really have been" ignorance and national fervor. Followers of Richard Spencer, Burt Colucci of the National Socialist Movement, Nicholas J. Fuentes, Lauren Chen, Alex Jones, Steven Crowder, the Institute for Historical Review, the Atomwaffen Division, white supremacist infiltration of law enforcement, far-right forces within the Southern Baptists, and the Klan itself increased under Trump.[52] Despite the shuttering of Stormfront, Don

Black's website, the Southern Poverty Law Center claimed white nationalist groups grew by more than half during Trump's term.[53] QAnon is now more popular than many longstanding religions, with 20 percent of adherents hoping for a biblical flood to "restore rightful leaders."[54] The FBI has reclassified neo-Nazi groups as being just as dangerous as ISIS, and the director of the Bureau said, "Not only is the terror threat diverse, it's unrelenting."[55] As we've seen following US invasions of Vietnam, or after coups or interference in Nicaragua, Mexico, Syria, and Salvador, America's refugee numbers balloon, and xenophobes respond with racist attacks or attempts at ethnic cleansing, often victimizing emigres fleeing communism or the very gangs right-wingers are afraid will spring up in their own communities.

In 1991, Beth Rickey prophesied that "a racist political victory could happen right now, in any area of the country." Duke, having "put an attractive face on racial resentment, and [thus] making it comfortable for people to express these feelings without social reprisal," would kick off a new political era of divisions along racial and xenophobic and "not class or economic lines."[56] The attacks on racial equity indeed came from all classes, including in upper crust liberal New York. Parents at the Dalton School wrote a letter complaining about "an obsessive focus on race and identity . . . a pessimistic and age-inappropriate litany of grievances in EVERY class." A dozen paragraphs later, they made a comment that could've been straight out of a Duke debate talking point: "To be clear, we abhor racism."[57]

Edwin Edwards watched all this and observed that Louisiana, since his first gubernatorial victory, had become "much more conservative . . . much more Republican. There was not one statewide Republican official . . . but as the sweep came across the South of conservatism, so did it come to Louisiana, and gradually . . . all of the major political figures of a statewide level are from the Republican Party."[58]

Said former LCARN leader Larry Powell, "Duke is somewhat of a spent force, trying to make himself relevant to the Alt-Right. He's always going to be on the fringes, and with such name recognition, he'll continue to get press attention, but he's viewed on the right as an opportunist. As for Trump, look at the hold he has on the Republican Party. Fortunately, he's a buffoon, stupid and lazy, and doesn't have the energy to build a movement, just for a few shakedowns. But still, he's dangerous."[59]

Retired LSU professor Wayne Parent feels similarly about Duke and Trump. "The Duke and Trump phenomenon is interesting," he said. "Duke was clearly associated with race politics, with a kind of a fuck-it-all [attitude during his] campaign. A lot of folks that I talked to that were Duke supporters said 'we're voting for him because you said we're stupid racists.' There was a little of that 'own the libs' stuff . . . that strain has gotten bigger in the Trump version of that kind of cultural populism."[60]

The supposed undercounted Duke support that didn't materialize for him in 1991 ironically became another kind of "hidden vote," as many Louisianans later downplayed their record of voting for the Republican. But as Parent noted, Louisiana had been the source of several of the "most dramatic changes in all of American politics" since the Second World War; for one thing, Democrats started to rely on high black turnout.[61] "I know there are a lot of Trump supporters, but I only saw Biden-Harris signs in Baton Rouge," said Parent of the 2020 election, suggesting a social stigma has developed around racist politicians, although others have solidified their power by dividing Americans along racial lines. While serving on the Tulsa Race Massacre Centennial Commission, the governor of Oklahoma signed legislation that effectively halted the teaching of "critical race theory."[62] As Louisiana came in dead last in a survey of educational quality, the legislature turned its efforts to banning abortion, and in Lakeview, near the New Orleans suburbs, homeowners tried to stop Robert E. Lee Boulevard from being renamed for African American musician Allen Toussaint.[63] Simultaneously, and in response to a rise of racist attacks on Asian people, President Biden called white supremacy "terrorism" in a landmark address to Congress.[64] He also honored legislators for passing an anti-hate crime bill to protect Asians and asked them to do him another solid: protect women and LGBT people.

But Rep. Steve Scalise, who once referred to himself as "David Duke without the baggage" and whose congressional district encompasses much of Duke's old turf, is the number two man for Republicans in the House of Representatives.[65] Josh Hawley, despite calls for his expulsion, is still a Missouri senator.[66] Three congressmen named by "Stop the Steal" organizer Ali Alexander as having "schemed [to put] maximum pressure on Congress while they were voting" are themselves still in Congress and, in Oregon, State Rep. Mike Nearman was seen on video providing "step-by-step" instructions on breaching the state capitol.[67] The GOP frontrunners for the 2024 presidential nomination are Trump acolytes, including Hawley, Tom Cotton, and Florida governor Ron DeSantis. All are on the Far Right.

The electorate and media are shifting in that direction too. In 2021, David Duke called Fox News' Tucker Carlson "our greatest ally" after the talking head pushed the "great replacement theory," a fictitious narrative trumpeted by Duke and white supremacists that posits that white Americans are being replaced by minorities through immigration.[68] The following year, a self-described "eco-fascist national socialist" allegedly shot and killed ten random shoppers in a predominantly black Buffalo neighborhood; earlier, he had posted a manifesto online that claimed black Americans were trying to "ethnically replace my own people."[69] It was the third in a string of recent massacres tied to the replacement theory.

"Clearly Duke's controversial views years ago have now become mainstream Republican values," said Michael Lawrence, who ran Duke's 2016 Senate campaign. "I think Trump and Duke are almost identical on immigration and the future of this country."[70] One editor noted in 1995, when Duke did not yet seem "finished" either, "the future of a new, not always latent racism as a campaign tactic in modern . . . politics 'depends on whether it is nurtured by our political leadership.'"[71]

Unquestionably, the tactic has never been better nurtured.

POSTSCRIPT

With the exception of Beth Rickey, the principal subjects of this book were living at the commencement of writing.

Buddy Roemer, who had been working in small-town banking for decades, passed away from complications of diabetes in May 2021, before I could interview him. "Duke and Edwards created a pincher move," in 1991, recalled Mark McKinnon. "You had a progressive and an extremist on the Right, with no room for the middle, which we're seeing today."[1] Carlos Sierra, an advisor on the former governor's passionate but little-noticed 2012 presidential campaign, had a different view of Roemer's place in the rise of the Far Right. "Believe it or not, Buddy actually liked Trump," Sierra said.[2] They were both underdogs and outsider presidential candidates, and had similar views on China, as Roemer was an economist and opponent of fair trade agreements, and he wanted the Chinese government sanctioned for allegedly manipulating their currency.[3]

Edwin Edwards passed away in 2021 at age ninety-three, leaving behind his third wife and a seven-year-old son. Edwards had a lackluster fourth term and tended to agree with experts about his inability to make fundamental change in the early 1990s. "Maybe they'll forget how bad I was," he said toward the end of his term.[4] They haven't, and certainly the US Attorney's Office did not. President Clinton named Eddie Jordan to Volz's old post in 1994 and, in 1999, the US prosecutor indicted the Silver Fox on twenty-six counts, including money laundering, extortion, and mail fraud, in a scheme with the owner of the San Francisco 49ers to sell riverboat gambling licenses. Among those who had applied for a license, albeit too late in the process: Donald Trump. (His liaison in Louisiana was none other than former Edwards campaign manager Bob D'Hemecourt.[5]) Edwards and his son Stephen were each convicted on more than a dozen counts and sentenced to multi-year prison terms. "The government asked the judge to sentence me to life or thirty-five to forty years. I'll take life," Edwards joked, "it's shorter."[6] Despite attempts by Dave Treen and Bennett Johnston to secure a presidential pardon for him, Edwards ended up doing eight years in Federal Corrections facilities. Perhaps most surprisingly, upon his release in 2011, nearly a third of Louisiana residents named him their best governor of the past thirty years; of course, he had been governor for nearly a third of them.[7]

In 2014, buoyed by a vacancy in the Sixth Congressional District, Edwards stunned the world by announcing he would run again at age eighty-seven. "I'm the only hope the Democrats have here," he quipped. He led in every jungle primary poll, but the district was heavily Republican and the seat's prior occupant, Bill Cassidy, had become the state's newest US senator. Buddy Roemer, though, admitted "yes, he can win."[8] Indeed, Edwards landed in first place on Election Night, with 30 percent of the vote; however, the state's primary system, instituted by Governor Edwards in the 1970s, worked against congressional candidate Edwards in 2014. Garret Graves solidified his Republican support and held Edwards to under 38 percent in the runoff, a near-mirror image of Edwards' 1991 victory. After his only general election defeat, he never ran again. After Edwards' successful reelection in 1975, four decades passed before a Democrat again won back-to-back gubernatorial races in Louisiana. His name was Edwards, too, although there is no relation.

On April 9, 2004, David Duke was released from prison in Big Spring, Texas, and was driven back to Louisiana in his daughter's SUV. (A year earlier, the former state representative had been sentenced to fifteen months for mail and tax fraud.[9]) His prison sentence for gambling using supporters' money overlapped with Edwards' jail term, however, the two never served time in the same facility. Today, Duke hosts a streaming radio show, sells merchandise, and puts out news through his website, and aside from Charlottesville, the controversial removal of Confederate monuments in New Orleans, and his 2016 US Senate race, has become relatively reclusive. "Only as the number of racially aware whites grows will we have the political power to accomplish some of these answers to our problems," he wrote in 1984.[10] He may have hit that magic number in the Trump era. "Trump really knows what his movement is based upon," said Duke, claiming he, not Trump, popularized several key campaign slogans, including "Make America Great Again." "Even that movie *Blackkklansman* . . . documented me saying that. He had to know that I ran my campaigns primarily on the immigration issue, on fair trade issues, on the issues of preserving American culture, on stopping the replacement of European Americans."[11] In 2021, Trump put Duke back in the news by saying, in Iowa, "One politician many years ago, came in second in a certain state, and he became famous for many, many years because he came in second." Duke, playing back a recording of Trump's Iowa speech on his show, suggested that the former president was saying he "believed that he couldn't get elected if he just laid out the fact that this tiny Jewish racist, ultra-racist, ultra-supremacist minority has supremacy over [the media.] Jews, they're Jews, Jews, and more Jews, and they're all connected."[12]

In one of her last public pronouncements regarding her war on bigotry, Beth Rickey reflected, "If conservatives don't speak out, then they're going to be smeared with the label of being racist. . . . It's a moral question. It's not something you say, oh, politically there may be a backlash. Some issues are beyond that. There are some things you have to say."[13]

Rickey's friend Kenneth Stern wrote of her, "No one I ever met was braver or more committed to fighting hatred . . . [she] more than anyone else, was responsible for the demise of David Duke."[14] After Duke's defeat in 1991, Rickey received the Cavallo Foundation Award, given for those "whose actions of moral courage benefit society despite personal risk," but the peak of her political career had passed. Rickey became a political science professor at her alma mater, UNO, a job a Governor Duke would have overseen as part of the state university system. Rickey told the *Texas Observer*. "We feel like we did what we set out to do, which was to defeat [Duke] soundly. I think he'll never be elected to statewide office. . . . So I'm going to sit back and watch, but stay vigilant."[15]

She became campaign manager for Lafayette area congressional candidate David Thibodaux, a Republican member of the Louisiana Coalition Against Racism and Nazism. Midway through the campaign, Rickey decided to keep her commitment to attend a Catholic mission trip to Mexico. Upon her return, she discovered Thibodaux had been in a motorcycle accident and was unable to campaign for ten days. She grudgingly took over his duties, making calls to supporters and contributors, speaking at campaign events (despite her fear of public speaking), and even challenging election results when Thibodaux was eliminated from the runoff by only twelve votes. All this while battling a virus caught on the mission trip, which came with a

103 degree fever. After her temperature dropped, however, Beth still seemed to become fatigued easily and early in the day.[16]

"Whatever she'd gotten on that mission trip never left her," Quin Hillyer lamented.[17] She had an autoimmune disorder and developed Crohn's Disease, an irritable bowel syndrome, and she would battle her own body for the rest of her life. "I think Beth never had a clear diagnosis and she spent a lot of time and money" trying to get a more accurate one, her brother Rob claimed.[18] Rickey piled up boxes of research on David Duke in her Coliseum Street apartment in anticipation of signing a book deal, to the point the space was almost unnavigable.[19] She strongly considered moving to DC to work for Democratic President Bill Clinton, whom she endorsed in 1992, but acceptable offers apparently never materialized.[20] Unable to work, she gave up her Coliseum Street apartment and, in and out of clinical care on an almost monthly basis, accepted spots on friends' couches and, after blowing through her family inheritance, borrowed money. "I last saw Beth in 2004 in Lafayette when she was in danger of becoming homeless," said her brother, who thought Beth struggled with mental illness as a result of her chronic, draining health issues.[21]

In the mid- to late 2000s, she accepted an offer to consult for the town of Jena as it dealt with the outcry following the arrest of six black teenagers for the alleged assault of a white classmate. Rickey found herself caught once more between the forces of racial justice and the Far Right. After one protest in support of the "Jena Six," an out-of-state Nationalist Movement chapter secured a permit to march on Martin Luther King Jr. Day in support of the victim and "as a centerpiece to abolish King Day." Rickey, embarrassed perhaps more than usual to speak to the press, feebly suggested that an ordinance that might have prevented the march would not go into effect in time. She apparently quit her post soon after.[22]

Kenneth Stern called Beth's situation "not only a health crisis but a financial one, and one made the other worse."[23] Stern, Hillyer, and journalist Jason Berry sent out fundraising pleas for Rickey, but "it was one crisis after another," Hillyer said. "She started getting mentally very unsure of herself and fragile. She would rally and seem to be getting well for three to four months, then she'd have a relapse."[24] Whichever friend had most recently spoken to her before each downturn would phone Hillyer and ask, "Did you hear that Beth is sick again?" Confined to friends' apartments, she would borrow money, then run up her hosts' phone bills.[25] During one call, she convinced Hillyer and his wife to see her just before they moved to Washington.

"We drove over and picked her up and had lunch," he said. "Beth was [seemingly] on top of the world. It was the Beth I knew twenty years earlier, when she was at the Republican National Convention, funny and smart. She was not a pitiful creature," Hillyer emphasized. "It was cyclical. When she was feeling better or the doctor came up with something that treated the symptoms, she would start acting like her old self. It was not a thirteen-year death march, but a thirteen-year death march interspersed with the old, wonderful Beth."[26] Less than a month later, however, Rickey suffered another relapse, one that took her six months to recover from. She went to New Mexico in July 2009 because, Hillyer believes, she figured the dry climate might be a invigorating change from humid Louisiana summers. But when friends came by to check on her, her shades would be drawn and she wouldn't answer the door.[27]

In her final interview, with the *Santa Fe New Mexican*, Rickey claimed that Duke, then living on the north shore of Lake Pontchartrain, was "still out there and his followers are, so that took a lot out of me, people calling me and threatening me. I had been through a lot with the Duke situation, and I wanted to move away and try to get my head cleared up. I moved here to kind of get away from the insanity that I had been through, and I had some health problems as a result. Santa Fe is an important place in my life even though I have not successfully found, you know, a niche, so to speak, but I feel it's a place where anything can happen."[28]

Friends located a philanthropist living near Rickey's Santa Fe motel and "debriefed her," as Hillyer put it.[29] The potential benefactor spoke with Rickey by phone, listened to her life story, and immediately agreed to help her get back on her feet financially, emotionally, and health-wise. They made an appointment to meet at the hotel the following morning. Hillyer was ecstatic, especially when the philanthropist informed him that Beth was in high spirits after speaking with friends all across the country. "She thought help was on the way," Hillyer said. "Beth realized how many people really cared about her. As far as we know, the last mood she was in, she was on an 'up,' perhaps not feeling well and physically ill, but she was content, reassured, touched and happy that she was hearing from all these people."[30]

No one answered the philanthropist's knock the next morning at the Silver Saddle Motel. Summoning first the hotel manager and then the police, the group broke into Rickey's room early on September 11, 2009, and found her collapsed on her back, still gripping a pitcher she had filled with iced tea for her guest. Beth Rickey was fifty-three.

A despondent Quin Hillyer tried to summarize her greatness four days later in the *Washington Times*, under the header "Beth, What Can We Do?" "There had been a time, back in the early 1990s, when journalists and academicians, Jewish leaders and evangelicals, conservative and liberal, all proclaimed her a heroine. They were right."[31] Ten years later, he would call her "the most courageous lady I've ever known in politics" and note that "she never withdrew from the fray, even though it was patently obvious that the effort was taking a serious toll on her.

"Beth did not have any particular animus against Duke personally; what motivated her . . . was a deep and loving belief in individual human potential without regard to race or religion."[32]

Kenneth Stern said, "She was a remarkable person. Many people were involved in pushing back against the bigotry Duke was trying to make mainstream—Stovall, Lance, Quin, and others. She was the sort of guiding light in many ways, and rightly so, a good public figure."[33] Holocaust survivor Anne Levy said: "I really admire what she did, she was gutsy, she was really gutsy, walking into the bookstore and buying books like she did. That was incredible."[34]

Lance Hill, in a little-noticed comment at a Coalition meeting in October 1989, speculated that "Duke's base is the belief in white supremacy. If Duke is eliminated, there are others. You can't have a strong racial society and have democracy. We must make that clear to the world."[35]

Today, thanks to a push from Stern, Bard College offers an annual honor to a person who "has taken sustained and effective action against hate."[36] It's called, of course, the Elizabeth "Beth" Rickey Award. The question remains: who in our political landscape is brave enough to qualify for it?

CAST OF CHARACTERS

Bernard J. "Ben" Bagert, state senator 1984–1992, Democrat turned Republican, Republican nominee for US Senate 1990

Don Black, friend of David Duke's, second husband of Chloe Duke, Imperial Wizard of the Ku Klux Klan, 1981–1987

Bob D'Hemecourt, 1991 Edwards for Governor campaign manager

David Duke, state representative, 1989 to 1992

Edwin Washington Edwards, Kingfish, "the Cajun Prince," city councilman, congressman, governor of Louisiana

Lance Hill, co-chair of LCARN with Beth Rickey

Quin Hillyer, journalist and member of LCARN

J. Bennett Johnston, US senator, ran for reelection in 1990 against David Duke and Ben Bagert

Louis Lambert, Public Service Commissioner and Democratic candidate for governor in 1979, member of the Louisiana Senate 1994–2004

Huey Long, Kingfish, senator and governor of Louisiana in the 1920s and '30s, assassinated in 1935

Carlos Marcello, reputed Mafioso in New Orleans

Wayne Parent, Russell B. Long Professor of Political Science at Louisiana State University

Larry Powell, history professor at Tulane University, on the LCARN board

Beth Rickey, co-chair of LCARN, member of the Republican State Committee in Louisiana, student, and campaign worker

Charles "Buddy" Roemer III, Edwards campaign staffer, congressman, and governor of Louisiana, 1988–1992

Charles E. Roemer II, a.k.a. "Budgie," Charles III's father, Edwards campaign staffer, convicted felon

John Treen, brother of governor Dave Treen, candidate for Louisiana State House seat in 1989

Bill Wilkinson, leader of the Invisible Empire Knights of the Ku Klux Klan, 1975–1981

NOTES

INTRODUCTION

Epigraph. Peter Applebome, "Duke: The Ex-Nazi Who Would Be Governor," *New York Times*, November 10, 1991, 1.

1. Huey Long and Castro Carazo, "Every Man a King," no recording date, thought to be public domain, 1935, see also Randy Newman, "Every Man a King," on *Good Old Boys*, Reprise Records, 1974.

2. Richard D. White, Jr., *Kingfish: The Reign of Huey P. Long* (New York: Random House, 2006), 174.

3. Hilary Moore and James Tracy, *No Fascist USA!* (San Francisco: City Lights Books, 2020), 34; Lawrence Lee Hewitt and Thomas E. Schott, *Lee and His Generals: Essays in Honor of T. Harry Williams*, (Knoxville: University of Tennessee Press, 2012), 5; Glen Jeansonne, "Challenge to the New Deal: Huey P. Long and the Redistribution of National Wealth," *Louisiana History: The Journal of the Louisiana Historical Association* 30, no. 4 (Autumn 1980), 284.

4. "Long Tells Klan Head to Stay Out of State," *New York Times*, August 18, 1934, 5.

5. History.com editors, "Huey Long," *History Channel*, March 9, 2019, https://www.history.com/topics/crime/huey-long; ushistory.org, "Roosevelt's Critics," *US History Online Textbook*, accessed July 21, 2021, https://www.ushistory.org/Us/49f.asp; speech by Huey Long, April 1945 radio address, http://historymatters.gmu.edu/d/5109.

6. Marcia Gaudet, "The Kingfish as Trickster Hero: Huey Long in Louisiana Culture," in *Louisiana Culture from the Colonial Era to Katrina*, ed. John Wharton Lowe, 231–44 (Baton Rouge: Louisiana State University Press, 2008), 239.

7. Long's heirs tried to live up to his standards on democratic socialism, with mixed results. His wife served out his Senate term in a special election. Her segregationist successor attacked Social Security as specifically designed to help black Americans, but after Long's brother Earl replaced Huey as governor, Huey's son Russell Long won election to the Senate at such a young age that he was constitutionally ineligible to serve for several weeks. Russell, the "poor man's friend" who "sneer[ed] at millionaires" (advertisement, *Minden Herald*, July 21, 1950, 3) spent forty years in Congress, often heading up the finance committee. He was therefore predominantly responsible for the expansion of social security to include disabled persons, the implementation of the earned income tax, and for locking down a National Football League team for New Orleans. One of his last moves as a political figure was to endorse Mary Landrieu for a Senate seat, saying that her Republican opponent would try to implement a terrible national sales tax plan to benefit the richest Americans.

8. "Edwin Edwards: High Times and Hard Times," Associated Press, November 12, 1991.

9. Parent qtd. in Elizabeth Kolbert, "The Big Sleazy," *New Yorker*, June 12, 2006, https://www.newyorker.com/magazine/2006/06/12/the-big-sleazy; Greg Hilburn, "Quips, Quotes from the Governor's Campaign Trail," *News Star* (Monroe, LA), September 25, 2015, https://www.thenewsstar.com/story/news/politics/2015/09/25/quips-quotes-governors-campaign-trail/72799590.

10. "A History of Key Abortion Rulings of the US Supreme Court," Pew Research Center, January 16, 2013, https://www.pewforum.org/2013/01/16/a-history-of-key-abortion-rulings-of-the-us-supreme-court; Thomas B. Edsall, "Gov. Roemer Struggles after Tax Issue Defeat," *Washington Post*, May 14, 1989, https://www.washingtonpost.com/archive/politics/1989/05/14/gov-roemer-struggles-after-tax-issue-defeat/71171b72-f41a-4f69-b831-4a0ff6584d08.

11. Keith Finley, "Late Twentieth-Century Louisiana," *64 Parishes*, August 19, 2013, https://64parishes.org/entry/late-twentieth-century-louisiana; John Maginnis, *Cross to Bear* (Baton Rouge: Darkhorse Publishing, 1992), 56, 135; see also Brett Barrouquere, "White Shadow: David Duke's Lasting Influence on American White Supremacy," *Hatewatch* (blog), Southern Poverty Law Center, May 17, 2019, https://www.splcenter.org/hatewatch/2019/05/17/white-shadow-david-dukes-lasting-influence-american-white-supremacy.

12. Maginnis, *Cross to Bear*, 19, 88, 74, 192

13. Anti-Defamation League, *A Dark and Constant Rage: 25 Years of Right-Wing Terrorism in the United States* (New York: Anti-Defamation League, 2017), https://www.adl.org/sites/default/files/documents/CR_5154_25YRS%20Right Wing%20Terrorism_V5.pdf; 116th Congress, House Meeting, "Meeting the

Challenge of White Nationalist Terrorism at Home and Abroad," US Government Publishing Office, September 18, 2019, https://www.govinfo.gov/content/pkg/CHRG-116hhrg37706/html/CHRG-116hhrg37706.htm.

14. Peter Applebome, "Blacks and Affluent Whites Give Edwards Victory," *New York Times*, November 18, 1991, 1; Jim Brown, "Edwards, Duke: 'The Race from Hell,'" *Ouachita Citizen* (West Monroe, LA), November 22, 2017, https://www.hannapub.com/ouachitacitizen/opinion/columns/jim-brown-edwards-duke-the-race-from-hell/article_fa048116-cfba-11e7-a1ce-47df205105fd.html.

15. Barry Eichengreen, *The Populist Temptation: Economic Grievance and Political Reaction in the Modern Era* (Oxford: Oxford University Press, 2018), 24.

PROLOGUE

Epigraph. Buddy Roemer, interview by unknown, "National Governors Association," CSPAN, July 29, 1990, https://www.c-span.org/video/?13330-1/interview-governor-roemer.

1. "Buddy Roemer," Gluxus, accessed July 21, 2021, https://www.gluxus.com/portfolio-items/buddy-roemer.

2. Maginnis, *Cross to Bear*, 259. See also "Bagert Gives Back Donation," *Shreveport Times*, October 13, 1991, 6.

3. Otis White, "Ex-Klansmen Draws La. Voters," *Tampa Bay Times*, 1991, https://www.tampabay.com/archive/1991/10/20/ex-klansman-draws-la-voters.

4. Maginnis, *Cross to Bear*, 259.

5. David Maraniss, "Edwards Cuts His Losses," *Washington Post*, October 26, 1987, https://www.washingtonpost.com/archive/politics/1987/10/26/edwards-cuts-his-losses/58bba235-c2d5-40e1-8bc2-fbdec9612688.

6. Richard E. Meyer, "The Rake, the Racist, and the New Age Reformer," *Los Angeles Times*, October 13, 1991, https://www.latimes.com/archives/la-xpm-1991-10-13-tm-1175-story.html.

7. Maginnis, *Cross to Bear*, 52, 47. Unwilling to live alone in the Governor's Mansion, the governor set up an extra bedroom and moved in adult daughter Caroline.

8. Maginnis, 190; "National Governors Association," CSPAN, July 29, 1990.

9. 1992 General Election Results: President, Georgia Secretary of State, https://sos.ga.gov/elections/election_results/1992/pres.htm.

10. In most of the US, party primaries determine a political party's nominee. However, in a system created in 1977 by Edwin Edwards, all of Louisiana's statewide candidates run together in a "jungle" primary. Unless one candidate crosses the 50 percent threshold, the top two finishers regardless of party affiliation head to a runoff.

11. Maginnis, *Cross to Bear*, 81, 197.

12. Paul West, "The Numbers from Louisiana Add Up, Chillingly," *Baltimore Sun*, November 18, 1991, https://www.baltimoresun.com/news/bs-xpm-1991-11-18 -1991322072-story.html.

13. "1991 World Series," Baseball Reference, accessed July 21, 2021, https://www. baseball-reference.com/bullpen/1991_World_Series#Game_1.

14. Leo Honeycutt, *Edwin Edwards: Governor of Louisiana* (Baton Rouge, LA: Lisburn Press, 2009), 293.

15. Tyler Bridges, *The Rise and Fall of David Duke* (Jackson: University Press of Mississippi, 2018), 248; see also Maginnis, *Cross to Bear*, 248, 355.

16. Maginnis, *Cross to Bear*, 261.

17. Josh Levin, "The Road to Hell," *Slow Burn*, Season 4: Episode 5 (podcast), released July 15, 2020. Transcript available on Slate, https://slate.com/transcripts/ ZytvR01nQzhDSDA1WmtQVW16dUhDelVwOG5ELosxRjBzZoVscWFlUjBkYzo=.

18. Wil Haygood, "A Messenger of Hope—or Hate?," *Buffalo (NY) News*, November 10, 1991, https://buffalonews.com/news/a-messenger-of-hope---or-hate-it -depends-on-your-point-of-view/article_a44ee05f-9fa8-5c49-84da-afbbc 262a50b.html.

19. Levin, "The Road to Hell."

20. Levin, "The Road to Hell."

21. Raymond Strother, phone interview, June 29, 2021.

22. Maginnis, *Cross to Bear*, 263.

23. Maginnis, *Cross to Bear*, 116, 282; see also Jewish Telegraphic Agency (JTA), "Louisiana GOP Refuses to Censure David Duke," *Daily News Bulletin*, March 14, 1990. Available through JTA Archive, https://www.jta.org/archive/ louisiana-gop-refuses-to-censure-david-duke.

24. Robin Toner, "Ex-Klan Leader's Vote Sends Message to a Pained GOP," *New York Times*, October 22, 1991, A1.

25. John Dillin, "Polls Show Duke Could Win Runoff," *Christian Science Monitor*, November 1, 1991. https://www.csmonitor.com/1991/1101/01031.html.

26. "LA Governor—Initial Election" (second chart), Our Campaigns, March 31, 2021, https://www.ourcampaigns.com/RaceDetail.html?RaceID=14413.

27. Mark McKinnon, phone interview, June 12, 2021.

28. Notes for a book proposal, Elizabeth Rickey Archives, American Jewish Committee, New York (hereafter Rickey Archive). Note that Rickey's papers in this archive have not yet been cataloged.

29. Maginnis, *Cross to Bear*, 69.

30. "The average White is more intelligent than the average black," Duke had written in *NAAWP News*. "There's only one country that's all-white, and that's

Iceland. And Iceland is not enough." *NAAWP News*, box 21, folder 2, Louisiana Coalition Against Racism and Nazism (LCARN) Records, 1943–1999, Amistad Research Center, Tulane University, New Orleans (hereafter LCARN Records); many of the documents in this archive have been cataloged and the finding aid is available at https://amistad-finding-aids.tulane.edu/repositories/2/resources/56. See also "Ex-Klan Leader Duke Finds Backers in Senate Race," *Orlando Sentinel*, June 3, 1990, https://www.orlandosentinel.com/news/os-xpm -1990-06-03-9006030246-story.html. In 1969, he'd written in the LSU newspaper, "What does National Socialism stand for? It stands for cultural, spiritual and racial values to become the primary emphasis of a system," and in 1986, he'd suggested "An American [*sic*] ruled by a majority of Blacks, Mexicans and other third world types will not be the America of our forefathers nor the kind of nation for which they struggled and sacrificed LCARN Archives, New Orleans, LA, Box 21, Folder 4; Maginnis, *Cross to Bear*, 192. See also "David Duke in His Own Words," in "A Special Double Issue on David Duke," ed. Ronnie Dugger and James Cullen, *Texas Observer* 84, nos. 1 & 2 (Jan. 17 & 31, 1992), 24–32.

31. "Louisiana GOP Won't Censure Duke," *Los Angeles Times*, September 24, 1989, https://www.latimes.com/archives/la-xpm-1989-09-24-mn-315-story.html. Duke blamed the bombing on a "gas explosion" in a conversation with Rickey. Phone call transcript, September 18, 1989, Rickey Archive; Maginnis, *Cross to Bear*, 60.

32. Letter to unknown addressee, Rickey Archive.

33. Personal observation. See also Maginnis, *Cross to Bear*, 25; Ronnie Dugger, "An Interview with David Duke," in Dugger and Cullen, "Special Double Issue," 24–32.

CHAPTER 1

Epigraph. Tyler Bridges, "Edwin Edwards, Louisiana Populist," *The Advocate* (Baton Rouge, LA), July 12, 2021, https://www.theadvocate.com/baton_rouge/news/politics/article_6c91c6a0-2bf2-11e9-b57a-0f28036ae840.html.

1. "Louisiana's Governor Struggles with His New Image," *Greensboro (NC) News & Record*, January 9, 1992. https://greensboro.com/louisianas-governor -struggles-with-his-new-image/article_c53ad070-0823-5470-a1ed-7ecd1edeadee. html.

2. In 1974, the *New York Times* referred to an unnamed state legislator (not Edwards), who had made a trip to Las Vegas: "He responded by saying he regretted having made the trip and would never do it again, and anyway he had only lost $35." Edwards himself claimed to have lost $5,000 in two decades of Vegas jaunts, but he swore, "I never go incognito. I never make any effort to

hide." He did, however, pay off massive debts in cash while traveling under a fake name; Roy Reed, "Louisiana's Gov. Edwards: Cajun With a Populist Tinge and Much Ambition," *New York Times*, February 14, 1974, 81.

3. "Louisiana's Governor Struggles."

4. Carroll Gazette, "Former Louisiana Gov. Edwin Edwards," *Avoyelles Today*, July 15, 2021. https://www.avoyellestoday.com/obituaries/former-louisiana-gov-edwin -edwards.

5. Honeycutt, *Edwin Edwards*, 16–17. Despite his insinuations, Edwin had no Cajun blood. Had this been more popularly known in Louisiana's 7th Congressional District, it might have hindered his chances at a House seat. Instead, the non-Cajun Baptists would become his biggest detractors, as the non-Catholics were for John F. Kennedy.

6. Honeycutt, *Edwin Edwards*, 16–17.

7. Bridges, "Edwin Edwards."

8. Honeycutt, *Edwin Edwards*, 23.

9. Estimates vary wildly, as no complete study was done at the time, but experts believe that, in today's dollars, the losses might total anywhere from $130 billion to $1 trillion; Susan Scott Parrish, "The Great Mississippi Flood of 1927 Laid Bare the Divide between the North and the South," *Smithsonian Magazine*, April 11, 2017.

10. Edwin Edwards 1987 campaign speeches, various; see also WVLA-TV, "'I Came Out on Top': Former Gov. Edwin Edwards, 91, Reflects on Life and Career," BRProud.com, May 10, 2019, https://www.brproud.com/news/local-news/ i-came-out-on-top-former-gov-edwin-edwards-91-reflects-on-life-and-career.

11. Honeycutt, *Edwin Edwards*, 24.

12. Frenchy Brouillette and Matthew Randazzo V, *Mr. New Orleans* (Metairie, LA, Mrv Entertainment LLC, 2014), 308.

13. Honeycutt, *Edwin Edwards*, 29–31.

14. Honeycutt, 29–31.

15. Honeycutt, 25–26.

16. Errol Laborde, "Edwin Edwards at 90," New Orleans, July 24, 2017, https://www. myneworleans.com/edwin-edwards-at-90-2.

17. On or close to the day Robert E. Lee was made Commander of the Army of Virginia, coincidentally.

18. The death of William Edwards partly prompted a funeral procession, notable for "the conduct of an individual not unknown in Washington City for her hostility to the Union. This person resides in St. Charles-street [*sic*], near the City Hall, and when the funeral procession passed her house, she, sitting in the gallery, rendered herself conspicuous by various actions, such as persons

delighted, and enthusiastic over a circus performance are wont to indulge in, mingling her derisive pantomime with hysterical bursts of laughter." William's great-great-grandson might have "wont to indulge in" a private meeting with this person; "The Funeral of Lieut. Dekay Disgraceful Exhibitions by the Rebel Sympathizers Resistance to Cotton-Burning-Shameful Outrages-Louisiana in a State of Anarchy," *New York Times*, July 13, 1862, 1.

19. Theresa Schmidt, "Edwin Edwards Returns to Crowley where His Political Career Began," *KPLC News*, May 8, 2018. https://www.kplctv.com/story/38144390/edwin-edwards-returns-to-crowley-where-his-political-career-began.

20. In 1991, he would say, "We'd watch the folks out of the corner of our eyes. If we saw them slapping, we'd know they weren't right" and that our preaching wasn't reaching them; Maginnis, *Cross to Bear*, 229.

21. WVLA-TV, "'I Came Out on Top.'"

22. Reed, "Louisiana's Gov. Edwards."

23. Elaine Schwartzenberg had undergone a reported twenty-six surgeries, according to Edwin's later recollections, by the time they met at thirteen. She had osteomyelitis and blushed when everyone stared at her "bum" leg. Edwin smoothly avoided fixating on her medical problems; Honeycutt, *Edwin Edwards*, 33–36.

24. Honeycutt, *Edwin Edwards*, 26.

25. Edwin's training was cut short by the two atomic bombs dropped on Japan in 1945; Honeycutt, *Edwin Edwards*, 25–39.

26. Edwin Edwards, personal correspondence, May 27, 2021.

27. The International Rice Festival was held there for many years and was even attended by future president John F. Kennedy and his wife.

28. "Solon Says Police Should Have Used Guns At Protests," *Daily Mail* (Hagerstown, MD), July 11, 1970, 13, https://www.newspapers.com/newspage/22145228.

29. Scott Laderman, "How Richard Nixon Captured White Rage—and Laid the Groundwork for Donald Trump," *Washington Post*, November 3, 2019, https://www.washingtonpost.com/outlook/2019/11/03/how-richard-nixon-captured-white-rage-laid-groundwork-donald-trump; Dave Leip, "1972 Presidential General Election Results - Louisiana," US Election Atlas, accessed July 22, 2021, https://uselectionatlas.org/RESULTS/state.php?year=1972&fips=22&f=1&off=0&elect=0.

30. Honeycutt, *Edwin Edwards*, 16.

31. George D. Haimbaugh Jr., "The TVA Cases: A Quarter Century Later," *University of South Carolina School of Law* 41, no. 2 (Winter 1996): 197, 205.

32. Jeff Wallenfeldt, "Dixiecrat," *Encyclopedia Britannica*, accessed July 22, 2021. https://www.britannica.com/topic/Dixiecrat; "Strom Thurmond: A Featured

Biography," United States Senate, accessed July 22, 2021, https://www.senate. gov/senators/FeaturedBios/Featured_Bio_Thurmond.htm.

33. In seven years in Congress, Edwards missed more than 47 percent of roll call votes. "Rep. Edwin Edwards," GovTrack.US, accessed July 22, 2021, https:// www.govtrack.us/congress/members/edwin_edwards/403760.

34. Honeycutt, *Edwin Edwards*, 28–29.

35. Honeycutt, 28–29.

36. Honeycutt, 64; see also Mercedez_Hall7, "Huey Fontenot," Quizlet, accessed July 22, 2021, https://quizlet.com/471181995/people-flash-cards.

37. Honeycutt, *Edwin Edwards*, 64; Mercedez_Hall7, "Huey Fontenot."

38. Clyde C. Vidrine, *Louisiana Political Hijinks* (Baton Rouge: Claitor's Publishing, 1985), 224–25.

39. Vidrine, 224–25.

40. Photograph of Edwards shaking hands in Opelousas, LA, by Dale Givens, 1971. Honeycutt, *Edwin Edwards*, following page 192.

41. Honeycutt, 50–51, 64.

42. "1 of 2 Baton Rouge Explosions Rips Capitol's Senate Chamber," *New York Times*, April 27, 1970, 29; see also Honeycutt, *Edwin Edwards*, 67.

43. Honeycutt, *Edwin Edwards*, 66.

44. Honeycutt, *Edwin Edwards*, 70–72.

45. Roy Reed, "Two Louisiana Reformers Win Runoff Spots in a 17-Man Race for Democratic Gubernatorial Nomination," *New York Times*, November 8, 1971, 19.

46. In those days, Louisiana held standard party primaries. Edwards suggested that it was unfair to force a candidate to win a party primary, then the runoff, and then have to go into a third bruising battle in the general election against yet another opponent. Four years later, the state instituted a "jungle" primary, in which candidates of all parties competed. Assuming no candidate hit the fifty percent mark, a runoff was then scheduled pitting the top two candidates against each other.

47. A. Roswell Thompson obituary, *New Orleans Times-Picayune*, February 16, 1976, 1, 12; and "Jerry P. Shinley Archive: HSCA Memo on Clay Shaw 9/77 (plus Thomas Beckham)," accessed June 29, 2022, http://www.jfk-online.com/jpsh scacs77b.html; see also Patsy Sims, *The Klan*, 2nd ed. (Louisville: University Press of Kentucky, 1996), 152–53.

48. B. I. Moody interview, Honeycutt, *Edwin Edwards*, 70; "Treen Says Louisiana Needs Two-Party System to Develop Leaders," *Minden Press-Herald*, September 3, 1971, 1. Treen campaigned as if unaware that a mere fraction of the state's voters were registered Republicans. When he crushed Vietnam vet-

eran Max Ross in the first- (and last-)ever closed Republican Party primary for governor, Treen began to creep up in polling.

49. William C. Havard, Rudolf Heberle, and Perry H. Howard, *The Louisiana Elections of 1960* (Baton Rouge: Louisiana State University Studies, 1963), 40; see also Gus Weill, *You Are My Sunshine: The Jimmie Davis Story: An Affectionate Biography* (Gretna, LA:. Pelican Publishing, 1991), 149, and "Two New Faces Top Primary in Louisiana," *Toledo Blade*, November 8, 1971, 2.

50. "The Campaign: George's General," *Time*, https://content.time.com/time/ subscriber/article/0,33009,902367,00.html, October 11, 1968.

51. Honeycutt, *Edwin Edwards*, 75–77.

52. Honeycutt, 70.

53. Maginnis, *Cross to Bear*, 7.

54. Reed, "Louisiana's Gov. Edwards," *New York Times*, February 14, 1974, 81.

55. Honeycutt, *Edwin Edwards*, 78.

56. Honeycutt, 71.

57. "Two New Faces Top Primary in Louisiana," *Toledo Blade*, November 8, 1971, 2.

58. Honeycutt, *Edwin Edwards*, 80

59. "Two New Faces Top Primary in Louisiana," *Toledo Blade*, November 8, 1971, 2.

60. "Two New Faces."

61. Bridges, *David Duke*, 170

62. Harnett T. Kane, *Huey Long's Louisiana Hayride: The American Rehearsal for Dictatorship 1928–1940* (Gretna, LA: Pelican Publishing, 1998 edition).

63. Brouillette and Randazzo, *Mr. New Orleans*, 309.

64. Honeycutt, *Edwin Edwards*, 84–85.

65. Michael Radcliff, "Remembering Dorothy Mae Taylor: The First Lady of 1300 Perdido St.," *Louisiana Weekly*, June 14, 2011, http://www.louisianaweekly.com/ remembering-dorothy-mae-taylor-the-first-lady-of-1300-perdido-st.

66. "New Faces Winning in Louisiana," *Miami News*, November 8, 1971, accessed June 28, 2012, see also: Honeycutt, *Edwin Edwards*, 85–86.

67. "1972 Gubernatorial General Election Results - Louisiana," US Election Atlas, September 14, 2014, https://uselectionatlas.org/RESULTS/state.php?f= 0&fips=22&off=5&elect=0&year=1972.

68. "Runoff Results Are Announced," *The Town Talk (Alexandria, LA)*, December 19, 1971, 6.

69. "1972 Gubernatorial General Election Results – Louisiana"; see also "GOP Doesn't Have a Chance, Edwards Says," *Minden (LA) Press-Herald*, January 7, 1972, 1.

70. "Democrat Is Winner in Louisiana," *New York Times*, February 2, 1972, 17.

CHAPTER 2

1. "La. Literature: 'Against the Klan' Recounts Small-Town Publisher's Fight," *The Advocate* (Baton Rouge, LA), Staff Report, March 7, 2021, https://www.theadvocate.com/baton_rouge/entertainment_life/books/article_0538ec86-779f-11eb-9a76-d348bb98703e.html.

2. "Lou Major Sr.'s Civil Rights Era Memoir Now Available for Purchase On-line," *Bogalusa (LA) Daily News*, March 30, 2021, https://www.bogalusadailynews.com/2021/03/30/lou-major-sr-s-civil-rights-era-memoir-now-available-online.

3. Patrick Richoux, "FBI: Former Gov. John McKeithen Arranged Payments to Ku Klux Klan to Quell Violence in 1960s," *The Advocate* (Baton Rouge, LA), April 27, 2016, https://www.theadvocate.com/baton_rouge/news/article_0cd51a58-e446-5be3-a566-128597814118.html; see also Andy Horowitz, "Hurricane Betsy and the Politics of Disaster in New Orleans's Lower Ninth Ward, 1965–1967," *Journal of Southern History* 80, no. 4 (November 2014): 893–934.

4. Astead W. Herndon and Sheryl Gay Stolberg, "How Biden Became the Anti-Busing Democrat," *New York Times Magazine*, July 15, 2019, A1.

5. William K. Stevens, "5 Ex-Klansmen Convicted in School Bus Bomb Plot," *New York Times*, May 22, 1973, 21; see also Matt Delmont, "In 1971, 6 members of the Michigan KKK were arrested for bombing 10 empty school buses in Pontiac, Michigan. They wanted to intimidate supporters of the city's school desegregation plan. Judge Damon Keith said, 'This case will not be settled in the streets of Pontiac.'" Twitter, 7:06 a.m., Oct. 9, 2020, https://twitter.com/mattdelmont/status/1314537595217555459.

6. Matt Delmont, "'Miserable Women on Television': Irene McCabe, Television News, and Antibusing Politics," *Camera Obscura* 29 no. 3 (January 2014): 33–63. https://doi.org/10.1215/02705346-2801507.

7. The *Times* credited her with electing Robert J. Huber of Michigan, although he apparently rescinded a job offer to McCabe as the public lost interest in blocking black kids from going to traditionally "white" schools; "Irene McCabe's Mothers' March to Washington," *Why Busing Failed*, American Crossroads (Berkeley: University of California Press, 2016), November 11, 2015, http://whybusingfailed.com/anvc/why-busing-failed-irene-mccabes-mothers-march-to-washington.

8. Barry Horn, "Mary Bacon Ran Out of Rides," *Dallas Morning News*, September 29, 1991, https://archive.seattletimes.com/archive/?date=19910929&slug=1308123.

9. Judy Klemesrud, "Women in Ku Klux Klan Move into the Male Power Structure," *New York Times*, May 22, 1975, 44.

10. "I didn't know this many Cajuns owned tuxedos," he joked at his inaugural ball. Kevin McGill, "Profile of Edwin Edwards," AP News, May 9, 2000, https://apnews.com/article/313daef597851df10fc7d2b561e8ca53.

11. Money was the focus of most discussion in the Edwards transition team meetings and household. The ex-Congressman would be making $28,750 per year, a huge pay cut. Honeycutt, *Edwin Edwards*, 112; Honeycutt, *Edwin Edwards*, 90.

12. Honeycutt, *Edwin Edwards*, 138–39; see also Reed, "Louisiana's Gov. Edwards."

13. Reed, "Louisiana's Gov. Edwards."

14. "Edwards Vows to Reward Blacks for Their Support," *New Orleans State-Times*, May 13, 1972, 6A.

15. Honeycutt, *Edwin Edwards*, 106–7; Forest C. Hammond-Martin Sr., once pardoned, wrote a book about his experiences, *With Edwards in the Governor's Mansion: From Angola to Free Man* (New Orleans: Pelican Publishing, 2012).

16. It was not without precedent. Huey Long's wife Rose replaced the Kingfish in the Senate, and Ellender had won the seat following that term; Dominic Massa, "Former La. First Lady, US Sen. Elaine Edwards dies," WWL-TV, May 18, 2018, https://tinyurl.com/SenElaineEdwards.

17. Robert D. McFadden, "Edwin Edwards, Flamboyant Louisiana Governor, Is Dead at 93," *New York Times*, July 12, 2021; the plane crash loss of Congressman Boggs, under consideration as the next Speaker of the House, was immeasurable for Louisiana. Without his seniority and experience, the state suffered a serious power vacuum in Washington.

    Asked if he was perhaps too old for public office or had suffered too many wounds, Edwards responded, "There are only two contingencies which I envision at this time that would inhibit me from completing this term. One of them is death, which I intend to resist to the bitter end, and the other is the possibility, no matter how slight it may be, that I could become a national official." G. E. Arnold, "NO.newspapers.070719_021.JPG," *The Advocate* (Baton Rouge, LA), October 26, 1975, https://www.theadvocate.com/image_f7a4acdc-3c51-5158-90b1-270b6b7872d0.html.

18. Honeycutt, *Edwin Edwards*, 157–58; see also Warren D. Smith, "Louisiana Governor Races 1975–2007 as a Testbed for Runoff Pathologies," *The Center for Range Voting*, April 2008, https://rangevoting.org/LAgovs.html.

19. Carter, Dukakis, Gore, Kerry, and Hillary Clinton are best remembered as presidential candidates for defending their past actions and positions, while the party's rare victories came when candidates like Obama and Bill Clinton talked up the need for progressive economic and cultural changes.

20. Selwyn Raab, *Five Families: The Rise, Decline, and Resurgence of America's Most Powerful Mafia Empires* (New York: St. Martin's Press, 2005), 133, 18.

21. Associated Press, "Carlos Marcello, 83, Reputed Crime Boss In New Orleans Area," *New York Times*, March 3, 1993, B12; see also Ronald Goldfarb, "What the Mob Knew about JFK's Murder," *Washington Post*, March 14, 1993, https://www.washingtonpost.com/archive/opinions/1993/03/14/what-the-mob-knew -about-jfks-murder/9803e911-f52f-4944-88f1-c26863e35867.

22. Associated Press, "Carlos Marcello, 83"; see also John Pope, "Charles 'Budgie' Roemer, 88, Top Aide to Former Gov. Edwin Edwards, Dies of Alzheimer's Disease," July 10, 2012, https://www.nola.com/news/politics/article_98781f1f-075b -53c3-81e3-1cc9398acd98.html.

23. Bridges, *Rise and Fall*, 196; Maginnis, *Cross to Bear*, 33–34.

24. "Charles Elson Roemer," *New Orleans Times-Picayune*, July 7, 2012, https://obits. nola.com/us/obituaries/nola/name/charles-roemer-obituary?pid=158421339.

25. AP, "AROUND THE NATION; Trial Opens in New Orleans for Reputed Mafia Leader," *New York Times*, March 31, 1981, A16.

26. Ed McHale, "'Brilab' Convictions Overturned," Associated Press, June 23, 1989, https://apnews.com/article/3c6d4494b803934182d1a3a2cb9b44ba.

27. Charles R. Babcock, "They Finally Nailed Tongsun Park," *Washington Post*, August 29, 1982, https://www.washingtonpost.com/archive/opinions/1982/08/29/ they-finally-nailed-tongsun-park/b1980588-51db-4525-adeb-a7ef2994017f.

28. Babcock, "Tongsun Park."

29. In 1982, following a verdict against him in tax court, the *Post* put out a headline: "They Finally Nailed Tongsun Park." However, he wouldn't truly get "nailed" by a prosecutor on criminal charges until the 1990s "oil-for-food" scandal, for which he was convicted of conspiracy in 2006; Babcock, "Tongsun Park."

30. "Korean Businessman Guilty in Oil-for-Food Case," *NBC News*, July 13, 2006, https://www.nbcnews.com/id/wbna13849968.

31. Elaine Edwards had never really wanted to be a political wife, let alone a politician.

32. "Louisiana Governor Says His Wife Was Given $10,000 by South Korean," *New York Times*, October 26, 1976, 14.

33. Vidrine, *Louisiana Political Hijinks*, 198–200; see also Honeycutt, *Edwin Edwards*, 115–17.

34. Steve Kornacki, "The Most Prophetic Statement Made by a Leader," *Hardball with Chris Matthews*, MSNBC, July 2, 2014, https://www.msnbc.com/hardball/ the-most-prophetic-statement-made-leader-msna361976.

35. Vidrine, *Louisiana Political Hijinks*, ix, 156, 160, and 198–200.

36. Vidrine, *Louisiana Political Hijinks*, 156.

37. Vidrine, *Louisiana Political Hijinks*, 198–200.

38. Eric Paulsen, "Edwin Edwards Reflects on His Life at 90-Years-Old," WWL-TV/ THV-11, August 4, 2017, https://www.thv11.com/amp/article/news/local/edwin -edwards-reflects-on-his-life-at-90-years-old/289-462100885.

39. The most bizarre aspect of *Louisiana Political Hijinks*, the self-published, ex- panded 1985 version of *Just Takin' Orders*, may be an anomaly, occurring in sev- eral copies. On page 21, several lines of text are redacted, seemingly by hand and using a thick black pen or magic marker. This section of the book deals with members of the Dave Treen administration, which took over following the 1979 election. Part of the blacked-out text reads, "Sting man Joseph Hauser posed as an agent for Prudential Insurance Company. He successfully paid [redacted] Lambert [redacted] $10,000, and Roemer was paid $25,000 to secure contracts for health insurance on state employees. Edwards was promised $50,000, which he never took because he got wind of the [authorities' sting] operation." Louis Lambert was the Democratic nominee for governor in 1979, but it is unclear if this is the "Lambert" referred to.

40. Reed, "Louisiana's Gov. Edwards."

41. A man named L. D. Knox was on the ballot, although under the name "None of the Above," as way to collect protest votes. "L. D. Knox, Who Tried to Give Vot- ers a Choice, Dies at 80," *New York Times*, May 28, 2009, https://www.nytimes. com/2009/05/29/us/29knox.html.

42. Honeycutt, *Edwin Edwards*, 124–26.

43. Martin Waldron, "2 Die in Clash with Police on Baton Rouge Campus," *New York Times*, November 17, 1972, 1; see also Gary Chambers, "Today is the 43rd Anniversary of Southern University Massacre where Denver Smith & Leonard Brown Were Killed," *Rogue Collection*, November 16, 2015, and Honeycutt, *Ed- win Edwards*, 121–26.

44. Waldron, "2 Die in Clash."

45. John Kifner, "Details of New Orleans Shootout Emerge, but Two Crucial Ques- tions Remain," Jan 15, 1973, 18; see also Honeycutt, *Edwin Edwards*, 131–32.

46. John Drabble, "From White Supremacy to White Power: The FBI, COINTEL- PRO-WHITE HATE, and the Nazification of the Ku Klux Klan in the 1970s," *American Studies* 48, no. 3 (Fall 2007): 61, https://core.ac.uk/download/pdf/ 162640719.pdf.

47. Jerry Thompson, *My Life in the Klan* (New York; Putnam, 1982), 77; "David Duke Protest - 1975," *The Carolina Story: A Virtual Museum of University History*, University of North Carolina, https://museum.unc.edu/exhibits/show/black -student-movement/david-duke-protest--1975.

48. John Drabble, "COINTELPRO-WHITE HATE, the FBI, and the Cold War Con- sensus," PhD diss., University of California at Berkeley/American Studies,

1996, 297–328; Judy Klemesrud, "Women in Ku Klux Klan Move into the Male Power Structure," *New York Times*, May 22, 1975, 44.

49. "Photos: A Look Back at the 1979 Greensboro Massacre 40 Years Later," *Greensboro News and Record*, October 30, 2019, https://greensboro.com/gallery/photos-a-look-back-at-the-1979-greensboro-massacre-40-years-later/collection_bcef3766-faac-11e9-bb5c-53b447a7885e.html.

50. "Photos: A Look Back."

51. The jury in the North Carolina trial said they believed the men had acted in self-defense.

52. "Photos: A Look Back."

53. Shaun Assael and Peter Keating, "The Massacre That Spawned the Alt Right," *Politico*, November 3, 2019, https://www.politico.com/magazine/story/2019/11/03/greensboro-massacre-white-nationalism-klan-229873.

54. Honeycutt, *Edwin Edwards*, 185.

55. Dominic Massa, "Former Louisiana Governor Edwin Edwards Has Died," July 12, 2021, https://www.wwltv.com/article/news/politics/former-louisiana-governor-edwin-edwards-has-died/289-19a34530-d2c5-431e-a970-754bd49 42b13; see also Honeycutt, *Edwin Edwards*, 185–86.

CHAPTER 3

Epigraph. Maginnis, *Cross to Bear*, 18.

1. Maginnis, 18

2. Michael Zatarain, *David Duke: Evolution of a Klansman* (Gretna, LA: Pelican Publishing Company, 1990), 44.

3. Henry C. Fong, *Media Manipulation in Electoral Campaigns: A Qualitative Look at David Duke's Political Career*, Working Paper 95-13 (Berkeley: Institute of Governmental Studies, University of California, Berkeley, 1995), https://escholarship.org/content/qt220212df/qt220212df.pdf.

4. Zatarain, *David Duke*, 46.

5. Lawrence N. Powell, "Slouching toward Baton Rouge: The 1989 Legislative Election of David Duke," in *The Emergence of David Duke and the Politics of Race*, Douglas D. Rose, ed., 12–40 (Chapel Hill: University of North Carolina Press, 1992), 18.

6. Maginnis, *Cross to Bear*, 28–29.

7. Maginnis, 28–29.

8. As it had during the Klan's second wave in the 1920s, the Klan's support again spread northward to counties whose makeup had been altered in the Great Migration of black people during the Civil Rights movement, to the point where, in the 1980s and beyond, much of Duke's financial support came from out-of-state and European whites. In 1980, Scotland, Connecticut, held its first Klan rally since the Great Depression to prepare "for the coming race war."

9. Powell, *The Emergence*, 26, 23.

10. Zatarain, *David Duke*, 44.

11. Moore and Tracy, *No Fascist USA!*, 103.

12. Introduction to *David Duke and the Politics of Race in the South*, eds. John C. Kuzenski, Charles S. Bullock III, Ronald Keith Gaddie (Nashville, TN: Vanderbilt University Press, 1995), xii; Ralph R. Hopkins: "Letters: The Real Reason David Duke Won His State House Election," *The Advocate* (Baton Rouge, LA), May 5, 2020, https://www.theadvocate.com/baton_rouge/opinion/letters/article_bae454d6-8c94-11ea-aedd-77b1ec64bdfc.html.

13. Zatarain, *David Duke*, 46–48.

14. Duke shouted, "Mr. Buddy Roemer, read my lips: no new taxes," a reference to President Bush—and Roemer's—supposedly broken campaign promises. Maginnis, *Cross to Bear*, 29. Historian Larry Powell believed the GOP had only themselves to blame for alienating working class voters: "Republican economic policies," he noted, "have helped shift wealth and opportunity upward [which prepared] the ground for Duke's racist insurgency." Powell, *The Emergence*, 7, 29; Maginnis, *Cross to Bear*, 29.

15. Zatarain, *David Duke*, 46.

16. "John has always worked for the traditional values and principles which you and I cherish." Ronald Reagan, Letter on Treen's behalf, circa January 1989, box 27, folder 10, LCARN Records.

17. Haygood, "Messenger of Hope."

18. "Friend, Ex-wife Say Duke Not Violent," *South Florida Sun-Sentinel*, February 23, 1989, 9; see also Anne Bohlen, Kevin Rafferty, and James Ridgeway, dirs., *Blood in the Face*, First Run Features, 1991.

19. Powell, *The Emergence*, 26.

20. Bridges, *The Rise*, 5.

21. Bridges, *The Rise*, 5

22. JoAnne Harrison, "David Duke: Dixie Divider: The Ex-Klansman Taps Well of Discontent to Win a Louisiana House Seat, and a Constituency," *Los Angeles Times*, March 21, 1989, https://www.latimes.com/archives/la-xpm-1989-03-21-vw-212-story.html.

23. Harrison, "David Duke."

24. Harrison, "David Duke."

25. Undated handwritten note, page 4, Rickey Archive.

26. "David Duke: In His Own Words," Anti-Defamation League of B'nai B'rith, Baylor University, accessed May 8, 2022, https://digitalcollections-baylor.quartexcollections.com/Documents/Detail/david-duke-in-his-own-words/808926.

27. Robert Caro, *The Years of Lyndon Johnson: The Path to Power* (New York: Random House, 1982), 85.

28. Zatarain, *David Duke*, 54.

29. Bridges, *The Rise*, 5.

30. Bill Turque, "The Real David Duke," *Newsweek*, November 17, 1991, https://www.newsweek.com/real-david-duke-201998.

31. During Duke's 1989 campaign for state representative, his campaign manager Howie Farrell argued in a letter to voters that Duke was not violent and had never supported violence, using statements by a right-wing talk radio host and an investigator with Klanwatch to prove it.

32. Turque, "The Real David Duke."

33. Turque, "The Real David Duke."

34. Presumably rock and roll and/or soul records.

35. "File:Dont Buy Ford Cititzens [*sic*] Council Flyer.jpg," Wikimedia Commons, Wikipedia, ca. 1963, uploaded September 27, 2011, https://commons.wikimedia.org/wiki/File:Dont_Buy_Ford_Citizens_Council_Flyer.jpg; "Help Save the Youth of America," Me.Me, March 19, 2017, 22:23, https://me.me/i/help-save-the-youth-of-america-dont-buy-negro-records-11561922.

36. Evelyn Rich interviews,, box 19, folder 18, LCARN Records.

37. Hayseed, "A Messenger of Hope or Hate?," *Buffalo News*, November 10, 1991, https://buffalonews.com/news/a-messenger-of-hope—-or-hate-it-depends-on-your-point-of-view/article_a44ee05f-9fa8-5c49-84da-afbbc262a50b.html.

38. Duke campaign letter, 1989, box 10, folder 1, LCARN Records; see also Evelyn Rich interviews; Hayseed, "Messenger of Hope or Hate?"; and Maginnis, *Cross to Bear*, 21.

39. Lawrence N. Powell, "When Hate Came to Town: New Orleans' Jews and George Lincoln Rockwell," *American Jewish History* 85, no. 4 (1997): 393–419, http://www.jstor.org/stable/23885627; see also "10 NAZIS SEIZED IN NEW ORLEANS; Rockwell-Led 'Hate' Group Tries to Pocket 'Exodus,'" *New York Times*, May 25, 1961, 22; Bob Dylan, "Talkin' John Birch Paranoid Blues," track 16 on *The Bootleg Series, Volumes 1–3*," 1963 (Columbia, 1991, compact disc).

40. Ta-Nehisi Coates, "Bigotry and the English Language," *Atlantic*, December 3, 2013, https://www.theatlantic.com/national/archive/2013/12/bigotry-and-the-english-language/281935.

41. Turque, "The Real David Duke."

42. Ryan Buxton, "Free Speech Alley Rich with History, Creating Legacy for Student Discourse, Debates," *Reveille*, August 27, 2009, https://www.lsureveille.com/news/free-speech-alley-rich-with-history-creating-legacy-for-student-discourse-debates/article_624b6342-55b6-551e-b5fd-3d89d924e55e.html.

43. Kenneth S. Stern, "David Duke: A Nazi in Politics," *Issues in National Affairs*, the American Jewish Committee, 1, no. 4, 1991, 1.

44. "The Alley was not only a place for solemn discourse," a student columnist wrote in the *Reveille* in 2009, by way of explanation. "Many students who took the podium did so with a sense of humor, like one student who satirically promoted his new political party, the International Sensualist Emergency Committee, which called for 'free love and nickel beer or free beer and nickel love.'"

45. "If blacks are inferior," Beth Rickey once unsuccessfully challenged him, "how can they be a threat?"

46. Buxton, "Free Speech Alley."

47. Maginnis, *Cross to Bear*, 15.

48. Hayseed, "A Messenger of Hope or Hate?"

49. His trip to Laos is not without controversy. In later years, he would suggest having flown on humanitarian "drops," although neither Tyler Bridges nor a *Buffalo News* reporter, both of whom looked into it, could find any witnesses or other hard evidence; B. G. Burkett and Glenna Whitley, *Stolen Valor: How the Vietnam Generation was Robbed of Its Heroes and History* (Dallas: Verity Press, 1998).

50. Hayseed, "A Messenger of Hope or Hate?"

51. Hayseed, "A Messenger of Hope or Hate?"

52. Bridges, *Rise and Fall*, 32.

53. Evelyn Rich Interviews, 1986–1991, box 19, folder 17, LCARN Records; see also Hayseed, "A Messenger of Hope or Hate?"

54. Bridges, *Rise and Fall*, 55; see also New Orleans States-Item articles by Lanny Thomas, including September 13, 1975; March 31, 1976, A1; April 1, 1976, A1; and April 2, 1976, A1—all cover Lindsay's widows murder trial and acquittal over a three-day period.

55. Hayseed, "A Messenger of Hope or Hate?"

56. Evelyn Rich Interviews, box 19, folder 17, LCARN Records.

57. Proof that Duke wrote the book, as was long rumored, came in the form of a registry of a claim to copyright, listing Chloê Hardin (his wife's name), aka "Muhammad X." In 1990, he said *African Atto* (or *African Attack*) "was nothing more than a spoof to expose black racism." Political advertisement, August 1990, box 19, folder 16, LCARN Records.

58. Copyright notice for African Atto, June 11, 1976, box 19, folder 16, LCARN Records; see also Wayne King, "Leader Says Klan, Not Black, Wrote Attack Book," *New York Times*, February 20, 1978, A12; "David Duke Timeline," KPLC-TV, December 19, 2002, https://www.kplctv.com/story/1055753/david-duke-timeline.

CHAPTER 4

1. Frederick James Simonelli, *American Fuhrer: George Lincoln Rockwell and the American Nazi Party* (Champaign, IL: University of Illinois Press, 1999), 131–135;

"On This Day; August 25," BBC, accessed July 24, 2021; http://news.bbc.co.uk/onthisday/hi/dates/stories/august/25/newsid_3031000/3031928.stm. See also "Ex-aide Is Held for Slaying of US Nazi Chief," *Lawrence Journal-World*, August 26, 1967.

2. After Patler's fourteen years in prison (including time for a parole violation), he told his son, "I should have been with Dr. King and the Civil Rights people back then. They were truly my people, not those Nazis." William H. Schmaltz, *For Race and Nation: George Lincoln Rockwell and the American Nazi Party* (Stillwater, Mn, River's Bend Press, 2013.)

3. His sister later told Duke biographer Tyler Bridges she didn't know how to save him after Rockwell and the Citizen's Council's teachings entered his belief system. (If he hadn't gone down that road, she believed, he could've been president of the United States.) Bridges, *Rise and Fall*, 4.

4. Zatarain, *David Duke*, 244–46.

5. *NAAWP Newsletter*, no. 31, 1984, box 21, LCARN Records.

6. Turque, "The Real David Duke."

7. "Ku Klux Klan Plans Border Patrol to Help Fight Illegal Alien Problem," *New York Times*, October 18, 1977, 80.

8. Turque, "The Real David Duke."

9. Maginnis, *Cross to Bear*, 217, 192.

10. "1920: Leander Perez's Rise to Power in St. Bernard, Plaquemines," *New Orleans Times-Picayune*, October 24, 2011; "Obituary: Leander Perez, Political Boss, Integration Foe," *Free Lance-Star* (Fredericksburg, VA), March 20, 1969, 5.

11. Wayne King, "David Duke: Cleaning up the Klan's Public Image," *New York Times*, reprinted in *St. Petersburg Times*, November 24, 1975, 3A.

12. King, "David Duke."

13. "David Duke," Anti-Defamation League, 2013, 1, https://www.adl.org/sites/default/files/documents/assets/pdf/combating-hate/David-Duke.pdf.

14. Fong, *Media Manipulation*, https://escholarship.org/content/qt220212df/qt220212df.pdf; see also the Anti-Defamation League of B'nai B'rith, *Hate Groups in America: A Record of Bigotry and Violence*, (New York: Anti-Defamation League of B'nai B'rith, 1988) and Moore and Tracy, *No Fascist USA!*, 12.

15. *Knights of K. K. K., Etc. v. East Baton Rouge*, 578 F.2d 1122 (5th Cir. 1978), https://casetext.com/case/knights-of-k-k-k-etc-v-east-baton-rouge.

16. John R. Vile, "Incitement to Imminent Lawless Action," MTSU, https://mtsu.edu/first-amendment/article/970/incitement-to-imminent-lawless-action.

17. Do You Wanna Know? (@Isitreallyfakenews), "45. David Duke," Facebook, October 1, 2020, https://www.facebook.com/permalink.php?id=104282044619824&story_fbid=173272147720813; see also Zatarain, *David Duke*, 225–27.

18. According to an unsubstantiated report, the Louisiana State Supreme Court later overturned Duke's conviction. Ronnie Dugger, "David Duke's Life and Work," in Dugger and Cullen, "Special Double Issue," 23; see also Stern, "David Duke: A Nazi in Politics," 8, and Julia Reed "His Brilliant Career," *New York Review*, March 12, 1992, https://www.nybooks.com/articles/1992/04/09/his-brilliant-career.

19. Harrison, "David Duke," *Los Angeles Times*, March 21, 1989; Do You Wanna Know? (@Isitreallyfakenews), "45. David Duke."; see also Zatarain, *David Duke*, 225–27.

20. The DNC endorsed his Republican opponent, who won the general election easily. In 1990, after the death of an Ethiopian man, an Oregon jury leveled a $5,000,000 penalty on Metzger and $5,500,000 against a white supremacist group for inciting the murder. Ken Stone, "Tom Metzger Dies at 82; Notorious KKK Boss, Supremacist Who Ran for Congress," *Times of San Diego*, November 10, 2020, https://timesofsandiego.com/life/2020/11/10/tom-metzger-dies-at-82-notorious-kkk-boss-supremacist-who-ran-for-congress/; see also Zatarain, *David Duke*, 225–27.

21. Moore and Tracy, *No Fascist USA!*, 15.

22. Kitty Kelley, "Rising out of Hatred," *Washington Independent Review of Books*, January 11, 2020, https://www.washingtonindependentreviewofbooks.com/index.php/bookreview/rising-out-of-hatred.

23. "Ku Klux Klan Representative David Duke," UNC Libraries, accessed July 24, 2021, https://exhibits.lib.unc.edu/exhibits/show/academic_freedom/campus-visitors/david-duke.

24. "Ku Klux Klan Representative David Duke."

25. He gave this interview in a moving black taxicab, as police officers had staked out BBC Studios to detain him; Zatarain, *David Duke*, 237–40.

26. "David Duke Timeline," KPLC-TV, December 19, 2002; E. James West, "Hunt the Wizard! Race, Immigration, and British Tabloid Coverage of David Duke's 1978 Tour," *Contemporary British History* 35, no. 1 (2021), 100–24, DOI: 10.1080/13619462.2020.1856081.

27. Rickey Archive.

28. Zatarain, *David Duke*, 242–43.

29. Fox News editors, "Woman with Ties to White Supremacists Represents School for Blacks and Hispanics," *Fox News*, July 30, 2008, https://www.foxnews.com/story/woman-with-ties-to-white-supremacists-represents-school-for-blacks-and-hispanics.

30. Heidi Beirich, "Stormfront Founder's Wife Fronts for Minority School," *Intelligence Report*, Fall 2008, https://www.splcenter.org/fighting-hate/intelligence-report/2008/stormfront-founders-wife-fronts-minority-school.

31. Hadley and Rickey, "Louisiana Republicans," 42; Zatarain, *David Duke*, 249–50; George A. Clark, "FBI Informant and Self-Appointed Imperial Wizard of the Invisible Empire, of the Knights of the Ku Klux Klan, Bill Wilkinson, Speaking at a Rally, Decatur, Alabama, June 17, 1979," photograph, AJCP221-043a, *Atlanta Journal-Constitution* Photographic Archive, Georgia State University Library. https://digitalcollections.library.gsu.edu/digital/collection/ajc/id/980.

32. John Drabble wrote, "Along with four other former American Nazi Party members, Duke fused Klan iconography with Nazi racialism, NSRP anti-FBI rhetoric, Minutemen paramilitarism, millennial Christian Identity, recruiting thousands to the Knights of the Ku Klux Klan. By 1978–1979, they would recruit thousands of young whites into their Nazi–Klan hybrid organization. By 1980, hybrid Nazi–Klan associations began to exceed membership in traditional Klan groups." The Far Right infiltrated disaffected youth groups in both Europe and the US, even giving out drinks at punk shows with labels saying, "This beer bought for you by the KKK." Drabble, "From White Supremacy to White Power," 61; Moore and Tracy, *No Fascist USA!*, 177.

33. "AROUND THE NATION; Klan Leader Reportedly Informed for F.B.I.," *New York Times*, August 31, 1981, A10.

34. NAAWP newsletter ads for Americana Books, various dates, 1980s, box 21, folder 2, LCARN Records; asked whether the NAAWP tried to address Jewish people Duke later said no, the "NAAWP is focused on the racial issue." The NAAWP instead wanted, he said, to "stop immigration and some of these programs that are going on," create separate black nation states within North America, and if they cannot, then "the Jewish issue's going to be moot anyway because there won't be any white people."

35. Moore and Tracy, *No Fascist USA!*, 41.

36. Turque, "The Real David Duke."

37. "The Ku Klux Klan: A Brief Biography," *Africana: The Encyclopedia of the African and African American Experience*, eds. Kwame Anthony Appiah and Henry Louis Gates Jr. (New York, NY, Basic Civitas Books, 1999), accessed May 11, 2022, through African-American Registry, https://web.archive.org/web/20120825005249/http://www.aaregistry.org/historic_events/view/ku-klux-klan-brief-biography; see also "Ex-Klansman Executed in Racial Slaying," *Washington Post*, Jun 6, 1997, https://www.washingtonpost.com/archive/politics/1997/06/06/ex-klansman-executed-in-racial-slaying/6a36e3a3-88a0-43c8-a0bf-aab8e6f95b7b.

38. Stephen Singular, "The Killers among Us," *Denver Post*, April 16, 2000, https://extras.denverpost.com/opinion/persp0416.htm.

39. Andrea Dukakis, "Murder of Colorado Radio Man Alan Berg Still Resonates 30 Years Later," *Colorado Public Radio*, June 18, 2014, https://www.cpr.org/

show-segment/murder-of-colorado-radio-man-alan-berg-still-resonates-30
-years-later.

40. Berg's murder and its aftermath inspired a pair of 1988 films, *Talk Radio* and *Betrayed*, from directors Oliver Stone and Costa-Gavras, respectively; *Nazi America: A Secret History*, dir. Greg DeHart, A&E Television Networks, 2000, https://video.alexanderstreet.com/watch/nazi-america-a-secret-history; "Alan Berg," *World Heritage Encyclopedia*, accessed July 25, 2021. http://community.world heritage.org/article/WHEBN0000512953/Alan%20Berg.

41. Alexandra Alter, "How 'The Turner Diaries' Incites White Supremacists," *New York Times*, January 12, 20212, C5.

42. Zatarain, *David Duke*, 254.

43. Bohlen, Rafferty, and Ridgeway, *Blood in the Face*.

44. Various NAAWP newsletters from 1985 to 1987 are available in the LCARN Archives at the Amistad Research Center, Tulane University, https://amistad -finding-aids.tulane.edu/repositories/2/resources/56.

45. Bridges, *Rise and Fall*, 2.

46. Zatarain, *David Duke*, 264, and Josh Levin, "David Duke's America," *Slate*, June 10, 2020, https://slate.com/news-and-politics/2020/06/david-dukes-political -rise-started-in-forsyth-county.html.

47. Levin, "David Duke's America."

48. In his newsletter, Duke lambasted Congress for making King's father's birthday a Federal holiday, calling the patriarch a "Communist sympathizer." Duke also made cracks about the order to seal King's FBI file for fifty years; John A. Bolt, "Up To 25,000 March for Racial Tolerance in Forsyth County," Associated Press, Jan 24, 1987, https://apnews.com/article/6974ae74eb05e21c0784dd 922442e57d.

49. David Duke, NAAWP News, no. 43, 1987, box 21, LCARN Records.

50. John A. Bolt, "Up to 25,000 March for Racial Tolerance in Forsyth County," Associated Press, January 24, 1987, https://apnews.com/article/6974ae74eb 05e21c0784dd922442e57d.

51. Bolt, "25,000 March."

52. John A. Bolt, "25,000 March."

53. David Duke, *NAAWP News*, no. 43, 1987, box 21, LCARN Records.

54. Zatarain, *David Duke*, 275.

55. Bridges, *Rise and Fall*, 133–38.

56. In the wee hours of September 10, 1957, on the morning the Hattie Cotton elementary school was integrated, hidden sticks of dynamite exploded and destroyed a wing of the building and blew out its windows, shuttering the school. John Kasper, a leader of the White Citizen's Council, had long been suspected

by the FBI but never stood trial. Betsy Phillips, "Nashville Desegregation and the Bombing of Hattie Cotton Elementary," *Nashville Scene*, September 7, 2017, https://www.nashvillescene.com/news/pith-in-the-wind/article/20974873/nashville-desegregation-and-the-bombing-of-hattie-cotton-elementary; see also Robert S. Griffin, "The Tale of John Kasper" http://www.robertsgriffin.com/TaleKasper.pdf.

57. Tim Wise, phone interview, May 1, 2021.

58. Zatarain, *David Duke*, 277–78; see also Bridges, *Rise and Fall*, 139–40.

CHAPTER 5

1. "Johnston Treads Warily in Trying to Defuse Opponent's Populist Movement in Louisiana," *Wall Street Journal*, August 29, 1990, 1.

2. Jeff Sadow, "Elizabeth Rickey: 1956–2009," *Between the Lines* (blog), September 2009, http://jeffsadow.blogspot.com/2009/09/elizabeth-rickey-1956-2009.html.

3. Rob Rickey, phone interview, October 9, 2021.

4. Notes for book proposal draft, Rickey Archive; see also Bridges, *Rise and Fall*, 160.

5. Rickey Archive, and Rob Rickey, phone interview, October 29, 2021.

6. Rickey Archive.

7. Sadow, "Elizabeth Rickey."

8. Rickey Archive.

9. "His death when Beth was 10 (I was 13) was traumatic for both of us," wrote Rob Rickey, "but Beth had had a fractious relationship with him and I think she felt guilty about it." Phone interview, October 29, 2021.

10. Duke had made the switch to the Populist Party ticket by that point.

11. Vitter had not lived in the district for a year, and would thus be disqualified from running in a prompt election. However, it should be noted that David Duke didn't even live within the borders of the district but still ran and faced no serious attempt to disqualify him.

12. Republicans made up 1.5 percent of the Louisiana electorate in 1964, 8 percent in 1980 and almost 20 percent—95.1 percent of whom were white—by the 1992 presidential race. These numbers were also deceptive: for instance, one-quarter of Louisiana *Democratic* chairpersons didn't consider themselves Democratic voters in national elections. Charles D. Hadley and Jennifer E. Horan, "Louisiana: Two-Party Conservatism," in *Southern State Party Organizations and Activists*, eds. Charles D. Hadley and Lewis Bowman, 145–64 (Westport, CT: Praeger, 1995), 4, 16; Bridges, *Rise and Fall*, 139.

13. Zatarain, *David Duke*, 20–27.

14. Bridges, *Rise and Fall*, 146.

15. Bridges, *Rise and Fall*, 145.
16. "Duke Endorsement Disputed," *New Orleans Times-Picayune*, January 20, 1989, https://www.nola.com/news/article_f6000771-bc85-5b4c-a6e1-86a87c406085.html.
17. Chevel Johnson, "New Orleans Breaks Its 1979 Murder Record," Associated Press, December 18, 1989 https://apnews.com/article/7395171cd8e385018cd34eb1c2eb66b0.
18. Mary T. Schmich, "Louisiana Klan Vet Stirs Furor," *Chicago Tribune*, February 12, 1989, https://www.chicagotribune.com/news/ct-xpm-1989-02-12-8903040837-story.html.
19. Charles D. Hadley and Elizabeth A. Rickey, "Louisiana Republicans and the 1987 Democratic Revolution: Continuing on the Road toward Realignment?," research paper (date unknown), Rickey Archive, 5.
20. Zatarain, *David Duke*, 27.
21. Zatarain, *David Duke*, 27.
22. Mary T. Schmich, "Louisiana Klan Vet Stirs Furor," *Chicago Tribune*, February 12, 1989, https://www.chicagotribune.com/news/ct-xpm-1989-02-12-8903040837-story.html.
23. Bridges, *Rise and Fall*, 146.
24. Mary T. Schmich, "Louisiana Klan Vet Stirs Furor," *Chicago Tribune*, February 12, 1989, https://www.chicagotribune.com/news/ct-xpm-1989-02-12-8903040837-story.html.
25. Philip Shenon, "F.B.I. Chief Warns Arabs of Danger," *New York Times*, December 11, 1985, A13; Dennis King, *Lyndon LaRouche and the New American Fascism* (New York: Doubleday, 1989), 243–51.
26. "Synagogue Cancels Rally Against KKK Candidate," *Tulsa World*, Jan 27, 1989, https://tulsaworld.com/article_e5c3601e-0cb5-5f03-b191-cd71ba97507f.html.
27. Jane Buchsbaum, phone interview, April 21, 2022.
28. Mordechai Levy, event flyer, circa January 1989, box 45, LCARN Records.
29. Stern, "David Duke," 13.
30. "The Velvet Underground in Boston," The Velvet Forum, user "velvetfan" comment, November 19, 2010, http://www.velvetforum.com/viewtopic.php?t=3654&start=70.
31. Jane Buchsbaum, phone interview, April 21, 2022; see also J. J. Goldberg, "Mordechai Levy vs the Klan," *Jerusalem Report*, July 2, 1992.
32. Schmich, "Louisiana Klan," *Chicago Tribune*, February 12, 1989.
33. Harrison, "David Duke," *Los Angeles Times*, March 21, 1989, 6A.
34. Bridges, *Rise and Fall*, 160.
35. Tim Wise, phone interview May 1, 2021.

36. LCARN meeting notes, June 11, 1990, Folder 5, box 6, "Meeting Agendas, Minutes and Notes, 1989–1992," LCARN records.

37. Hadley and Rickey, "Louisiana Republicans," 24.

38. Tim Wise, phone interview, May 1, 2021.

39. Rickey Archive.

40. LCARN meeting notes, October 17, 1989, "Meeting Agendas, Minutes and Notes, 1989–1992," Folder 5, box 6, LCARN Records.

41. Elizabeth A. Rickey, "The Nazis and the Republicans: An Insider View of the Response of the Louisiana Republican Party to David Duke," in *The Emergence of David Duke*, ed. Douglas D. Rose, 59–79 (Chapel Hill: University of North Carolina Press, 1992), 62–64; Untitled research paper, page 13, Rickey Archive; for other perspectives on Rickey's trip to Chicago, also see Zatarain, *David Duke*, 285–86; Bridges, *Rise and Fall*, 154–56; and John P. Avlon, *Independent Nation: How Centrists Can Change American Politics* (New York: Three Rivers Press, 2005), 99, 108.

42. Notes from Populist Party convention, undated, 1989, Rickey Archive.

43. Notes from Populist Party convention, undated, 1989, Rickey Archive.

44. Rickey, "Nazis and Republicans," 63–64.

45. Rickey, "Nazis and Republicans," 64.

46. "Duke Says He's Sorry," *Orlando-Sentinel*, March 5, 1989, 7.

47. In an August 1990 push poll on Duke's United States Senate run, 62 percent said his propensity to hire neo-Nazis or ex-Nazis made them less likely to support him, while only 42 percent had the same answer after learning of his membership in the Klan.

48. Maralee Schwartz, "Republican Ex-Klan Member Might Challenge Sen. Johnston," *Washington Post*, December 6, 1989, https://www.washingtonpost.com/archive/politics/1989/12/06/republican-ex-klan-member-might-challenge-sen-johnston/90e3f512-ccd3-4c4e-b13e-3bd0d63cdf33.

49. Schwartz, "Republican Ex-Klan Member."

50. Rickey, "Nazis and Republicans," 65–66.

51. Rickey, "Nazis and Republicans," 65–68.

52. David Duke, "Why I Oppose Race Mixing," *NAAWP News*, no. 42, 1986, 1.

53. Caroline Moorehead, *A House in the Mountains: The Women Who Liberated Italy from Fascism* (New York: HarperCollins, 2019), 140.

54. Notes for a book proposal, page 20, Rickey Archive.

55. John Treen campaign analysis, page 55, author unknown, Rickey Archive.

56. Hadley and Rickey, "Louisiana Republicans," 54.

57. Barbara Perry, *In the Name of Hate: Understanding Hate Crimes* (Oxfordshire: Taylor & Francis, 2001), 167.

58. Rickey claims the same friend went back later that week and acquired the Rockwell tape, as well as books on racial differences, ethnic group differences, and *Did Six Million Really Die?*, among other controversial works.

59. Jane Buchsbaum, phone interview, April 21, 2022; and Anne Levy, phone interview, April 7, 2022.

60. Lawrence N. Powell, "The Rise and Fall of David Duke: How Holocaust Memory Broke the Code of Right-Wing Populism," *American Scholar* 74, no. 4 (Fall 2005): 60–72.

61. Lawrence N. Powell, *Anne Levy, the Holocaust, and David Duke's Louisiana*, (Chapel Hill: University of North Carolina Press, 2019, 2nd ed.), 2–4, 10–11, 19; see also Bridges, *Rise and Fall*, 158–59.

62. Anne Levy, phone interview, April 7, 2022.

63. Bridges, *Rise and Fall*, 163–66.

64. From Duke's perspective, this was rather rich, as Atwater came to power (and infamy) for creating George H. W. Bush's game-changing 1988 campaign ad highlighting a black convict named Willie Horton, whom Bush's opponent had inadvertently allowed out on a work release program, whereupon he murdered someone. The ad was as close to a literal "dog whistle" as one could imagine.

65. Bridges, *Rise and Fall*, 162–63.

66. Rickey, "Nazis and Republicans," 64.

67. Powell, *Anne Levy*, 462–63.

68. Bridges, *Rise and Fall*, 163–66.

69. Kenneth Stern, phone interview, June 25, 2021.

70. Powell, *Anne Levy*, 19.

71. Note to Kenneth Stern, page 2, Rickey Archive.

72. Tyler Bridges, "Neo-Nazi Books Sold at Duke's Office," *New Orleans Times-Picayune*, June 8, 1989, 5.

73. Bridges, "Neo-Nazi Books."

74. Bridges, *Rise and Fall*, 163.

75. June 1989 telephone call transcript, Rickey Archive. At the same time, Duke had not pieced together the full scope of Rickey's animosity. "How does he get all this stuff?" Duke howled about the dossier, imagining John Treen being behind it.

76. Bridges, *Rise and Fall*, 163.

77. Undated essay, Rickey Archive.

78. Undated essay, Rickey Archive.

79. Lawrence Stern, phone interview, June 25, 2021.

80. John Naland, phone interview, August 14, 2021.

81. Quin Hillyer phone interview, May 12, 2021.
82. In the 1980s, with video recording prohibitively expensive and no internet searches, if Duke wanted to cover the tracks of a racist past, he might only need a paper shredder.
83. Maginnis, *Cross to Bear*, 57.
84. Maginnis, *Cross to Bear*, 57–58; Bridges, *Rise and Fall*, 159; see also Powell, *Anne Levy*, 445.
85. The British novelist had gone into hiding after the Supreme Leader of Iran ordered Rushdie's assassination.
86. Rickey, "The Nazis," 72–73; Ronnie Dugger, "Beth Rickey Replies to Duke," in Dugger and Cullen, "Special Double Issue," 32.
87. "Louisiana GOP Refuses to Censure David Duke," Jewish Telegraphic Agency, March 14, 1990, https://www.jta.org/1990/03/14/archive/louisiana-gop-refuses -to-censure-david-duke; see also Zatarain, *David Duke*, 292.
88. Meeting notes, folder 5, box 6, Meeting Agendas, Minutes and Notes, 1989– 1992, LCARN Records.
89. Quin Hillyer, phone interview, May 12, 2021.
90. November 20, 1989 meeting notes, folder 5, box 6, Meeting Agendas, Minutes and Notes, 1989–1992, LCARN Records.
91. Handwritten letter, addressee unknown, June 23, 1989, Rickey Archive; Quin Hillyer, phone interview, May 12, 2021; Lawrence N. Powell, phone interview, May 17, 2021. LCARN still hadn't announced its name, as most of its members assumed Duke and the movement to stop him would fizzle out in tandem once "the truth" came out.
92. 1990 diary entry, Rickey Archive.
93. Maginnis, *Cross to Bear*, 71; see also Rickey, "The Nazis," 71.

CHAPTER 6

1. Maginnis, *Cross to Bear*, 71; see also handwritten letter, addressee unknown, June 23, 1989, Rickey Archive.
2. Phone call transcript, September 18, 1989, Rickey Archive.
3. Maginnis, *Cross to Bear*, 58–61, 71; handwritten letter, addressee unknown, June 23, 1989, Rickey Archive; see also Bridges, *Rise and Fall*, 163–65.
4. Maginnis, *Cross to Bear*, 71, and Peter Applebome, "Duke: The Ex-Nazi Who Would Be Governor," *New York Times*, November 10, 1991, 1.
5. Duke told her genetic disparities between the races lead to economic collapse and criminal activity. He also claimed "there's ten times more whites who suf- fer from minority-visited violence—than blacks." David Duke and Elizabeth Rickey, phone conversation, September 19, 1989, Rickey Archive.

6. Danny Duncan Collum, "Fascism with a Facelift," *Sojourners*, January 1992, https://sojo.net/magazine/january-1992/fascism-facelift.

7. Anna Quindlen, "Public & Private: (Same Old) New Duke," *New York Times*, November 13, 1991, A25.

8. He would soon tell the Los Angeles *Times*, "I never got a face lift. . . . I had a broken nose repaired and I had some scarring here, which he (the doctor) fixed. . . . I had some precancerous conditions that I had worked on a little bit." Meyer, "The Rake."

9. Maginnis, *Cross to Bear*, 277.

10. Jane Buchsbaum, phone interview, April 21, 2022.

11. Hadley and Rickey, "Louisiana Republicans," 40–41.

12. Dugger, "Beth Rickey Replies."

13. Quin Hillyer, phone interview, May 12, 2021.

14. Bridges, *Rise and Fall*, 164.

15. Maginnis, *Cross to Bear*, 58.

16. Maginnis, *Cross to Bear*, 58; diary entry, July 8, 1989, Rickey Archive.

17. Rickey, "The Nazis," 72–73; Dugger, "Beth Rickey Replies."

18. Diary entry, August 8, 1989, Rickey Archive.

19. John Naland, phone interview, August 14, 2021.

20. Bridges, *Rise and Fall*, 165; see also Hadley and Rickey, "Louisiana Republicans," 40–41; Maginnis, *Cross to Bear*, 58–60.

21. Maginnis, *Cross to Bear*, 59.

22. Powell, *Anne Levy*, 46.

23. Mary Sanchez, "Sanchez: Elizabeth Rickey: An Unsung Hero Passes," *The Gazette* (Cedar Rapids, IA), Sep. 29, 2009, https://www.thegazette.com/opinion/sanchez-elizabeth-rickey-an-unsung-hero-passes.

24. Rickey, "The Nazis," 72–73; Dugger, "Beth Rickey Replies."

25. Maginnis, *Cross to Bear*, 59.

26. AP, "Former Leader of Klan Narrowly Wins Contest in Louisiana," *New York Times*, February 19, 1989, 27; Bridges, *Rise and Fall*, 139–40; Maginnis, *Cross to Bear*, 27–28, 54, 63.

27. Maraniss, "Winning Support," *Washington Post*, October 26, 1987.

28. Maraniss, "Winning Support."

29. Maginnis, *Cross to Bear*, 118.

30. Maginnis, 48–49.

31. Maginnis, 48–49, 192; Frances Frank Marcus, "Louisiana Crushes Tax Overhaul in a Defeat Damaging to Governor," *New York Times*, May 1, 1989, A12.

32. Maginnis, 48–49, 192; Marcus, "Louisiana Crushes."

33. Maginnis, *Cross to Bear*, 70; Bridges, *Rise and Fall*, 171.

34. Fong, *Media Manipulation*, 15.

35. Bridges, *Rise and Fall*, 191.

36. Bridges, *Rise and Fall*, 169; see also Maginnis, *Cross to Bear*, 65–66.

37. Maginnis, *Cross to Bear*, 84–85.

38. Wayne Parent, *Inside the Carnival* (Baton Rouge: Louisiana State University Press, 2004), 45.

39. Bridges, *Rise and Fall*, 170, 187–91.

40. J. Bennett Johnston campaign mailer, 1990, Rickey Archive.

41. Bridges, *Rise and Fall*, 191.

42. Bridges, *Rise and Fall*, 177–81.

43. Lucian K. Truscott IV, "Hate Gets a Haircut," *Esquire*, November 1989, https://classic.esquire.com/article/1989/11/1/hate-gets-a-haircut.

44. Bridges, *Rise and Fall*, 176–78.

45. Tim Wise, phone interview, May 1, 2021.

46. Tim Wise, phone interview, May 1, 2021.

47. Maginnis, *Cross to Bear*, 69–70.

48. David Duke interview by Evelyn Rich, circa 1986, box 19, folder 17, LCARN Records.

49. Tim Wise, phone interview, May 1, 2021.

50. October 17, 1989 LCARN Meeting Notes, box 6, folder 5, Meeting Agendas, Minutes and Notes, 1989–1992, LCARN Records.

51. UNO poll, University of New Orleans, 1990, Rickey Archive; see also "Affirmative Action in Louisiana," *Public Policy in Louisiana*, Ballotpedia.org, accessed July 26, 2021, https://ballotpedia.org/Affirmative_action_in_Louisiana.

52. Maginnis, *Cross to Bear*, 66–68.

53. Jason Berry, "The Louisiana Racists Who Courted Steve Scalise," *Daily Beast*, January 3, 2015, https://www.thedailybeast.com/the-louisiana-racists-who-courted-steve-scalise.

54. Duke, curiously, didn't bring on friends Ralph Forbes, Western chair of the American Nazi Party, or Don Black, who married Chloê years after her divorce from Duke.

55. Truscott, "Hate Gets a Haircut."

56. Paul West, "With Duke in Senate Race, Old Passions," *Baltimore Sun*, October 1, 1990.

57. Maginnis, *Cross to Bear*, 77–78.

58. Internal memo, J Bennet Johnston campaign materials, folder 11, box 27, LCARN Records; see also "Senate Fund-Raising, 1989–90 and Candidates' Cash on Hand, June 30, 1990," *Christian Science Monitor*, September 18, 1990, https://www.csmonitor.com/1990/0918/asen3.html.

59. Bridges, *Rise and Fall*, 180.

60. Bridges, *Rise and Fall*, 182–84; "Duke's Affirmative Action Ban Passes Louisiana House," Associated Press, May 30, 1990.

61. Brides, *Rise and Fall*, 182–83.

62. Robert Suro, "Behind Duke's Success, Campaign without End," *New York Times*, October 27, 1991, 22; see also Bridges, *Rise and Fall*, 183–85.

63. Suro, "Behind Duke's Success."

64. When callers dialed up the 1-900 number, his campaign automatically received a contribution via the caller's phone bill. In his FEC filing, Duke claimed to have lost $150,000 in donations because of the phone company's decision. When he employed this strategy again, his campaign did not bill via the phone company.

65. Bridges, *Rise and Fall*, 187; "Louisiana to Choose Duke or Edwards Today," *Greensboro News & Record*, November 15, 1991, https://greensboro.com/louisiana-to-choose-duke-or-edwards-today/article_c53486ee-2c94-5bda-bfb3-75fd3a3086b6.html; see also FEC letter, request for "proper disposition of funds held pursuant to its 900 services," Washington, Perito & Dubuc, October 29, 1990, https://www.fec.gov/files/legal/aos/1991-02/1083048.pdf.

66. Senator Pat Moynihan fundraising letter for Senator J. Bennett Johnston, box 27, folder 11, LCARN Records.

67. Moynihan fundraising letter, LCARN Records.

68. Analysis for J. Bennett Johnston 1990 US Senate campaign, unknown author, box 27, folder 12, LCARN Records.

69. Interviews from February 1986, March 1985, and others in Anti-Defamation League, *David Duke in His Own Words* (New York: Anti-Defamation League, 2012), 3–5, https://www.adl.org/sites/default/files/documents/assets/pdf/combating-hate/David-Duke-long-article.pdf.

70. "Voice Script — Duke/Fields/Rich Interview, 1986," prepared by LCARN, July 17, 1991, Rickey Archive; see also "David Duke in His Own Words."

71. "Voice Script — Duke/Fields/Rich Interview, 1986."

72. In 1992, he clarified, "This idea that blacks tend to act more in anti-social ways, well, I think crime figures tend to bear that out. That's not stating anything other than what the fact is." Chris Tucker, "Parting Shot: David Duke's Media Problem—and Everyone's," *D Magazine*, March 1992, https://www.dmagazine.com/publications/d-magazine/1992/march/parting-shot-david-dukes-media-problem-and-everyones.

73. Maginnis, *Cross to Bear*, 68–70.

74. Years later, Stovall said they were still sitting on unused dirt on Duke.

75. Tucker, "Parting Shot."

76. Undated flyer, circa 1990, LCARN Records.

77. Peter Applebome, "Republican Quits Louisiana Race in Effort to Defeat Ex-Klansman," *New York Times*, October 5, 1990, A1.

78. Bridges, *Rise and Fall*, 192–93.

79. Bridges, *Rise and Fall*, 192–93.

80. Bridges, *Rise and Fall*, 192–93; Leonard Zeskind, "Opinion: For Duke, Just a Start?," *New York Times*, October 9, 1990, A25.

81. Zeskind, "For Duke, Just a Start?"

82. Maginnis, *Cross to Bear*, 86.

83. Zeskind, "For Duke, Just a Start?

84. Maginnis, *Cross to Bear*, 86–89.

85. Tim Wise, *White Like Me* (Berkeley, CA: Soft Skull Press, 2008), 43. Tim Wise was later pulled over by the police because, he suggested, he had an anti-Duke sticker on his car. When Wise, who was white, rolled down the window, the officer simply said, "Oh." Wise, *White Like Me*, 83.

86. October 17, 1989 meeting notes, box 6, folder 5, Meeting Agendas, Minutes and Notes, 1989–1992, LCARN Records.

87. Maginnis, *Cross to Bear*, 87.

88. Although it wouldn't immediately affect his poll numbers and prospects, Roemer ended up splitting his female support. The Women For Roemer group, which had backed him as a pro-choice Democrat in 1987, stayed aboard in 1991, but female conservatives bailed on him. Frances Frank Marcus, "Roemer Is Silent on Abortion Bill," *New York Times*, July 10, 1990, A17.

89. "Duke Enters Governor's Race," *New York Times*, March 14, 1991, A19.

90. Robin Toner, "Louisiana Is Bracing for Politics with Gusto," *New York Times*, May 29, 1991, A17.

CHAPTER 7

Epigraph. Debbie Elliott, "Edwin Edwards, the Larger-Than-Life Former Louisiana Governor, Dies at 93," NPR, July 12, 2021, https://www.npr.org/2021/07/12/1015250354/edwin-edwards-former-governor-of-louisiana-dies.

1. Lauren McGaughy, "Edwin Edwards' Best Quotes: A Look Back as We Look Ahead to His Congressional Run," *Times Picayune*, March 17, 2014, https://www.nola.com/news/politics/article_baa97dao-8d95-5c6a-8d3b-9feobbebc216.html.

2. Maginnis, *Cross to Bear*, 166; John Maginnis, *The Last Hayride* (Baton Rouge, LA: Gris Gris Press, 1984), 334.

3. The record has since been broken. Kenneth F. Warren, "Encyclopedia of U.S. Campaigns, Elections, and Electoral Behavior" (Thousand Oaks, CA: Sage, 2008), 381.

4. Honeycutt, *Edwin Edwards*, 177–79.

5. Honeycutt, 185.

6. Honeycutt, 213–14; "Incentive Pay System Could Replace PIPs," *Minden Press-Herald*, October 12, 1984, 1; see also Maginnis, *Cross to Bear*, 48, 134; "Louisiana Governor Gambols on Tightropes to Be Governor," *Washington Post*, August 16, 1983; and "Treen Supports Oil, Gas Tax," *Minden Press-Herald*, May 7, 1982, 5.

7. S. L. Alexander, *Courtroom Carnival: Famous New Orleans Trials*, (Gretna, LA: Pelican Publishing, 2011), 205

8. Paul Taylor, "Colorful Governor Hopes to Return to Power in Louisiana," *Washington Post*, October 20, 1983, https://www.washingtonpost.com/archive/politics/1983/10/20/colorful-former-governor-hopes-to-return-to-power-in-louisiana/ce6908f2-0fe8-4d89-85a6-37c618a8a77a; see also: "Bubba Henry Says Edwards Creating a 'Smoke Screen,'" *Minden Press-Herald*, March 25, 1982, 1.

9. Honeycutt, *Edwin Edwards*, 216.

10. "Edwards Denies Wrongdoing—Keeps Running," *Minden Press-Herald*, March 15, 1982, 1.

11. Honeycutt, *Edwin Edwards*, 194–96.

12. Honeycutt, *Edwin Edwards*, 196.

13. Of Treen's own campaign manager, the challenger quipped, "I asked Gus why he abandoned the Concorde to climb aboard the Titanic."

14. Honeycutt, *Edwin Edwards*, 194.

15. Nancy Lemann, *The Ritz of the Bayou* (New York: A.A. Knopf, 1987), 107.

16. "WWL-TV News 1983, Bob Hope, Dave Treen and Edwin Edwards," WWL-TV, New Orleans, YouTube video posted by Classic New Orleans TV, Nov 14, 2015, https://www.youtube.com/watch?v=ol6nUpqm9xY.

17. Maginnis, *Last Hayride*, 54–55.

18. Maginnis, *Last Hayride*, 54–55, and Edwin Edwards, phone interview, May 27, 2021; see also "Marion Edwards: Obituary," *The Advocate*, January 12, 2013, https://obits.theadvocate.com/us/obituaries/theadvocate/name/marion-edwards-obituary?id=11416915.

19. Maginnis, *Last Hayride*, 54–55, and Edwin Edwards, phone interview, May 27, 2021.

20. Maginnis, *Last Hayride*, 211.

21. Maginnis, *Last Hayride*, 211; Honeycutt, *Edwin Edwards*, 201–3.

22. "WINGATE v. NATIONAL UNION FIRE INS. CO.," Leagle, accessed May 14, 2022, https://www.leagle.com/decision/19831029435so2d5941808; Maginnis, *Last Hayride*, 213.

23. Maginnis, *Last Hayride*, 211; see also Honeycutt, *Edwin Edwards*, 201–3.

24. Honeycutt, *Edwin Edwards*, 202.

25. Maginnis, *Last Hayride*, 218.

26. WWL-TV estimated the fundraiser would earn the campaign $1,800,000, of which Hope would receive a $60,000 appearance fee, part of a $5 million fund-raising haul for 1983."WWL-TV News 1983, Bob Hope, Dave Treen and Edwin Edwards," WWL-TV, New Orleans, YouTube video posted by Classic New Orleans TV, Nov 14, 2015, https://www.youtube.com/watch?v=ol6nUpqm9xY.

27. Alexander, *Courtroom Carnival*, 204–6.

28. "Jambalaya," *Washington Post*, October 26, 1983, https://www.washington post.com/archive/politics/1983/10/26/jambalaya/989b5c1c-58a8-45d7-8e71 -35205c1805b6.

29. Honeycutt, *Edwin Edwards*, 198.

30. Honeycutt, *Edwin Edwards*, 199.

31. "Campaign 1983: The Treen/Edwards Debates, No. 1," Louisiana Public Broadcasting, YouTube, posted July 14, 2021, https://www.youtube.com/watch?v= vAPyonbbt50.

32. "Treen/Edwards Debates, No. 1."

33. "Treen/Edwards Debates, No. 1."

34. The first question, however, dealt with the environment and came from Treen, who told Edwards, "You allowed toxic waste . . . to pile up in Louisiana. . . . We're paying the price of your neglect. Do you know what it's going to cost to clean up?" It would be bizarre to witness such a moment today, with a conservative Republican attacking a New Deal liberal on the environment. Edwards suggested, "For three years, you were governor and you did very little to stop it. It is true that, in this election, you finally cleaned up one of the waste dumps, for which I congratulate you." "Treen/Edwards Debates, No. 2."

35. "Treen/Edwards Debates, No. 2."

36. Honeycutt, *Edwin Edwards*, 199.

37. Eric Benson, "Return of the Guv," *National Journal*, July 12, 2014, https://www. nationaljournal.com/s/72604/return-guv; "Blagojevich Fatigue? Get Used to It," *New York Times*, August 22, 2010, A23.

38. Maginnis, *Last Hayride*, 287–88.

39. Meyer, "The Rake."

40. Edwin Edwards, phone interview, May 27, 2021.

41. Maginnis, *Last Hayride*, 344.

42. Maginnis, *Last Hayride*, 314; Honeycutt, *Edwin Edwards*, 207.

43. Maginnis, *Last Hayride*, 314; Honeycutt, *Edwin Edwards*, 207.

CHAPTER 8

1. "Louisiana Governor Going to Trial. Fraud Charges against Edwards Stem from Hospital-Permit Scheme," *Christian Science Monitor*, Sept. 16, 1985, https://www.csmonitor.com/1985/0916/agov.html.

2. Kenneth O'Brock, "Happy Edwin Edwards Day!," *Shreveport News*, August 7, 2014, https://www.shreveportnews.com/shreveport-politics/edwin-edwards -day/751.

3. Reporter Nancy Lemann said the defense pushed for the gag order to stop Edwards from potentially incriminating himself.

4. "WATCH: The Life of Former Louisiana Governor Edwin Edwards," WVUE-TV, July 12, 2021, https://www.facebook.com/watch/?v=347402883648585.

5. The case took up four weekdays per week, leaving only Fridays for state business, which lead to suggestions that Edwards resign, guilty or otherwise, to spare the state the slowdown. In his press conference, the governor claimed that, regardless of his own innocence, had he felt that he would be *found* guilty, he would have resigned. Massa, "Former Louisiana Governor."

6. April Siese, "Before Trump, This Governor Set the Gold Standard for Outrageous Politicians," *Times-Picayune*, November 4, 2016, https://narratively.com/ before-trump-this-governor-set-the-gold-standard-for-outrageous-politicians.

7. One prosecution witness stated that Edwards had repaid a gambling debt with $200,000 in a suitcase. Maginnis, *Cross to Bear*, 8.

8. Lemann, *Ritz*, 109.

9. Lemann, *Ritz*, 90, 146.

10. J. Michael Kennedy, "Gov. Edwards Jury Deadlocks; Mistrial Called," *Los Angeles Times*, December 19, 1985, https://www.latimes.com/archives/la-xpm-1985 -12-19-mn-30340-story.html.

11. Lemann, *Ritz*, 13.

12. Frances Frank Marcus, "Louisiana's Governor Acquitted in 2d Trial on Fraud Charges," *New York Times*, May 11, 1986, 18.

13. Lemann, *Ritz*, 40–41.

14. Lemann, *Ritz*, 118.

15. Marcus, "Governor Acquitted."

16. Lemann, *Ritz*, 122.

17. Matt Labash, "Conviction Politician," *Washington Examiner*, December 7, 2014, https://www.washingtonexaminer.com/weekly-standard/conviction-politician -820730.

18. Lemann, *Ritz*, 122.

19. Honeycutt, *Edwin Edwards*, 244.

20. Honeycutt, *Edwin Edwards*, 209–11.

21. Honeycutt, *Edwin Edwards*, 209–11; Maginnis, *Last Hayride*, 339.

22. Honeycutt, *Edwin Edwards*, 209–11; Maginnis, *Last Hayride*, 339.

23. Honeycutt, *Edwin Edwards*, 214–24.

24. CSPAN rebroadcast of Louisiana Public Broadcasting gubernatorial debate, Sept, 28, 1991, https://www.c-span.org/video/?21627-1/louisiana-gubernatorial -debate.

25. In 1984, she told the *Shreveport Times* that in the early years, with Edwards working late, she admitted to suffering "long, lonely days . . . I'd find myself crying on the shoulders of the maid." "Elaine Edwards, Former Louisiana First Lady, Senator Dies," *Shreveport Times*, May 14, 2018, reprinted from 1984, https://www.shreveporttimes.com/story/news/local/louisiana/2018/05/14/ elaine-edwards-former/608714002.

26. Honeycutt, *Edwin Edwards*, 250.

27. Vidrine, *Louisiana Political*, ix.

28. "One-Time Bodyguard to Gov. Killed by Apparent Jealous Husband," Associated Press, December 16, 1986, https://apnews.com/article/3085fa97104bb1d7f232e5 6272001bbd; "Jealousy Called Motive in Shooting Death of Ex-Gubernatorial Confidant," Associated Press, December 17, 1986, https://apnews.com/article/ 02f88767cb460dda4f6c576e254ac48a.

29. "E006 Buddy Roemer at Asphodel 1987," People Like Us/Louisiana Public Broadcasting, 1987, https://www.youtube.com/watch?v=mC4U-u4e6Uc.

30. Sarah Crawford, "Gov. Roemer Tells of Bossier Childhood in New Book," *Shreveport Times*, September 3, 2017, https://www.shreveporttimes.com/story/ news/2017/09/03/gov-roemer-tells-bossier-childhood-new-book/616815001.

31. Brian Boyles, "An Interview with Governor Buddy Roemer," *64 Parishes*, accessed July 27, 2021, https://64parishes.org/an-interview-with-governor-buddy-roemer.

32. Boyles, "Interview with Governor Buddy Roemer."

33. Perhaps the most pertinent detail in this case is that the prosecutor was John Volz.

34. "'Brilab' Convictions Overturned," Associated Press, June 23, 1989, https://ap news.com/article/3c6d4494b803934182d1a3a2cb9b44ba.

35. Maginnis, *Cross to Bear*, 33–34.

36. Jonathan Fuerbringer, "Washington Talk: Avocations; Networking at the Poker Table," *New York Times*, June 10, 1987, A24.

37. John Maginnis reported that, returning home after his second grand jury appearance, Buddy crashed into a parked state police vehicle, apparently because of insulin shock, the first major incident tied to the diabetic condition that later ended his life. Maginnis, *Cross to Bear*, 34.

38. Maginnis, *Cross to Bear*, 34–36; see also Honeycutt, *Edwin Edwards*, 263.

39. Fuerbringer, "Avocations."

40. "Remembering Louisiana's Ex-Gov. Buddy Roemer: Bright, Quirky, 'and a Good Man,'" WBAP, May 18, 2021, https://www.wbap.com/news/remembering -louisianas-ex-gov-buddy-roemer-bright-quirky-and-a-good-man.

41. Maginnis, *Cross to Bear*, 39.

42. Quin Hillyer, phone interview, May 12, 2021.

43. Remarks by Caroline Roemer and Chas Roemer, Governor Charles Elson "Buddy" Roemer III funeral service, Baton Rouge, LA, May 17, 2021, author notes.

44. Boyles, "Interview with Governor Buddy Roemer."

45. Remarks by Chas Roemer, "Buddy" Roemer funeral service.

46. Raymond Strother, phone interview, June 29, 2021.

47. Mark McKinnon, phone interview, June 12, 2021.

48. Mark McKinnon, phone interview.

49. "Buddy Roemer - 1987 Campaign for Governor," Roemer for Governor Committee, 1987, lessig, posted to YouTube March 2, 2011, https://www.youtube.com/ watch?v=SH8UISKwXxs.

50. Raymond Strother, phone interview, June 29, 2021.

51. During the 1991 race, Edwards suggested his campaign "play back those silly stupid commercials of his" opponent's and throw Roemer's own words back in his face, but Strother is convinced the first one, coupled with newspaper endorsements, actually turned the tide in 1987. Maginnis, *Cross to Bear*, 13; Raymond Strother, phone interview, June 29, 2021.

52. "E006 Buddy Roemer at Asphodel 1987," YouTube, raw footage from *Louisiana Boys* documentary, released by People Like Us - The CNAM Channel, July 19, 2017, https://www.youtube.com/watch?v=mC4U-u4e6Uc.

53. Rob Hinton (host), "Buddy Roemer Elected Governor (1987)," *Louisiana: The State We're In*, broadcast October 30, 1987, Louisiana Public Broadcasting, Louisiana Digital Media Archive, http://ladigitalmedia.org/video_v2/asset-detail/ LSWI-1105.

54. Raymond Strother, phone interview, June 29, 2021. and Mark McKinnon, phone interview, June 12, 2021.

55. "Debate 1987: The Governor's Race," Louisiana Public Broadcasting, September 25, 1987, Louisiana Digital Media Archive, http://ladigitalmedia.org/video_ v2/asset-detail/LGUBD-19870925. To much snickering, Edwards responded, "Well, Bob, unemployment is down three percent from the time the last Republican governor served us."

56. "Debate 1987."

57. Mike Hasten, "Roemer: I'll Slay the Dragon," *Daily Advertiser* (Lafayette, LA), October 14, 1987, 21; "Buddy Roemer," *The Town Talk*, October 14, 1987, 1.

58. Raymond Strother, phone interview, June 29, 2021.

59. Raymond Strother, phone interview, June 29, 2021; and Honeycutt, *Edwin Edwards*, 264–71.

60. Maginnis, *Cross to Bear*, 30.

61. Frances Frank Marcus, "Edwards Spurns Runoff Election After Placing 2d," *New York Times*, October 26, 1987, p. A12

62. Marcus, "Edwards Spurns Runoff."

63. Honeycutt, *Edwin Edwards*, 270; see also Jack Wardlaw, "Roemer Plays New Hand Close to Vest," *Times-Picayune*, October 26, 1987.

64. Edwin Edwards, phone interview, May 27, 2021.

65. "I wonder what's going to happen to him," Edwards said, seemingly genuinely concerned for the apparently incorruptible young Roemer. "I don't envy him." Hinton, "Buddy Roemer Elected Governor (1987)."

66. Mark McKinnon, phone interview, June 12, 2021.

67. Maginnis, *Cross to Bear*, 12.

68. Leman, *Ritz*, 87.

69. Maginnis, *Cross to Bear*, 12; see also William Poundstone, *Gaming the Vote: Why Elections Aren't Fair (and What We Can Do about It)* (New York: Macmillan, 2009), 10.

CHAPTER 9

1. "David Duke: From Klansman to Politician," WWL-TV (*NBC News* rebroadcast), January 13, 2015, https://www.nbcnews.com/video/david-duke-from-klansman -to-politician-379422787648.

2. Maginnis, *Cross to Bear*, 122.

3. Maginnis, *Cross to Bear*, 98.

4. Maginnis, *Cross to Bear*, 69–70

5. Jack Anderson and Dale Van Atta, "Skeletons in Duke's Closet Loom Larger," *Washington Post*, September 17, 1990, https://www.washingtonpost.com/ archive/lifestyle/1990/09/17/skeletons-in-dukes-closet-loom-larger/a6c63904 -3c6d-46c8-9129-0220325f5804; and "Report on David Duke Research" by Beth Rickey, J. Bennet Johnston campaign materials, folder 11, box 27, LCARN Records. Sample line from *Finderskeepers*: "Many actually develop a taste for [blowjobs]. That's quite a bedtime snack. At least it's low on calories." Maginnis, *Cross to Bear*, 25.

6. The Archbishop of New Orleans mailer, January 30, 1989, box 27, folder 10, LCARN Records.

7. Maginnis, *Cross to Bear*, 88.

8. Maginnis, 89.

9. Wayne Parent, phone interview, May 8, 2021.

10. Lawrence Powell, phone interview, May 17, 2021.

11. Maginnis, *Cross to Bear*, 91.

12. A. J. Liebling, "The Rise of Earl Long," *New Yorker*, May 28, 1960, https://www.newyorker.com/magazine/1960/05/28/i-the-great-state-waiting-for-the-imam.

13. Honeycutt, *Edwin Edwards*, 274; Maginnis, *Cross to Bear*, 52.

14. Carlos Sierra, phone interview, June 10, 2021.

15. Raymond Strother, phone interview, June 29, 2021.

16. Exceptions for the life of the mother, he said, "are very important to me and, I believe, important to the women of Louisiana whose rights and lives must be protected." Garry Boulard, "Abortion Bill Veto Override in Louisiana Fails," *Los Angeles Times*, July 8, 1990, https://www.latimes.com/archives/la-xpm-1990-07-08-mn-327-story.html.

17. Holloway had snuck into Congress from a heavily Democratic district by defeating a liberal black woman.

18. Clancy Dubos, "Clancy: Buddy Roemer's Legacy Endures," WWL-TV, May 18, 2021, https://www.wwltv.com/article/news/local/clancys-commentaries/clancy-buddy-roemers-legacy-endures/289-69f2e835-4726-481e-affd-bd34c8bed4c0.

19. Chas Roemer, Governor Charles Elson "Buddy" Roemer III funeral service, Baton Rouge, LA, May 17, 2021, author notes.

20. Strother noted that Roemer preferred to sit with his back to the dining room at one restaurant and refused to walk around, glad handling, as Edwards and Duke might. Raymond Strother, phone interview, June 29, 2021.

21. Bridges, *Rise and Fall*, 203–4.

22. Bridges, *Rise and Fall*, 204.

23. Bridges, *Rise and Fall*, 204–5; Robert Buckman, "Louisiana's Roemer Gets a Mild Rebuke from His New Party," *Christian Science Monitor*, May 17, 1991, https://www.csmonitor.com/1991/0517/17041.html.

24. Parent, *Inside the Carnival*, 44

25. Maginnis, *Cross to Bear*, 116.

26. Raymond Strother, phone interview, June 29, 2021.

27. Analysis of the Louisiana Republican Party, 1991, Rickey Archive.

28. Jack W. Germond and Jules Witcover, "Louisiana's Buddy Roemer and the Race Factor," *Baltimore Evening Sun/New York Daily News*, March 14, 1991, https://www.nydailynews.com/bs-xpm-1991-03-14-1991073139-story.html.

29. In a 1991 speech, Duke proclaimed he was against abortion but suggested that Norplant could help reduce the country's rates of terminated pregnancies by

thousands per year. "Norplant and Birth-Control Tyranny," *Baltimore Sun*, November 5, 1991, https://www.baltimoresun.com/news/bs-xpm-1991-11-05-1991309 147-story.html.

30. Bridges, *Rise and Fall*, 206.
31. Maginnis, *Cross to Bear*, 95, 171.
32. "I'm 64 years old, and it is very flattering. Some people say that at 64 years old a man should be looking for a nurse. Others say that he ought to be looking for the best-looking young lady he can find." After a comic pause, he added, "I've combined the two." Maginnis, *Cross to Bear*, 2.
33. "You have sixty days to get people registered. If you don't think they will vote right, don't encourage them." Maginnis, *Cross to Bear*, 169.
34. Maginnis, *Cross to Bear*, 169.
35. A campaign aide zinged Roemer: "I really hate talking about the dead." Another: "I don't know what lie will be his downfall." Edwards tops them: "His downfall," he said, "was his inability to deliver on his Big Lie of four years ago." Maginnis, *Cross to Bear*, 179.
36. Lawrence Powell, phone interview, May 17, 2021.
37. Tim Wise, phone interview, May 1, 2021.
38. Dugger, "An Interview with David Duke."
39. Dugger, "Beth Rickey Replies."
40. Elizabeth A. Rickey, "The Duke Phenomenon," *Dallas Morning News*, November 24, 1991; see also "How 'It Can't Happen Here' Almost Happened in Louisiana: A Study of the David Duke Phenomenon in the 1990 Senate Race, an executive summary conducted by Garin-Hart Strategic Research, 1991 March," box 41, folder 3, LCARN Records, https://amistad-finding-aids.tulane.edu/repositories/2/archival_objects/17244.
41. June 11, 1990 meeting notes, folder 5, box 6, Meeting Agendas, Minutes and Notes, 1989–1992, LCARN Records.
42. Mary Cross, "100 People Who Changed 20th-Century America" (Santa Barbara, CA, ABC-CLIO, 2013), 537. On another *Downey* episode that season, a black man in a suit and a White Aryan Resistance leader wearing white supremacist cross and Confederate flag patches debated at Harlem's Apollo Theater. "If not for all those cops outside," the black man intoned, "you would not go home today." Downey blamed "liberal rule" for "trying to get the blacks and whites going at each other," to huge cheers from the mixed audience. White Aryan Resistance Youth leader Tom Metzger objected to the use of the term "hate" to describe his efforts to get the Aryan Youth movement going in the US, calling it "love" for the white race. However, he also said, "we support that declaration of war" that the Order had launched on the US government. By the

end of the hour, the show had descended into chaos, with a gentile woman screaming at the neo-Nazi, "You should be shot!" and Downey inches from Metzger's face, yelling: "You shut up! You shut up!" while Metzger gave the host the finger. "Morton Downey Jr Show: White Supremacy," *Morton Downey Jr Show*, YouTube, posted June 5, 2016, https://youtu.be/E8tGbAO7u1M.

43. One woman alerted him to something happening in New York City: "White woman was raped + beaten by about 30 blacks in Central Park, Wed. 4-19. She is in a coma + the blacks are free. Nothing is being done & they are saying it's not a racial thing." "Phone Message Book," 1989, box 20, folder 17, LCARN Records.

44. Asked whether he believed Jewish people overstated the death totals of the Holocaust, Duke said in that appearance, "Of course there were terrible atrocities in Europe and I condemn that and there were terrible atrocities as well in the Soviet Union. And I oppose any oppression of people. And I think there is a lot of bullshit. The closest thing that I know to the policies of Germany in this country is the so-called affirmative action or quota systems. They had quotas in Germany as well on the basis of race. I don't think you should have racial preferences." Robert Suro, "The 1991 Election: Louisiana; Bush Denounces Duke as Racist and Charlatan," *New York Times*, November 17, 1991, B18.

45. "Duke Wins Case on Collection," *Buffalo News*, October 14, 1993, https://buffalo news.com/news/duke-wins-case-on-collections/article_81c35b58-ec48-5cb1 -9a2e-36da32937e39.html.

46. "The Right to a Free Exchange of Ideas," *CSPAN*, March 28, 1991, https://www. c-span.org/video/?17361-1/free-exchange-ideas; see also "Hecklers Disrupt Talk by Former Klan Leader," *New York Times*, March 29, 1991, p. B6, https://www.ny times.com/1991/03/29/us/hecklers-disrupt-talk-by-former-klan-leader.html.

CHAPTER 10

1. Raymond Strother called Roemer's poker playing among "the best" he'd ever seen; Honeycutt, *Edwin Edwards*, 278; Raymond Strother, phone interview, June 29, 2021; and Jonathan Fuerbringer, "Washington Talk: Avocations; Networking at the Poker Table," *New York Times*, June 10, 1987, A24; see also Tyler Bridges, "Buddy Roemer, Reform Governor Who Switched Parties and Lost Re-election Bid, Dies at 77," *The Advocate* (Baton Rouge, LA), May 17, 2021, https://www.theadvocate.com/baton_rouge/news/article_4e8cd89e-3676-11eb -b2fc-eb5c23580375.html.

2. Maginnis, *Cross to Bear*, 94.

3. Maginnis, *Cross to Bear*, 94.

4. Bridges, *Rise and Fall*, 209; see also Maginnis, *Cross to Bear*, 144, 194, and 248.

5. Raymond Strother, phone interview, June 29, 2021; see also Maginnis, *Cross to Bear*, 194–95; Bridges, *Rise and Fall*, 210.

6. Raymond Strother, phone interview, June 29, 2021; see also *Cross to Bear*, 188; Bridges, *Rise and Fall*, 210–12.

7. Raymond Strother, phone interview.

8. Gordon Russell, "How an Environmental Regulator Became Known for Protecting Industry," *Pro Publica*, December 19, 2019, https://www.propublica.org/article/how-an-environmental-regulator-became-known-for-protecting-industry; Mike Bayham, "The Rise, Fall, And Rebirth of Buddy Roemer, Louisiana's Dragon-Slayer," *The Hayride*, May 19, 2021, https://thehayride.com/2021/05/bayham-the-rise-fall-and-rebirth-of-buddy-roemer-louisianas-dragon-slayer.

9. Maginnis, *Cross to Bear*, 236.

10. Bridges, *Rise and Fall*, 213–15.

11. John Fund, "Bayou Boy Wonder," *Wall Street Journal*, October 22, 2007, https://www.wsj.com/articles/SB122546719987488231.

12. Maginnis, *Cross to Bear*, 162–64.

13. His campaign-advisor father later told a reporter, "At first we were going to start [campaigning] July 6. Then we pushed back to August 6. We were thinking of waiting until September 6, but we didn't think we could do that." It should be noted that the primary was set for October 19, thirty-three days later. Maginnis, *Cross to Bear*, 186.

14. Maginnis, *Cross to Bear*, 162–64.

15. Maginnis, *Cross to Bear*, 133.

16. Raymond Strother, phone interview, June 29, 2021.

17. Maginnis, *Cross to Bear*, 214–16.

18. Maginnis, *Cross to Bear*, 214.

19. "Remarks at a Fundraising Dinner for Governor Buddy Roemer in New Orleans, Louisiana," George H. W. Bush Memorial Library & Museum, September 30, 1991, https://bush41library.tamu.edu/archives/public-papers/3446.

20. "Remarks at a Fundraising Dinner."

21. Maginnis, *Cross to Bear*, 216.

22. Robert Suro, "Roemer's New Tack for Old Problems," *New York Times*, January 20, 1991, 20.

23. Maginnis, *Cross to Bear*, 253; Edwards had campaign workers attend Roemer events and do a "true" accounting of attendees. He claimed that in Lake Charles, eighty-nine Roemer supporters showed up at an event for which one thousand had been expected. Maginnis, *Cross to Bear*, 253–54.

24. Maginnis, *Cross to Bear*, 224.

25. Maginnis, *Cross to Bear*, 237.

26. Maginnis, *Cross to Bear*, 237–39; see also Robert Suro, "Ex-Klan Chief Has Even Odds in Governor's Race," *New York Times*, October 19, 1991, 1.

27. Anne Levy, phone interview, April 7, 2022.

28. Maginnis, *Cross to Bear*, 238; see also Suro, "Ex-Klan Chief."

29. Maginnis, *Cross to Bear*, 238.

30. Maginnis, *Cross to Bear*, 239.

31. Suro, "Ex-Klan Chief."

32. Maginnis, *Cross to Bear*, 239.

33. Maginnis, *Cross to Bear*, 240.

34. Suro, "Ex-Klan Chief."

35. Maginnis, *Cross to Bear*, 241.

36. Dan Even, "Spirited Governor's Race Opening Pocketbooks across the Nation," Associated Press, November 15, 1991, https://apnews.com/article/b7cb5 b358159309c995aab27a67982cf.

37. Meyer, "The Rake."

38. Bridges, *Rise and Fall*, 206.

39. Maginnis, *Cross to Bear*, 243, 251.

40. Tom Stokes phone interview, May 28, 2021; see also Tom Stokes and Edwin Edwards photograph from 1991, Tom Stokes, "Me and Double 'E' . . ahh I was so young and good looking in 1991 . . Now I am old and good looking HA #EWE14," Edwin Edwards: A True Louisiana Legend Facebook group, Facebook, August 3, 2014, https://www.facebook.com/groups/2220682290/perma link/10152282566127291.

41. Tom Stokes, phone interview, May 28, 2021.

42. Tom Stokes, phone interview, May 28, 2021.

43. Maginnis, *Cross to Bear*, 231.

44. Bridges, *Rise and Fall*, 215; see also an earlier poll with Duke at 12 percent: "UNO Poll, September 17–24," 1991, Box 31, "Polling and Results/Stats," LCARN Records; Maginnis, *Cross to Bear*, 52.

45. Duke/Fields/Rich interview transcript, February 17, 1986, Rickey Archive; see also Maginnis, *Cross to Bear*, 228.

46. Duke/Fields/Rich interview transcript, February 17, 1986, Rickey Archive.

47. "Like Hitler," *Texas Observer*, January 17 and 31, 1992, 17–19.

48. Kenneth Stern, phone interview, June 25, 2021.

49. Dugger, "Beth Rickey Replies."

50. Kenneth Stern, phone interview, June 25, 2021.

51. Maginnis, *Cross to Bear*, 248–49.

52. Maginnis, *Cross to Bear*, 233.

53. Maginnis, 233.

54. James Gill, "Keeping the Unthinkable in Mind," *Times-Picayune*, October 11, 1991, B7.

55. Maginnis, *Cross to Bear*, 233.

56. Maginnis, *Cross to Bear*, 249–50.

57. Maginnis, *Cross to Bear*, 255–58.

58. Maginnis, *Cross to Bear*, 259.

59. Duke had once again expressed his support for Thomas the night before, accusing Democrats of slandering Thomas with harassment allegations.

60. "Chet Edwards on C-SPAN Call-in Show," C-SPAN, YouTube, October 19, 1991, https://www.youtube.com/watch?v=RXWUfcrhoFo.

61. Bridges, *Rise and Fall*, 178, fig. 41.

62. Maginnis, *Cross to Bear*, 260.

63. Maginnis, *Cross to Bear*, 260.

64. Bridges, *Rise and Fall*, 216; Maginnis, *Cross to Bear*, 259–62.

65. Maginnis, *Cross to Bear*, 262.

66. Maginnis, *Cross to Bear*, 262.

67. mightyflynn, "'The box score is the catechism of baseball, ready to surrender its truth to the knowing eye.' Stanley Cohen," *It's a Long Season* (blog), Tumblr, accessed November 20, 2021, https://mightyflynn.tumblr.com/post/5569264618/the-box-score-is-the-catechism-of-baseball-ready.

68. Warren D. Smith, "Louisiana's Famous 1991 'Lizard versus Wizard' Governor Race," RangeVoting, accessed July 28, 2021, https://rangevoting.org/LizVwiz.html.

CHAPTER 11

1. Dillin, "Polls Show."

2. Toner, "Ex-Klan."

3. Dillin, "Polls Show."

4. Dillin, "Polls Show."

5. Wayne Parent, phone interview, May 8, 2021.

6. Dillin, "Polls Show."

7. Toner, "Ex-Klan."

8. Toner, "Ex-Klan."

9. Maginnis, *Cross to Bear*, 268; Princess Weekes, "*Slate*'s Podcast Miniseries about David Duke's 1991 Louisiana Gubernatorial Run Is the Essential Pre-Election Listen," *Mary Sue*, July 22, 2020, https://www.themarysue.com/slates-podcast-mini-series-david-dukes-1991-louisiana-gubernatorial-run.

10. Maginnis, *Cross to Bear*, 268.

11. Weekes, "*Slate*'s Podcast."

12. Fox Butterfield, "THE 1991 ELECTION: Election Roundup; Wave of Voter Discontent Sweeps Many from Office," *New York Times*, November 7, 1991, B18.

13. Josh Levin, host, "The Road to Hell," *Slow Burn* (podcast), season 4, episode 5, July 15, 2020, https://slate.com/podcasts/slow-burn/s4/david-duke/e5/david-duke-1991-campaign-governor.

14. Levin, "The Road to Hell."

15. Maginnis qtd. in Peter Applebome, "Rogue or Reformer, Edwards Seeks Louisiana Vindication," *New York Times*, November 11, 1991, A1.

16. Suro, "Ex-Klan."

17. Maginnis, *Cross to Bear*, 241–42.

18. Maginnis, *Cross to Bear*, 264.

19. "Louisiana Voters," Associated Press, October 22, 1991, and Bridges, *Rise and Fall*, 218.

20. Maginnis, *Cross to Bear*, 270.

21. Maginnis, *Cross to Bear*, 270.

22. "Strategy Guideline Statement," 1991, folder 1, box 6, LCARN Campaign Materials, LCARN Records.

23. The ads inspired misbehavior from Edwards fans too. One sent Duke's campaign a soiled condom. Box 4, folder 6, "Hate Mail," LCARN Records.

24. "Hate Mail," box 4, folder 6, LCARN Records.

25. "Hate Mail," box 4, folder 6, LCARN Records.

26. "Hate Mail," box 4, folder 6, LCARN Records.

27. "Hate Mail," box 4, folder 6, LCARN Records.

28. Tim Wise, phone interview, May 1, 2021.

29. Strategy Guideline Statement, box 6, folder 1, LCARN Campaign Materials, 1991, LCARN Records.

30. Tim Wise, phone interview, May 1, 2021.

31. Tim Wise, phone interview, May 1, 2021.

32. Diary entry, August 16, 1989, Rickey Archive.

33. Letter to LCARN, box 5, folder 18, LCARN Records.

34. In 2021, Edwards called the Coalition's board "all good, loyal people who spoke the truth." Edwin Edwards, personal correspondence, May 27, 2021.

35. Maginnis, *Cross to Bear*, 289.

36. Maginnis, *Cross to Bear*, 289.

37. Roemer Says He'll Vote for Edwards," *Deseret News*, November 1, 1991, https://www.deseret.com/1991/11/1/18949312/roemer-says-he-ll-vote-for-edwards.

38. Edwin Edwards, personal correspondence, May 27, 2021.

39. Maginnis, *Cross to Bear*, 287.

40. "I want you to write the check to DemoPac," he told a maxed-out donor. "They are coordinating election day activities. You can make it out to them and send it to us here. And come down for the election, we're gonna have some fun. Thank you and good luck to Walgreens." Maginnis, *Cross to Bear*, 317.
41. Maginnis, *Cross to Bear*, 287.
42. "Louisiana Has Two Living Ex-Governors: An Old Ex-Con and a Young Has-Been," *New York*, May 19, 2021, https://nymag.com/intelligencer/article/edwin-edwards-bobby-jindal-louisiana-living-ex-governors.html.
43. Maginnis, *Cross to Bear*, 131.
44. Maginnis, *Cross to Bear*, 131.
45. A variation: "I, too, have been called a wizard under the sheets." Joe Murray, "David Duke Makes It Acceptable to Hate," *Town Talk* (Alexandria, LA), November 14, 1991, 8; see also *The Record* (Hackensack, NJ), May 23, 1991, 54; *Daily Advertiser* (Lafayette, LA), November 8, 1991.
46. Not to be outdone, Duke closed by warning Edwards, "You may be surprised who you're in a runoff with." Maginnis, *Cross to Bear*, 131. Beth Rickey and the Coalition were nauseated by this debate, blaming Duke's opponents and the moderator for "normalizing" the hatemonger.
47. "Louisiana Gubernatorial Debate," C-SPAN, September 28, 1991, https://www.c-span.org/video/?21627-1/louisiana-gubernatorial-debate#.
48. "Louisiana Gubernatorial Debate," Sept. 28, 1991, 2:15 to 3:10.
49. "Louisiana Gubernatorial Debate," Sept. 28, 1991, 6:20 to 7:15. Meredith had been an informal activist during the Civil Rights movement, becoming the student who integrated the all-white University of Mississippi before switching to a hard right stance on affirmative action and other civil rights platforms.
50. Duke was quoting James Russell Lowell, "A Fable for Critics," published in 1848.
51. "Louisiana Gubernatorial Debate," Sept. 28, 1991, 7:16 to 8:36.
52. "Louisiana Gubernatorial Debate," Sept. 28, 1991, 18:36 to 18:46.
53. "Louisiana Gubernatorial Debate," Sept. 28, 1991, 22:22 to 24:29.
54. "Louisiana Gubernatorial Debate," Sept. 28, 1991, 27:37 to 33:05.
55. "Louisiana Gubernatorial Debate," Sept. 28, 1991, 1:02:57 to 1:03:20.
56. Backstage and unreported at the time, the campaigns, all flailing, sniped. "This is weak, pushy shit," one Roemer staffer said of Edwards' performance. Edwards' campaign manager Bob D'Hemecourt snapped back, "Yeah, well, there's more to come, pal." Another got up in D'Hemecourt's face, hissing, "We're going to slit your throat." D'Hemecourt: "That jerk gets near me I'll whip his ass." Maginnis, *Cross to Bear*, 202.

57. Maginnis, *Cross to Bear*, 271–73; Bridges, *Rise and Fall*, 223–24.

58. Bridges, *Rise and Fall*, 223–24.

59. "Edwards, Duke Sling Charges in Debate," *Times of Shreveport*, November 3, 1991; see also Bridges, *Rise and Fall*, 225.

60. Salary hikes had gone into effect prior to Duke's election to the State House.

61. "Edwards, Duke Sling Charges."

62. Bridges, *Rise and Fall*, 225.

63. "Edwards, Duke Sling Charges."

64. Maginnis, *Cross to Bear*, 274.

65. Maginnis, *Cross to Bear*, 334.

66. Maginnis, *Cross to Bear*, 300.

67. "Louisiana Gubernatorial Debate," C-SPAN/Louisiana Public Broadcasting, November 6, 1991, https://www.c-span.org/video/?22521-1/louisiana-guberna torial-debate; see also Maginnis, *Cross to Bear*, 300–304; Bridges, *Rise and Fall*, 226–27; "Duke, Edwards Face Off in Television Debate," UPI, November 6, 1991, https://www.upi.com/Archives/1991/11/06/Duke-Edwards-face-off-in-television -debate/3749689403600.

68. "Louisiana Gubernatorial Debate," Nov. 6, 1991, 3:18 to 4:44.

69. "Louisiana Gubernatorial Debate," Nov. 6, 1991, 55:29 to 55:42.

70. "Louisiana Gubernatorial Debate," Nov. 6, 1991, 52:33 to 53:09.

71. "Louisiana Gubernatorial Debate," Nov. 6, 1991, 10:17 to 13:45.

72. "Louisiana Gubernatorial Debate," Nov. 6, 1991, 34:57 to 35:04.

73. "Louisiana Gubernatorial Debate," Nov. 6, 1991, 32:14 to 32:48.

74. Maginnis, *Cross to Bear*, 302.

75. "Louisiana Gubernatorial Debate," Nov. 6, 1991, 36:03 to 36:14.

76. "Louisiana Gubernatorial Debate," Nov. 6, 1991, 36:22 to 36:45.

77. "Louisiana Gubernatorial Debate," 37:45 to 38:42.

78. "Louisiana Gubernatorial Debate," 49:52 to 50:05.

79. Maginnis, *Cross to Bear*, 300–304.

CHAPTER 12

1. Tim Russert, host, "David Duke, Edwin Edwards," *Meet the Press*, NBC, NBC News transcript, November 10, 1991; see also John Pope, "David Duke vs. Edwin Edwards: A 1991 Election Reflection," *Times-Picayune*, November 14, 2017, photo 18 of 22.

2. Russert, "David Duke, Edwin Edwards."

3. "Russert, "David Duke, Edwin Edwards."

4. Robert Suro, "THE 1991 ELECTION: Louisiana; Bush Denounces Duke as Racist and Charlatan," *New York Times*, November 7 1991, B18.

5. Robert Suro, "Moderates Seen as Key to Louisiana's Election," *New York Times*, October 22, 1991, A10.

6. Roberto Suro, "Rivals in Louisiana Intensifying Pace and Vitriol," *New York Times*, November 14, 91, A1.

7. Wayne Parent, phone interview, May 8, 2021.

8. *Resource Packet: The Politics and Background of David Duke*, 5th ed., Dec. 1991, New Orleans, LA: LCARN, 1991, https://archive.org/details/DavidDukeResource Packet.

9. Bill McMahon, "Tulane Researcher Calls Duke Candidacy an Effective Political Masquerade," *State Times* (Baton Rouge, La.), July 20, 1990, 13A.

10. Meyer, "The Rake."

11. Applebome, "Rogue or Reformer."

12. Applebome, "Rogue or Reformer."

13. Murray, "Duke Makes It Acceptable to Hate"; Meyer, "The Rake."

14. Russell McDermott, "Edwin Edwards Has New Life, New Wife," *Texarkana Gazette*, November 13 2013, https://www.texarkanagazette.com/news/opinion/editorial/story/2013/nov/13/edwedwards-hnew-life-new-wife/297253. During the primary, Edwards claimed, "The best thing that can happen to me is to win the election and to die the next day." Maginnis, *Cross to Bear*, 374.

15. Honeycutt, *Edwin Edwards*, 299.

16. Bill Nichols, "Edwin Edwards' last stand," *Politico*, April 10, 2014, https://www.politico.com/story/2014/04/edwin-edwards-louisiana-2014-elections-105563.

17. Maginnis, *Cross to Bear*, 280.

18. Bridges, *Rise and Fall*, 234.

19. Honeycutt, *Edwin Edwards*, 299

20. Suro, "Moderates Seen."

21. Edwin Edwards, phone interview, May 27, 2021.

22. Lawrence Powell, phone interview, May 17, 2021; Quin Hillyer, phone interview, May 12, 2021.

23. Honeycutt, *Edwin Edwards*, 300.

24. Robert Suro, "Duke Recasts His Religious Claims, *New York Times*, A12.

25. Staff Editorial, "The Only Choice," *New Orleans Times-Picayune*, November 16, 1991, https://www.nola.com/article_80bb8e62-e0ba-11ea-a588-f316e3585b7b.html.

26. Honeycutt, *Edwin Edwards*, 300.

27. Bridges, *Rise and Fall*, 230–31.

28. Kenneth Stern, phone interview, June 25, 2021, and Quin Hillyer, phone interview, May 1, 2021.

29. Maginnis, *Cross to Bear*, 318, 335.

30. Galvez Street is named for the Spanish governor of Louisiana who assisted in the American Revolution.

31. WSB-TV poll of 1992 race, box 31, folder 1, Polling and Results/Stats, LCARN Records.

32. Bridges, *Rise and Fall*, 234–35.

33. A reporter said, "win or lose, David Duke has already won important credibility as a voice on the right." "CBS Evening News - 1991-11-16," CBS, November 16, 1991, https://tvnews.vanderbilt.edu/broadcasts/335909.

34. "Louisiana Gubernatorial Runoff Election: Election Coverage, WDSU-TV, New Orleans," CSPAN, November 16, 1991, 3:20 to 3:23, https://www.c-span.org/video/?22755-1/louisiana-gubernatorial-runoff-election.

35. WSB-TV poll, box 31, folder 1, Polling and Results/Stats, LCARN Records.

36. "Louisiana Gubernatorial Runoff Election,"4:02 to 4:08.

37. "Louisiana Gubernatorial Runoff Election," 3:56 to 4:20.

38. "Louisiana Gubernatorial Runoff Election," 4:49 to 5:06.

39. "Louisiana Gubernatorial Runoff Election," 7:28 to 7:30.

40. "Louisiana Gubernatorial Runoff Election," 52:40 to 55:26.

41. "Louisiana Gubernatorial Runoff Election," 18:12 to 19:02.

42. Quin Hillyer, phone interview, May 1, 2021.

43. Kenneth Stern, phone interview, June 25, 2021.

44. Kuzenski, *David Duke*, 21.

45. James Cullen, "Giving the Devil His Due," in "A Special Double Issue on David Duke," in Dugger and Cullen, "Special Double Issue," 35.

46. Honeycutt, 301.

47. "Southern voters don't like David Duke," a 1992 presidential poll by WSB-TV concluded, "but they're looking for someone who talks like him. Nearly half of all Southern men expressed appreciation for Mr. Duke's message, perhaps in response to the pressure of affirmative action." "Quality of Life in Orleans and Jefferson Parish, April 1990" UNO Survey Research Center report, Dr. Susan Howell, director, box 31, folder 1, Polling and Results/Stats, LCARN Records.

48. Robin Toner, "Buchanan, Urging New Nationalism, Joins '92 Race," *New York Times*, December 11, 1991, B12.

49. Maginnis, *Cross to Bear*, 346–47.

50. Toner, "Buchanan."

51. Kenneth Stern, phone interview, June 25, 2021.

52. Peter Applebome, "The 1992 Campaign: Far Right; Duke's Followers Lean to Buchanan," *New York Times*, March 8, 1992, p. 26.

53. Applebome, "Far Right."

54. Kathleen Belew, "The History of White Power," *New York Times*, April 18, 2018, https://www.nytimes.com/2018/04/18/opinion/history-white-power.html.

55. Marcia Nelson, "When Geraldo Comes to Town: KKK Fight Put Janesville in National Spotlight," *GazetteXtra* (Janesville, WI), August 2, 2015, https://www.gazettextra.com/archives/when-geraldo-comes-to-town-kkk-fight-put-janesville-in-national-spotlight/article_5b7688c5-7ac2-5926-a7a1-aea24oba5a1d.html.

56. Tony Horwitz, *Confederates in the Attic* (New York: Pantheon Books, 1998), 294.

57. Belew, "The History."

58. Jo Thomas, "Behind a Book That Inspired McVeigh," *New York Times*, June 9, 2001, A7.

59. "Rudolph Agrees to Plea Agreement," CNN, April 12, 2005, http://www.cnn.com/2005/LAW/04/08/rudolph.plea.

60. "Violent History: Attacks on Black Churches," *New York Times*, June 18, 2015, https://www.nytimes.com/interactive/2015/06/18/us/19blackchurch.html.

61. Doug Willis, "Arson Caused Calif. Synagogue Fires," Associated Press, June 18, 1999, https://apnews.com/article/2303dc721dd4bbd70c48020ef30b781a; Danny W. Davis, *The Phinehas Priesthood: Violent Vanguard of the Christian Identity Movement* (Praeger Security International, 2010), 181.

62. David Baudner, "Interviews with Racist Aired on TV," Associated Press, July 8, 1999.

63. Rick Hepp, "Shooting Victim Sues White Supremacist," *Chicago Tribune*, April 4, 2000, https://www.chicagotribune.com/news/ct-xpm-2000-04-04-0004160022-story.html.

64. Columbine was originally planned to coincide with the anniversary of the Oklahoma City bombing one day prior and ended up occurring on what would have been Hitler's 110th birthday.

65. "Inspiring Extremist Crimes," ADL, archived on September 25, 2012, accessed June 15, 2016.

66. "National Alliance, Holocaust Deniers React to 9/11 Attacks," Southern Poverty Law Center, March 5, 2002, 2002 Spring Issue, https://www.splcenter.org/fighting-hate/intelligence-report/2002/national-alliance-holocaust-deniers-react-911-attacks.

67. "Post 9-11 Backlash," SAALT, accessed July 29, 2021, https://saalt.org/policy-change/post-9-11-backlash.

68. Just as the blue wall in the South appeared deceptive in 1991, it is deceptive now. Despite governorships in Louisiana and Kentucky, a majority of state Democratic parties have hemorrhaged power since Obama's election.

69. "Ku Klux Klan Burns Cross in Black Neighborhood in Alabama," Equal Justice Initiative, May 8, 2009, https://calendar.eji.org/racial-injustice/may/08.

70. Mary Neal, "Black Teen Found Dead, Organs Missing," FreeSpeakBlog, September 4, 2012, http://freespeakblog.blogspot.com/2012/09/black-teen-found-dead-organs-missing.html.

71. "KKK Joins Immigration Debate with Calls for 'Corpses' on the Border," SPLC, July 31, 2014, https://www.splcenter.org/hatewatch/2014/07/30/kkk-joins-immigration-debate-calls-corpses-border.

72. Rebecca Hersher, "What Happened when Dylann Roof Asked Google for Information about Race," NPR, January 10, 2017, https://www.npr.org/sections/thetwo-way/2017/01/10/508363607/what-happened-when-dylann-roof-asked-google-for-information-about-race.

73. Jason Wilson, "White Nationalist Hate Groups Have Grown 55% in Trump Era, Report Finds," *Guardian*, March 18, 2020, https://www.theguardian.com/world/2020/mar/18/white-nationalist-hate-groups-southern-poverty-law-center.

74. Several members of the Klan were blamed for the 1995 fire. The church sued the Klan and won a $37.8 million judgment, which the jury awarded due to a belief the Klan's platform inspired the men to carry out the arson. "Violent History."

75. Mark Potok, "The Year in Hate and Extremism," SPLC, February 17, 2016, 2016 Spring Issue, https://www.splcenter.org/fighting-hate/intelligence-report/2016/year-hate-and-extremism.

76. Cynthia McFadden, Victoria Thompson, Jon Meyersohn, "Klan Group Heralds Rise of New KKK, Calls for Segregation," ABC News, October 26, 2012, https://abcnews.go.com/US/klan-group-heralds-rise-kkk-calls-segregation/story?id=17572788.

77. McFadden, Thompson, and Meyersohn, "Klan Group."

78. McFadden, Thompson, and Meyersohn, "Klan Group."

79. Yilu Zhou, Edna Reid, Jialun Qin, Hsinchun Chen, and Guanpi Lai, University of Arizona, Tucson, "U.S. Domestic Extremist Groups on the Web: Link and Content Analysis," July 9, 2010, 1–22, https://web.archive.org/web/20100709003315/http://ai.arizona.edu/intranet/papers/Zhou_Domestic_MainText.pdf.

80. "Rome Sentences 24 for Hate Comments on 'Stormfront' Forum," InfoMigrants, February 12, 2020, https://www.infomigrants.net/en/post/22714/rome-sentences-24-for-hate-comments-on-stormfront-forum.

81. Hunter Walker, "Stormfront Founder Don Black Says White Supremacists Thought Ron Paul Was 'One of Us,'" *New York Observer*, December 28, 2011, https://observer.com/2011/12/stormfront-founder-don-black-says-white-supremacists-thought-ron-paul-was-one-of-us-2.

82. Arlie Russell Hochschild, *Strangers in Their Own Land: Anger and Mourning on the American Right* (New York: New Press, 2016), 227.

83. Raymond Strother, phone interview, June 29, 2021.

84. Zack Staton, "The Rise of the Biden Republicans," *Politico*, March 4, 2021; see also Mark Danner, "Reality Rebellion," *New York Review of Books*, July 1, 2021, 14.

85. "Donald Trump and David Duke Are Sinister Soul Brothers," *Daily Beast*, March 24, 2018, https://www.thedailybeast.com/donald-trump-and-david -duke-are-sinister-soul-brothers.

86. Dorothy Thompson, qtd. in Lesley M. M. Blume, "Truth Is the First Casualty of War. These Reporters Tried to Save It," *New York Times*, March 16, 2022, https:// www.nytimes.com/2022/03/16/books/review/last-call-at-the-hotel-imperial -deborah-cohen.html.

87. Hochschild, *Strangers*, 222–26.

88. David Firestone, "A Dealing with David Duke Haunts Louisiana Governor," *New York Times*, June 22, 1999, A18.

89. Firestone, "Dealing with David Duke."

90. Bridges, *Rise and Fall*, 266–67.

91. In both races, Foster defeated black Democratic Congressmen, with the vote generally splitting along racial lines.

92. Tim Wise, phone interview, May 1, 2021.

93. "Patrick Joseph Buchanan, 'Culture War Speech: Address to the Republican National Convention' (17 August 1992)," Voices of Democracy: The U.S. Oratory Project, accessed May 13, 2022, https://voicesofdemocracy.umd.edu/buchanan -culture-war-speech-speech-text.

94. Tim Wise, phone interview, May 1, 2021.

95. "KKK Bitch," another Ice-T song written for Body Count that year, was designed to provoke censors like Gore, who is mentioned in the lyrics, as well, but the talk didn't engender nearly so much controversy. Detractors found it difficult to discuss its extremely explicit lyrics of sleeping with a young white woman whose father is head of the local KKK, although that may have been by design. Ice T, as told to Heidi Sigmund, *The Ice Opinion: Who Gives a Fuck?* (New York: St. Martin's Press, 1994), 99–101, 108, 166–180.

96. Tim Wise, phone interview, May 1, 2021.

CHAPTER 13

Epigraph. A. J. Liebling, *The Earl of Louisiana* (Baton Rouge: Louisiana State University Press, 1961, reprinted 2008), xiii.

1. Eric Hananoki, "How Trump Acknowledged David Duke on CNN in 1991: 'I Hate Seeing What It Represents,'" *Media Matters*, February 29, 2016, https:// www.mediamatters.org/donald-trump/how-trump-acknowledged-david-duke -cnn-1991-i-hate-seeing-what-it-represents.

2. Hananoki, "How Trump."

3. "Pat Moynihan: A Racist?" *Oklahoman*, November 26, 1991, https://www.oklaho man.com/article/2376387/pat-moynihan-a-racist; Richard Lacayo, "Down on the Downtrodden," *Time*, December 19, 1994.

4. Julian E. Zelizer, "The Partisan," *New York Times*, May 2, 2021, 10 (Sunday Book Review.)

5. Bob Grant, a right-wing talk show host, took that message and ran with it, saying, among other things, that he wished some Haitian refugees had drowned instead of reaching US shores. Iver Peterson, "Whitman Rebukes Bob Grant on the Air," *New York Times*, November 18, 1994, B7, https://www.nytimes.com/1994/11/18/ nyregion/whitman-rebukes-bob-grant-on-the-air.html; Zelizer, "The Partisan."

6. Zelizer, "The Partisan."

7. "2000 Republican Party Platform," UCSB, https://www.presidency.ucsb.edu/ documents/2000-republican-party-platform.

8. Morgan Watkins, "From Apartheid to Affirmative Action: Sen. Mitch McConnell's Complicated History on Race," *Louisville Courier-Journal*, August 13, 2020, https://www.courier-journal.com/story/news/politics/elections/kentucky/ 2020/08/13/mcconnell-has-a-complicated-history-when-it-comes-to-race/ 3291516001.

9. EJ Montini, "Joe Arpaio Ran a Self-Proclaimed 'Concentration Camp' for Years. Where Was GOP Outrage?," *AZCentral*, June 20, 2019, https://www.azcentral. com/story/opinion/op-ed/ej-montini/2019/06/20/joe-arpaio-self-proclaimed -concentration-camp-ocasio-cortez/1508251001/.

10. Jeremy Alford, "Much of David Duke's '91 Campaign Is Now in Louisiana Mainstream," *New York Times*, January 5, 2015, A12.

11. Alana Abramson, "How Donald Trump Perpetuated the 'Birther' Movement for Years," *ABC News*, September 16, 2016, https://abcnews.go.com/Politics/ donald-trump-perpetuated-birther-movement-years/story?id=42138176.

12. Abramson, "How Donald Trump."

13. In a 2020 Instagram post, former First Lady Michelle Obama wrote, "Donald Trump had spread racist lies about my husband that had put my family in danger." Michelle Obama (@michelleobama), Instagram, November 16, 2020, https://www.instagram.com/p/CHqZ-ylrqJd. A *USA Today* headline said "Trump used words like 'invasion' and 'killer' to discuss immigrants at rallies 500 times." John Frize, "Trump Used Words Like 'Invasion' and 'Killer' to Discuss Immigrants at Rallies 500 Times: USA TODAY Analysis," *USA Today*, August 8, 2019, https://www.usatoday.com/story/news/politics/elections/2019/08/08/ trump-immigrants-rhetoric-criticized-el-paso-dayton-shootings/1936742001. In 1989, the year of Duke's election to the State House in Louisiana, Trump

told interviewer Bryant Gumbel "A well-educated black has a tremendous advantage over a well-educated white in terms of the job market." "Is Donald Trump Racist?" *Fortune*, June 7, 2016 https://fortune.com/2016/06/07/donald-trump-racism-quotes.

14. Michael Wilson, "Trump Draws Criticism for Ad He Ran after Jogger Attack," *New York Times*, October 23, 2002, B3.

15. Steven A. Holmes, "Member of 'Central Park 5' Blasts Trump," *CNN*, October 7, 2016, https://www.cnn.com/2016/10/06/politics/reality-check-donald-trump-central-park-5.

16. Christina Coleburn, "Donald Trump on Racist Endorsement: 'I Don't Know Anything about David Duke,'" NBC News, February 28, 2016, https://www.nbcnews.com/politics/2016-election/donald-trump-racist-endorsement-i-don-t-know-anything-about-n527576.

17. In 1991, Beth Rickey wrote that Duke voters' racism hand been "prompted by economic concerns." Mary Schmich, "David Duke and Donald Trump and the Long Ties of History," *Chicago Tribune*, August 15, 2017, https://www.chicagotribune.com/columns/mary-schmich/ct-david-duke-mary-schmich-20170815-column.html.

18. George W. Goodman, "For Starrett City, An Integration Test," *New York Times*, October 16, 1983, section 8, 7. https://www.nytimes.com/1983/10/16/realestate/for-starrett-city-an-integration-test.html.

19. Andrew Kaczynski, "He's 'Certainly the Best of the Lot' Running For President," *BuzzFeed News*, August 25, 2015, https://www.buzzfeednews.com/article/andrewkaczynski/david-duke-on-trump-hes-certainly-the-best-of-the-lot-runnin#.pnMB24G4n, see also: Jeremy Diamond, "David Duke on Trump: He's 'the Best of the Lot,'" *CNN*, August 25, 2016, https://www.cnn.com/2015/08/25/politics/david-duke-donald-trump-immigration/index.html.

20. He would finish in the single digits and far from the runoff.

21. Mark Ballard, "Anti-David Duke Group Reboots for US Senate Race," *Tuscaloosa News*, September 2, 2016, retrieved October 25, 2021, https://www.tuscaloosanews.com/news/20160902/anti-david-duke-group-reboots-for-us-senate-race.

22. During the debate, Democrat Foster Campbell said: "I have nothing in common with David Duke except probably that we're both breathing." Tom Boggioni, "Ex-Klan Head David Duke Goes Bonkers at Raucous Senate Debate: 'Hillary Should Get the Electric Chair!,'" *Raw Story*, November 2, 2016, https://www.rawstory.com/2016/11/ex-klan-head-david-duke-goes-bonkers-at-raucous-senate-debate-hillary-should-get-the-electric-chair.

23. Jennifer Agiesta, "Most Say Race Relations Worsened under Obama, Poll Finds," *CNN*, October 5, 2016, https://www.cnn.com/2016/10/05/politics/

obama-race-relations-poll/index.html. Bill Wilkinson, another former Grand Wizard and Duke's old rival, believed there wouldn't be a race war over George Floyd's murder because, he said, Black Lives Matter and antifascists movement amounted to "nothing." Ryan Perry, "EXCLUSIVE: Former Imperial Wizard of the Ku Klux Klan Claims There Won't Be a Race War in America because the BLM Movement Is 'Nothing' and Says the Killings of George Floyd and Rayshard Brooks Are 'Totally Justified,'" *Daily Mail*, June 29, 2020, https:// www.dailymail.co.uk/news/article-8470747/Former-Imperial-Wizard-Ku-Klux -Klan-says-killings-Black-men-justified.html.

24. But simply calling someone a racist, as Edwards and Rickey learned, didn't taint a candidate in the eyes of the public. One had to show, rather than tell, why Duke and his kind were unfit for office.

25. "Election 2016 Favorability Ratings," *Real Clear Politics*, accessed September 17, 2021, https://www.realclearpolitics.com/epolls/other/president/clintontrump favorability.html; Jeffery M. Jones, "Hillary Clinton Favorable Rating at New Low," Gallup, December 19, 2017, https://news.gallup.com/poll/224330/hillary -clinton-favorable-rating-new-low.aspx.

26. Michael L. Kurtz, "Louisiana at the End of the Century, 1987–2000," *Louisiana: A History*, 6th ed., edited by Bennett H. Wall and John C. Rodrigue, 418–53 (Malden, MA: Wiley Blackwell, 2014), 426.

27. Jason Bourne (@TheOriginalWTH), "James Comey handed the presidency to Trump when he double-whammied Hillary. He broke FBI procedures to announce the re-opening of the 'Hillary's email' BS. He did NOT announce that Trump was under investigation at that time for his Russia collusion. She never had a chance." Twitter, November 28, 2021, 3:30 p.m., https://twitter.com/the originalwth/status/1465070691208728579.

28. Kenneth Stern, phone interview, June 25, 2021.

29. Tyler Bridges, phone interview, May 8, 2021.

30. Megan L. Wood, "Trump Racist Policies, An Incomplete—and Very Long— List of the Most Racist Policies the Trump Administration Has Tried to Enact," *Courier*, August 12, 2020, https://couriernewsroom.com/2020/08/12/ trumps-most-racist-policies.

31. Elizabeth Rickey Papers, untitled note, June 21, 1991, AJC, June 21, 1991.

32. Sarah Sidner, "Klansman Gets 4 Years in Prison for Firing Gun at 'Unite the Right' Rally," CNN.com, August 22, 2018, https://www.cnn.com/2018/08/22/us/ kkk-unite-the-right-richard-preston-sentence/index.html.

33. "David Duke among Kessler's Planned Speakers for Unite the Right Anniversary Rally in D.C.," *Richmond Times Dispatch*, August 6, 2018, https://richmond.com/ david-duke-among-kesslers-planned-speakers-for-unite-the-right-anniversary

-rally-in-d-c/article_c80fb489-04a1-5825-a1a4-6f569b786679.html; and Holly Yan, Devon M. Sayers and Steve Almasy, "Virginia Governor on White National-ists: They Should Leave America," CNN, August 14, 2017, https://www.cnn.com/2017/08/13/us/charlottesville-white-nationalist-rally-car-crash/index.html; see also Moore and Tracy, *No Fascist USA!*, 27.

34. Libby Nelson, "'Why We Voted for Donald Trump': David Duke Explains the White Supremacist Charlottesville Protests," *Vox*, August 12, 2017, https://www.vox.com/2017/8/12/16138358/charlottesville-protests-david-duke-kkk.

35. Nelson, "'Why We Voted."

36. "Two Years Ago, They Marched in Charlottesville. Where Are They Now?," ADL, August 8, 2019, https://www.adl.org/blog/two-years-ago-they-marched -in-charlottesville-where-are-they-now.

37. Michael E. Miller, "'Shocking': Neo-Nazis Fly Swastika Flag, Salute at Vir-ginia Shopping Center where Leader Was Killed," *Washington Post*, August 25, 2017, www.washingtonpost.com/news/retropolis/wp/2017/08/25/shocking-neo -nazis-fly-swastika-salute-at-shopping-center-where-leader-was-killed.

38. The COVID-19 pandemic also undermined his chances at reelection, although Trump still far outperformed his 2016 numbers and was only narrowly de-feated in several battleground states.

39. "Six Facts About Threats to The Jewish Community," *ADL*, January 16, 2022, accessed May 21, 2022, https://www.adl.org/blog/six-facts-about-threats-to-the -jewish-community.

40. Merrit Kennedy, "'Pizzagate' Gunman Sentenced to 4 Years in Prison," NPR, June 22, 2017, https://www.npr.org/sections/thetwo-way/2017/06/22/533941689/ pizzagate-gunman-sentenced-to-4-years-in-prison.

41. She has also allegedly spoken at white nationalist conferences. "Romney: Mar-jorie Taylor Greene a 'Moron' for Speaking at White Nationalist Event," *Guard-ian*, February 27, 2022, https://www.theguardian.com/us-news/2022/feb/27/mitt -romney-marjorie-taylor-greene-paul-gosar-morons; Lauren Gambino, "Who Is the Republican Extremist Marjorie Taylor Greene?," *Guardian*, February 6, 2021, https://www.theguardian.com/us-news/2021/feb/06/who-is-marjorie-taylor -greene-republican-qanon.

42. "Freshman Congresswoman Mary Miller says 'Hitler was right,'" @rose.warfare, Instagram, January 6, 2021, https://www.instagram.com/p/CJuhtzJBdg9.

43. "Sierra Club Calls for Expulsion of Hawley," Sierra Club, January 12, 2021, https:// www.sierraclub.org/missouri/blog/2021/01/sierra-club-calls-for-expulsion -hawley.

44. "Capitol Riots Timeline: The Evidence Presented against Trump," BBC News, February 13, 2021, https://www.bbc.com/news/world-us-canada-56004916.

45. Anonymous, January 6, 2020, Instagram Message.

46. Anonymous, January 6, 2020, and January 7, 2020, Instagram Message and Facebook Messenger.

47. *Blood in the Face*, produced and directed by Kevin Rafferty, James Ridgeway, and Anne Bohlen, Right Thinking Productions, 1991, available on Letterboxd, https://letterboxd.com/film/blood-in-the-face.

48. Duke referred to it on his May 28, 2021, internet radio show. "The whole YouTube shutdown, it wasn't a lot of the other so-called 'radical right,'" he said. "I was the first big target of [their] censorship." He also suggested the Israeli government and the ADL were hypocritical for promoting "open borders" in the US but supported a race-based entry or residency requirement in Israel. "Dr Duke & Mark Collett of UK on Jewish Supremacy & First Major JewTube Censorship – Which Was against David Duke in UK," David Duke radio show, May 28, 2021, https://davidduke.com/friday210514-2-2.

49. Annie Karni, "N.A.A.C.P. Files Federal Suit against Trump and Giuliani," *New York Times*, February 17, 2021, A12.

50. Richard Hine (@richardhine), "One week before the election, 31% of Americans considered themselves Republicans. Four months after the insurrection, only 26% do. #RIPGOP (via @GallupNews)," Twitter, May 12, 2021, 11:17 a.m., https://twitter.com/richardhine/status/1392514364649967618.

51. Jason Wilson, "Revealed: Neo-Confederate Group Includes Military Officers and Politicians," *Guardian*, June 28, 2021, https://www.theguardian.com/us-news/2021/jun/28/neo-confederate-group-members-politicians-military-officers. At a 2021 meeting, Georgia Republicans roundly booed their right-wing governor, Brian Kemp, for refusing to overturn the state's 2020 election results. "Georgia governor Brian Kemp gets loudly booed at the state's Republican convention. The crowd is upset he didn't illegally overturn the 2020 election in favor of Donald Trump," @werdmouf, Reddit, May 2021, https://www.reddit.com/r/PublicFreakout/comments/nszw4z/georgia_governor_brian_kemp_gets_loudly_booed_at.

52. The website of the National Socialist Movement calls black people "truly ridiculous clowns" and refers to President Biden as "China Joe." Julia Harte, "Neo-Nazi Leader Arrested in Arizona for Aggravated Assault," Reuters, April 20, 2021, https://www.reuters.com/world/us/neo-nazi-leader-arrested-arizona-aggravated-assault-2021-04-20; see also National Socialist Movement, https://www.nsm88.org. Nicholas J. Fuentes is a white nationalist and, according to the ADL, a white supremacist. "Nicholas J. Fuentes: Five Things to Know," American Defamation League, July 8, 2021, https://www.adl.org/blog/nicholas-j-fuentes-five-things-to-know. Lauren Chen hosted a three-part

interview with Richard Spencer that helped the neo-Nazi achieve a degree of legitimacy. She asked if the US really should "have intervened" in WWII, criticized open borders and abortion, referred to LGBT people as degenerates, and believes the book *The Bell Curve* proves blacks and whites have markedly different average IQs.) See, for example, Lauren Chen, "Should America have intervened in WWII? A surprising amount of people say NO. Is this a manifestation of the 'America First' principle that sees preoccupation with foreign interests as a detriment to Americans? And what about humanitarianism? Full vid: https://youtu.be/3ebzDG9xeAM," Twitter, June 5, 2021, 11:32 a.m., https://twitter.com/TheLaurenChen/status/1401215363669442562. On July 4, 2021, Alex Jones said, "On average, whites have the highest IQ." @blassic liberal, "Y'all cheering for Alex Jones in a beef with Joe Budden when he says Blacks have low IQ? Couldn't be me!," July 4, 2021, 7:19 p.m., https://twitter.com/blassicliberal/status/1411842192495181827. After George Floyd's murder by a Minneapolis police officer, Steven Crowder posted a mocking reenactment of his death. @podofthrones, "I wonder if any evangelical conservatives out there are seeing irony in Steven Crowder making fun of someone being asphyxiated, and then getting a collapsed lung not far in the future. Maybe the Lord's ways aren't always mysterious," July 27, 2021, 6:41 p.m., https://twitter.com/podofthrones/status/1420167417200742401. @rollingstone, "The FBI warned in 2006 that white supremacists were actively trying to infiltrate the military and law enforcement," Instagram, May 12, 2021, https://www.instagram.com/p/COxmMWatUzg/?igshid=kqh49043cjoa. An FBI informant who exposed multiple KKK murder plots claimed that police officers made up a substantial portion of Florida's Klan membership. Jason Dearen, "He Wore a Wire, Risked His Life to Expose Who Was in the KKK," Associated Press, December 23, 2021, https://apnews.com/article/florida-race-and-ethnicity-racial-injustice-veterans-ku-klux-klan-fa0ec412o0b1457f56c527108074795b5.

53. Stormfront, called "the murder capital of the internet," had been linked to dozens of killings. Jay Reeves, "Oldest White Supremacist Site, Stormfront, Based in Florida, Shut Down after Complaint," *Orlando Sentinel*, August 28, 2017, https://www.orlandosentinel.com/news/os-oldest-white-supremacist-site-based-in-florida-shut-down-after-complaint-20170828-story.html; see also Alex Hern, "Stormfront: 'Murder Capital of Internet' Pulled Offline after Civil Rights Action," *Guardian*, August 29, 2017, https://www.theguardian.com/technology/2017/aug/29/stormfront-neo-nazi-hate-site-murder-internet-pulled-offline-web-com-civil-rights-action; Jason Wilson, "White Nationalist Hate Groups Have Grown 55% in Trump Era, Report Finds," *Guardian*, March 18, 2020, https://www.theguardian.com/world/2020/mar/18/white-nationalist-hate-groups-southern-poverty-law-center.

54. Giovanni Russonello, "QAnon Now as Popular in U.S. as Some Major Religions, Poll Suggests," *New York Times*, May 27, 2021, https://www.nytimes.com/2021/05/27/us/politics/qanon-republicans-trump.html.

55. Erin Donaghue, "Racially-Motivated Violent Extremists Elevated to 'National Threat Priority,' FBI Director Says," CBS News, February 5, 2020, https://www.cbsnews.com/news/racially-motivated-violent-extremism-isis-national-threat-priority-fbi-director-christopher-wray.

56. Undated newspaper clipping, likely from the *Times of Houma/Thibodaux*, circa December 1991, Rickey Archive.

57. "Loving Concern @ Dalton / An Open Letter to The Dalton Community," January 2021, unsigned, https://freebeacon.com/wp-content/uploads/2021/01/FILE_5439-1-2.pdf.

58. "Edwin Edwards First TV Interview during a Public Appearance in 10 Years," Foundation for Historical Louisiana Preservation Awards, 2011, Louisiana Hometown, YouTube, www.YouTube.com/watch?v=Mq2NVcMSZIw.

59. Larry Powell, phone interview, May 17, 2021.

60. Wayne Parent, phone interview, May 8, 2021.

61. Parent, *Inside the Carnival*, 44.

62. Kevin Canfield, "Tulsa Race Massacre Centennial Commission Asks Stitt to Veto Bill on 'Critical Race Theory,'" *Tulsa World*, May 4, 2021, https://tulsaworld.com/news/state-and-regional/govt-and-politics/tulsa-race-massacre-centennial-commission-asks-stitt-to-veto-bill-on-critical-race-theory/article_7d30aa30-ac38-11eb-9ad1-f715fbb09cdd.html.

63. Tom Shackleford, "New Orleans City Council Proposes Robert E. Lee Blvd. to Be Renamed for Allen Toussaint," *Live For Live Music*, March 14, 2021, https://liveforlivemusic.com/news/new-orleans-proposes-robert-lee-blvd-renamed-allen-toussaint.

64. Matthew Brown, "'White Supremacy Is Terrorism': Biden Urges Vigilance against Home-Grown Violence after Jan. 6 Attack," *USA Today*, April 28, 2021, https://www.usatoday.com/story/news/politics/2021/04/28/biden-calls-white-supremacy-terrorism-speech-congress/4884034001.

65. Tyler Bridges, phone interview, May 8, 2021. In 2002, Scalise spoke at Duke's European-American Unity and Rights Organization meeting, railing against taxes, and when he was confronted in 2014 about that appearance, he expressed regret and claimed to disdain racism and anti-Semitism.

66. "Sierra Club Calls for Expulsion of Hawley," Sierra Club, January 12, 2021, https://www.sierraclub.org/missouri/blog/2021/01/sierra-club-calls-for-expulsion-hawley.

67. Ali went by Ali Akbar when he lived in Baton Rouge and worked to defeat Senate Democrat Mary Landrieu in 2014 and failed to elect Jay Dardenne governor

in 2015. Lamar White, Jr., "Theater of the Absurd: How A Louisiana Extremist Helped the Trump Campaign Manufacture Outrage," Bayou Brief, November 8, 2020, https://www.bayoubrief.com/2020/11/08/theater-of-the-absurd-how-a-louisiana-extremist-helped-the-trump-campaign-manufacture-outrage. Emma Mayer, "Calls to Fire GOP Lawmaker Grow after Video Shows Him Hint at Opening Oregon Capitol Door to Protesters," *Newsweek*, June 5, 2021, https://www.newsweek.com/calls-fire-gop-lawmaker-grow-after-video-shows-him-hint-opening-oregon-capitol-door-protesters-1597887.

68. Dean Obeidallah, "Tucker Carlson's Fox News Host Salary Is Bankrolled by You," *NBC News*, November 16, 2021, https://www.msnbc.com/opinion/tucker-carlson-s-fox-news-host-salary-bankrolled-you-n1283754; "How could I be an evil guy" if Carlson is repeating "all the fundamental things" of my argument, Duke asked rhetorically. Kieran Press-Reynolds, "A Former Leader of the KKK Celebrated Tucker Carlson 'Finally' Sharing the White-Supremacist 'Great Replacement' Conspiracy Theory," *Insider*, October 22, 2021, https://www.insider.com/tucker-carlson-replacement-theory-david-duke-kkk-trump-2021-10.

69. Ellie Hall, "'I'm Only Shitposting IRL': The All-Too-Familiar Online Ideology of the Alleged Buffalo Shooter," *BuzzFeed News*, May 17, 2022, https://www.buzzfeednews.com/article/ellievhall/buffalo-shooter-online-influence-4chan; Nicholas Confessore and Karen Yourish, "A Fringe Conspiracy Theory, Fostered Online, Is Refashioned by the G.O.P.," *New York Times*, May 15, 2022, https://www.nytimes.com/2022/05/15/us/replacement-theory-shooting-tucker-carlson.html.

70. "David Duke's Former Campaign Manager Says Trump and the Former KKK Leader Are 'Identical,'" *Vice*, February 13, 2017, https://www.vice.com/en/article/qkxpdb/david-dukes-former-campaign-manager-says-trump-and-the-former-kkk-leader-are-identical.

71. Parent, *David Duke*, xiv.

POSTSCRIPT

1. Mark McKinnon, phone interview, June 12, 2021.
2. Carlos Sierra, phone interview, June 10, 2021.
3. Roemer also disliked Clinton and Obama, the former for signing a bill allowing commercial and investment banks to incorporate under the same umbrella, and the latter for not running as promised on public financing. Carlos Sierra, phone interview, June 10, 2021.
4. Honeycutt, *Edwin Edwards*, 303.
5. Tyler Bridges, "Donald Trump, Businessman, Not Always as Successful in Louisiana as Donald Trump, President-Elect," *The Advocate* (Acadiana, LA), November 15, 2016, https://www.theadvocate.com/acadiana/news/politics/elections/article_654bc48c-ab7e-11e6-be81-0730b00a7bdf.html.

6. Expecting to die in prison, Edwards divorced Candy, his second wife, saying she had "suffered enough" already. "Edwin Edwards," *FamPeople*, May 18, 2019, https://fampeople.com/cat-edwin-edwards_4?amp.

7. Natalie Shepherd and Dominic Massa, "WWL-TV/Advocate Poll: Edwards, Jindal Named State's Best, Worst Governors," *USA Today*, October 2, 2015, https://www.usatoday.com/story/news/politics/2015/10/02/wwl-tvadvocate-poll-edwin-edwards-bobby-jindal-named-states-best—worst-governors/73169648.

8. Boyles, "An Interview with Governor Buddy Roemer."

9. "David Duke Released from Prison," KPLC-TV, April 9, 2004, https://www.kplctv.com/story/1774083/david-duke-released-from-prison.

10. NAAWP editorial document, *NAAWP Newsletter*, no. 31, 1984, box 21, LCARN Records.

11. @change_the_system3.0, "David Duke says Trump modeled his platform after him #trump #davidduke," April 22, 2022, TikTok, https://www.tiktok.com/@change_the_system3.0/video/7089472793892392238.

12. Eric Kleefeld, "White supremacist David Duke: I inspired Donald Trump — and Tucker Carlson, too," Media Matters, October 20, 2021, https://www.mediamatters.org/white-nationalism/white-supremacist-david-duke-i-inspired-donald-trump-and-tucker-carlson-too

13. Dugger, "Beth Rickey Replies."

14. Kenneth Stern, "Elizabeth Rickey, Derailed David Duke," *Forward*, September 16, 2009, https://forward.com/news/114205/elizabeth-rickey-derailed-david-duke.

15. James Cullen, "Louisiana's Lesson: Don't Take Duke for Granted," in Dugger and Cullen, "Special Double Issue," 37.

16. Quin Hillyer, phone interview, May 1, 2021, and Kenneth Stern phone interview, June 25, 2021.

17. Quin Hillyer, phone interview, May 1, 2021.

18. Rob Rickey, phone interview, October 29, 2021.

19. Jane Buchsbaum, phone interview, April 21, 2022; Notes for a book proposal, Rickey Archive.

20. John Naland, phone interview, August 14, 2021. In December, the president-elect sent her a form letter thanking her for her "help in our campaign." Bill Clinton to Elizabeth Rickey, December 19, 1992, Rickey Archive.

21. Rob Rickey, phone interview, October 29, 2021.

22. "Supremacists Will March in Jena, La. without Bond," *Tuscaloosa News*, January 12, 2008, https://www.tuscaloosanews.com/article/DA/20080112/News/606100456/TL; Sadow, "Elizabeth Rickey."

23. Kenneth Stern, phone interview, June 25, 2021

24. Quin Hillyer, phone interview, May 1, 2021.

25. Jane Buchsbaum, phone interview, April 21, 2022.

26. Quin Hillyer, phone interview, May 1, 2021.

27. Jane Buchsbaum, phone interview, April 21, 2022.

28. Tom Sharpe, "Elizabeth Ann 'Beth' Rickey, 1956–2009: David Duke Nemesis Dies in Santa Fe," *Santa Fe New Mexican*, September 13, 2009, https://archive.is/20130104135539/http://www.santafenewmexican.com/Local%20News/Elizabeth-Ann--Beth--Rickey---1953-2009-David-Duke-nemesis-dies.

29. Quin Hillyer, phone interview, May 1, 2021.

30. Quin Hillyer, phone interview, May 1, 2021.

31. Quin Hillyer, "Beth, What Can We Do?" *Washington Times*, September 15, 2009, https://www.washingtontimes.com/news/2009/sep/15/beth-what-can-we-do.

32. Quin Hillyer, "Bard Has New Award for Beth Rickey, Heroine against Hate," *Washington Examiner*, September 12, 2019, https://www.washingtonexaminer.com/opinion/bard-has-new-award-for-beth-rickey-heroine-against-hate.

33. Kenneth Stern, phone interview, June 25, 2021.

34. Anne Levy, phone interview, April 7, 2022.

35. LCARN meeting minutes, October 17, 1989 folder 5, box 6, Meeting Agendas, Minutes and Notes, 1989–1992, LCARN Records.

36. "Beth Rickey Award," Bard College, Center for the Study of Hate, accessed July 29, 2021, https://bcsh.bard.edu/beth-rickey-award.

ACKNOWLEDGMENTS

First off, I want to thank you for reading this, whoever you are, Mysterious and Beloved Stranger.

Numerous friends and other unsavory characters helped with the drafting of this book. Andrea Dube was an excellent volunteer research assistant when one was desperately needed, and lent books from her library on Southern and American political history (separate subjects, by the way), took copious notes, and contributed her campaign finance expertise; I thank her and Tom Hill for the cocktails. Kathryn Donahoe read the manuscript in a near-complete version and provided great copyediting. Valentina Flores of the Bard College / Hannah Arendt Center program served as my physical presence at the American Jewish Committee (AJC) Archives and Records Center, and Sarah deVeer at Bard and Charlotte Bonnelli, Ken Stern, and the rest of the AJC staff facilitated access to Beth Rickey's unseen archival material. Phillip Cunningham and Lisa Moore at the Amistad Research Center at Tulane University offered seemingly limitless assistance with their archives. Rob Rickey was instrumental in shedding light on his sister's early years, providing great archival material and answering a barrage of questions at the last minute, and Quin Hillyer repeatedly donated his time to shed light on Beth's later years. I'm indebted to Larry Powell and Lance Hill for help facilitating interviews and providing long-sought archival materials; Marco Ceglie, Andrew Boyd, Dan Katz, and especially Kurt Opprecht helped talk me through everything and brought some levity (a.k.a. vicious ribbing) to the proceedings; Wylie Stecklow, my fearless attorney, graciously volunteered his help with contracts and other irritations; and Anita Vatshell and Carreen Maloney were instrumental in the proposal becoming an actual book by talking me off a ledge and out of a dangerous hot sauce choice at Rosalita's Backyard Tacos, and crucially and accidentally helped me reframe my pitch.

Thank you to everyone at Vanderbilt University Press, especially Betsy T. Phillips, editor, confidante, passionate collaborator, and source of two or three of my Top 10 favorite emails of all time, and copyeditor Joell Smith-Borne. Also, a thank you to the three freelance editors who helped tweak the original proposal that started this project: Susanne Schotanus, Steffanie Moyers, and Quata Diann Merit. At *Business Insider*, Grace DeGraaf and Bob Bryan accepted and published my first piece about Edwards and Duke.

Thank you to my booster club: Diane Fairbanks, Scott Fairbanks, Dana Fairbanks, Cathy Phillips Fairbanks, Terry Linton, Erika Wiese, Marquela Stevenson, Andy Brooks, Matthew Penwell, Emily Floyd, Lyz Lenz, John Bowers, Meghan Garhan, Joe Reckley, Lisa Wade, Jennifer Pincus, Melissa Sands, Conor Donohue, Brock LaBorde, Mac Lemann, Tiana Nobile, Zachary Belway, Katie Lyon-Hart, Kelsy Yeargain, Margaret Quick, Noah Tapper, Sydney Shivers, and Yasin "Frank" Southall.

And my deepest thanks to interview subjects Jason Berry, Tyler Bridges, Jane K. Buchsbaum, Edwin Edwards, Debra Holden, Leo Honeycutt, Quin Hillyer, Anne Levy, Mark McKinnon, John K. Naland, Wayne Parent, Lawrence N. Powell, Rob Rickey, Plater Robinson, Caroline Roemer, Chas Roemer, Mary Schmich, Carlos Sierra, Kenneth Stern, Tom Stokes, Ray Strother, and Tim Wise. David Duke did not return my emails or letters requesting an interview.

CPSIA information can be obtained
at www.ICGtesting.com
Printed in the USA
LVHW011804121022
730564LV00003B/274